ADVENTURES IN CHILDHOOD

Adventures in Childhood connects modern intellectual property law and practice with a history of consumption. Structured in a loosely chronological order, the book begins with the creation of a children's literature market, a Christmas market, and moves through character merchandising, syndicated newspaper strips, film, television, and cross-industry relations, finishing in the 1970s, by which time professional identities and legal practices had stabilised. By focusing on the rise of child-targeted commercial activities, the book is able to reflect on how and why intellectual property rights became a defining feature of twentieth century culture. Chapters trace the commercial empires that grew around *Alice in Wonderland, Peter Rabbit, Meccano, Felix the Cat, Mickey Mouse, Peter Pan, Eagle Magazine, Davy Crockett, Mr Men, Dr Who, The Magic Roundabout* and *The Wombles* to show how modern intellectual property merchandising was plagued with legal and moral questions that exposed the tension between exploitation and innocence.

Jose Bellido is Reader in Law at Kent Law School, University of Kent (UK). He is particularly interested in the history of intellectual property law and has additional research interests in legal theory, evidence and legal history. His most recent book project as editor and contributor is *Landmark Cases in Intellectual Property Law* (Hart Publishing, 2017).

Kathy Bowrey is a Professor of Law in the School of Law, Society and Criminology, Faculty of Law & Justice, University of New South Wales, Sydney, Australia. She is a legal and cultural historian interested in how cultural commodification operates on a global scale. Her most recent works include *Copyright, Creativity, Big Media and Cultural Value: Incorporating the Author*, (Routledge, 2021). She is a Co-Director of the International Society for the History and Theory of Intellectual Property.

CAMBRIDGE INTELLECTUAL PROPERTY AND INFORMATION LAW

As its economic potential has rapidly expanded, intellectual property has become a subject of front-rank legal importance. Cambridge Intellectual Property and Information Law is a series of monograph studies of major current issues in intellectual property. Each volume contains a mix of international, European, comparative and national law, making this a highly significant series for practitioners, judges and academic researchers in many countries.

A list of books in the series can be found at the end of this volume.

Adventures in Childhood

INTELLECTUAL PROPERTY, IMAGINATION AND THE BUSINESS OF PLAY

JOSE BELLIDO
University of Kent

KATHY BOWREY
University of New South Wales

CAMBRIDGE
UNIVERSITY PRESS

CAMBRIDGE
UNIVERSITY PRESS

University Printing House, Cambridge CB2 8BS, United Kingdom

One Liberty Plaza, 20th Floor, New York, NY 10006, USA

477 Williamstown Road, Port Melbourne, VIC 3207, Australia

314–321, 3rd Floor, Plot 3, Splendor Forum, Jasola District Centre, New Delhi – 110025, India

103 Penang Road, #05–06/07, Visioncrest Commercial, Singapore 238467

Cambridge University Press is part of the University of Cambridge.

It furthers the University's mission by disseminating knowledge in the pursuit of education, learning, and research at the highest international levels of excellence.

www.cambridge.org
Information on this title: www.cambridge.org/9781108485913
DOI: 10.1017/9781108641968

First published 2022

A catalogue record for this publication is available from the British Library.

Library of Congress Cataloging-in-Publication Data
NAMES: Bellido, Jose, author. | Bowrey, Kathy, author.
TITLE: Adventures in childhood : intellectual property, imagination and the business of play / Jose Bellido, University of Kent; Kathy Bowrey, University of New South Wales.
DESCRIPTION: Cambridge, United Kingdom ; New York, NY: Cambridge University Press, 2022. | SERIES: Cambridge intellectual property and information law | Includes bibliographical references and index.
IDENTIFIERS: LCCN 2021060682 (print) | LCCN 2021060683 (ebook) | ISBN 9781108485913 (hardback) | ISBN 9781108725347 (paperback) | ISBN 9781108641968 (epub)
SUBJECTS: LCSH: License agreements–English-speaking countries. | Intellectual property–English-speaking countries. | Children's mass media–English-speaking countries. | Children's paraphernalia–English-speaking countries. | Child consumers–English-speaking countries.
CLASSIFICATION: LCC K1405 .B45 2022 (print) | LCC K1405 (ebook) | DDC 346.04/8–DC23/eng/20220204
LC record available at https://lccn.loc.gov/2021060682
LC ebook record available at https://lccn.loc.gov/2021060683

ISBN 978-1-108-48591-3 Hardback

Contents

Figures

Cover image credit:
Felix the Cat toy – Nielsen Park Beach, Sydney, NSW, 1926. L to R: Edna Rule, June Ditchburn. Courtesy SLNSW. Photographed by a street photographer.

Acknowledgements

This book would have not been possible without the assistance of many archivists, librarians, colleagues and others who gave us their time and insights. We gratefully acknowledge their collegiality, help and generosity. In particular, we would like to thank Nick Baldwin, Amy Schireson, Antonio Palouzié, Vanessa McElduff, Max Williams, Jane Kirsty Tuckwell, Tasmin Overton, Peter Firmin, Emma Robertson, Juan Hermida, Jessica Hogg, Margaret Simpson, Antony Neufeld, Chris Crouch, Kelly McAnnaney, Richard Culley, Robert Beebe, Emm Johnstone, David Cardwell, Didier Ghez, Ross Carder, Adam Hargreaves, Will McNally, Malcolm Langley, Michael Barrier, Shaqui Le Vesconte, Josianne Wood, John Maher, Marie Selwood, Jerry Lewin, Chris Wentzell, Matthew Chipping, Keith Bales, Cara Levey, Tom Hercock, Kris McKie, Robert Egby and David Hale Hand.

Our gratitude also goes to the Strong National Museum of Play at Rochester, the Centre for Intellectual Property and Information Law at the University of Cambridge, the Engelberg Center on Innovation Law & Policy at New York University and the International Society for the History and Theory of Intellectual Property (ISHTIP). We would also like to thank the institutions we were working at while the book was being researched and written for their support: the University of New South Wales, Birkbeck College and the University of Kent. Finally, our thanks go to our editor at Cambridge University Press, Matt Gallaway, and his team, who have been wonderfully understanding and patient throughout this project.

Abbreviations

AHOEPM	Archivo Histórico de la Oficina Española de Patentes y Marcas, Madrid
AMPAS	Academy of Motion Picture Arts and Sciences, Special Collections
ANC	Arxiu Nacional de Catalunya, Sant Cugat del Vallès, Barcelona
AP	Antonio Palouzié's private archive, Barcelona
BBC WAC	BBC Written Archives Centre, Reading
BL	British Library
BPL	*Beatrix Potter's Letters: A Selection by Judy Taylor* (Frederick Warne, 1989)
BTA	Bendy Toys' private archive, Ashford, Middlesex
BTHA	British Toy & Hobby Association, London
COWAC	City of Westminster Archives, London
DL	Dodgson's Letters in Morton N. Cohen and Anita Gandolfo (eds.), *Lewis Carroll and the House of Macmillan* (Cambridge University Press, 1987)
GOSH	Great Ormond Street Hospital Archives
HA	Hogarth Puppets' Private Archive, Devon
HAT	History of Advertising Trust Archives, Norwich
ITA	Independent Television Authority, Archives & Special Collections, Bournemouth University
JCAC	The John Canemaker Animation Collection, New York University

LCD	*Lewis Carroll's Diaries: The Private Journals of Charles Lutwidge Dodgson*, Edward Wakeling (ed.) (The Lewis Carroll Society, 1993): the first complete version of the nine surviving volumes with notes and annotations
LMA	London Metropolitan Archives
MAL	Maritime Archives & Library, National Museum, Liverpool
MHC	Modern History Centre, University of Warwick
MM/CUA	Papers of Marcus Morris (1915–1989), Special Collections & Archives, Cardiff University
NAA	National Archives of Australia
NARA	National Archives and Records Administration, USA
NCCB	Seven Stories, the National Centre for Children's Books, Newcastle-upon-Tyne
NRS	National Records of Scotland
PA	Parliamentary Archives, London
QMIPA	Intellectual Property Archive, Queen Mary University of London
RL	Roberta Leigh's Private Archive, Oxford
SLNSW	State Library of New South Wales
SRO (NSW)	New South Wales State Archives & Records, Kingswood, Australia
TA	Walter Tuckwell's private archive, Brighton
TGA	Tate Gallery Archive, London
TNA	The [UK] National Archives, Kew
UARM	Unilever Archives and Record Management, Port Sunlight
UoR FW	Frederick Warne Archive, Archives & Special Collections, University of Reading
UoR MAC	Records of Macmillan and Co., Archives & Special Collections, University of Reading
UoR RKP	Routledge & Kegan Paul Archive, Archives & Special Collections, University of Reading
V&A	Victoria & Albert Museum, Special Collections, London
WB/AHC	William Boyd Papers, American Heritage Center, University of Wyoming

WBA/USC	Warner Bros Archives, University of Southern California
WBP	Leslie Linder, *A History of the Writings of Beatrix Potter* (Frederick Warne & Co, 1971)
WYAS	West Yorkshire Archive Service, Wakefield
ZSL	Prince Philip Zoological Library & Archives, London

Introduction

Children play, learn and grow immersed in a commercialised world where distinctive toys and character merchandise cater for special occasions, idle moments, training for adulthood or just for the sake of making the mundane more enjoyable. Unsurprisingly, many intellectual property cases today centre around the intangible rights claimed over toy helmets, juvenile T-shirts, or ride-on kids' suitcases, as there is a profitable industry based on children's entertainment and their special attachment to the commodities associated with that entertainment.

This book explores how the business of play and the development of modern intellectual property evolved together, and alongside concerns about children's consumption becoming a legitimate source of revenue and profit. Or, in other words, how that industry and children's special attachment to it gradually emerged. In so doing, it considers the paradox in the relationship between the growth of intellectual property and the presumed innocence of childhood that initially underpinned controversies about the construction of the child as a consumer. As is apparent throughout the book, our main argument is neither moralistic nor regulatory. Rather, our concern is to explore how, since the late nineteenth and through to the twentieth century, attempts to come to terms with this paradox were embedded in many issues and contexts. In tracing those entangled relationships, we think it is possible to see how modern authorship, entrepreneurship and even the child as a consumer, all came into simultaneous existence through a process of the mutual conferring of reality. In other words, intellectual property is not only a product of statutes. It includes a layer of activities and cultural presumptions that capture attention and generate goodwill around a particular set of creations.

From the obvious paternalistic connotations of authorship to the wireless technique of 'uncling', one of the ways in which these dynamics took off was with the emergence of the industrial author. By connecting ideas of childhood as a state of imagination and innocence to business practices, some creators began to entertain the possibility of becoming entrepreneurs in light of the many possible kinds of commodities that could arise from their creations. The book traces the commercial practices of Lewis Carroll and queries the legendary status of Beatrix Potter as the founder of British character merchandising. The late Victorian and Edwardian business practices of these authors are differentiated from the more extensive transatlantic licensing of the film cartoon character 'Felix the Cat' and the world's most famous rodent, 'Mickey Mouse'. Carroll and Potter were mostly able to effectively assert legal rights in a way that maintained an intimate relationship between the author and the eventual children's gift products. However, in the 1920s and 1930s, the craze for character merchandise unleashed by film led to a far more undisciplined consumption. For the most part, the formal designation of legal rights – copyright, design, passing-off and trademark law – failed to protect the exclusive interests imagined by the enterprise originators. Nevertheless, a cultural distinction between authorised and unauthorised merchandise began to take hold, enabling manufacturers, retailers and consumers to choose the closeness of their affiliation with a brand family. This leads to the question of whether the modernisation of intellectual property law came about more through shifting entrepreneurial practices and associated development of new forms of expertise than as a direct consequence of legislative reform or judicial innovation.

Our history complicates conventional understandings about how creativity became industrialised and challenges conventional wisdom about the legal evolution of intellectual property rights to prevent free-riding and support investment in product development. We show how licensing practices became normalised after the 1930s. By the 1960s, the scope of licences entered into had become a yardstick to measure the extent of an enterprise's property claim. Through detailed cultural, legal and business case studies, the book traces how effective international commercial licensing infrastructures were built, which included exposure to preferred protocols of consumption, with a premium attached to authorised products that created a profitable environment to exploit and grow the global trade in character merchandise. The book identifies a tension between a latent concern for protecting the innocence of the child and increasingly sophisticated strategies aimed at recruiting consumers into the commercialisation of play. We try to avoid the negative connotation that is often attached to profiting from child-related ventures, focusing instead on how intellectual property practices tended to blur the distinction between the institutions of the family and the market, as well as between gift and commodity.

For readers interested in the institution of law, this book adds to and interacts with the standard histories of intellectual property law. Firstly, it highlights the importance of studying the twentieth century to understand modern intellectual property law. As the law evolved alongside the maturing of international consumer markets, it was the most significant period of development in modern intellectual property law. In that sense, this work offers a critical point of departure from existing historiographies that have emphasised and fetishised the eighteenth and nineteenth centuries when explaining the 'origins' of intellectual property. Much contemporary scholarship on intellectual property history ends the discussion with early twentieth-century codifying events (e.g. the 1911 Imperial Copyright Act), even though modern international cultural trade was barely established at that time. By looking at the emergence of commercial expansion and the development of cross-industry dynamics, the book is a clear departure from those that look for the mythical origins of intellectual property law in earlier centuries.

Secondly, one of the aims of this book is to shed some light on the way different branches of intellectual property law (copyright, design, trade mark and patent) coalesce creatively to foster merchandising opportunities and develop business strategies. We look at the permeable boundaries between different intellectual property rights and how all rights could be engaged to protect different aspects associated with trade in the authorised product. It is the intersection of rights that facilitates opportunities for brand extension, rather than the discrete limits to protection, that is of particular interest here.

Thirdly, the book draws attention to the relevance of corporate structures and history as key resources to aid understanding of how intellectual property law was imagined and managed in practice. Rather than prioritising the 'law on the books', this work highlights how legal relations were constructed and enforced in businesses, showing the emergence of 'workarounds' and other innovations to overcome formal impediments to corporate ambition.

Lastly, the book shows the emergence of the child as a particular kind of consumer, crossing the boundary between play and education, and how intellectual property law was fundamental to that. One of the notable features of the child-related entertainment industry was its capacity to invest in audience and consumer participation. The children were not constructed as 'passive' consumers but were expected to engage deeply in imaginary play and role-play centred around their toys and playthings. Franchise holders also supported platforms for membership, participation and club enrolment. Where educational value became a marketing tool, the business of play helped reconstitute the identity of the child through socialisation. Thus, the way in which you instructed a child incorporated recruitment into broader agendas of social and cultural inclusion that signalled that imitation and copying were appropriate when associated with authorised consumption.

This history provides an important context to help better our understanding of late twentieth-century debates about piracy, copyright infringement and 'user rights'. We argue that the success of some corporations in regulating piracy relied on their capacity to understand, anticipate and domesticate channels of child and consumer participation. Engaging with the terms of play has always been part of intellectual property history, but for most of the twentieth century it was primarily viewed opportunistically, rather than as a threat to enterprise.

This work pays special attention to the logic of derivatives (tie-ins, merchandising, syndication and licensing schemes) as the main setting from where intellectual property practices emerge. We suggest that in conventional intellectual property literature, licensing is constructed as a mere contractual arrangement. Based on archival research, we develop a different view, arguing that intellectual property licensing entails a relationship based on trust and investment in a fantasy, creating extended relationships that transcend traditional delineations of producer, distributor or consumer. We also investigate how this trust relationship posed particular difficulties for public broadcasters whose charters posit a different kind of engagement with their audiences.

Combined, the themes of the book expose the capacity of the law to imagine and bring into being new markets, new kinds of business association and new kinds of cultural activity. Thus, it provides an alternative framing to the conventional view of the law as based on 'protection' of intangible property rights. The analysis is attentive to insights from literary studies, mass communications, sociology, cultural studies and social anthropology. However, we are not seeking to bridge the disciplines of humanities/social sciences and law.

For readers interested in publishing history and commodity culture, we historicise and problematise the construction of authorship and its relevance to intellectual property relations in the late nineteenth century and into the twentieth century. The literary text is not approached as a bounded cultural object, a vessel that transmits an authorial expression that can be further analysed or deconstructed to reveal a deeper hidden subtext, perhaps also revealing insights into the subjectivity of the author. Instead, we consider the text in the context of its circulation in the market. However, we also depart from histories of print capitalism that treat the book as an object of trade, its central characteristics exposed in narratives about the exploits of entrepreneurs, their commercial intentions and successes in expanding readerships. Instead, in our view, literary texts are conceived of as communication devices that carry multiple kinds of significations that produce intellectual property law's subjects and objects, transgressing public and private spheres, and reconstituting the institutions of the market and the family.

We are aware that there is criminological and psychoanalytical literature that critically engages with the idea of the child, family, innocence and predatory behaviour. The motivations of those who profess to be lovers of children or are intensely engaged in the world of the child are judged with reference to ideas of propriety and concern for criminal behaviour. This book is not concerned with those debates or concerned with drawing the line between appropriate and inappropriate standards of conduct. Rather, chapters are attentive to the child as an audience, with reference to the specifics of mass communications technologies. We are especially interested in film distribution and radio and television broadcasting as technologies that mediate relations between the family and the market. The focus is not merely on the construction of audiences *for* radio, television and film programmes, as defined by distribution contracts and broadcast licensing agreements. We are also interested in the multiple ways in which audiences are assembled and interacted with. Our contention is that the notion of audience is hypermobile, with possibilities of its constitution extended through new consumption practices inflected with judgements about the types of gift or commodity that are suitable for a child.

In discussing the idea of 'the child', we draw upon sociological literature, in particular histories about the construction of childhood in the twentieth century, the family and the gift. This literature largely engages in discussion of innocence, exploitation and commodification through a critical reading of the circulation of media products and their marketing. This can lead to a reification of commodity relations, which assumes that there is an object of contractual exchange regulated by law. This positioning is often adopted in commodification critiques without reading the business and legal records associated with commercial activity. The inaccessibility of business and legal records and the difficulty associated with interpreting them has contributed to this problem.

Our primary sources – the business and legal artefacts that document specific pathways of commodity relations – provide the original foundation to our analysis. This material includes business correspondence, confidential memorandums, corporate minutes, trade association records and journals, as well as conventional legal artefacts such as intellectual property registrations and litigation. We draw upon all these sources to explore how legal and business practices and discourses were deeply implicated in the emergence of constructs that, as a society of consumers, we have come to take for granted. The subject positions interrogated include that of the child, consumer, creator, author, entrepreneur, manager, agent, audience and fan. We posit that these were not merely private subjectivities that interacted with consumerism and branding through audience participation, product purchases or self-identification as a fan. Rather, our contention is that, in the age of global mass communications, the family became a market and, at one and the same time, the market became a family. Intellectual property law was central to this dynamic, not through the creation of intangible property rights or their deeper penetration into culture, but because law produced and regulated the connections between subjects, objects and institutions. Where the family was the site of consumption, the circulation of a commodity or gift depended upon reference to notions of trust, exploitation, protection, competition, affiliation and individualisation. The institutions of the family and the market became inseparable from their configuration and reconfiguration as actors navigated commercial paths, opportunities and aspirations.

Each chapter explores different sites where aspects of these dynamics can be traced. The focus is not always directly linked to the production of a particular toy or franchise. As is explained in the chapter previews below, which actors are considered as key protagonists, and the specific assemblages that emanate from quandaries around commercial opportunities and limits to trade, varies. While there are recurrent themes, we are not seeking to expose a 'new origin' of intellectual property or trace the sequential development of the infrastructure that supports character merchandising across the twentieth century. Our selection highlights different tensions around particular practices and discourses that, with the passage of time, were managed, in particular, through professionalisation and recourse to ideological ideas of the function of intellectual property rights.

This book is not only relevant to critical thinkers interested in the business of play and the child as a special kind of consumer. The methodology and themes explored have broader relevance for understanding the intersection of media, culture and law, and the reproduction of commodity relations in the age of mass communications. Many of the dynamics explored are also relevant to contemporary debates about social media, self-branding and the death of privacy discussed in relation to the lack of regulatory oversight over the design of platform technologies and techniques of surveillance capitalism. While the communications technologies may have changed, and we do not explore these more recent developments, there are continuities with processes of commodification that evolved across the twentieth century. In understanding this earlier age, we are better able to appreciate the shape of the world today and our place within it.

PREVIEW OF BOOK CHAPTERS

Chapter 1 explores one of the most enduring popular works for children, Lewis Carroll's *Alice's Adventures in Wonderland* (1865). Charles Dodgson (1832–1898) wrote it at a time when the very conception of childhood as a distinctive and cherished stage of human development was being explored and, through the popularity of Dodgson's penmanship, being promulgated. Dodgson's interest in children is also apparent from his (now controversial) photographs of children and from his obsessively detailed exchanges with his publisher, Frederick Macmillan, over the presentation of *Alice* and other works for children. Dodgson sought to curate the way young readers entered into and experienced the fantasy realm. He wanted to be recognised as the author Lewis Carroll, father of the *Alice* universe, and used copyright to assert his paternity of the creative representations of *Alice*. He appeared to draw the line at ventures he judged could dilute the fantasy, such as mass-manufactured goods produced outside of Victorian artistic creative industries. Dodgson wrote at a time when authors could and did control the terms of engagement with their fantasy through the exercise of copyright. Managers, agents and lawyers would supersede this authorial power and authority in the following century.

Through tracing the character merchandising of Beatrix Potter (1866–1943), Chapter 2 explores why Potter should be considered as both a creative and an industrial author. She directly engaged with the idea of childhood where the parent was a consumer, an idea that affected the direction of her creativity. We also consider the extent to which she relied upon intellectual property laws to support her merchandising interests. Potter's forethought in registering copyright and design rights is much commented on by her biographers. However, at that time, intellectual property law struggled with the very idea of an 'industrial author'. And, although

Potter engaged and popularised an expanded idea of authorship and intellectual property, she never used her rights defensively to protect the exclusivity of the 'Peter Rabbit' range of merchandise from imitations and piracies. Rather, particularly incensed by the loss of her copyright over *The Tale of Peter Rabbit* in the United States and frustrated by her dealings with British doll-makers, she was drawn into debates about British manufacturing, the politics of international trade and the reform of tariff law. Potter's legacy was to encourage the practice of authorising iterations of popular character designs across an ever-increasing range of goods circulating as appropriate gifts for children and decorative embellishment for the home.

Chapter 3 unpacks the pivotal idea of instruction in making up a particular type of subjectivity: the 'Meccano Boy'. This construction toy schooled the child in scientific education, social participation, civic roles, life within a profession and in building the material infrastructure of modernity. Playing with Meccano encouraged translation of an intangible idea represented in two dimensions into material forms through the production of three-dimensional compositions of machinery or models. We compare the legal interpretation of this form of play with its broader cultural significance. Branding strategies attached to the toys and the paraphernalia collected and exchanged by community members, sensitivity towards group identity and a distinctive approach to piracy were all tied together in the attempt to create a base of socially connected consumers, orchestrated to extract commercial value from educational play. Meccano did not involve free play or simply making educational models. A toy for making toys, Meccano was marketed as training for adulthood. Through the establishment of Meccano guilds and the relevance of the *Meccano Magazine*, children, their fathers and a wider brotherhood were interpellated as active developers of Meccano. It was a brand and activity Meccano designed for international appeal and where the child was happily engaged in play that supported a later life that contributed to international industrialisation.

Chapter 4 explores the powerful creation of Felix the Cat and Mickey Mouse, simple anthropomorphic characters represented on film and embraced by fans, which formed the foundation of extended business activities and tie-ins in the 1920s and 1930s. The term 'animated properties' acknowledges that these popular fictional representations were attributed subjecthood and, as such, came alive outside the celluloid frame. This overlaid the idea of the family with entrepreneurial dimensions. Felix and Mickey were regularly visited in the cinema, pre-packaged as family-friendly viewing. Doll effigies and other merchandise literally took the characters into the heart of the home to be present in the daily lives of the entire family unit. We are interested in the tensions that arose between authors, film distributors, entrepreneurs and merchandising agents who sought to step into the role of the parent entitled to control interactions and the staging of further public appearances of Felix and Mickey.

The chapter goes on to discuss the ambivalent role of intellectual property registration in stabilising the character merchandising trade in this era, exploring what was particularly distinctive about the Disney Corporation's industrial system of production and distribution. As Disney was unable to rely upon legal enforcement of imagined rights, the successful strategy was an organisational one with cultural ambitions, engaging franchise managers and licensees in educating children and the trade about the protocols of consumption attached to play. It involved building a portfolio of characters based upon traditional fare for children, while standardising the visual identity of Disney products. The new international infrastructures of exploitation entirely displaced lingering concerns for protecting the innocence of children from the marketplace. The Disney brand came to signify child-friendly cultural content of all kinds, with trust in the name secured by the deployment of a new legal creation, the phenomenon of 'world rights' exploited by a new managerial class, Disney Enterprises' agents.

In 1929, J. M. Barrie (1860–1937) made a bequest to the Great Ormond Street Hospital for Sick Children of his most popular creation, 'Peter Pan'. Chapter 5 explores the dynamic of gift-giving specifically for the benefit of vulnerable children and how this translated into licensing practices. A *Peter Pan* movie, to be directed by George Cukor with Audrey Hepburn as the main protagonist, was never made because of the bitter relationship that developed between the licensor, the Great Ormond Street Hospital, and its licensee, the Disney Corporation, which resulted in litigation in the 1960s. By looking at the misfortune of a film that was never made, the chapter shows how licensing intangible properties involved not only a question of contract and property but also a more complicated question of trust, sociality and the etiquette of managing commercial opportunities. The chapter engages the reader in a deeper consideration of the impact of the Disney Corporation, not just in creating a highly effective managerial infrastructure to exploit and construct the child as a consumer but also in developing intellectual property strategies to gain a privileged position with consumers, who were now conceived of as being included within the Disney family.

A key phenomenon of the twentieth century is the rise of merchandising agents as a distinct and independent profession in the United Kingdom. While previous chapters have discussed merchandising practices, the development of these activities was always attached to specific corporations such as Meccano Ltd, Pat Sullivan Studios and Disney Corporation. Chapter 6 traces the rise of merchandising agencies and focuses on the most influential independent British agency of the period, Walter Tuckwell & Associates. A former Disney employee, New Zealander Walter Tuckwell (1913–1980) fostered a network connecting and linking commercial and legal opportunities offered by television programmes and the emerging demand for child-related products. The chapter discusses the specific relationship between content creation and marketing that arises with the earliest days of television. This entails a discussion of Tuckwell's role at the British Broadcasting Corporation (BBC) and, in particular, how objections to the development of merchandising inside the corporation were managed. We then show how the arrival of commercial television changed agendas, leading to stabilisation in contractual practices between broadcasters, licensing agencies and sectors such as the toy, publishing and food industries, all of which were eager to capitalise on the new communication medium. By the late 1960s, children's participation in commodification was fully promoted and fortified in intellectual property practice and was an integral part of television culture, regardless of the character of the broadcast licence.

The tangled beginnings of the establishment of merchandising at the BBC is further developed in Chapter 7. The most troubling question for the corporation was how, in line with the organisation's traditional public values and duties as expressed in its charter and broadcasting licence, it should respond to the exploitation of radio identities such as 'Uncle Mac', a persona linked to the radio star and BBC employee Derek McCulloch, that were, without authority, also being commercialised on everyday consumer goods by outsiders to the corporation. Internal dynamics at the BBC were further impacted by the development of commercial television and the unexpected success of television programmes such as *Doctor Who*. Expectations shifted. Rather than being criticised for commercialisation, the public corporation's failure to pursue profit is what became contentious. One outcome was the development of a new management unit separate from programming, the BBC Exploitation Department, later renamed as BBC Television Enterprises, which served as merchandising agent for third-party productions such as *The Magic Roundabout* and *The Wombles*. Both instances resulted in litigation.

The book's conclusion returns to the commercialisation of *Alice in Wonderland* to draw together thoughts about how attitudes towards childhood have changed and how controversies about this continue to be negotiated outside of public view. It reconnects with discussion of Dodgson's nineteenth-century conception of 'the child' and its boundary with adulthood, as set out in Chapter 1, by considering the controversy surrounding Jonathan Miller's 1966 *Alice* film, screened by the BBC at Christmas. It was not specifically targeted for a child audience. Thus, a representation that was highly unlikely to have concerned Dodgson at all was considered controversial enough to be discussed in the British Parliament. Commissioned by the BBC's drama department, the art film offered a surreal Victorian dreamscape of childhood, as much for an erudite adult audience as for a child audience. This representation of the 'children's classic' provoked public responses of hostility and incomprehension, attracting protests about a liberality that ought to be banned.

This controversy allows us to reference changed understandings of childhood, particularly in light of Disney's rendition of *Alice* and the development of the BBC's institutional role in the 1960s, where there is ready acceptance of the children's department remit, with the imagery of the child overlaid with expectations of marketing and age-appropriate merchandise. Many issues that vexed the BBC in this period are rooted in the paradox that underpins the whole book: the tension between exploitation and innocence; family and market; public and private; and the normalisation of the logic of commercialisation tied to intellectual property.

1

Commercialisation and the Innocent Child

Alice's Adventures in Wonderland (1865) was written by Charles Dodgson (1832–1898), under the pen name Lewis Carroll, at a time when the very concept of childhood as a distinctive and cherished stage of human development was being explored. He had a romantic vision of childhood that is hard for us to grasp today, especially since our understanding of *Alice* and Lewis Carroll is now coloured by the ongoing popular and commercial re-imaginings of 'Alice', contemporary musings about Alice Liddell – the supposed inspiration for the character – as well as the propriety of the author himself. This chapter offers a new perspective of Dodgson, connecting his idea of childhood as a state of imagination and innocence to his practice as a commercial actor.

Dodgson was deeply involved in the design and production of his signature works for his friends and the public. His interest was not just limited to the completion of a text; his negotiations with publishers, illustrators, composers, actors, designers, manufacturers and retailers affected how his works would engage and interest children and their parents. Through the manner in which he exercised his rights, Dodgson sought to curate the way young readers entered into and experienced the fantasy realm. The early exploitation of *Alice* was cautious and considered, in line with the connection the author wanted to create with child audiences. What makes Dodgson particularly interesting to us is that, while copyright provided a legal foundation to control the circulation of *Alice*-connected wares bearing his pen name, he sustained an ongoing interest and engagement with his fantasy and his audiences that transcended any particular text. The construction of his commercial transactions was overlaid with romantic concerns for character formation of the child, the protection of a state of innocence and a time for play and imagination. This invested his authorship with a parental ambition that would be increasingly challenged in a commercial society flooded with toys available for purchase as gifts for children of all classes, produced on an industrial scale.

1.1 A PASSION FOR CHILDREN'S LITERATURE

He thought of his childhood, left far behind,
That blissful and innocent state.

Lewis Carroll, *The Hunting of the Snark* (1871)

Alice is only one of many works that provide an insight into Victorian attitudes towards children. The mid-nineteenth century was a period during which a large number of whimsical, nonsense and fantasy stories about children and for children were published. Their popularity has been taken as a significant indicator of the social changes that occurred in mid-Victorian society. Well-known works still considered significant today include the publication now credited as the first full-length children's fantasy, F. E. Paget's *The Hope of the Katzekopfs* (1844), along with Edward Lear's *Book of Nonsense* (1846); John Ruskin's *The King of the Golden River or the Black Brothers: A Legend of Stiria* (1851), illustrated by Richard Doyle; Julia Corner's adaptations of fairy tales, written as rhyming couplets, *Little Plays for Little People* (1854); William Makepeace Thackeray's Christmas book, *The Rose and the Ring; or, The History of Prince Giglio and Prince Bulbo. A Fireside Pantomime for Great and Small Children*, a work he also illustrated and published under the pseudonym Mr M. A. Titmarsh (1855); Frances Browne's continuation of the Grimm tradition, *Granny's Wonderful Chair and its Tales of Fairy Times* (1857); Dinah Maria Mulock's *Craik's Fairy Book* (1863); Charles Kingsley's *The Water Babies. A Fairy Tale for a Land Baby* (1863); Charles Dickens' *The Magic Fishbone*, illustrated by F. D. Bedford (1867); Dodgson's friend and literary adviser, George MacDonald's *The Light Princess* (1864) and his collection of stories, *Dealing with the Fairies* (1867) illustrated by Arthur Hughes; and Jean Ingelow's *Mopsa the Fairy* (1869), an early successful book inspired by Lewis Carroll's *Alice's Adventures in Wonderland* (1868).[1] The Victorian era also saw a surge in the publication of children's works beyond the fantasy genre and in boys' and girls' magazines.

Dodgson was a driver of the early dissemination of *Alice*. Eleven thousand copies were printed between 1865 and 1870.[2] Despite concern over the difficulty of translating nonsense verse and puns, as a result of Dodgson's own efforts and contacts, translations into French and German had begun by 1867.[3] When William W. Appleton returned to New York with the copies of the original

[1] The importance of these works can be ascertained by the fact that they have current entries in Daniel Hahn (ed.), *The Oxford Companion to Children's Literature*, Oxford University Press, 2015.

[2] Edward Wakeling (ed.), *Lewis Carroll's Diaries: The Private Journals of Charles Lutwidge Dodgson (Lewis Carroll)*, The Lewis Carroll Society, 1993 (hereafter LCD): vol. 6, 50–51, n 72 (Number 10, 24 August 1868).

[3] Ibid.

'disgraceful printing' by Clarendon Press (rejected by John Tenniel)[4] for sale in the United States, it was felt, at first, that he had made a bad buy.[5] While reviews were generally positive,[6] *Alice* was arguably more radical, challenging and enigmatic than other children's books of its time. Some considered it controversial, arguing that it was not a real children's book. The American journal, *The Nation*, described it as a book designed for adults: 'children care little or nothing for it, and it is to grown people that it is so charming'.[7] *The Atheneum* added that 'any real child might be more puzzled than enchanted'.[8] Others noted it was a work only for children who would enjoy the nonsense verse,[9] while Tenniel's illustrations, based on Dodgson's sketches, were considered to appeal to both young and old.[10] In 1929, Virginia Woolf noted that 'these are not books for children; they are books in which we become children'.[11]

The publication of *Alice* unsettled some readers' expectations about the qualities of works for children because of Dodgson's departure from the more conventional format of a moral lesson or a straightforward adventure story. For many, this was clearly one of *Alice*'s strengths, allowing an exploration of what it meant to be a child. The book entertained and perplexed, leading to the very large body of parodies, sequels, spin-offs and 'imitations' that emerged between the late 1860s and the 1920s.[12] Dodgson personally collected early *Alice* imitations.[13] He was clearly interested in tracing other's playfulness with his fantasy work.

Alice lends itself to many different interpretations. With an engaging origin story, playfulness with fantasy-states and reality, and an author taken to be ageless himself – 'a mixture of credulity, acumen, and innocence which we call a child'[14] – biography, psychology and, from the 1930s, psychoanalytical readings, all have become very influential in constructing the significance of *Alice*. It has become conventional

4 These copies were originally destined for wastepaper; see LCD: vol. 5, 100–101 (Number 9, 2 August 1865).

5 Flodden H. Heron, 'The Appleton "Alice"' (1936) 3(1) *The Colophon* 422–7; Grant M. Overton, *Portrait of a Publisher and the First Hundred Years of the House of Appleton*, D. Appleton & Co, 1925, 7.

6 LCD: vol. 5, 12, n 2 (Number 9, 13 September 1864).

7 As quoted by Michael Hancher, 'Alice's audiences' in James Holt McGavran (ed.), *Romanticism and Children's Literature in Nineteenth Century England*, University of Georgia Press, 1991, 194.

8 'Children's books', *The Atheneum* 1900, 16 December 1865, 844, as cited in Carol Sigler (ed.), *Alternative Alices: Visions and Revisions of Lewis Carroll's Alice Books*, University Press of Kentucky, 1997, xii.

9 See, e.g., the discussion in *The Standard* (6 October 1888); LCD: vol. 8, 430, n 693 (Number 12, 25 October 1888).

10 Hancher, above n 7, 195–6.

11 Virginia Woolf, 'Lewis Carroll' (1929), as cited in Sigler, above n 8, xiv.

12 Ibid. xvi.

13 LCD: vol. 8, 579, n 925 (Number 12, 11 September 1891).

14 F.J. Harvey Darton, *Children's Books in England: Five Centuries of Social Life*, (1932), Cambridge University Press, 2011, 267.

to read the text with reference to Dodgson's well-documented relationship with Alice Liddell and other child friends, not only for whom he wrote but whom he also photographed. Much of the *Alice* scholarship constructs his books and images as 'texts', where the significance is found in the author's representation of childhood in the texts and images. His images are considered to be particularly polarising.[15] Carol Mavor describes his works as 'delicious confections made of little girls (and little boys); we can safely eat them with our eyes, without using our mouths'.[16] Any contextualisation of Lewis Carroll that attempts to reveal the truth of his private motivations and the propriety of his authorship inevitably draws on limited sources. For example, although a large number of his diary entries of various length and detail survive, these have been tampered with. Of a large number of letters, estimated by Morton N. Cohen at over 100,000, saved by the addressees, only one half of the correspondence can now be found;[17] the reconstructed recollections of family members and friends, all sources now read from considerable distance.

There is an enormous volume of writing about Dodgson, clearly fascinating to many scholars who are drawn to explain the author, Lewis Carroll, his significance as a photographer and a writer, and *Alice*'s cultural importance. However, what strikes us as interesting is that Dodgson is rarely credited as a significant Victorian commercial and legal subject, and his intellectual property practices, though noted, are not properly explored. Yet, to fully appreciate Dodgson's mark as a Victorian who, unwittingly or otherwise, contributed to the conceptualisation of childhood and the market for children's literature, we need to look well beyond his texts as literary and artistic works and consider the economic and legal conditions attached to his productions as part of his negotiation of the conception of childhood.

The very idea of Dodgson as a commercial or legal subject might initially seem rather odd. Dodgson's identity is usually related to his dual role as mathematician and logician at the University of Oxford and author of numerous fiction and non-fiction works. He combined both roles. Such was the commercial success of *Alice* that from 1870 he was able to reduce his lecturing commitments.[18] It is generally accepted that 'Dodgson was not an easy man to work with. He was very specific about his publishing requirements and his approach was exacting and often pedantic'.[19] Dodgson's relationships with his publishers are described as indicative of a 'difficult' man, 'fanatically anxious', 'exceedingly fussy', 'demanding, indeed an

15 This was the main focus of the BBC 2 documentary, broadcast to celebrate the 150-year anniversary, *The Secret World of Lewis Carroll*, Clare Beavan (dir), 2015.

16 Carol Mavor, 'Forgetting to eat: Alice's mouthing metonymy' in Denis Denisoff (ed.), *The Nineteenth Century Child and Consumer Culture*, Ashgate, 2008, 103, n 13.

17 Dodgson's letters to Macmillan are held at the Rosenbach Museum and Library, Philadelphia; Macmillan's letters to Dodgson are at the British Library, but also collected in Morton N. Cohen and Anita Gandolfo (eds.), *Lewis Carroll and the House of Macmillan*, Cambridge University Press, 1987 (hereafter DL).

18 LCD: vol. 6, 131, n 201 (Number 10, 17 October 1870).

19 Edward Wakeling, *Lewis Carroll: The Man and His Circle*, I.B. Taurus & Co. Ltd, 2015, 53.

exhausting, author', a 'hypercritical taskmaster' or the outcome of an 'Evangelical ethic and his high aesthetic standards'.[20] However, to read Dodgson's relationship with his publishers as only revealing details about the author's character prevents an opportunity to explore how his dealings over the presentation of his works to the public document a change in the understanding of the exploitation prospects of fantasy worlds.

1.2 TAKING PHOTOGRAPHS

Dodgson is usually credited as a professional author yet also considered an amateur photographer. This shorthand serves to cleave consideration of his photographic practice from his literary endeavours, leading to a misleading picture of how he positioned himself in the cultural marketplace. There was, however, considerable slippage between professional and amateur status in the Victorian era. Sylvia Wolf notes that the professionals did more than make money from their work. They made a contribution to the arts:

> In the 1860s, a 'professional' was a man of breeding and education who was appointed to a position of some authority .... In the arts, professionals were distinguished from artisans and amateurs by their contribution to human achievement.[21]

However, during this period, wealthy amateurs were similarly engaged. Indeed, 'amateur study of the arts and sciences ... was considered a noble enterprise, one which expanded an individual's understanding of the physical world and allowed for the passing of idle hours in productive and creative amusement'.[22] It is clear that Dodgson was interested in photography as an art form. He attended exhibitions, purchased works of photographers he admired and, when it came to his own practice, engaged in extensive preparation for photographic opportunities and in staging the images. He also, on occasion, took photographs at the request of friends and charged reasonable sums for the prints.[23]

Dodgson actively pursued young children, especially girls, to photograph through friends and 'chance' meetings in parks and at the seaside. He went to great lengths to entertain his young friends with dolls, toys, puzzles, musical inventions, and

[20] DL: 17–18.

[21] Sylvia Wolf, '"Mrs Cameron's Photographs, Priced Catalogue": a note on her sales and process' in her book *Julia Margaret Cameron's Women*, Art Institute of Chicago/Yale University Press, 1998, 208–16, 216.

[22] Ibid.

[23] For example, George McDonald requested Dodgson to take photographs of his daughter Irene and then ordered prints for which he paid seven shillings per copy, 'a substantial sum at this time'. See LCD: vol. 5, 81–2, n 126 (Number 9, 18 June 1845).

novelties. He accompanied them to the theatre, carefully selecting performances that were not 'vulgar, coarse or irreverent'.[24] He sent letters in mirror-writing (a primitive form of cypher by writing letters in reverse), told stories and drew comics. Amusements were used to placate his subjects as he sought to clothe them and get them to pose for photographs.[25] At one point he alarmed his publisher, Macmillan, by requesting they include a slip in the forthcoming edition of *Alice*, requesting that children send in photos of themselves.[26] Children served as playmates, readers, audience, participants and inspiration. One clearly needs to take care not to separate out Dodgson's literary and photographic practices, even though discussion of his texts has primarily been left to literary scholars, and his imagery, to those from the visual arts.

One difficulty in analysing Dodgson's commercial and legal practice, however, is that his photography left few enduring marks on the business and legal worlds. His amateurish status is especially apparent when his practice is compared to that of his contemporary, Julia Margaret Cameron (1815–1879). Dodgson's photography is very similar to Cameron's works: portraits of famous artists, actors and other influential figures; tableaux with subjects dressed up and staged as archetypal personae; and sensual imagery of children. Dodgson also met with Cameron to compare their photographs of children[27] and, incidentally, she had also photographed Alice Liddell.[28] Cameron was a member of the Royal Photographic Society of Great Britain, established in 1853 to promote the art and science of photography. She entered into a business relationship with the art dealership and print-sellers Colnaghi & Co. in 1864, when photography was yet to be widely considered an art.[29] Her copyright practice was extraordinary, resulting in the registration of five hundred images between 1864 and 1875, at a time when this was uncommon.[30] A cursory glance at the relevant registers reveals that the brothers Oliver and Napoleon Sarony also frequently registered their photographs. However, in contrast to Cameron, they had established a strong commercial infrastructure to support the

[24] Charles C. Lovett, *Alice on Stage*, Meckler, 1990, 12. Lovett notes he would write to the theatre manager asking for material he found offensive be removed.

[25] He was primarily interested in little girls. For example, in response to the suggestion of a colleague bringing around a little boy to visit he wrote: 'I am fond of all children, but I am not omnivorous like a pig. I pick and choose'. Further, 'I confess I do not admire naked boys. They always seem to me to need clothes—whereas one hardly sees why lovely forms of girls should ever be covered up'. See Helmut Gernsheim, *Lewis Carroll: Photographer*, Dover Publications, revised edn, 1969, 18–21.

[26] DL: 84, n 4.

[27] Gernsheim came to consider Carroll's photography following his study of Cameron. See Gernsheim, above n 25, 28–30.

[28] Wolf, above n 21, 54; LCD: vol. 6, 274, n 446 (Number 10, 24 April 1873).

[29] Timothy Clayton, 'From fireworks to old masters: Colnaghi and print-selling, c.1760–1880' in Jeremy Howards (ed.), *Colnaghi: A History*, Colnaghi, 2010, 11.

[30] Wolf cites 508 registrations: above n 21, 216; Julian Cox cites 505 in 'Introduction', *In Focus: Julia Margaret Cameron*, J. Paul Getty Museum, 1996, 7.

activity, running studios, galleries and selling celebrity cartes de visite, arguably the most commonly pirated images at this time.[31] It is not clear why Cameron used copyright as she did. She sold reproductions experimenting with various formats – including cartes de visite and cabinet-card formats – and entered into an agreement with the Autotype Company to produce carbon prints on her behalf when she was in Ceylon.[32] When it came to selling her works, her pricing policy for prints took into account the popular appeal of a given image and the cost of the material that went into its making.[33] However, a commercial logic is clearly not the motivation behind her copyright registration practice. Curator Julian Cox argues that 'registering her photographs for copyright was a way for her to organise her work, contend with the competition, and define her output'. If so, it was a poor method. Cameron tended to register blocks of images at a time that would have been administratively convenient for her to do when in London. However, there is no apparent order to it: the register itself required so little information that it is ill-suited as a tool to define one's catalogue, amounting to little more than a bare assertion of ownership of a visual artefact as indicated by a (tentative) title. Her registration practice appears to have been less a commercially or legally prudent measure and more of a credentialing mechanism, indicating her aspiration to be taken seriously as a professional artist. Cameron engaged the law politically and symbolically, in order to affirm a social and cultural status that attested to her public life as a serious artist, through which her photographs are overtly projected as glorious works of fine art, belonging with the other subject matter protected under the Fine Arts Copyright Act 1862.

Turning back to Dodgson, he used to attend photographic exhibitions, but he only publicly exhibited once, in 1858 – and, even then, only four images.[34] He never joined the Photographic Society of London and did not produce cartes de visite nor images for sale. It has been estimated that he produced over 3,000 images, of which, no more than 1 per cent were nudes.[35] Furthermore, Amy Leal notes that, at the time, it was Dodgson's presence amongst the unchaperoned children, rather than the nudity, that raised the most hackles.[36] Dodgson's images were kept in albums for private use. They circulated amongst the families and friends of his sitters, and he instructed that the nudes be returned to the sitter or destroyed after his death. Given the personal and limited scope of circulation, as his biographers note, it is unlikely he saw photography as more than a fabulous hobby. Thus, although Mavor observes that, in the Victorian era, 'the child and the photograph were commodified,

[31] Steve Edwards, *The Making of English Photography: Allegories*, Pennsylvania State University, 2006, 78, 84–5.

[32] '"Real and ideal": the photographs of Julia Margaret Cameron', in Cox, above n 30, 110.

[33] Wolf, above n 21, 216.

[34] Gernsheim, above n 25, 31.

[35] Wakeling, above n 19, 163.

[36] Amy Leal, 'Lewis Carroll's little girls' (2 November 2007) 54(10) *Chronicle of Higher Education* B16–B19.

fetishised, developed alongside each other: they were laminated and framed as one',[37] the fact that there was no commercial side to Dodgson's photographic practice is significant. The photographs evidence Dodgson's interest in exploring the visual imagination even though the poses and creative framing do not support any particular fixed point of connection with the *Alice* fantasy. Leal says that

> writing, child-befriending, and the 'black art' of photography (so dubbed for the stains it left on the hands) were frequently interdependent in Dodgson's life .... Looking through Dodgson's vast assemblage of photographs, ... one sees a kinship between them and the stories he immortalized in his books. ... They are not fetishistic embarrassments by a beloved author, but inextricable from his aesthetic vision of childhood.[38]

If Dodgson elected not to exhibit or reproduce his photographs for public circulation, the reasons may lie in his interest in keeping them private. However, given that many of his images are similar in subject matter to Cameron's, rather than assume there is some manipulative, potentially deviant motive behind this, we should look more carefully for other reasons. For instance, his 'amateur' status already indicates a special relationship to the child. One of the hallmarks of a professional is reference to a set of agreed ethical standards as to the boundaries, limits and external oversight of appropriate conduct. With the etymological origins of the word 'amore' or 'love' still present in the meaning of 'amateur', the child is not a commercial object, but an object of love.

1.3 THE NOM DE PLUME: LEWIS CARROLL

As noted above, the Victorian public/private and professional/amateur distinction was not straightforward. Cameron, for example, in so many regards a professional photographer, still noted her occupation on the 1861 and 1871 census as 'wife' and legally, until the passage of the Married Women's Property Act 1870, was denied the right to own property.[39] For a bourgeois gentleman, already with a public and professional identity and status as 'an Oxford man', there were also complications that would come from his amateur productions entering the public domain. There is a reason why Dodgson used the Lewis Carroll nom de plume for non-academic writing throughout his life. His nom de plume was invented in 1856 when he sought to first publish verse, prose and humorous pieces in a Victorian home magazine,[40] although it is worth noting that he was also happy to refer to himself as Lewis Carroll

[37] Quoted in Catherine Robson, *Men in Wonderland: The Lost Girlhood of Victorian Gentleman*, Princeton University Press, 2001, 130.

[38] Leal, above n 36.

[39] Wolf, above 21, 216.

[40] Stuart Dodgson Collingwood, *The Life and Letters of Lewis Carroll*, Century, 1898, x.

where this assisted in him meeting personally with little girls, and, later in his life, occasionally when he was seeking to influence public affairs by writing to the newspapers.[41] Even toward the end of his life, a factor that discouraged him from pursuing legal action against an English *Alice* imitation in 1895 was the fear that he would have to appear in court and reveal his identity; 'that would be worse for me than any money loss which the sale of the book could entail'.[42] Dodgson strove to keep the persona of the Oxford mathematician and the children's author distinct with respect to the public at large. The nom de plume was one of the more obvious strategies he devised which suggested a public/private distinction. However, a nom de plume was also a particularly useful device for addressing his relationship with children, where both the author and young readers sought to share Alice's world together, a space where the distinction between real and imaginary realms is effaced. This connection opens up a secret door to innocence, where the background noise and corruption of imagination that Dodgson associated with adulthood is shut out.

Dodgson also discriminated between the gifts he made with and for children he knew and the works that were for sale to the general public. The original version of *Alice's Adventures in Wonderland*, the handwritten and hand-illustrated manuscript 'Alice's Adventures Under Ground' (1864), was presented to Alice Liddell complete with the dedication 'A Christmas gift to a Dear Child in Memory of a Summer's Day'. It concluded with a hand-drawn picture of Alice but was overlaid with the photograph on which the drawing was based, which Dodgson clearly felt was superior to his own sketch.[43] When he agreed to the publication of a facsimile edition in 1886, changes were made to the text:

> Lewis Carroll omitted from it the photograph of Alice, which necessitated rewriting the last line – 'Happy summer days' – after which he handed 'The End' on a slip of paper, which was fastened over the portrait . . . .
>
> We can only surmise his reasons for not including the photograph in the published facsimile. The manuscript of Alice's Adventures Under Ground was essentially personal, inspired by and presented to his 'ideal child friend'. On the other hand, the published facsimile was impersonal, and the author may not have wanted to limit its appeal to all children by associating it with the photograph of one particular child. Another reason, perhaps the weightier of the two, may have been the fact that the public was now thoroughly familiar with Tenniel's Alice, modelled on Mary Hilton Badcock, who bore no resemblance to Alice Liddell.[44]

41 Robson, above n 37, 139; Jean Gattegno, *Lewis Carroll: Fragments of a Looking-Glass – From Alice to Zeno*, George Allen & Unwin, 1977, 230.

42 Morton N. Cohen, *Lewis Carroll: A Biography*, Macmillan, 1995, 126; Gernsheim, above n 25, 50.

43 Lewis Carroll's 'Alice's Adventures Under Ground': www.bl.uk/onlinegallery/ttp/alice/accessible/pages90and91.html#content.

44 Gernsheim, above n 25, 49–50.

It is possible that Dodgson saw his photographs in a similar light to the manuscript of 'Alice's Adventures Under Ground'. He kept records of the seventy-six people to whom he sent copies of the published edition of *Alice*, as well as copies of some of the personal inscriptions.[45] With his photographs he staged, captured and developed the images. These were portraits of people with whom he was personally acquainted, whom he often sought to maintain a connection with. All artists can have difficulties with 'letting go' of their works, yet it seems that Dodgson did not see any benefit to himself in circulating images beyond his circle of acquaintances. A photograph could circulate as an image of beauty, a captured innocence, but to Dodgson it also documented a point in time and experience he, as a photographer, had actually shared with his subject. It is possible that, because of his personal connections with the subjects, he did not consider the photographs as (potentially) commodities. Dodgson's abortive request to have children send their images to him also suggests an apparent discomfort with a degree of distance from his readers. He directly appealed to the readers of his 1876 Easter edition of *Alice* to imagine a personal relationship with the author, Lewis Carroll:

> Please fancy, if you can, that you are reading a real letter, from a real friend whom you have seen, and whose voice you can seem to yourself to hear wishing you, as I do now with all my heart, a Happy Easter.[46]

The author's direct form of address imagines him in communication with children as if they were in company one-to-one in the home, as if the book was *his gift*. A nom de plume provides a means of presenting himself as part of the child's family, while distancing the realm of commercial relationships that made the production of the book and its purchase by a parent or friend of the child possible.

1.4 COMMERCIALISING *ALICE*

One of the problems with characterising *Alice* as a literary work by the author Lewis Carroll is that this construction already presumes too much in highlighting a legal view of the relationship between author and text, publisher and public, without considering whether Dodgson prioritised the relations that stemmed from his creation in this way. The idea of *Alice* as a literary work is based on a proprietary relationship between a person and a thing – the author and his manuscript – which founds the legal idea of copyright and permits the author and their publisher to determine the terms on which the public consumes the work. We now take for

[45] LCD: vol. 6, 92, n 142 (Number 10, 3 September 1869).

[46] Quoted in Helen Groth, 'Projections of Alice: anachronistic reading and the temporality of mediation' (2012) 26 *Textual Practices* 667–86, 669. Dodgson often included personal 'seasonal' notes to his child readers, which led to him receiving letters from them. See, e.g., a reference to receiving from Menella Smedley 'approval' of his Christmas message – LCD: vol. 6, 189, n 293 (Number 10, 22 October 1871).

granted this legal construct, which some literary historians date from the late eighteenth century,[47] so that it displaces more nuanced ways of thinking about the author and their work.

Dodgson was not unknowledgeable about or unperturbed by copyright. Indeed, he retained his literary property right to *Alice* and, after seeking advice on a stage adaptation, registered copyright in a dramatic version.[48] However, when a text is viewed from a contemporary copyright perspective, the audience tends to be homogenised and flattened, becoming an undifferentiated 'public', constructed at a distance from the work from the outset, overshadowed by the figure of the author as owner and controller of the text. It is clear that this author sought to control reception of *Alice*, but he preferred a playful and involved way of connecting with his child readers, whom he saw as his primary audience, and he used his rights accordingly.

While his retention of the copyright – entitling the publisher, Macmillan, to a 10 per cent commission[49] – was not unusual for the time, Dodgson considered that this entailed more than a printing and distribution arrangement with Macmillan. As he was paying the costs of printing, illustrating and advertising himself, he believed he should have his own way in how the book was produced. When he later realised this liberty could not be guaranteed through these copyright arrangements with publishers, he insisted on including a clause in his contract with Macmillan so that 'it is understood that the author has the control, and that no details will be carried out without his actual or implied consent'.[50] Further, although he kept close tabs on his expenses, when it came to decision-making, cost was rarely a determining factor. He cared very much about matters of presentation, well aware that children could attach great importance to aesthetic details. Dodgson remained involved in the production process, even as *Alice* rapidly evolved through multiple editions. His decision about the colour of the cover came about because he viewed red cloth as 'most attractive to childish eyes',[51] and he paid more for his preference for cream-coloured rather than stark-white paper. Dodgson personally negotiated over Tenniel's illustrations and bore these costs, including the 'monumental' loss of six hundred pounds on the first print-run when the illustrator protested about the 'disgraceful printing', which led to reprinting.[52] His legendary persnicketiness over

47 Mark Rose, *Authors and Owners: The Invention of Copyright*, Harvard University Press, 1993.

48 Copyright Registration Number 3251, Registered 12 December 1872. See LCD: vol. 6, 241–3, nn 384, 386 (Number 10, 21 December 1872).

49 Cohen and Gandolfo, above n 17, 14–15.

50 Charles Dodgson to Alexander Macmillan, 24 June, 1883, DL: 171.

51 Charles Dodgson to Alexander Macmillan, 11 November, 1864, DL: 35.

52 The loss was partially recouped by selling the inferior pages for sale in the American market and by Clarendon Press accepting a small loss; see Morton N. Cohen and Edward Wakeling (eds.), *Lewis Carroll and His Illustrators: Collaborations and Correspondence 1865–1898*, Cornell University Press, 2003; and Warren Weaver, *Alice in Many Tongues: The Translations of Alice in Wonderland*, University of Wisconsin Press, 1964, 24.

the printing – complaints about lists of corrections to mistakes that had crept into later editions not being addressed, notation of reduced margin widths, questioning the substitution of cheaper paper, wanting new plates produced to maintain the clarity of lines in the illustrations – tell us more about Dodgson than just his obsessive personality. Inferior works rejected as unsuitable for the British market were gifted to hospitals and charities or sold to 'colonials'. He was very particular about how *Alice* should be experienced by middle-class British readers. However, while he was in some ways acting as the archetypical 'author as owner', it was neither the literary work in a narrow copyright sense nor protection of his economic interest that he was most exercised about. While Dodgson clearly saw *Alice* as his own creation, the way he negotiated the publication of the text reveals that he saw himself as directly engaging with children and their understanding of the world. He produced not what copyright would view as a literary expression that incorporated artistic works – where the story could be dramatised for stage and adapted for film and broadcast – but a more complex creation where the sounds of the verse, the images, and layout of the text were designed so that they fell out of their separate courses and worked together to amuse and entertain. In other words, he was more interested in creating a fun experience for his audience than in adhering to genre rules about the construction and printing of a literary text. He pushed the boundaries of the medium. Many of his instructions were more in the spirit of seeking to curate *Alice* as an experience of childhood.

Dodgson's dealings with his publishers and collaborators suggest that he sought to engage his child audience in a similar manner to when he was in their company in person – combining jokes, puzzles, nonsense, and aural and visual puns. Dodgson played with the form of the narrative, drawing the original versions of the illustrations and page layouts. As the biographer Edward Wakeling says:

> Indeed, to Lewis Carroll the illustrations were part of a story – which explains why, when he decided that he could not draw well enough himself, he treated his various artists – Tenniel and Furniss in particular – almost as workmen engaged to carry out his own designs.[53]

The layout created visual puns and stretched credulity – such as the mouse's tail that escaped the page and the drawing of Alice's absurdly long neck. Hancher notes:

> Twice the narrator urges the reader to consult an illustration of Tenniel's to resolve an indeterminacy in the text .... Even without such advice the pictures would tend to dominate the text, because the reader would normally see them before reading the words. Someone to whom the story were read aloud would have greater imaginative freedom and responsibility – unless she were shown the pictures.[54]

[53] LCD: vol. 1, 20 (Number 2).

[54] Hancher, above n 7, 190–207, 195.

The verse in *Alice* was penned with familiar tunes in mind. In drawing upon the shared oral traditions of his times, Dodgson was forging another connection with his assumed audiences, who would understand that in places the rhyme parodied existing popular music, while drawing attention to the humour in his own phrasing. His inventive references to tunes that were well known at the time posed a considerable challenge for those, such as Arthur Sullivan and Walter Slaughter, who sought to compose original music for dramatic productions.[55] Dodgson gave permission for his verse to be set to new music but doubted the sense of the venture:

> Several of the songs are parodies of old Nursery songs, that have their own tunes, as old as the songs probably. I would much prefer, if you introduce any of these, that the old air should be used. The whole of the poetry, in both books, has been already published, with music, many times: people are constantly applying for leave to do this: and they have simply spoiled such pieces as 'Will you walk a little faster' by writing new airs. It would take a very good composer to write anything better than the sweet old air of 'Will you walk into my parlour, said the Spider to the Fly'.[56]

Dodgson via his communications over his productions and his instructions to his collaborators is akin to an auteur-director, more commonly linked today to the creative vision behind a modern film. He was trying to ensure that *Alice* was experienced as he had personally envisioned and heard as he wrote it. In other words, he was more than an author in relation to his text, but rather an orchestrator of the *Alice* experience.

1.5 REACHING THE AUDIENCE

Dodgson was committed to disseminating his creation so that it would reach as large an audience as possible. The original version of *Alice* was priced at six shillings.[57] In the mid-1860s an engineer would earn seven shillings and sixpence (7/6) a day; a bricklayer, carpenter, mason or smith 6/6; and a common labourer only 3/9.[58] Thus it was a significant purchase for the lower-middle class. In 1869, he sought to release a 'cheap edition', which Macmillan persuaded him to call the 'People's Edition':

> In view of the coming Easter season, I want you to consider once more the idea I once suggested to you – of bringing out a 'cheap edition' of Alice. My reasons for wishing for it are not commercial, strictly speaking – as a commercial speculation, it may very likely not be profitable, or even may be at a loss – but that I do not care

55 Lovett, above n 24, 27–31, 36–8; Cecily Raysor Hancock, 'Musical notes to the annotated Alice' (1988) 16 *Children's Literature* 1–29.

56 Hancock, above n 55, 2: note omitted.

57 Wakeling notes that he sold 86,000 of the original six-shilling edition total in his lifetime, netting approx. £4,125 profit total; see LCD: vol. 6, 50–51, n 72 (Number 10, 24 August 1868).

58 Dale H. Porter, *The Thames Embankment: Environment, Technology, and Society in Victorian London*, University of Ohio Press, 1998, 176.

> about. My feeling is that the present price puts the book entirely out of reach of many thousands of children of the middle classes, who might, I think, enjoy it (below that I don't think it would be appreciated). Now the only point I really care for in the whole matter (and it is a source of very real pleasure to me) is that the book should be enjoyed by children – and the more in number, the better.[59]

His disinclination to consider the children of the working class arguably relates to his presumption that their lack of education and experience would mean many of the cultural references in *Alice* would not be understood or enjoyed, even if they had leisure time, income for books and aptitude for reading.[60] Dodgson's friend, a fellow 'girl-lover' John Ruskin,[61] had similarly observed: 'The man who likes what you like, belongs to the same class with you, I think. Inevitably so'. Ruskin went on to note that if you could make the scavenger or costermonger (street-seller) like Dante and Beethoven, you would make a gentleman of him, and 'he won't like to go back to his costermongering'.[62] Dodgson, amongst others, felt comfortable speaking with authority about the taste of his own class and also middle-class children as a subset of this group.

Dodgson noted that for the first *Alice* editions a breakdown on returns was as follows: expenses, 60 per cent; publisher, 10 per cent; and author, 30 per cent. Whereas to keep the price of the People's Edition low without losing too much in quality, the cut he agreed to be was as follows: expenses, 90 per cent; publisher, 10 per cent; author, 0 per cent. His forgoing of a copyright royalty in order to keep costs down for the People's Edition[63] speaks volumes about his genuine desire to entertain greater numbers of children and his relative disinterest in using *Alice* as a vehicle of profit. In 1876, he began discussing with Macmillan the possibility of producing a cheaper edition of *Alice* with a sturdy binding to be distributed to sick children in hospitals.[64]

The release of a cheaper green cloth-covered People's Edition also allowed Dodgson to pursue piracies in the UK without raising moral qualms, for example,

[59] Charles Dodgson to Alexander Macmillan, 15 February 1869, 20 February 1869, 7 October 1887, DL: 77–9, 237.

[60] Similarly, Frankie Morris observes that 'writing for the child whose lessons, servants, toys, amusements and pet animals comingle with every part of the story, Carroll might understandably question its fitness for those who had never owned a dollhouse, seen a lantern show, been taken to a pantomime', in *Artist of Wonderland: The Life, Political Cartoons, and Illustrations of Tenniel*, University of Virginia Press, 2005, 180.

[61] It is worth noting that Alice Liddell also fascinated Ruskin; see Nina Auerbach, 'Alice in Wonderland: a curious child' (1973) 17(1) September *Victorian Studies* 31–47, 34, n 7; 'The stones of childhood: Ruskin's "lost jewels"', in Robson, n 37 above, 94.

[62] John Ruskin, *Traffic* (1864), Penguin, 2015, 5–6.

[63] DL: 237, n 1.

[64] See LCD: vol. 6, 473, n 780 (Number 10, 6 July 1876). Hospitals were also recipients of inferior productions unsuited to public sale. The practice of children's book authors attentiveness and generosity to children impacted by illness is explored further in relation to J. M. Barrie's gift to the Great Ormand Street Hospital for Sick Children in Chapter 4.

when not long after a weekly paper, *Happy Hours*, began printing parts of the book as weekly instalments.[65] He also instructed his American agent to buy up plates of rival American 'piracies', prints published legally in the United States but without his permission. These were purchased at Dodgson's own expense and subsequently destroyed.[66] As well as removing unwelcome competition in a jurisdiction where he could not enforce his copyright, this also helped ensure that his work was experienced in the manner he intended. Dodgson further approved *The Nursery Alice* (Macmillan & Sons, 1891); a sixpence edition (Macmillan & Sons, 1898); a *The Lewis Carroll Picture Book* (T. Fisher Unwin, 1899); and an abridged Little Folks Edition (Macmillan, 1907). As with the first publication, he took great care with the illustrations for *The Nursery Alice*:

> He not only makes the tiny tot concentrate on the picture, but he awakens and prods the child's curiosity by asking questions that a youngster should be able to answer just by looking at the picture and by reflecting upon his or her small well of experience. He makes sure the child can recognize colors; he makes the child examine the picture's details and tries to help develop habits of close observation.[67]

He also delayed this publication as the pictures were 'far too bright and gaudy, and vulgarise the whole thing. None must be sold in England'.[68] As with the first printing of *Alice*, he thought this sub-standard printing might be appropriate for the American market. Charles Macmillan recalls that 'they were offered and declined, as not being gaudy enough'.[69] Yet, Cohen revealed that 4,000 of the badly printed edition were sold in America, 100 in Australia, and a further 10,000 of a new printing in Britain. Dodgson considered *The Nursery Alice* a financial failure, although Cohen suggests that this is unlikely to be true, given that over 14,000 copies were circulated.[70]

1.6 PERFORMING *ALICE*

Dodgson's sense of proprietorship did not prevent others from engaging with his creation across other mediums, leading to the exercise of varying degrees of control over a number of *Alice* productions. Dodgson was interested in new entertainment technologies and their potential to spark the imagination, including to broaden the ways to experience *Alice*. For instance, Dodgson referenced magic-lantern technology with his 'dissolving view' of the Cheshire Cat. In the 1860s he also exhibited his

65 Charles Dodgson to Alexander Macmillan, 1 May 1870, DL: 86–7.
66 Charles Dodgson to Alexander Macmillan, 22 August 1876, DL: 204–205.
67 Morton N. Cohen, 'Another wonderland: Lewis Carroll's The Nursery "Alice"' (1983–84) 7(8) *The Lion and the Unicorn* 120–6, 123.
68 Charles Dodgson to Alexander Macmillan, 23 June 1889, DL: 257.
69 Charles Macmillan, *The House of Macmillan, 1843–1943*, as cited in Weaver, above n 52, 25.
70 Cohen, above n 67, 124.

own magic-lantern or dissolving-view shows of *Alice* as family entertainment.[71] He attended 'fairy shows' with fellow writer George McDonald and numerous others at the Royal Polytechnic of London,[72] and, in 1875, he was approached by a Leeds magic-lantern-maker, W. L. Breare, who sought permission to reproduce *Alice* illustrations as slides. A magic-lantern show was not usually a stand-alone visual representation of scenes, but rather it was a multimedia experience that brought the story to life. Thus, Dodgson assumed Breare was seeking a copyright licence for a dramatic performance – a recitation of scenes from *Alice* accompanied by Breare's projected images. However, it appears that these slides did not eventuate.[73]

A year later, in 1876, Dodgson authorised W. R. Hill, who worked for the Royal Polytechnic Institute, to produce an *Alice* series of slides. The Polytechnic was a private company established in 1838 to display scientific and technological exhibitions to educate the public.[74] Popular interest in optical experimentation led to the development of evermore sophisticated projection techniques and instruments. The institute established a permanent projection theatre in 1848 to stage shows to enthral and delight 'optical theatre' goers. Programmes included magic-lantern shows with dissolving views, with romantic effects such as moonlight on rippling water, as well as other unique kaleidoscopic experiences like the chromotrope, where two glass discs with patterns on them were rotated in opposite directions, and the eidoscope, which created a moving pattern based on metal discs, rather than painted glass. The popularity of these innovations drew in talented artists who learnt to paint on glass in order to create the unique slide experiences, raising the quality of the education and the entertainment.[75] The Polytechnic's magic-lantern displays were well suited to literary adaptations. As part of its 1866 Christmas programme, it staged a dramatic reading of Dickens' *A Christmas Carol* (1843), with a succession of ghosts appearing on stage.[76] The following year the institute exhibited a sequence from *The Pickwick Papers* (1836–1837), set to commissioned music. Such was the popularity of these shows that *The Times* referred to the dissolving-view shows as 'the backbone of the Polytechnic' in 1878.[77] The stories were meant to be experienced, and scenes from *Alice* were well suited to visual projection. The Polytechnic's magic-lantern *Alice*

71 See, e.g., LCD: vol. 6, 463 (Number 10, 23 May 1876).

72 Morris, above n 60, 174, 178.

73 On 20 March 1876, Macmillan noted that the printer Craik had been approached by the magic-lantern-maker, but it appears no terms were ever settled: Charles Dodgson to Alexander Macmillan, 17 March 1876, n 4, DL: 122, 126.

74 They held demonstrations, lectures and evening classes, including demonstrations of photography. Under the stewardship of former coal merchant Richard Beard, they opened Europe's first commercial photographic portrait studio on the roof of the Polytechnic in 1841. Patent licences underpinned this entrepreneurial practice and in profiling the latest scientific advances the Institute was heralded as a London centre for technological innovation.

75 Brenda Weeden, *The Education of the Eye: History of the Royal Polytechnic Institution 1838–1881*, Granta Editions, 2008, 43–50, 80.

76 Ibid.

77 Ibid. 91.

slides, hand-painted by Hill, featured designs inspired by scenes from the book – Alice in a garden with roses; an owl, a dodo, a parrot and other birds in a pool of water; looking at playing cards sitting on a table; the jury scene with the white rabbit and Alice being swarmed by the flying pack of cards – and the institute did not actually need a licence from Dodgson to produce these images. The production was originally entitled 'a lecture for children' on Dodgson's books – something to which he did not object.[78] However, when the Polytechnic wrote to Macmillan that the work was described very differently as 'an entertainment founded upon the story of *Alice*', Dodgson suggested that, if it was anything in a dramatic form, he wanted more details before he would consent, informing the Polytechnic that he held dramatic copyright to *Alice*.[79] Dodgson's view was that a licence was required for 'a tableaux interspersed with appropriate readings of songs' at the Royal Polytechnic Institute, as well as the music. He thus asserted legal rights that, for reasons discussed below, were somewhat limited. However, he ended up being quite successful in controlling how *Alice* was performed. He wrote in his diary that the show

> lasted about 1¼ hours. A good deal of it was done by dissolving views, extracts from the story being read, or sung to Mr Boyd's music; but the latter part had a real scene and five performers (Alice, Queen, Knave, Hatter, Rabbit) who acted in dumb show, the speeches being read by Mr Buckland.[80]

William Boyd wrote the music in consultation with Dodgson, and with the latter's permission.[81] Stuart Collingwood, the author's nephew biographer, wrote that 'Mr Dodgson exercised a rigid censorship over all the extraneous matter introduced into the performance'.[82] This included his request for removal of a song 'for the Cat, about a footman and housemaid ... so out of place'.[83] Collingwood says the song was about the drowning of kittens, which Dodgson felt was a subject unsuitable for humour, especially for a child audience. Similarly, in response to Savile Clarke's request to make an operetta out of *Alice* and the *Looking Glass* in 1886, he

78 It is perhaps due to the purported educational objective of the institute and because he was well known to the Polytechnic that it was initially suggested that Dodgson could pay the institute £500 to present *Alice* as part of a public lecture – a prospect that alarmed and amused Macmillan. However, by the 1870s the Polytechnic's educational objectives had dissipated, replaced by more commercially productive ventures. Traditional educational activity struggled to be recognised in a programme that had come to include 'vulgar and depraved' phantasmagoria and various other novel forms of light family entertainment, including singing, impressionists, ventriloquists, bird imitations, wire-balancing feats, juggling and conjuring. Charles Dodgson to Alexander Macmillan, 1 March 1876 in DL: 122–3; Weeden, above n75, 90; Simon During, *Modern Enchantments: The Cultural Power of Secular Magic*, Harvard University Press, 2002, 145–6.

79 LCD: vol. 6, 451–2, n 742 (Number 10, 29 February 1876).

80 LCD: vol. 6, 457, n 752 (Number 10, 18 April 1876). The note contains an extract of a review of the show in *The Times*.

81 LCD: vol. 6, 132, n 203 (Number 10, 17 November 1870).

82 Collingwood, above n 40, 174; Lovett, above n 24, 25–7.

83 LCD: vol. 6, 132, n 203 (Number 10, 17 November 1870).

consented, 'on condition of "no suggestion ever of coarseness in libretto or in stage business"'.[84]

Soon after this exhibition, Dodgson learnt of a 'pirated' dramatic work being performed by the Ellisons, 'a family of Burlesque entertainers' in Brighton. He was told it was inspired by the book, not based on his script. He sought legal advice and was informed that his copyright registration of the dramatic work 'only secured the drama from being copied, not the book, so we cannot interfere with the Ellison family'.[85] Dramatic copyright proved problematic throughout the late nineteenth century as a novel could be dramatised in the form of a script or public performance without the need for obtaining authorial consent for the adaptation. The 1878 Copyright Commission noted that this practice 'has given rise to much complaint, and considerable loss, both in money and reputation'.[86] It recommended that the right to dramatise a work be reserved to the author. However, the legislation that supported this change was not passed until 1911. Writers, such as Dodgson and Wilkie Collins, tried to prevent adaptations of their novels by registering their own dramatic works. Another practice involved seeking to perform the dramatic work before the novel was produced, making it harder for imitations to compete with the original dramatic release. However, unless a script (the text and stage directions) could be proven as copied, it was impossible to prevent performances of competing original adaptations of literary works.[87] Dodgson attended a performance by the Ellisons, finding it 'third-rate', inaudible, with the singing out of tune. Yet, thereafter he took to visiting the family and befriending their daughter, actress Clara Ellison. It appears that, despite the provocation and unwelcome news that he could take no legal action to prevent an unauthorised performance, he did not hold a grudge against the family.

Dodgson collaborated on the 1888 Clarke operetta and was involved in discussion of the use of particular tunes.[88] He suggested stage instructions and italicised words in the script to convey his intended emphasis on particular words. Yet, his royalty share in the work was only one-sixtieth,[89] copyright in the dramatic work being retained by Clark and in the musical work by Slaughter. Thus, while being directly involved, Dodgson was not acting here in the guise of the legal or commercial

[84] LCD: vol. 8, 291 (Number 12, 2 September 1886). He also made suggestions about the staging. See vol. 8, 304, n 504 (Number 12, 30 October 1886). His sensitivity and sense of propriety is also indicated by a letter of complaint to the *Pall Mall Gazette* for publishing lurid articles about child prostitution that he thought would influence the minds of men and boys, contrary to the editor's intention; see LCD: vol. 8, 222–5, n 381 (Number 12, 22 July 1885).

[85] Charles Dodgson to Alexander Macmillan, 1 March 1876, DL: 122–3.

[86] Copyright Commission, *Laws and Regulations Relating to Home, Colonial and Foreign Copyrights* (1878), xv.

[87] See further Barbara Lauriat, 'Charles Reade's roles in the drama of Victorian dramatic copyright' (2009) 33 *Columbia Journal of Law & the Arts* 1–26.

[88] Hancock, above n 55, 2–3.

[89] Charles Dodgson to Alexander Macmillan, 24 March 1889, DL: 252.

owner of *Alice*. Again, his interest was in something other than controlling *Alice* as his commercial and legal property.

1.7 AUTHORISED CURIOSITIES AND COLLECTIBLES

Over time, a large number of *Alice*-inspired works emerged.[90] Mainly these involved the fictional characters from *Alice* and *Through the Looking Glass* and are an extension of the Wonderland universe. As early as 1875, Dodgson developed the idea of an *Alice* puzzle book and contracted Tenniel to draw the frontispiece, but the project never came to fruition.[91] While today it might be taken for granted that a successful story would lead to toys and collectibles, arguably Dodgson did not see these developments as 'tie-ins' or mere exploitation. He was interested in exploring novel ways that children could engage with his fictional universe. However, two products that came on the scene in the final decade of his life suggest a shift that is closer to modern franchising: a Wonderland postage-stamp case and an *Alice* biscuit tin, both of which also featured Tenniel's illustrations.

The stamp case accompanied Dodgson's manual *Eight or Nine Wise Words about Letter-Writing*. The cover proclaimed the price to be one shilling and that it was 'invented by Lewis Carroll'. The case provided the child with 'pictorial surprises', a simple form of animation that included an inventive element:

> You don't see why I call them 'Surprises'? Well, take the Case in your left-hand, and regard it attentively. You see Alice nursing the Duchess's Baby? (An entirely new combination, by the way: it doesn't occur in the book.) Now, with your right thumb and forefinger, lay hold of the little book, and suddenly pull it out. The Baby has turned into a Pig! If that doesn't surprise you, why, I suppose you wouldn't be surprised if your own Mother-in-law suddenly turned into a Gyroscope![92]

Books with moveable effects caused by slipping or uncovering slides were well known, having been marketed as dissolving-view books by Dean & Sons in 1856.[93] Kathleen Blake argues that this work should be categorised within the large body of articles written by Lewis Carroll about games. She suggests that it demonstrates Dodgson's view of communication itself as a form of gameplay:

> Almost without exception, Carroll's rules are predicated upon a general assumption: whatever miscarriages of communication can happen, will .... Carroll expresses extreme suspicion of the accuracy and reliability of language as it issues from two different mouths or pens .... The line between work and game is dim here .... The idea behind Eight or Nine Words is that every stratagem must be used

[90] Weaver notes twenty-seven, above n 52, 12.

[91] LCD: vol. 6, 381–2, n 627 (Number 10, 1 March 1875).

[92] Lewis Carroll, *Eight or Nine Wise Words about Letter Writing*, Emberlin & Sons, 1890, 5.

[93] Morris, above n 60, 177.

> to ensure, against tremendous odds, the understanding of the reader, however ordinary his interpretative ability.[94]

Wakeling also notes that mathematical games and logical puzzles were part of the narratives of *Alice's Adventures in Wonderland* and *Through the Looking Glass*.[95] Thus, Carrollians tend to see this product essentially as an extension of his interest in puzzles and mathematical games.

However, despite the text elucidating the author's interest in communication rules that could be described as a game, unlike with the magic-lantern slides, in *Eight or Nine Wise Words* a stamp case references the image of Alice and other characters accompanied by a text, but otherwise the product does not refer to the *Alice* narrative at all. The sections of the booklet are 'On stamp cases', 'How to begin a letter', 'How to go on in a letter', 'How to end a letter' and 'On registering correspondence'. There is also a long list of Lewis Carroll's in-print publications and their prices at the end of the booklet.

The tenuous connection between the subject matter of the booklet and the stamp case is referred to in the opening paragraph, 'On stamp books':

> Some American writer has said 'the snakes in this district may be divided into one species—the venomous'. The same principle applies here. Postage-Stamp-Cases may be divided into one species, the 'Wonderland'. Imitations of it will soon appear, no doubt: but they cannot include the two Pictorial Surprises, which are copyright.[96]

In this instance, Dodgson wields an abstract legal and economic right to assist in selling a booklet that becomes an *Alice*-branded commodity. With this novel product, the author is clearly experimenting with using the characters from the *Alice* story, the Duchess's Baby and the disappearing Cheshire Cat, as valuable commercial assets. He reminds his audience that these animations are artistic works to which he owns the copyright, and he playfully references the coercive force of the state, a poisonous snake, who will strike out to protect his exclusive rights.

The 1892 biscuit tin, made by Barringer, Wallis & Manners for W. R. Jacob & Co, is a further example of the commodification of *Alice* (see Figure 1.1). It is similar in design to other chocolate-box imagery that was so popular in Victorian Britain, some of which featured works of fine art. For example, Dodgson's friend, the painter John Everett Millais, had permitted his painting *A Child's World* to be used in a Pear's soap advertisement entitled 'Bubbles' in 1886.[97] However, this new 1892 *Alice*

[94] Kathleen Blake, *Play, Games and Sport: The Literary Works of Lewis Carroll*, Cornell University Press, 1974, 77–83.

[95] Edward Wakeling (ed.), *Lewis Carroll's Games and Puzzles*, Dover Publications, 1992, xiii.

[96] Carroll, above n 92, 5.

[97] Mallais was at first apprehensive but 'mollified by the high quality of the proofs'. He was paid a very large sum – £2,200. The commercial use was subject to much criticism in *The Times*. An *Alice*-inspired advertisement appeared in 1904. See Tim Shackleton, 'Bubbles' in Mike

product was particularly innovative. A metal box-maker was looking to publicise its new offset lithographic technique of tinplate printing that allowed for the transfer of complex images from rubber onto the surface, rather than requiring printing directly onto the tin.[98] Mary Manners, the sister of one of the firm's partners, had a connection with Dodgson. He had written to her in 1885 praising her for some verses she had published in a women's journal. She wrote to ask if the firm might use Tenniel's illustrations on a box. Dodgson was impressed with the result: 'The *Alice* tin is indeed a great success . . .. I've not the least idea how such a thing could be done, they look as if painted by hand'.[99] The front surface of the lid carried the inscription 'By kind permission of the Author Lewis Carroll'. However, when he was later sent the product as provided to the trade, he found out that the tin also bore branding for Jacob's biscuits, including an *Alice*-themed advertisement on the underside of the lid. He objected to this manner of presentation as it was not his intention 'to vulgarise the boxes by turning them into advertising mediums'. After much correspondence, he was placated by the presentation of a quantity of tins that he insisted 'go out empty' to his list of friends as gifts. After the initial supply of fifty was exhausted, he then requested a hundred more.[100]

Dodgson was, thus, happy to allow *Alice* to be associated with the tin, which was at that time, a distinctive novelty item. He was also likely to have been impressed by the use of advanced printing technology, nor did he object to the *Alice* universe extending to new mediums, especially where he had assessed the product as aesthetically pleasing, representing 'quality'. However, he was uncomfortable with this connection extending further to encompass an additional association with a mass-produced product like biscuits. Metal-tin aficionado, Michael J. Franklin, suggests this may have been because Lewis Carroll was a Huntley & Palmer biscuit man. Yet, jokes aside, even though the first royal commemorative tins date from 1887, commercially produced biscuits may still have been considered 'vulgar' in their ubiquity. In removing the biscuits in the boxes sent to his personal networks, Dodgson was arguably seeking to erase the trace of his engagement in everyday commodity relations. Perhaps he was uncomfortable being associated with a commercial transaction between a biscuit seller and its consumers, two parties with whom he had no personal connection, advertised by the slogan 'with kind permission of the Author'.

Dempsey (ed.), *Bubbles: Early Advertising Art from A&F Pears Ltd*, William Collins & Sons Co, 1978, 3–4, 47.

98 Denise Amos, 'Barringer, Wallis and Manners – Metal Box Company – Crown specialty packaging', Nottinghamshire Heritage Gateway: www.nottsheritagegateway.org.uk/themes/metalbox.htm.

99 Michael J. Franklin, *British Biscuit Tins 1868–1939: An Aspect of Decorative Packaging*, Methuen, 1980, 21–22.

100 Robert Douglas-Fairhurst, *The Story of Alice: Lewis Carroll and the Secret History of Wonderland*, Harvill Secker, 2015, 323–4.

FIGURE 1.1 *Alice in Wonderland*, biscuit tin, 1892.
Courtesy of V&A Museum, London

Dodgson wanted to be recognised as the author Lewis Carroll, father of the *Alice* universe. He permitted others to represent his characters and story only with approval. He used copyright to assert his paternity over creative representations of Alice, and he appeared to draw the line over ventures that he judged as potentially diluting the fantasy, such as mass-manufactured goods outside of the Victorian artistic creative industries.

1.8 ALICE IN THE LAND OF TOYS[101]

In late 1840s Britain, a remarkable trend began to emerge. Alongside a growing interest in childhood, evidenced by the growing body of children's literature and entertainments such as pantomime, there were increasingly direct references made to children's pastimes and toys within these works themselves. Tenniel also engaged

[101] Morris, above n 60.

with this trend via his illustrations featuring Alice and her universe.[102] And, on one level, the riddles and puzzle books of Lewis Carroll can also be read as toys for the literate, as *Alice* spin-off products. However, we need to be careful here about what we mean by 'toys'.

In the nineteenth century, the 'toy' lexicon changed. It shifted from meaning '"a petty commodity, a trifle, a thing of no value; a plaything or a bauble . . . to becoming a synecdoche for childhood" . . .. Toys were bought for the specific purpose of teaching children skills and concepts'.[103] This move reflected changes in the idea of childhood and the importance of education and play. However, in the nineteenth century, the idea of appropriate education and play was also constructed with reference to changes in commodity culture. As Maria Edgeworth wrote in *Practical Education* (1796):

> A boy who has use of his limbs and whose mind is untainted with prejudice would, in all probability, prefer a substantial cart in which he could carry wood, earth and stones up and down hill to the finest frail coach and six that ever came out of a toy shop.[104]

In this example, Edgeworth argued that the child had selected the coach because of parental interference that directed him to purchase the 'prettiest' toy on display:

> Instead of attending to his own sensations and learning from his own experience, he acquires the habits of estimating his pleasures by the tastes and judgement of those who happen to be near him.[105]

She argued that no harm would be caused 'as long as a child has sense and courage to destroy the toys'. A generation later, Dodgson did not share Edgeworth's prescriptive view of education and productive play. As Davidoff surmises, 'The commercial dream that Edgeworth's toys were to help propagate had, by the end of the century, been reconceived by many as a perpetual dissatisfaction inherent in consumer culture'.[106]

Dodgson was not against trade, but against commodifying his relationship to children. As we have seen, he participated in the making of books, theatre, games, puzzles and even biscuit tins. Yet, he subscribed to the romantic idea of children as innocents, 'precious vehicles of virtue and promise'.[107] 'Play' was not a trivial concern to Dodgson and other 'child lovers'. This affected Dodgson's engagement with the world of toys. He wrote notes on the children's theatrical performances that

[102] Ibid. 170–81, 375, n 1.
[103] Teresa Michals, 'Experiments before breakfast: toys, education and middle-class childhood', in Denisoff, above n 16, 29–42, 32. References omitted.
[104] Maria Edgeworth, *Practical Education*, vol. 1, J. Johnson, 1798, 2.
[105] Ibid. 3.
[106] Dennis Denisoff, 'Introduction: small change – the consumerist designs of the nineteenth century child', in Denisoff, above n 16, 12.
[107] Ibid. 8.

he attended, but what he commented on was their professionalism and easy performance of adult identities. He did not especially dwell on their innocence, purity or vivacity.[108] Furthermore, he protested legislation designed to protect the educational rights of child performers that prohibited theatre owners from employing those aged under ten, arguing that the law went too far. The Prevention of Cruelty to Children Act 1889[109] debarred children from a 'healthy and innocent occupation that they dearly love'.[110] He refused to recognise stage employment as labour.[111] Instead, he thought performing and more generally, imaginative play, were essential to character formation.[112] He wrote at a time when the rights of children were being debated in Parliament. Education and childish pastimes were seen to impact upon British nationhood. However, Dodgson had a broader ideal of education and placed more importance on creative play than was represented in the child protection debates in Parliament. Dodgson was critical of the Elementary Education Act of 1870, which established free, compulsory and non-religious education for all children in England and Wales aged between five and thirteen. He argued that this reform had contributed to a disturbing secularisation of society. It led to moral decay, enslavement of weaker brethren, degradation of women and animal cruelty. His fear was that the future would become

> an age when all religious thought shall be things of the past; when chemistry and biology shall be the A B C of a State education forced upon on all; when vivisection shall be practised in every college and school; and when the man of science looking forth over the world which will then own no other sway than his, shall exult . . . that he has made of this fair green earth, if not a heaven for man, at least a hell for animals.[113]

Newspaper advocacy against vivisection, published using the pen name Lewis Carroll, set him against the evolutionary notion where animals occupied a 'lesser order' of God's creation. Dodgson was neither anti-science nor objectionable to evolutionary theory in the way that is familiar to us in religious fundamentalism of the twenty-first century. Rather, his Christian commitment, concern for the welfare of humanity and animals, love of mathematics and hidden order, and belief in the

[108] Marah Gubar, 'The drama of precocity. Child performers on the Victorian stage', in Denisoff, above n 16, 68.

[109] Section 3(c) prohibited children under ten from being present on premises licensed for entertainment and theatre owners needed permission of a school board to employ children aged seven. Licence conditions addressed child safety and hours of employment; Prevention of Cruelty to Children Act 1889.

[110] He also noted that the income was a godsend to poorer families: Jean Gattégno, *Lewis Carroll: Fragments of a Looking-Glass – From Alice to Zeno*, George Allen & Unwin, 1977, 269. For further discussion of the legislation see Tracy C. Davis, 'The employment of Children in Victorian theatre' (1986) 2(6) *New Theatre Quarterly* 117.

[111] Gubar, above, n 108, 74.

[112] Imaginative play was also a concern of Gramsci. See Chapter 3, 70.

[113] Lewis Carroll, 'Vivisection as a sign of the times' (1875) quoted in Cohen, above n 42, 391.

power of humour and imagination were seen as all linked. He feared that a domestication of imagination would be the result of formal state education and training.[114]

Dodgson valued literature, performance and toy theatres, though he also collected some mechanical inventions, including, of course, optical toys like magic lanterns and kaleidoscopes. Liz Farr notes that juvenile drama in the form of toy theatre was a space for cultural education where boys usually took the lead in the role of the 'stage manager', with girls taking up subsidiary roles. This play explicitly linked art, cultural education and commerce. The miniature shows with printed cardboard cut, coloured and arranged in fantasy scenes mimicked the spectacular forms of entertainment of the day. Toy theatre also fascinated many of his friends and peers including Aubrey Beardsley, Dickens, Millais, Robert Louis Stevenson, Ellen Terry and Jack B. Yeats. This kind of creative play was noted as having a formative influence on the aesthetic practice of these cultural elites.[115] Imaginative play was not valued for its own sake or thought of as an indulgence pursued by the young and the idle; it mattered for the good of society. Meanwhile, Dodgson's child friends helped keep his imagination active, enabling him to maintain a connection with 'an otherworldly realm that was also the source and affirmation of the dominant moral order'.[116]

The toy emporiums that came to prominence in major retail districts in the late 1800s, such as the world's most famous toy store, Noah's Ark (which would become Hamley's), were productive in creating new commercial desires through their eye-catching presentation windows, displays and demonstrations, where the child's visit to the store became a special 'event'. However, for the most part, buying gifts for children was usually limited to birthdays and increasingly, as the century progressed, Christmas.[117] Children were not to be 'spoilt'. Victorian psychologist, and one-time vice president of the British Child Study Association, James Sully advised in 1895 that young children's hedonistic impulses needed to be curtailed:

> What is better marked, for example, than the boundless greed of the child, his keen desire to appropriate and enjoy whatever presents itself, and to resent others' participation in such enjoyment? For some time after birth the child is little more than an incarnation of appetite which knows no restraint.[118]

[114] He was not alone in this regard. For a discussion of the false religion of consumption, including discussion of the religious view of children's writer Charles Kinglsey, see Victoria Cunningham, 'Goodness and goods: Victorian literature and values for the middle-class reader' (1992) 78 *Proceedings of the British Academy* 109–27.

[115] Liz Farr, 'Paper dreams and romantic projections: the nineteenth-century toy theatre, boyhood and aesthetic play', in Denisoff, above n 16, 43–5.

[116] Denisoff, above n 16, 8.

[117] Edward Newmark, 'British toys' (1968) 116(5138) January *Journal of the Royal Society of Arts* 135–54, 136–7.

[118] Quoted in Denisoff, above n 16, 8.

There was a class and gender dimension to this attitude. As leisure time and to some extent, disposable income, came within the purview of the lower-middle classes, concerns proliferated about the corrupting influence of pulp literature and other novelties that stimulated private pleasure, especially that which indulged the whims of young poorly educated men. Further, children's participation in the circulation of cheap wares was taken to also negatively impact on their parents.[119] Yet, in a liberal society where free trade, free religion, free art and free self-culture stand and fall 'all bundled together',[120] the state cannot control what is on display for purchase.

In the toy trade, cheap wares and trivialities were the domain of street vendors, whereas in toy stores and toy emporia what was on display were very different dolls, stuffed animals, dolls houses, puzzles, cards, board games, toy trains and complex mechanical toys.[121] These toys were often imported from the Continent. Manufacturing orders were placed based upon British retailers viewing continental samples, assisted by displays at annual toy fairs in the large British towns such as Manchester and Brighton.

As this chapter has shown, one of the limitations of the more extended commercialisation of *Alice*, and in particular the authorisation of *Alice*-franchised toys and other goods, stemmed from Dodgson's apparent discomfort with the idea of circulating Lewis Carroll products in spheres in which he had limited engagement with the makers and limited control over how the goods would be experienced. In essence, he baulked at allowing intrusions that could disrupt an imaginary personal link between the author Lewis Carroll and the children he wrote for. A Victorian patriarchal sensibility disrupted this expansion. He was not driven by a modern economic rationality, and he had no apparent real interest in building a commercial franchise in the modern sense. Imaginative play was too important to him to turn *Alice* into a 'triviality'.

Even if further product lines had occurred to him, given the way the British toy trade was constructed at this time, to make an Alice doll this Oxford don would have needed to forge connections with those 'in trade'. In publishing, he remained at a distance from the printer, leaving Macmillan to deliver instructions and manage the logistics of distribution and shop business. Some large department stores manufactured certain goods, such as clothing, as well as retailing,[122] but in the main quality toys and designs for new toys for the British public came from abroad. Although he

[119] Ibid. 6.

[120] Matthew Browne, *Views and Opinions* (1866), quoted in Peter Bailey '"A mingled mass of perfectly legitimate pleasures": the Victorian middle class and the problem of leisure' (1977) 21 (autumn) *Victorian Studies* 7–28, 17.

[121] The UK copyright design and patent registers are an excellent source of information about high-end toys.

[122] Gareth Shaw, 'The evolution and impact of large-scale retailing in Britain' in John Benson and Gareth Shaw (eds.), *The Evolution of Retail System c1800–1914*, Leicester University Press, 1992, 135.

was particularly invested in design as it related to character formation, the pragmatics of manufacturing and retailing were entirely alien to Dodgson and of no interest. Such matters did, however, interest and vex Beatrix Potter, the author and illustrator most commonly attributed with the development of British character merchandise. Her participation in the commodity market for children and her views on the importance of building a quality toy industry in Britain are explored in Chapter 2.

2

Books, Toy Books and the Artfulness of Consumption

One child who was enthused by Lewis Carroll's *Alice's Adventures in Wonderland*, in particular the illustrations, was six- or seven-year-old Beatrix Potter (1866–1943).[1] She was moved to produce her own illustrated version of the story.[2]

There were similarities between the ways Potter and Charles Dodgson exercised authorship, including an interest in corresponding with children. Both authors were inspired to publish stories that were originally written to amuse children with whom they were acquainted. Potter's *The Tale of Peter Rabbit* (1902) was based on a letter written in 1893 to a sick child, five-year-old Noel Moore,[3] whose mother, Annie Moore, Potter's former lady companion, is credited as the first to suggest that her letters might well be made into books.[4] Both Dodgson and Potter transformed private correspondence addressed to children into publications. Like Dodgson, Potter was concerned about the colour, quality and cost of her books and quite adamant about the work's presentation. She adopted many features that subtly broke with tradition for books for small children, based on her own observations about current trends and interests. As Katherine R. Chandler puts it, Potter 'accomplished her "revolution" in genre, illustration, form, and prose much as Lewis Carroll did: quietly'.[5] However, what sets Beatrix Potter apart was that she is credited as more than an innovative and accomplished artist and book writer. Her commercial

1 Judy Taylor, *Beatrix Potter: Artist, Storyteller and Countrywoman*, Frederick Warne, revised ed., 1996, 25.

2 Katherine R. Chandler, 'Thoroughly post-Victorian, pre-modern Beatrix' (2007) 32(4) Winter *Children's Literature Association Quarterly* 287–307, 288; Linda Lear, *Beatrix Potter: The Extraordinary Life of a Victorian Genius*, Penguin, 2007, 34.

3 Annie Carter (Moore), only three years her senior, was engaged as a lady companion and German teacher prior to marriage to Mr Moore in 1886. Leslie Linder, *A History of the Writings of Beatrix Potter*, Frederick Warne & Co., 1971 (hereafter WBP), 4.

4 Taylor, above n 1, 20–8, 50. For the discrete origins of the later stories and the process of illustrating and editing texts for print, see WBP, 4.

5 Chandler, above n 2, 288 (note omitted).

ambitions led the Victoria and Albert Museum to describe her as 'the first fully to exploit the merchandise possibilities of fiction. Peter Rabbit became a popular cultural phenomenon twenty-five years before Walt Disney conceived his screen icon, Mickey Mouse'.[6]

This chapter argues the case for Beatrix Potter as both a creative and an industrial author. Entrepreneurial aspirations changed the character of childhood in the late Victorian era. Furthermore, commercial developments, like the craze over advertising characters 'Sunny Jim' and the 'Golliwogg',[7] came to inform how Potter produced and disseminated her artistic and literary works. She directly engaged with an idea of childhood where the parent was a consumer, which affected the direction of her creativity. We also consider the extent to which she relied upon intellectual property laws to support her merchandising interests. Potter's forethought in registering copyright and design rights is much commented on by her biographers, including Linda Lear and Leslie Linder. However, as we explain in this chapter, copyright and design law did not clearly underpin or support the commercial enterprise that grew up around Peter Rabbit and his friends. Potter's political and legal practice did not lead to changes in British statutes or any landmark case law, and her advocacy failed to impact the free trade debate. Nonetheless, she did make a very significant contribution to the future of character franchises. Potter's business connections were also family connections. Private relationships provided a foundation for her participation in industry. Together they successfully engineered what were, in reality, quite limited property rights, demonstrating to a wide range of manufacturers the benefit of pursuing profitable 'side-shows'. For some, it showed the productivity of forging personal links with the 'original author' whose works excited the visual imagination of the masses. Potter's legacy was to encourage the practice of authorising iterations of popular character designs across an ever-increasing range of 'cultural' goods – a phenomenon that only expanded with the cinematic release of 'Felix the Cat' and 'Mickey Mouse' in the 1920s.

2.1 POTTER'S SOCIAL REALISM

Both Dodgson and Potter developed innovative stories that allowed children to safely explore the mysterious world around them. Dodgson offered a child's view – where readers are immersed in his characterisation of a state of innocence, a world where space and time are directly experienced as mutable and unpredictable. We share Alice's alarm and fear of being too big or too small for the doorway, that, alongside Alice, we want to enter – where the solution to life's challenge comes from

6 See Victoria and Albert Museum, 'Beatrix Potter: Leighton, Room 102', www.vam.ac.uk/content/articles/b/beatrix-potter-business-of-books.

7 This chapter adopts the spelling of 'Golliwogg' throughout as represented by the author Florence K. Upton, rather than the more contemporary 'Golliwog'.

exploration and logical experimentation with the resources to hand. Potter, too, encouraged discovery, but her books, designed for a younger audience, promoted a different way of knowing to Dodgson. It was an introduction into the world that adults and children share:

> 'Her characters are entirely animal', Nicholas Tucker states, 'as befits a skilled natural historian, both in their looks and behaviour. They are also absolutely human in their clothes, language and particular concerns'. . . .
>
> [Yet] None of these tales is told with an 'and the moral is' kind of ending. Often the conclusions leave readers with a sense that the disruptive behavior will be repeated or that the laugh is on the character who is the authority figure.[8]

Potter's biographer Linda Lear attributes the author with reinventing a traditional form of storytelling for children, the animal fable. In Potter's version of this genre,

> the anthropomorphized animals behave always as real animals with true animal instincts and are accurately drawn by a scientific illustrator. . .. In 'The Tale of Peter Rabbit', Potter achieves a seamless harmony between animal and human nature. It is an imaginary tale for children that leaves no doubt that such a rabbit as Peter exists in nature now, and has existed in nature forever.[9]

Of late there has been a renewed celebration of Potter's prowess as a woman scientist and naturalist and of her artistic credentials.[10] Alison Lurie points to her innovation in 'portray[ing] the world from a mouse's or rabbit's or small child's eye view. The vantage point in her exquisite watercolours varies from a few inches to a few feet from the ground, like that of a toddler'.[11] Her skill and accuracy help sustain the interest of her young readers in the story and, in so doing, to understand the world outside the book. Yet, as Lear realises, Peter's world is not an entirely fictional universe: 'It is a triumph of fantasy rooted in fact'.[12] Potter's characters served to help children interact with and relate to an imaginary British natural and social order. However, unlike Dodgson, Potter melds fictional characters with social realism, mediated by a strong desire to teach children how to read and interact with the adult world. Potter's characters face 'real-world' challenges, but the stories teach essential natures and immutable characteristics. Peter Rabbit will continue to return to Mr McGregor's vegetable patch despite the dangers he experiences and his mother's sage advice. While Peter may ignore his mother's warnings, the child learns to trust that a Potter story will resolve satisfactorily. The author will guide the child through

[8] Chandler, above n 2, 288–9.
[9] Lear, above n 2, 153.
[10] See, e.g., 'Beatrix Potter – author and amateur pioneer mycologist', *The Science Show*, Australian Broadcasting Corporation, 9 May 2015, www.abc.net.au/radionational/programs/scienceshow/beatrix–potter-e28093-author-and-amateur-pioneer-mycologist/6456308.
[11] Cited in Chandler, above n 2, 290.
[12] Lear, above n 2, 155.

the beastly order of the world that it is in Peter's nature to investigate, confident that at the conclusion the adventurer will return to the hearth and safety.

Throughout her life, Potter engaged in political activity, including around farming matters. Whereas we saw in Chapter 1 that Dodgson's opposition to vivisection linked animal cruelty with a loss of humanity and a secularisation of society, Potter had a far less sentimental view. In one draft letter, she criticised a regulation attached to the Protection of Animals Act 1911. She referred to it as a 'grandmotherly legislation', and her protest reveals something of her particular attitude towards childhood and the animal kingdom. The new law consolidated existing animal cruelty laws and regulation of knackeries, with the latter provisions seeking to ensure that animals delivered for slaughter were fed, watered and killed within two days and not killed within the sight of other animals. It also made it illegal for children under sixteen to be present in the knacker's yard.[13] It appears she misunderstood the regulation, believing it stopped children being present at the slaughter and butchering of animals on farms, about which she had fond reminiscences. She suggested the legislation hid children from the realities of life, so that they were being 'reared upon tea – and slops'.[14]

It was the horrors of Victorian animal cruelty and the trade in carcasses not meant for human consumption that was the target of this particular legislation, not farming communities. Potter's claim that fifteen-year-old farm lads would be prevented from helping cut up the pigs because 'there had once or twice been one or two serious accidents where [children] have tried to imitate the scene in play' shows an extremely unemotional view of childhood exploration and innocence. Potter believed that children should not be shielded from the realities of life, danger and death. She had a markedly different motivation in engaging the childish imagination. Her authorship was teaching very different lessons about the world from Dodgson's flights of fantasy.[15] Dodgson sought to draw the child's imagination back to the *Alice* universe to sustain their innocence and separation from the world outside. This affected the form of his address to the child, his language choices – what it sounded like being read aloud, the visual puns, and his broader motivations of creating the *Alice* universe as a sanctuary from the secular world. Potter's interest was in a much more worldly form of play, threaded with education about the natural order and consequences flowing from social interactions.

A child learning about the world through exposure to Peter Rabbit books gifted to them by family and friends also gained an introduction into the world of commerce

[13] Section 5, Protection of Animals Act 1911. Section 15 clarifies 'that the expression "knacker" means a person whose trade or business it is to kill any cattle not killed for the purpose of the flesh being used as butcher's meat and the expression "knacker's yard" means any building or place used for the purpose, or partly for the purpose, of such trade or business'.

[14] Beatrix Potter (draft letter) 1911, in Judy Taylor, *Beatrix Potter's Letters. A Selection by Judy Taylor*, Frederick Warne, 1989 (hereafter BPL), 190–1.

[15] Ibid.

markedly different to the relationship curated by Dodgson. To fully appreciate how this occurs, we need to consider in more detail the idea of bookmanship, in particular the commercial packaging of books as gifts, a backdrop to understanding the significant difference between Dodgson's gift editions and the distinctive production values of Potter's 'toy books'.

2.2 CHRISTMAS WISHES

In the late nineteenth century, English people had some of the highest per capita incomes in Europe. Disposable income was available to be used on leisure and in decoration of the home.[16] Yet, it was still considered morally wrong, as well as gauche, for those with 'new money' to parade their wealth.[17] In this context, family-centred consumption and the indulgence of children, especially on 'special occasions', were more socially acceptable ways of enjoying and sharing prosperity. The emergence of the Christmas book market is emblematic of a wider social transformation in Victorian society.

Dodgson's 'Alice's Adventures Under Ground' (1864) was a Christmas gift to Alice Liddell, and the commercial release, *Alice's Adventures in Wonderland* (1865), was also prepared for sale as a Christmas book, with subsequent editions targeting the Christmas and Easter markets.[18] There was a commercial logic to distinguishing books by their covers which goes beyond solely enhancing visual appeal to potential customers by increasing sales. Whereas scaling could lead to lower unit costs in the printing industry, Alexis Weedon argues that 'for the publisher, the benefits of manufacture were not necessarily in the quantity or speed of production, but in various "finishes" the printer and binder could provide'.[19] In a mass market, presentation is an important feature that adds impetus to the cycle of objects.[20] Goods may remain entirely fit for purpose in terms of their function, but an advertising premium is attached to 'newness' and 'distinctiveness'. Goods come to be judged in terms of manufactured properties: hallmarks of quality that encode previous iterations of the 'same goods' by marking them out as designated for particular niche groups and classes, as superseded stock or as deliberately unfashionable. Product

[16] John Benson, *The Rise of Consumer Society in Britain 1880–1980*, Longman, 1994, 11–34; Lori Anne Loeb, *Consuming Angels: Advertising and Victorian Women*, Oxford University Press, 1994, 8–9.

[17] The mid-Victorian era heralds the rise of a new genre – the etiquette book – to assist the middle class in the cultivation of manners and good taste: see Andrew Maunder, '"Alone into the wide, wide world": Trollope's Miss Mackenzie and the mid-Victorian etiquette manual' (2000) 26(2) *Victorian Review* 48–74.

[18] Tara Moore, *Victorian Christmas in Print*, Palgrave Macmillan, 2009, 109.

[19] Alexis Weedon, *Victorian Publishing: The Economics of Book Production for a Mass Market, 1836–1916*, Ashgate, 2003, 75.

[20] Jean Baudrillard, 'The system of objects' in John Thackara (ed.), *Design after Modernism: Beyond the Object*, Thames & Hudson, 1988, 171–82.

differentiation in the form of the wrapping or the art of bookmanship – special papers, bindings, cloths and illustrations – was a method of expanding the range of price points and moving 'new stock' to different classes of consumers, while minimising production costs.[21]

To the extent that bookmanship targeted traditional religious days such as Christmas and Easter, it encouraged a change in the meaning of 'gift'. While gift-giving still attested to the personal connection between the giver and recipient, the meaning of this relationship came to be overlaid with secular significations reflecting the circulation of these 'special' commodities. Dodgson's direct Easter message to children (discussed in Chapter 1) was an attempt to suppress the reality that, with these kinds of special editions, the distinction between gift and commodity was diluted. Gift-givers also engage in this dynamic by taking into account the publisher's wrapping when selecting from particular products on display, then literally papering over that commercial positioning by rewrapping the goods in additional decorative garb, often with the addition of a suitable gift card to 'personalise' the presentation of the commodity.

The idea of a Christmas book market had grown in significance from the 1820s onwards. Until around the 1860s, literary annuals dominated this trade, often containing little seasonal content. They were conveniently post-dated so copies could continue to sell into the following year.[22]

> Annuals were intended to supply the need for presents at once intimate and proper, but saying that ignores the degree to which they were widely publicized to create the very need they claimed to answer.[23]

These gifts were made for keeping. However, by the 1860s, literary annuals were supplanted by other gilt-edged presentation editions that could serve the same commercial purpose. Publishers faced tensions over producing 'quality' works for a smaller readership and meeting popular demand, especially where a publisher might be required to give the bookseller a large discount on seasonal fare.[24] While a copy might be handed around, not all books had the same expectation of longevity. From the mid-nineteenth century, the October–December window for release of books grew in significance. By the close of the century, it was the busiest season for the release of new titles, with publishers eventually targeting October as the most important month. Closer attention to the timing of releases allowed for more

21 Weedon, above n 19, 75.

22 Moore, above n 18, 9–10.

23 Peter J. Manning, 'Wordsworth in the Keepsake, 1829' in John O. Jordan and Robert L. Patten (eds.), *Literature in the Marketplace: Nineteenth Century British Publishing and Reading Practices*, Cambridge University Press, 1995, 45.

24 'Concerning books for boys' (1901) 11(1) *The Author* 34. Macmillan explained to Dodgson that the average bookseller also needed to get discounts from authors because of the Christmas trade, as 'he is obliged to offer [leftover stock] for 6d. or 1s. under the ordinary price so that at next Christmas he may have quite fresh copies': in Moore, above n 18, 110.

efficient stock management and advertising impact.[25] Social and cultural change is apparent from shifts in book subject matter made available for sale. In the first half of the nineteenth century, religious books comprised approximately 20 per cent, whereas fiction and juvenile literature combined made up 16 per cent of titles. By the first decade of the twentieth century, religious books made up only 9 per cent, whereas fiction and juvenile literature now comprised 30 per cent of all titles.[26] One study, by the Society of Authors, of books released in 1889 found that of 828 new works of fiction 'at least half' were characterised as 'children's books or goody books'.[27]

In the late Victorian period, children's, boys' and girls' own annuals – large volumes containing a mix of popular short stories, colour and black-and-white pictures, educational features, simple puzzles and games, wrapped in an eye-catching cover, released in time for Christmas – became standard fare of all major publishers. These issues were often compiled from commissioned material that had already been published in children's periodicals throughout the year – an efficient reuse of works in which the publisher owned the copyright outright. As the mid-nineteenth century progressed, book reviews also began to move beyond commentary on what one should read to improve one's self-education to recommending books one should buy for others. With this development, reference to book titles and authors' names starts to do more than convey useful information about the content of the publication. Titles and names function as a signal to consumers that the distinguished titles are worth buying. Reviews also began to comment on the physical commodity itself:

> 'The vast and glittering array of Christmas books' became 'an infallible sign' of Christmastime. Another *Times* reviewer said of the bright, enticing books for sale, 'Christmas would not be recognized without them'.[28]

More serious commentary reflected anxiety about the social costs of consumer culture. Correspondence about the subject published in the Society of Authors' journal, *The Author*, was generated by public discussion in the newspapers at the time:

> To keep him quiet we pack boys off with 'half-a-dozen gaily illustrated wanton misrepresentations of facts of every sort', and his purse is tempted by those who unscrupulously trade on his simplicity with cheap wiggeries and sham introductions to life. Then 'we proceed to wonder at the fatuity of his views'.
>
> 'Any trash will do', says a writer in the *Guardian* and this sentiment is apparently endorsed by publishers and reviewers. The very manner in which the 'gift book'

[25] Simon Eliot, 'Some trends in British book production' in Jordan and Patten, above n 23, 34–8.

[26] Eliot's study compares titles listed in *Bibliotheca Londinensis* in 1800–1850 and *Publishers' Circular* in 1900–1909: ibid., 34–8.

[27] 'Leaflet III: on paying for publication' (1890) 1(1) *The Author* 75.

[28] Moore, above n 18, 102–3.

makes its annual appearance on the market is sufficient to rank it as something equal in value to Christmas crackers and candied fruit'.[29]

By the end of the century, reviews of Christmas fare were referred to as 'altogether a farce'.[30]

Even serious publishers like Longmans, who claimed to be disinterested in the market for bestsellers, were lured into servicing the lucrative children's market. Asa Briggs notes that the house published children's poetry such as Robert Louis Stevenson's *A Child's Garden of Verses* (1885) and Walter de la Mare's (pseud. Walter Ramal) *Songs of Childhood* (1902). These works were accompanied by specially commissioned illustrations even though the inclusions went against the wishes of both Stevenson and de la Mare, who believed that 'pictures only confuse and distract the reader's own constantly fleeting pictures'.[31] Here we see the author's concern for curating reception of their work displaced by commercial logics. Illustrated volumes of poetry were a staple of the Christmas trade.[32] The inclusion of illustrations in both de la Mare's and Stevenson's books, regardless of their wishes, symbolises a shift in power from author to publisher, and the blurring of the statuses of reader and consumer. Whereas Dodgson used illustrations and visual puns to amuse, entertain and connect with middle-class children, visual interest was increasingly dictated by publisher perceptions of what purchasers might think was appealing to children and their parents. With this trend, the relationship between authorship and aesthetics was transformed. Through the changes in practices of bookmanship and marketing of works as 'especially designed for children', it becomes harder to access and value creativity unfiltered from the imagining of a children's market and the place of a particular commodity within it. While the attribution of creativity or originality to authorial genius was increasingly popularised through agitation for international copyright law reform in the 1880s, the intrusion of far more complex decision-making and production values coming to inform the significance of a literary work and its popular reception was obscured.

The growth and change in the marketplace were supported by changes in distribution and retail arrangements and in copyright licensing. The Society of Authors, founded by writer Walter Besant in 1883, sought to play a significant role in educating writers about the pitfalls of publishing in this time of transition. Standard contractual terms had become common, reducing the scope of authorial negotiations. The Society of Authors sought to educate the public about many of the author–publisher agreements in circulation. In 1890, the society launched a journal, *The Author*, to nurture the business literacy of authors, 'to promote recognition of

29 'Concerning books for boys', above n 24 13, 34.

30 Ibid., 34.

31 Longmans also produced Andrew Lang's *Blue Fairy Book* (1889), which was 'converted' in 1890 into a series of coloured class readers for school: Asa Briggs, *A History of Longmans and Their Books 1724–1990: Longevity in Publishing*, British Library & Oak Knoll Press, 2008, 361.

32 Moore, above n 18, 121–40.

the fact, hitherto most imperfectly understood, that literary property is a real a thing as property in every other kind of business. … [The Society] has always asked for one thing only – just and honest treatment, fair and open agreements, and honourable observation of those agreements'.[33]

Beatrix Potter initially saw herself as an illustrator rather than an author, but, like many Edwardian women who were coming to think of themselves as professionals,[34] Potter chose to take charge of her own commercial dealings. Her interest in the world of commerce was not simply, as has been emphasised by her biographers and the film *Miss Potter* (directed by Chris Noonan, 2006), driven by her desire to achieve independence from her parents. From the earliest days, she was very interested and actively involved in developing a market for her works, understanding that business was conducted through family firms and their connections.

2.3 BOOKS AS TOYS

In 1890 Beatrix Potter made her first commercial sale of illustrations to the printer Hildescheimer & Faulkner. These were used on Christmas and New Year cards and in a book of rhymes. Her uncle had made the initial approach to the publisher on her behalf, but this interest prompted her to seek to place other images, which in turn led her to the publisher Frederick Warne & Co., who encouraged her to submit ideas in book form.[35] When she later took her plans for a small-sized book to Warne, as well as many other publishers, she was 'repeatedly turned away, each publisher wanting something larger and with illustrations'.[36] She stood her ground. Potter's desire to publish a small-sized Peter Rabbit story book was based on her observations of the latest trends in children's books. She was influenced by the success of Helen Bannerman's small-format *Little Black Sambo* (Grant Richards, 1899).[37] Bannerman's text followed on from the earlier success of the Christmas release of Florence K. Upton and Bertha Upton's *The Adventures of Two Dutch Dolls – and a Golliwogg* (Longmans, Green & Co., 1895).[38] The wide appeal of Florence Upton's illustrations of the 'Golliwogg' character led to Longman publishing new stories each Christmas until 1909, for which the authors received a yearly

33 (1890) 1(1) *The Author* 1, 2.

34 E.g. a series of articles, 'Women who work', based on a statistical analysis of the 1881 census data, was published in the *Pall Mall Gazette* from 1884 to 1886. See 'Women who work No XVI: their numbers and employments' *Pall Mall Gazette*, 3 October 1884.

35 BPL, 28.

36 BPL, 50.

37 Lear, above n 2, 144–5.

38 For the time, the terms agreed to with Longmans were very favourable, including a graduating royalty of 10 per cent on retail price for the first 5,000 copies, and 15 per cent above that; plus 10 per cent on American sales and a £50 advance; see Norma S. Davis, A *Lark Ascends: Florence Kate Upton, Artist, and Illustrator*, Scarecrow Press, 1992, 15–16.

royalty of £1000.[39] Florence Upton's illustrations of the wooden dolls and the *Golliwogg* figure were modelled on cheap toys. She had purchased a collection of inexpensive poseable 'penny-woodens' in sizes from an inch to over a foot. These were most likely cottage productions. The model for her Golly doll came from an American toy fair. It had long lived in the Upton household.[40] The first story was set in a toyshop where all the toys come to life on Christmas eve. It was novel to include the Golly in the plot, although the book came into being at a time when racist African American inspired caricatures were very commonly represented on Victorian toys.[41] It is frequently reported that Upton failed to profit from the craze, which saw the production of postcards, toffees, perfumes, dolls, china, chintz and, later, the adoption of a Golliwogg logo by Robertson's marmalade, because of a failure to copyright or patent her work.[42] However, this is not a well-thought through argument.

Upton's Golliwogg was undoubtedly innovative subject matter for a children's book, and her drawing style, utilising simple lines, bright colours and negative space was innovative in terms of the fashions of Victorian children's literature.[43] However, as discussed below in relation to Peter Rabbit, there are a multitude of problems with the view that intellectual property registration could have assisted her. British copyright was not dependent upon registration at this time. There was no British case law that allowed copyright, design or trademark protection to be extended to characters per se to prohibit this kind of unauthorised trade extension. The idea that copyright in a simplified two-dimensional drawing, a Golliwogg illustration, itself based on an existing Golliwogg doll, extended to the manufacture of other dolls, such as Steiff's 1908 doll (with seal hair), entirely lacked legal precedent.[44] The commercial attraction of the Golly design was in part related to the context – Upton's stories projected a 'child-like' view of the world.[45] But Golly's personality and the narrative position assumed by the author, however effective in emotionally connecting with the public and child readers, were not protectable under any intellectual property regime.

39 Adaline Piper, 'Florence K. Upton: an appreciation of her work' (1923) 14(9) September *American Magazine of Art* 487–92, 488.

40 Davis, above n 38, 8–12.

41 One study of the 103 toys from the Victorian/Edwardian era reveals 80.5 per cent depicted African American figures: Christopher P. Barton and Kyle Somerville, 'Play things: children's racialized mechanical banks and toys, 1880–1930' (2012) 16 *International Journal of Historical Archaeology* 47–85, 60.

42 Jan Nederveen Pieterse, *White on Black: Images of Africa and Blacks in Western Popular Culture*, Yale University Press, 1992, 157; Briggs, above n 31, 361; Edith Lyttelton, *Florence Upton: Painter*, Longmans/Green & Co, 1926, 11; Davis, above, n 38, 23.

43 Davis (above, n 38, 17) argues her style was inspired by the celebrated children's illustrator, Walter Crane.

44 This is discussed in Chapter 4 ('Animated Properties').

45 Davis, above, n 38, 19.

Further, it was design law, not copyright, that applied to manufactured articles of trade like dolls. While design rights did require registration, protection was limited. The right really only extended to the particular design applied to a specified class of manufactured good and protection was limited in time.[46] Trademark also required registration, and trademark law may not have prohibited others' registration of Golliwogg marks, nor use of Golliwogg imagery as designs. Additionally, as discussed in the conclusion to Chapter 1, due to the state of British toy manufacturing, it may have proven very difficult to find a local maker of authorised Golliwoggs in Britain if Upton had thought to authorise doll production. With respect to German doll-makers whose wares dominated the quality doll trade, Britain lacked any developed infrastructure to control channels of supply in the 1890s. Lastly, the very power of a widely circulated racist stereotype vests in it referencing shared cultural values, where 'we' are collectively empowered to recognise, and in this case, also infantilise, 'them'. There was a fashion for racialised toys at this time, and there were no commercial ethics in place[47] that suggested the need for permission to reuse popular and racist motifs in trade, even where the heritage of the design could be attributed to a named author.

It is not clear whether Potter was provoked by the Golliwogg trade to consider a Peter doll prototype in 1903. Golliwogg dolls were not commercially manufactured at any scale until the German company Steiff began importing them in 1908. However, there is plenty of evidence to suggest that Potter was an observer of popular culture, carefully watching these trends in department stores. Potter's letters mention visits to Hamley's toy store, Whiteley's (London's first department store), Harrods and the British stuffed toymaker J. K. Farnell, where she inspected stock and engaged staff in discussion of new lines. Potter mentions a German origin velveteen 'Policeman' doll on sale as inspiration for her Peter Rabbit doll design. She also wrote to her publisher:

> 'Harrod's said they were bringing out a doll *like the advt. of "Sunny Jim", there is a run on toys copied from pictures*'. And Beatrix was aware that others were starting to benefit from the success of her books. 'My father has just bought a squirrel in the Burlington Arcade, it was sold as "nutkin"; it is prettier than the rabbits, but evidently the same make. I wonder how soon we may expect to see mice'.[48]

The Tale of Peter Rabbit was published at a time when the nature of toys available for sale in Britain was changing. Popular culture, including exposure to advertising, was starting to drive interest in character merchandise. 'Sunny Jim' was a fictional character created in the United States by writer Minnie Maud Hanff and artist

[46] The Patent, Design and Trade Mark Act 1883 limited protection of registered designs to five years. Protection was extended to fifteen years by optional renewal under the Patents and Designs Act 1907.

[47] The importance of commercial ethics is later elaborated in British 'passing off' law. See 249–54.

[48] Taylor, above, n 1, 92 (our italics).

Dorothy Ficken for the advertising agent Earnest Elmo Calkins. Sunny Jim was used in a very innovative advertising campaign for Force brand cereal. Rather than extolling the health virtues of the grain, Sunny Jim was used to communicate the emotional benefits of the brand: 'Jim Dumps became Sunny Jim after eating "Force". Without ever specifying why Jim had been depressed and listless beforehand, or what qualities in "Force" caused his transformation, she created light, humorous jingles depicting the change'.[49] This was considered a radical advertising campaign. The light humour caused controversy in an emerging advertising industry that was seeking to claim scientific marketing expertise and credentials.[50] As the campaign expanded, the public learnt about Sunny Jim's family, cook, janitor and the girl upstairs. The character caught the popular imagination so much that the public began developing their own jingles about Sunny Jim. The phenomenon created a desire for Sunny Jim merchandise, including buttons, cereal spoons, a booklet about the character and, as mentioned by Potter, a bestseller Force cereal Sunny Jim doll to be retailed by Harrods in London.[51] This development did not simply reflect changes in mass media practices.

Toys were also beginning to be differentiated by distinctive invented names that came to notice through globally syndicated news. In 1902, 'Teddy Bears' had emerged, replacing their more realistic looking forebears. These cuddly anthropomorphic creatures were inspired by a news story and a strip[52] which was a popular caricature of the soft-hearted US president, Theodore Roosevelt, who took pity on a bear when on a hunting expedition. Teddies were launched at the Leipzig Trade Fair in 1903. Teddies were also made by the German company Steiff, in association with Harrods.[53] 'Cultural products' – manufactured goods of interest to consumers because of their emotional appeal, with direct reference to shared media experiences and commercially fabricated memories – were increasingly on show for stockists and parents to buy. Having seen what toy and department stores were interested in stocking, in late 1903, Beatrix Potter began experimenting with making her own Peter Rabbit doll using rabbit fur.[54] She soon also started work on a Peter Rabbit board game.[55] A few months later, having received a letter requesting permission to produce 'badly drawn' rabbits intended as wallpaper friezes, she began

[49] Eileen Margerum, 'The case for Sunny Jim: an advertising legend revisited' (2001–2002) XII 1&2 fall/spring *Sextant: The Journal of Salem State College*: https://web.archive.org/web/20050209031952/http://www.salemstate.edu/sextant/volXII_2/SEXT-essay-sunny-jim.htm; Poster – '"Force". The wheat-malt cereal' (1903): http://collections.vam.ac.uk/item/O74356/force-the-wheat-malt-cereal-poster-benson-s-h.

[50] Stephen Fox, *The Mirror Makers: A History of American Advertising and its Creators*, University of Illinois Press, 1997, 46–8.

[51] Sunny Jim Doll http://collections.vam.ac.uk/item/O93823/sunny-jim-doll-unknown.

[52] The significance of cartoon serialisation is discussed at 112–4.

[53] Deborah Jaffe, *A History of Toys: From Spinning Tops to Robots*, Sutton Publishing, 2006, 150.

[54] Beatrix Potter to Norman Warne, 10 December 1903, BPL: 83.

[55] Beatrix Potter to Norman Warne, 7 December 1904, BPL: 110.

experimenting with her own wallpaper designs.[56] Thus, she both initiated and reacted to commercial approaches from manufacturers.

When *The Tailor of Gloucester* and *The Tale of Squirrel Nutkin* were to be published by Frederick Warne in 1903, a decision was made to include special pictorial end-papers including Potter characters.[57] Thereafter, more animal tales adopting the same illustrative style would appear. Despite these titles being based on new animal characters, the original works were executed by the author and, through attention to bookmanship, presented as part of a 'Peter Rabbit Book series'. The fantasy universe Potter created was loosely based on a shared narrative about the countryside and village life, featuring a range of small animal and human characters with common themes of predation and chase. But what all the books in the series had most in common was the way that the name of the author was emphasised by its distinctive placement on the cover and frontispiece and their common design style and visual wrapping. Individual tales were later combined and sold as 'nursery collections'. There were translations, children's stationery (wrappers, greeting and Christmas cards, calendars), wall pictures, pocketbooks, almanacs and jigsaw puzzles. One new character, Jemima Puddleduck, followed the success of the Peter doll, emerging as a soft toy designed by Potter.[58] She also negotiated agreements for china and statuettes.[59] And there were three painting books in 1911, 1917 and 1924.[60] During World War I, as well as further developing the game, there was discussion about a pincushion,[61] handkerchiefs, embroidered bibs and feeder cups.[62] In the 1920s and 1930s there were rubber toys, papier mâché figurines, plays and music books.[63] Throughout the decades, Potter corrected advertising copy,[64] negotiated contractual terms and reviewed the quality of the merchandise. Her royalties ranged from a 'standard' request for 10 per cent on retail price, reduced to 5 per cent, depending upon the kind of goods.[65] Manufacturers reminded her that the higher the

56 Beatrix Potter to Norman Warne, 14 February 1905, BPL: 113.

57 WBP: 112–14,137.

58 Frederick Warne Publishers Ltd, UoR FW: MS5337.

59 Beatrix Potter to Harold Warne, 18 January 1908, BPL: 157; Chris Wrigley, 'Hilltop, Beatrix Potter and a tale of much merchandise' (1996) 52 Winter *The Historian*, 14 17, 17.

60 WBP: 267–73.

61 J. K. Farnell to Mrs Heelis, 2 February 1915; V&A: W1, 860L, 204.1915.2 Farnell-BP 2.2.1915; Beatrix Potter to Mr Warne, 20 June 1925; W1, 864L, 200.1905.38, BP-Warne 20.6.1905.

62 Beatrix Potter to Fruing Warne, 1 September 1917, Frederick Warne to Messrs AC Cavalier, V&A: W1.865L, 207.1928.1, Warne-AC Cavalier 25.6.1928; V&A: W1.866L, 205.1926.1, Warne-AC Cavalier, 10.10.1926; w1.867L, 207.1926.1, Warne-AC Cavalier 11.10.1926.

63 WBP, 276, 288–9.

64 E.g. 'I think the catalogue design would have looked better if the ribbon had been pink, the lettering being red. It seems rather a jumble of colour. I like the simple fleur-de-lis pattern very much'. Beatrix Potter to Norman Warne, 5 December 1904, BPL: 110.

65 E.g. she received 10 per cent from Steiff on the *Peter* soft toy originally, but consented to 5 per cent on a run in 1910, as the rabbit had already 'had a fair sale'. Beatrix Potter to Harold Warne, 22 April 1910, BPL: 179. One exception was the game. This was further developed in 1917 with Fruing Warne's wife, Mary, following Harold Warne's arrest for fraud. She offered to gift the royalties to Mary, but it appears that the firm was not able to commercialise the prototype.

royalty, the higher the cost of the wares, which would affect volume sales, especially on items like handkerchiefs, where margins were very low and designs turned over rapidly. A lower royalty could thus yield higher returns in some cases.

Although this merchandising provided Potter with the comfortable income and the financial independence she had sought, the need to constantly draw for commercial purposes appears to have frustrated her at times. With respect to the sequel, *The Tale of Benjamin Bunny* (1904), Lear notes:

> At the time the book was conceived, she had few alternatives for backgrounds since by her own admission she had run out of ideas and consequently had to spend time making new sketches of rabbits in gardens. She was also consciously catering both to the public's demand and to her publisher's desire for another commercial success, while suffering some of the familiar pains of trying to write a sequel to 'an original work of genius'.
>
> The repeated red of the carnation, the foxgloves and the red pocket handkerchief that Peter repeatedly drops are calculated to catch a child's eye in a book that is once again predominantly rabbit-brown and garden-green. It was indeed [as she described it to Warne] a 'pretty book'.[66]

As the years passed, many letters to her publishers note her eyes being too tired to draw well, along with her lack of motivation once her existing series of books had given her financial security. Later in life she rather acerbically noted:

> I think the vogue of children's books in this country is too much governed by shop keepers; and mine have always been toy books – not literature. Certainly my English publishers considered the pictures first; and the words a poor second. The shop keepers like something comic and showy … it does seem such a pity that children should be encouraged to like things grotesquely ugly.[67]

What is missing from this observation, of course, is any acknowledgement of her own role in the development of 'toy books' and the industrial conditions for successful children's authors. She clearly contributed to the progress of commercialisation – reading marketplace trends, reinterpreting traditions and creating new fashions and product lines for children – working closely with her publisher and with manufacturers who contacted them.

2.4 LEGAL TECHNICALITIES

Beatrix Potter frequently referred to her ownership of copyright and design rights as the basis of this character trade. Though her father was trained as a barrister, it

Their energies were directed to managing bankruptcy proceedings and company restructuring, which saw Potter ending up with shares in the new company. Beatrix Potter to Fruing Warne, 3 September 1917, BPL: 236–7; Lear, above n 2, 284–7.

66 Lear, above n 2, 183–4.

67 Beatrix Potter to Mrs Coolidge, 9 December 1929, BPL: 324.

appears he did not spend a great deal of time in practice, largely living off family money generated from the textile printing trade. Copyright registration of textile designs was established in the eighteenth century and Potter's family connection to the trade may have given her a general awareness of this technical area of law and its importance to manufacturing. A successful textile printing business had been established in Manchester by her paternal grandfather, Edmund Potter (1802–1893), who also had a keen interest in arts education and advocated its importance for the working man. He was the president of the Chamber of Commerce and the Manchester School of Art at a time when these were highly influential fora for discussion of intellectual property rights. He also served as a Liberal Member of Parliament (1861–1874).[68]

Potter's family background, her general understanding of commercial matters and ready access to her father assisted her in negotiating most of the legal aspects of her business. She was practically minded, forward-looking and resilient, with an eye to creating commercial opportunities and anticipating how these might be exploited. Undeterred by the initial lack of commercial interest in *Peter*, she paid £11 for a printing of the book in black and white by Strangeways & Sons in September 1901. She also arranged for a colour frontispiece from Hentschel. The first print run was 250 copies. However, she had the foresight to order 500 of the frontispiece so that she could arrange a reprint quickly if needed. It was. She ordered a reprint in February 1902.[69] At the same time, negotiations were afoot with Warne & Co. for a wider release of *Peter Rabbit*, which included reducing the number of illustrations but colouring them all. It was through her association with the publisher that she met her fiancé, Norman. This led to continuity from her upbringing, where personal connections and business realms intersected, providing her with expertise and opportunities of real value to a woman engaged in business.

Initially, Warne & Co. offered her a deferred royalty arrangement, based upon a standard Publishers Association agreement. This was a form of agreement where she was asked to contribute to the cost of the printing by forgoing royalties on the first 3,000 copies, and thereafter would receive a 10 per cent royalty on the retail price for the remainder.[70] The Society of Authors' assessment of deferred royalty agreements was that her royalty should have been higher than 10 per cent given the contribution already made.[71] Warne & Co. suggested this arrangement was necessary due to high printing costs related to her demands. Not only did their edition have more coloured illustrations than her first version, they used the new method of producing three colour blocks, developed by Hentschel. She commented on Hentschel's work as being superior to that of Warne's traditional printer, Edmund Evans.[72]

68 Lear, above n 2, 10–13; Taylor, above n 1, 14.
69 Lear, above n 2, 145.
70 Norman Warne to Beatrix Potter, 7 May 1902; 26 May 1902; 29 May 1902; WBP: 103–105.
71 'Matters for consideration' (1897) 5(1) *The Author* 17.
72 Beatrix Potter to Warne & Co., 11 September 1901, 15 July 1902, BPL: 64.

Like Dodgson, Potter wanted her book to stand out by emphasising its superior visual appeal. She approached aesthetics in a similar way, informed by an interest in drawing the child into engagement with the fantasy and based on an understanding of what she believed small children liked. She also differentiated between the books for her child friends and those for the general public, and, in the early days, she distrusted Warne's assessment of the children's market. Following *Peter Rabbit*, she self-published another title, *The Tailor of Gloucester* (Strangeway & Sons, 1902), which was based on an illustrated story, a Christmas gift to Freda Moore in 1901. She had done this assuming Warne would not be interested in another title so soon, and also because she assumed that they would have demanded she cut out some of her rhymes.

However, soon Potter learnt to accept her fiancé's advice on revisions of the text and illustrations. She explicitly considered the need for her work to stand out in a crowded marketplace for children's literature; her decision-making involved keen anticipation of what an imagined consumer would like and could afford. She wrote in an illustrated letter to ten-year-old Marjory Moore that 'she would rather make two or three little books costing 1/- each, rather than one big book costing 6/- because she thinks little rabbits cannot afford to spend six shillings on one book, and would never buy it'.[73] Therefore, she insisted on the retail price of one shilling, refusing, however, to sign the publishers' agreement until they clarified the copyright arrangements for future editions, including her right to the blocks if Warne discontinued the printing.

After the tragic death of her fiancé Norman Warne (1865–1905), brothers Harold and Fruing took over the management of the 'Bunny business', as they called it. She was generally satisfied with the printing of her books, with quality being overseen by Warne & Co's production manager, W. A. Herring. However, the firm did not initiate connections of tie-ins with manufacturers. Largely, they were reactive to inquiries that came to the firm, and Potter found their dealings with outside manufacturers and the accounting of royalties less satisfactory. She complained about Harold's 'mishandling' of doll production arrangements in 1910–1911, advising them that from now on she preferred 'to manage the dolls myself'. Her judgement of the firm's competency shows her entrepreneurial attitude and confidence in dealing with trade. She made numerous appeals to both brothers over delayed royalty payments, before, during and after the war. She had negotiated with Norman for monthly payments so that she would have a steady flow of income to live off. Knowing the brothers personally, she did not hold back in reminding them of their financial obligations, at the same time apologising for putting them under pressure. In 1917, Harold was convicted for financial fraud and, when the firm was sold to creditors, Potter ended up with shares in the restructured company. Coming out of this affair, she insisted on arrangements to return all original illustrations to her or,

[73] Beatrix Potter to Marjory Moore, 13 March 1900, in Lear, above n 2, xvi–xvii.

alternatively, for them to go to a library, and she demanded an end to open-ended copyright assignments to the firm[74] as such agreements could lead to a significant loss of control over future productions.

It is likely that she had thought to register a design for her Peter Rabbit doll in 1903,[75] due to her general knowledge of the importance of design protection to 'quality' manufacturing.[76] Further, Hildescheimer & Faulkner, to whom Potter had sold illustrations for use as postcard designs, also occasionally registered copyright in these productions, though there are none that credit her authorship. As regards the first publication of her book, it is likely she retained her copyright in the Strangeways & Sons edition of *Peter Rabbit*, given that it was self-published. However, negotiating copyright matters with Frederick Warne was a little complicated over *Peter* as she was confidently anticipating the publishing of 'editions' from the outset. She pressed Norman for clarity:

> I do not quite understand about the copyright. Do you propose that the copyright remains mine; you agreeing to print an edition of 5,000 – and having – as part of the agreement the option of printing more editions if required? . . . For instance, who would hold the copyright in the event of your not wishing to print a second edition? I have not spoken to Mr Potter, but I think Sir, it would be well to explain the agreement clearly, because he is a little formal having been a barrister.[77]

Though agreeing to assign her copyright to the firm in 1902, she insisted from the outset on a clause that gave her a right to repurchase her work. She understood that the value of the copyright was both linked to the quality of her illustrations, text and the book design and also affected by the vagaries of the manufacturing process. She was confident of her ability as an artist, but her income would dry up if her works were widely pirated or if things went awry at the reproduction end. The first editions of *Peter* include the words 'COPYRIGHT' in large bold typeface at the bottom of the front cover and title page. This appears to be an unregistered copyright. UK copyright registration records of the relevant time period include volumes of original copyright entry forms from 1842 to 1912.[78] There is also a register of assignments of copyright,[79] the Stationer's Company Register for Literary Works[80] and the Fine

74 Taylor, above, n 1, 121; 138–9; Lear, above n 2, 284–5.

75 Design Registration Number 423888, Peter Rabbit Doll, 28 December 1903; TNA: BT 51/118; BT 50/531.

76 In 1905, more than 6,000 of 7,000 registered printed textile designs came from Manchester and, though she was not living in the town, the importance of design rights in the manufacturing trade would have been common knowledge. It was argued that there was a need for a design registry to be established in the city because of the degree of registration activity. Mr Astbury, 'Patent and Design Bill 1907' (Hansard, 17 April 1907).

77 Beatrix Potter to Frederic Warne & Co., 18 December 1901, BPL: 56.

78 TNA: COPY 1 (1 January 1837–31 December 1912).

79 TNA: COPY 3/100 (22 November 1901–18 March 1924).

80 TNA: COPY 3/30–COPY 3/62 (Literary works, 1883–1924).

Arts Register.[81] Despite diligent searches, we were unable to locate any entry under the publisher and proprietor names of Strangeways & Sons or Frederick Warne & Co. for the title *The Tale of Peter Rabbit*, or for Beatrix Potter, Strangeways & Sons, Frederick Warne & Co. as copyright owner of this literary or artistic work.[82]

This was perfectly acceptable practice in the book trade at the time. As the entry form 'Instructions for Registration of Books[83] first published within the British Dominions' notes:

> **Necessity of Registration**. – Copyright is created by Statute, and does not depend upon registration, which is permissive only and not compulsory, but no proprietor of copyright in any book can take proceedings in respect of any infringement of his copyright unless he has, before commencing his proceedings, registered his book.

Subsistence of copyright and registration were treated as separate matters.[84] Failure to register did not invalidate the right, but it was not possible to bring an infringement action without providing proof of proprietorship in the form of a stamped copy of the register entry. Once registered, proprietors could then proceed to enforce rights from the date of first publication.[85] This technicality only further complicates searching UK copyright records because the date of the copyright registration may not coincide with the date of publication. It can occur much later, initiated because of a desire to bring legal proceedings.

The entry form requires the proprietor of the copyright to certify to being the 'first publisher' of the title. While it was possible for authors to lodge the registration, this requirement may also have been difficult for Potter to comply with. There would be little reason for Strangeways & Sons to assist her in registering a small print run of an experimental work. Their failure to register also had implications for Warne & Co. Though the title was soon proven widely popular and successful, Warne & Co. was publisher of subsequent editions only. As they were not the 'first publisher', they could not have honestly complied with this technical legal requirement and registered the copyright on Potter's behalf. However, there are copyright registrations by Warne & Co. for many of the later tales.[86] Potter also asked that copyright be

[81] TNA: COPY 3/119–COPY 3/163 (Paintings & Drawings, 1883–1912).

[82] Original entry forms were checked for the period 1 August 1901 to 31 March 1903. The assignment of copyright register was checked for 22 November 1901 to 18 March 1924. The Stationer's Company Register for literary works was checked for 9 January 1901 to 4 June 1903 and the Register for Fine Arts (Paintings & Drawings) from 24 October 1901 to 21 May 1903.

[83] The full title is 'Instructions for Registrations of Books first published within the British Dominions under the Provisions of the Copyright Acts, 5 and 6 Vict, c45, and 49 and 50 Vict, c33'. Copyright Entry Form (UK), dated 1901.

[84] See *Walter v Howe* (1881) LR Ch D 708; *Trade Auxiliary Co. v Middlesbrough and District Trademen's Protection Association* (1888) LR 40 Ch D 425; *Cate v Devon and Exeter Constitutional Newspaper Company* [1899] 60 Ch D 500.

[85] Section 24, Copyright Act 1842. *Goubard v Wallace* (1877) 36 LT 704; 25 WR 604.

[86] There are many registration receipts in Copyright Receipts March 1900–February 1930, UoR FW: MS 5337.

registered in her 1904 version of the Peter Rabbit board game, and, although correspondence between Beatrix and Norman suggests he complied, we could also find no trace of this registration.[87]

2.5 AMERICAN PIRATES

Published in the 1860s, Dodgson's *Alice* did not have the direct benefit of copyright protection in the United States, but an English author could still obtain a copyright by way of 'trade courtesy' in this market if they could arrange for their book to be printed in the United States before any British printings had emerged.[88] A new multilateral international copyright treaty came into force in 1886 which simplified trade relations for publishers. The Berne Convention meant that when *Peter Rabbit* was first published in 1901, the book was automatically protected in all convention countries – not just in the UK and its dominions.[89] Though not a signatory, the United States passed the International Copyright Act (the Chace Act) in 1891, which further improved the situation for British authors and publishers.[90] The combined effect of these legal changes was to facilitate an infrastructure to support an international book market that increased the potential value of copyright assignments to publishers. Common author agreements sprang up that routinely sought assignment of 'Serial, American, Colonial, Continental, Translation and Dramatic Rights'. Some common agreements suggested a 50 per cent share in any royalties from such sources. The Society of Authors considered this as unfair, given that for many of these editions the publisher was only acting as agent, for which a commission of 10–15 per cent was the industry standard.[91] The society established its own Author's Syndicate in 1890 for the purpose of syndicating or selling serial rights of authors in magazines, journals and newspapers. This included links with an American agent.

Frederick Warne alerted Potter to the possibilities of sales in the US market. In 1902 the firm had set up an office and agent in the United States, and copies of the book were sent to the New York office between October and December of that year. An attempt was then made to register the US copyright, but there were technical problems with Frederick Warne's attempts to register *The Tale of Peter Rabbit.*

[87] Lear, above n 2, 175.

[88] This was why William Appleton was looking to the British market for new unpublished works. Flodden H. Heron, 'The Appleton "Alice"' (1936) 1(3) *The Colophon* 422–7; Grant M. Overton, *Portrait of a Publisher and the First Hundred Years of the House of Appleton, 1825–1925*, Appleton & Co, 1925, 7.

[89] Berne Convention for the Protection of Literary and Artistic Works 1886. In 1901 signatories included Belgium, France, Germany, Italy, Japan, Luxembourg, Monaco, Norway, Spain, Switzerland, Tunisia and the UK. See further, Ronan Deazley, 'Commentary on International Copyright Act 1886' in L. Bently and M. Kretschmer (eds.), *Primary Sources on Copyright (1450–1900)*, www.copyrighthistory.org, 2008.

[90] International Copyright Act (The Chace Act), Washington DC (1891).

[91] 'Matters for consideration' (1897) 5(1) *The Author* 19.

Under the Chace Act, authors had to comply with strict copyright formalities. There were four conditions precedent to protection:

(1) registration of the title with the Library of Congress *on or before the date of publication*;
(2) deposit of copies was required on or before the date of publication with no grace period allowed for in the 1891 statute, although as per previous Acts some late deposit was allowed in practice;
(3) books had to be printed in the United States; and
(4) a copyright notice had to be included on all copies.

A report by the Copyright Office from this time notes numerous 'inequalities of exchange' in the internationalisation of rights, including that

> there may be an important practical difference in the ease or difficulty of compliance with obligatory formalities, depending upon whether the author is a citizen or a foreigner. It is not as easy, for example, for a foreign as for a native author to arrange for the filing of his title page at Washington before publication, and it is obviously a much less difficult matter for an American than for a foreign author to arrange to have his book type-set in the United States before the day of first publication, which may mean for the alien author the burden of a double printing of his work, abroad and in the United States.[92]

Frederick Warne was unable to secure a US registration for *The Tale of Peter Rabbit* because the book was already in print. The book appears to be the firm's first failed experiment with US registration, although, by the end of 1902, a registration was achieved for an unrelated title.[93]

In 1904, a Philadelphia publisher Henry Altemis published a version of *Peter Rabbit* with minor textual changes to the Warne originals and duly registered his copyright in January 1904. Two deposit copies were received by the Library of Congress on 23 June 1904. However, Altemis was also unable to enforce his copyright.[94] Due to Warne's failure to comply with US copyright formalities, the title had already entered the public domain. These technical formalities were soon relaxed in the United States with the 1909 copyright revision.[95] While the United States may have been belatedly identified as a 'secondary' market for *Peter*, the

92 Library of Congress, Copyright Office, *Report on Copyright Legislation*, Washington, 1904, 28–9.

93 The full entry reads 'Knowlson, T[homas] Sharper, *The Art of Success*, New York & London, Frederick Warne & Co., 1902, xi, 163 pages, 19 cm. 2– 26498. 6662a. Copyright by Frederick Warne & Co. New York, N.Y. Class A, XXC, no 44092, October 20, 1902; 2 copies rec'd, Nov 7, 1902'.

94 John Turner, *A Bibliography of Unauthorised American Editions of The Tale of Peter Rabbit by Beatrix Potter 1904–1980*, Ian Hodgkins & Co. Ltd, 2012, 1–2.

95 See Tyler T. Ochoa, 'Protection for works of foreign origin under the 1909 Copyright Act' (2010) 26 *Santa Clara Computer & High Technology Law Journal* 285.

inexperience of Warne & Co. proved very costly. Not only did the loss of an American copyright lead to lost royalties in that market, the situation contributed to many battles against 'pirate' printings as traders sought to import American editions into markets where the work remained in copyright. The experience brought home to Potter the importance of professional management of copyright, though from a reading of surviving business records in the UK it appears that Warne & Co. continued to manage registration very casually.[96] The enormous challenge of preventing American piracies from entering the UK market can be seen from correspondence with the commissioner for customs and excise. Assistance was sought to seize a number of works in 1939. The offending titles were

> 'The Tale of Peter Rabbit' by Milo Winter. Merill Publishing Co, Chicago. Size: 13 x 9 ¾ inches. The text is entirely copied; the illustrations are adapted from Beatrix Potter's work.
>
> 'Peter Rabbit'. On the title page, 'The Story of Peter Rabbit' by Beatrix Potter. Illustrated by Ruth Easthill. Whitman Publishing Company, Wisconsin. Size: 5 5/8 x 6 5/8 inches. The text has been somewhat abridged. The illustrations are adapted from Beatrix Potter's work.
>
> 'A Picture Story Book for Children' designed by Maywell Dudley. Containing the story of 'Peter Rabbit', 'Red Riding Hood' etc. Whitman Publishing Company, Wisconsin. Size: 9 ½ x 12 inches. The text is complete. The illustrations are adapted from Beatrix Potter's work.[97]

It is worth noting that alleged piracies frequently altered Potter's original illustrations. As *Peter* was in the public domain in the United States, these changes were not executed to try and evade infringement. US publishers were free to adapt the work as they liked. Changes to the imagery in the book related to trying to maintain visual interest in what was by now a familiar story book, a commodity that had been continuously in print for almost forty years. It was precisely these changes that created a hurdle for the customs officials. Under section 14 of the Copyright Act 1911, in conjunction with the Customs Consolidation Act 1876, customs officers were only permitted to seize foreign 'copies' of copyright works. Distinguished copyright lawyer E. J. MacGillivray noted that this section probably meant that customs were only empowered to seize identical or verbatim copies. 'Colourable

[96] E.g. there is no particular order to the company copyright records. It is not searchable by title. The relevant book is a compendium of miscellaneous correspondence, including 'random' pasted in original receipts from Stationer's Hall, and the record has no index. See Copyright Receipts March 1900–February 1930; UoR FW: MS 5337. Further, as noted earlier, despite Norman Warne advising her that the firm had registered her idea for a board game in 1904, no registration can be found.

[97] 'Copyright infringement of The Tale of Peter Rabbit, by Beatrix Potter: Copyright Act 1911 s14' TNA: Cust 49/2910.

imitations', and even translations, may not be caught.[98] A concern was communicated to Warne & Co. that customs were not readily able to judge if these were in fact infringements. In reply the firm furnished copies accompanied by the claim that the written texts were 'entirely the same'. An order was subsequently made allowing customs officials to seize these offending copies.

On inheriting Potter's copyrights in 1943, Warne & Co. instructed solicitors to track down pirate commodities across the globe. The same infringing copies referred to in 1939 were again imported into Britain and the Commonwealth after World War II. Customs informed Warne & Co. that, although the earlier titles had not been removed from the seizure list,

> it will be appreciated, however, that Customs Officers cannot examine every package of goods imported as freight or by post, or every piece of passenger's baggage, and some copies of copyright works inevitably escape detection.[99]

Details were also furnished of other allegedly infringing copies. These imitations had been sourced from various US publishers and appeared in stores in Bermuda, New Zealand, Johannesburg and Calcutta. On receipt of complaints from Warne & Co's solicitors, department stores in Commonwealth countries invariably apologised and the offending stock was removed. But it was thought likely that the same titles would, if not already in circulation, also be imported into the UK. In pursuing the matter, a customs official noted: 'We shall then have a miniature copyright list (of 17 works) for "Peter Rabbit" alone! But that can hardly be helped'. Another had scribbled on the margin, 'British publishers are entitled to the highest degree of protection we can give'.[100] The firm also sought to restrain importation of a further thirteen titles published by the Platt & Monk Co, New York, as part of the 'Wee Books for Wee Folks' series. These books had deceptive titles such as *How Peter Rabbit Goes to Sea*, *Peter Rabbit and Jack-the-Jumper*, *Peter Rabbit's Easter*, and *Peter Rabbit's Christmas*. The illustrations were claimed to be based on Potter's characters and, as the solicitors put it, the books adopted a similar 'make-up and form' to the copyright works. The titles were also considered 'colourable imitations', the concern being that the public could be deceived into thinking that this new *Peter Rabbit* series was associated with the now-deceased author, Beatrix Potter. Again, very sympathetic, customs carefully avoided opening up discussion as to whether copyright was actually the correct body of law to rely upon here to restrain importation. It seems doubtful that the texts had any relation to any existing Potter story. At least some, and probably most, of the illustrations were drawn to fit the new narratives. Passing-off law, not copyright, would have been the more relevant body of law as it protects the public against deception caused by misleading titles and packaging 'get-up'.[101] Warne & Co's solicitors were

[98] E. J. MacGillivray, *The Copyright Act 1911: Annotated*, Stevens & Sons, 1912, 108.
[99] H. A. Parker to Messrs Guscotte, Fowler & Cox, 5 August 1948; TNA: Cust 49/2910.
[100] File Ref: 57915/48; TNA: Cust 49/2910.
[101] This is discussed in more detail in Chapter 4.

attempting to use copyright because, with sympathetic customs officers onside, it had proven efficient in the past. However, as already mentioned, copyright does not exist in mere titles or characters, nor does it entirely rule out making 'adaptations' of illustrations, and copyright did not protect the 'make up and form' of books, at least in the vague sense indicated by Warne & Co.[102] If contested, a court would need to judge the extent of the deviation from the original drawings to work out if the offending works involved infringement. It was for this reason that MacGillivray had warned that customs were probably only empowered to seize identical 'copies' of the original. But the officials deftly skirted around the rather large foundational problem with Warne & Co's allegation. They simply deferred consideration, focusing on more immediate minor procedural matters. They advised the solicitors to comply with the letter of the copyright regulation, submit the appropriate statutory declaration where Warne & Co. asserted these works did infringe copyright and be prepared to lodge a bond if any goods were seized. The thirteen titles were then added to their list.

2.6 IMITATIONS

As discussed above with respect to the Golly dolls, as a matter of law it was notoriously difficult to prevent 'imitation' toys free-riding on the back of an author's success. In 1905, the British firm Dean's Rag Book Co. launched the 'Knock-About' toy range. The company had pioneered a method of colour-fast printing on cotton, using technology to print children's rag books with edges cut with a zig-zag 'cloth-making shears' pattern. These were sold as 'Dean's Patent Rag books' and 'Hygienic A1 Toys' – washable works for small children. The 'Knock-About' range was comprised of colourful cloth-sheets of printed pattern pieces, with instructions for cutting out and sewing into soft cloth dolls. The range included traditional and then currently popular fare: the Pussy Cat, the St Bernard Puppy, the Bunny, the Coloured Ball, Little Red Riding Hood, Dolly Dimple, the Rocking Horse and the Elephant, A Little Dutch Doll and Little Pete Coon Doll. The range fitted in envelopes for easy mailing to customers.[103] The 1905 'Bunny' design was a stylised squatting rabbit without any adornment, printed with mottled brown and white 'fur'. However, a decade on this toy was completely restyled. Still called 'Bunny', the finished doll was now presented standing upright on its two hind legs, like the Steiff Peter Rabbit doll. It had also acquired distinctive clothing: dressed in pants, waistcoat, a jacket with brass buttons, and a jaunty bowtie. His waistcoat was printed in green.

[102] The typographic layout of a book was first protected by the Copyright Act 1956 (UK). For the history of this exception, see *Newspaper Licensing Agency Ltd v Marks and Spencer plc* (2001) UKHL 38 (HL).

[103] Dawn Cope and Peter Cope, *Dean's Rag Books and Rag Dolls*, New Cavendish Books, 2009, 24.

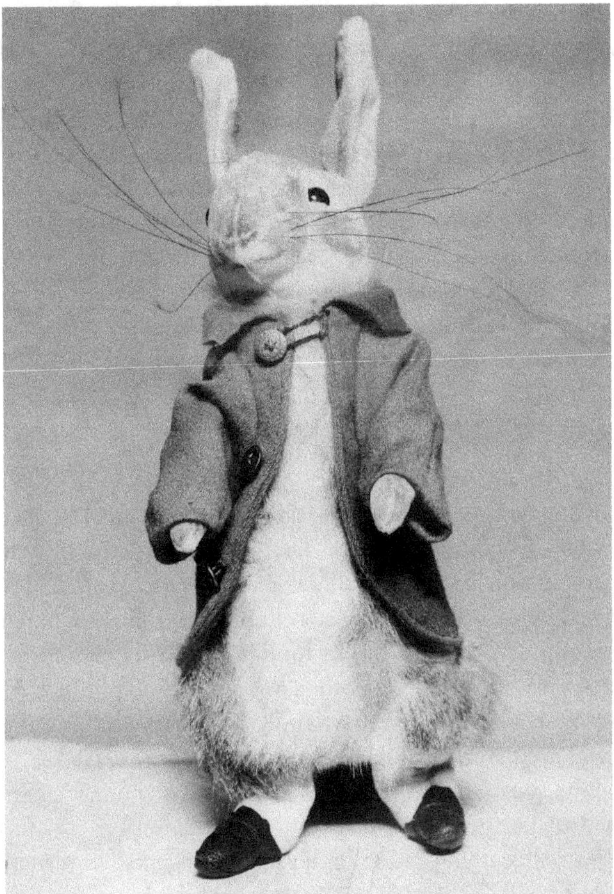

FIGURE 2.1 *Peter Rabbit* doll design registration, 1903
Courtesy of National Archives, UK

Potter had a design right for a Peter Rabbit doll. Though her authorised doll was manufactured as a plush toy, design protection was not limited to dolls made of any particular material. The design right covered any similar looking doll. However, here Dean's Rag Book Co's doll-sheet dissected the dressed rabbit into pieces so that it did not look like any particular Potter illustration or any particular rabbit. And Dean's was not actually selling a doll, only two-dimensional pattern pieces that would be cut, sewn and stuffed by the purchaser.[104] Dean's was not infringing Potter's copyright nor any design right. 'Rabbit' could be legally transformed so it far more closely resembled the eponymous Peter. In this regard, the decision to

[104] Today this could lead to a discussion as to whether Dean's Rag Book Co. was authorising the copyright infringement of the cloth sheet purchaser.

change the colour of the waistcoat from sky blue to green is interesting. Perhaps the professional artist employed by the toy company felt uncomfortable with setting out to baldly copy such a famous design by a well-respected artist.

It appears that Warne & Co. noticed 'Bunny's' new look. In the following year, 1917, Dean's Rag Book Co. began production of a stuffed doll called Peter Rabbit, part of the 'Puddleduck Series'.[105] It was in both parties' interests to collaborate. And Dean's mail order and advertising would be far more effective if the product name clearly indicated a connection with the creations of the famous Beatrix Potter, even though there was no registered trademark for Peter Rabbit or Beatrix Potter. A commercial imperative trumped any worry over whether a licence was actually required to manufacture some of these particular toys or call them Peter Rabbit.[106]

2.7 BRITISH QUALITY

From very early on, Beatrix Potter anticipated consumer interest in her characters beyond the format of traditional books. Though not particularly interested in the mechanics of production processes, she cared about the quality of material goods that bore a visual association with Peter Rabbit and her own name. She was particularly annoyed at being unable to find a British manufacturer for her Peter Rabbit doll in 1903, forcing her to appoint a foreign firm to produce it because there was simply no firm available within her family or Warne's sphere of contacts, or in the cities beyond their networks. Her chosen collaborator, Steiff, associated with quality doll-making, was familiar to customers in Britain.

In only a few years, the situation at home had improved. In 1906 the British toymaker J. K. Farnell started producing plush 'teddy bears', in response to demand for this new style of doll.[107] After disagreements over Harrods' arrangements, Potter sought out Farnell to produce her Jemima doll in 1910 – 'the only side show which I arranged personally and accounted for'. This included registering a design right in her own name.[108] However, other correspondence she had with Farnell over dolls never came to anything, leading to her conclusion that the then leading British manufacturer of soft toys was a 'semi charitable amateur toy maker'.[109] In a similar vein, unable to source appropriate housing for his lead model soldiers, the writer H. G. Wells noted in 1913 that 'the toy shops are just the merciless mercenary

[105] Cope and Cope, above n 103, CD ROM: Serial No D227.

[106] This market dynamic is discussed further in Chapter 4.

[107] www.vam.ac.uk/moc/collections/j-k-farnell. The total production of British-made toys remained modest. In 1907, it was only valued at £217,000, but the trade was expanding. Edward A. Newmark, 'British toys' (1968) 16(5138) January *Journal of the Royal Society of Arts* 135–54, 137.

[108] Design Registration Number 564811, Jemima Puddleduck Doll, 20 July 1910; TNA:BT52/239.

[109] Beatrix Potter to Fruing Warne, 30 April 1917, BPL: 233–4.

enemies of youth and happiness'.[110] Toy traders complained that with no import tax on toys it was very difficult for local toymakers to get established or compete with the German toy imports.[111] And British printers also complained about their being shut out of much of the US market due to manufacturing clauses. As the free trade debate heated up in 1910, Potter became involved in political debate over protectionism and British manufacturing, agitating for tariff reform.

Potter argued that British toymakers were disadvantaged by having to not only compete with foreign imitations that were untaxed, but these 'piracies' were made by German labour not subject to the same restrictions on working hours and fair wages as achieved by the Factories Acts – 'We are fighting with one arm tied, so long as there is no import duty. The London toy shops are choked with foreign toys'.

British printers were also thwarted by US tariffs on imported books (estimated as high as 25 per cent)[112] and by the tying of copyright protection to US book manufacturing. Potter argued that the situation was so dire that 'in 1909 there was a serious proposal [that Warne & Co] print ALL copies in future in America, and ship part of them back from America to England for use here'. This, she estimated, would have led to a loss of £2,000 a year in British wages:

> The working man can safely give Tariff Reform a trial without being frightened by the bogey of dear bread.
>
> Let us have honest British and Colonial goods even if we have to pay a little more for some of them. We shall at least have the satisfaction of knowing that our money is being spent in British wages.[113]

Her advocacy included designing and hand-illustrating posters such as the 'Camberwell Beauties', a drawing of a limp doll leaning against a gravestone with the inscription 'Here lies the Camberwell Wax Doll killed by Free Trade with Germany'.[114] Another poster design was a picture of a Peter Rabbit doll, price tag attached, with a banner 'Made in Germany'. This poster was accompanied by a note that German ships were being built on profits of German trade with England. However, she chose not to forward the copy to the printer. She did baulk at Harold Warne's suggestion that they print a booklet, 'Peter R. on Politics' – 'It should savour of advt [advertisement]; and don't you see it would do the thing you dislike – drag the little book into radical politics'. But she also noted rather dryly that she had not received any royalties from Steiff for the Peter Rabbit doll for over two

[110] H. G. Wells, 'Floor games' quoted in Newmark, above n 107, 141.

[111] Newmark, above n 107, 135, 137–9.

[112] B. Zorina Khan, 'An economic history of copyright in Europe and the United States', *Economic History Association*, https://eh.net/encyclopedia/an-economic-history-of-copyright-in-europe-and-the-united-states.

[113] Beatrix Potter, Election Pamphlet, 1910, in WBP: 402–3.

[114] Ibid. 398–9.

years and that she no longer had 'an atom of affection' for Peter Rabbit. While she had done well from *Peter*, now she was 'done with him'.[115]

Given Potter's experience with Peter Rabbit imitations and piracies, why did her efforts focus quite narrowly on a call for trade protection and not include a call for stronger intellectual property protection for her designs?

Tariffs were a traditional avenue for indirectly regulating distribution channels to promote the interests of local manufacturers. It may be that she engaged with tariff reform, rather than intellectual property reform, for this reason. If there were no suitable British toymakers to negotiate with, the value of her design rights in Britain was limited. Britain was the children's market she understood, had helped define and where she could personally oversee trade connections. Nonetheless, it was also a time of major copyright law reform leading to the Copyright Act 1911. Further, the recent report of the Copyright Committee had suggested that 'there is no reason why the author of a work of fine art applied to industrial purposes should not receive the protection of the [Berne] Convention, and also be able to obtain protection which will be afforded by the Patents and Designs Act, 1907'.[116] That is, the committee anticipated that the author should receive both copyright and design protection. This was a radical suggestion that, if implemented, could have been particularly beneficial to authors such as Potter in Britain.

2.8 AN INDUSTRIAL AUTHOR

To understand what was at stake in intellectual property law reform for industrial authors like Potter, we need to look quite closely at the political debate around the passing of the Patents and Designs Act 1907. Sherman and Bently argue that in the early twentieth century the two international intellectual property treaties to which the UK was a signatory – the Berne Convention for the Protection of Literary and Artistic Property (1886) and the Paris Convention for the Protection of Industrial Property (1883) – had contributed to a bifurcated understanding of legal rights and, along with this, a distinction between original authors and inventors.[117] Patent and design were conceived of as directly linked to questions of manufacturing and international trade, in ways that copyright discourse was generally not. Although it was still commonplace to refer to 'design copyright' at the turn of the century, from an intellectual property law viewpoint, the copyright regime served 'authors', while design registration and other formalities were required for 'inventors of designs'. Potter was both an author in a copyright sense and an inventor in a design sense at a time when an imagined order to the international intellectual property regime

[115] Beatrix Potter to Harold Warne, 8 January 1910, BPL: 174.

[116] Report of the Committee on the Law of Copyright (1909) (Cd 4976), 10.

[117] Brad Sherman and Lionel Bently, *The Making of Modern Intellectual Property Law: The British Experience 1790–1911*, Cambridge University Press, 1999, 162.

appeared to cleave these two statuses. However, while the Copyright Committee considered this situation unfair to creators, especially given the increasing value of aesthetics to manufacturing,[118] the Board of Trade was mostly concerned with intellectual property monopoly rights inhibiting British manufacturing. International patent and design law were criticised as a cause of industrial malaise and of stifling British innovation.

The Paris Convention (1883) had come about due to concerns over theft of inventions when nations were promoting their manufacturers at the great international trade exhibitions of the nineteenth century. Signatories agreed to protect the patent, trademark and industrial designs of nationals of convention countries, on the same terms as available to their own citizens.[119] Further, owners who had first registered in their home country were afforded a 'right of priority', giving them the benefit of the earlier filing date, if they subsequently filed in another member country within a specified time. This flexibility meant that foreign inventors did not have the same struggles in achieving a foreign registration as had beset British copyright owners in the United States. Though not a member of the Berne Convention until 1989, the United States had signed the Paris Convention in 1887. Germany joined in 1903. It was United States and German inventors who were the focus of British complaint. The president of the Board of Trade, Lloyd George, claimed in Parliament that 'out of 14,700 patents issued last year, 6,500 are foreign'.[120] It was also asserted that German and North American 'syndicates' had developed whereby foreign manufacturers with strengths in a particular field were creating patent blocs.[121] It was alleged that UK registrations were secured by the syndicate to drive local firms out of business. This included not working the invention in the UK but preventing UK manufacturers from competing with them by adopting improvements in mass production techniques. The allegation was of a deliberate strategy designed to make the UK dependent on importation of manufactured wares and to stifle local innovation. The introduction of patent blocs especially stressed traditional business organisation centred on the family firm, as transatlantic licensing of intellectual property rights, rather than localised personal trade

[118] See, generally, Clare Pettit, *Patent Inventions: Intellectual Property and the Victorian Novel*, Oxford University Press, 2005, 84–148.

[119] In 1907, the signatories included Belgium, Brazil, Cuba, Denmark, Dominican Republic, France, Germany, Great Britain, Italy, Japan, Netherlands, Norway, Portugal, Serbia, Spain, Sweden, Switzerland, Tunisia and the United States.

[120] HC Deb, 19 March 1907, vol 171, cols 683–7. Most of these would have been directly filed in the UK by foreign companies. In 1907, 29,040 patent applications were filed in the UK; only 2,286 were convention filings (819 Germany; 587 US; 548 France). 'Patents and trade marks. grants and registrations in 1907 – Annual Report of the Comptroller' *The Financial Times*, 9 June 1908, 3.

[121] See, e.g., Lionel Bently, 'Singer sewing machine' in C. Op den Kamp and D. Hunter (eds.), *A History of Intellectual Property in Fifty Objects*, Cambridge University Press, 2019, 72–9.

networks, would reconfigure industry relations, with traditional trade alliances disrupted by foreign cherry-picking amongst local firms.

The main impetus for patent reform came from Manchester's textile trade impacted by the manufacture and sale of chemical dyestuffs and struggling to catch up with German innovation. It was argued that German syndicates had patented every possible chemical combination, even where they had not tried them or put them in operation anywhere in the world. Also, vague and trivial patents, such as over a typewriter ribbon mechanism, were used to prevent British companies making whole machines. It was claimed that the foreign syndicates had the advantage over smaller British firms as they had deeper pockets to defend their patents.

German and North American syndicates were accused of applying for patents 'on a very great scale'; using 'obscure and vague terms so as to cover any possible invention that may be discovered afterwards'; and 'employing "the most expensive counsel at the British Bar, and the best scientific experts"', giving a distinct advantage in litigation. They also used anti-competitive licence conditions to tie the local manufacturer to the syndicate for long periods, so that 'he will not be allowed to put improved machinery into his works'. Lloyd George introduced the Patents and Designs Bill 1907 as a significant reform

> in the interest of free trade. I am not afraid of foreign competition as long as British trade is free to fight it. I would free British trade from impossible conditions abroad and from equally stupid tariff systems at home .... Many British industries have been completely wiped out by privileges conceded by British institutions to foreigners.[122]

Shifts in the international balance of trade were causing serious concern in Britain. Germany and the United States were experiencing a surge in exports and, as both economies were protected by high tariffs, imported British goods were uncompetitive.[123] The 1907 Act sought to restrict patent rights, requiring the invention to be worked in Britain on a commercial scale within four years or risk the patent being revoked. There were additional provisions to make it easier for British manufacturers to revoke patents outside the UK.[124]

In terms of design, the main anti-competitive practice complained of was the marking of goods as subject to a registered design, when registration had in fact lapsed. It was suggested that goods should be required to include the date of design registration.[125] This suggestion was not enacted; however, section 57 provided that,

[122] HC Deb, 19 March 1907, vol 171, cols 683–7.

[123] Percy Ashley, *Modern Tariff History: Germany, United States, France*, John Murray, 3rd edn, 1920; Douglas A. Irwin, 'Historical aspects of US trade policy', NBER Reporter, Research Summary www.nber.org/reporter/summer06: www.nber.org/reporter/summer06/irwin.html.

[124] Patents and Designs Act 1907, ss24, 27. See, generally, George Schuster, 'The Patents and Designs Act 1907' (1909) 19 (76) December *Economic Journal* 538–51.

[125] J. D. White, HC Deb, 17 April 1907, vol 172, cols 1012–56.

on payment of a fee, the comptroller would furnish the public with information whether the registration was still valid and contact details of the registered proprietor. While the outbreak of war makes it difficult to determine the efficacy of the 1907 reforms, one analysis of trade figures does not credit it as leading to any significant immediate boost to British manufacturing or to the development of new industries. Schuster's 1909 study concluded that 'the original evil was greatly exaggerated' and that the 'problem was the traditional apathy of the British manufacturer'.[126]

Clearly, the strength of British manufacturing and problems with balance of trade were not wholly or mainly attributable to intellectual property laws. However, there is no doubt that reform debates were caught up in the nationalist fervour of the times. Despite the recommendation of the Copyright Committee, the Copyright Act 1911 contained a new provision that sought to police the imagined boundary between copyright and design regimes. Alongside the creation of a new category of copyright, the 'work of artistic craftsmanship', to protect high-quality manufacturing processes that integrated aesthetics into production processes – generally affecting the quantity of goods that could be produced – mass-produced goods were afforded lesser protection as 'designs'. This demarcation was imagined as improving the situation for British manufacturers, in the context where, overall, British design as adopted in mass manufacturing was considered inferior to that on the Continent.[127]

Section 22 removed copyright protection for designs used, or intended to be used as patterns to be multiplied by any industrial process, where these were capable of being registered under the Patents and Designs Act 1907. The intention was to promote competition by limiting protection for industrial designs to a maximum of fifteen years; otherwise these works might retain the regular term of copyright life plus fifty years. MacGillivray noted that the Act probably removed copyright protection of Christmas cards, as these productions were applied designs, 'a combination of words and pictures blend together to form a picturesque whole' – the design being applied to the folded cardboard.[128] But he anticipated serious difficulties in the application of the provision given its wording, noting that advertising posters and even some Christmas cards might still retain artistic copyright where the design was embodied on a flat surface, such as an advertising billboard. Here, the entire design of the poster was adhered to the billboard, but the design was not 'applied to an article'. As such, he mused, it probably fell outside of the ambit of section 22, though was intended to have been caught.

The technical language attempted to quarantine copyright for 'artistic' endeavours, while, in the interest of competition, leaving designs with more limited protection. This caused difficulties in application. Historically, the UK copyright

[126] Schuster, above n 124, 545.
[127] See Kathy Bowrey, 'Art, craft, good taste and manufacturing: the development of intellectual property laws' (1997) 15(1) *Law in Context* 78.
[128] MacGillivray, above n 98, 137–8.

register was full of all sorts of industrial works. The books of entry forms and the Stationers' Company Register for literary and artistic works are dominated by registration of various stationery formats, including sets of instructions, charts, race cards, telephone directories, calendars, advertising literature, product labels and trademarks. It had been a trade practice to register very mundane printed works lacking in much discernible literary or artistic quality, presumably with the hope that the act of registration would bolster a rather dubious copyright claim. Now section 22 was supposed to remove any copyright protection afforded to many of these kinds of productions where it could be claimed to be an 'applied' design. Manufacturers, in contrast, would continue to want to retain the commercial advantage of longer copyright protection without need for design registration and would argue that this new section did not apply to their wares, especially where they were 'flat designs'.[129] The legal idea that the copyright and design regimes serviced different kinds of creations underpinned the logic of section 22. However, the reform only served to obscure the reality of a very significant transformation of creative authorship, already apparent to creators such as Potter. As visual appearance came to be of increased importance in late Victorian and Edwardian commodity markets, and as the literary work took form as a 'toy-book', recognisable for a distinctive graphic style and bookmanship and instantly related to a family of merchandise that bears similar visual qualities, it is impossible to distinguish the creative from the industrial author.

By 1910 Potter was both a noted and distinguished creative artist and author and, at the same time, also an experienced industrial author. With the exception of the Jemima doll that she handled herself, *Peter Rabbit* series characters were being carefully redesigned by an array of commercial artists employed by the various chintz, stationer, wallpaper, doll and china manufacturers who sought to produce wares that bore Potter's and Peter Rabbit's names. Potter had carefully approved the design of some of these renditions, but she did not directly 'author' them, in the copyright sense of 'authorship'.[130]

2.9 THE FAMILY AS A MARKET

Potter's authorship developed into business relationships that were essentially supervisory in nature. Her industrial authorship brought into being a 'family' of wares. She used her limited intellectual property rights to support what she hoped would result in quality British-manufactured, authorised products that bore her name and displayed images associated with her signature style: toy books, cards, posters, dolls, cloth and china – mostly products for decorating and 'personalising' the nursery. On

[129] This is discussed further at Chapter 4, 121–2.

[130] The term 'author' remained defined by common law, and there was no attempt to confine it by statute: see *Walter v Lane* [1900] AC 539.

display in the home these helped reinforce the idea of a distinctive children's market, synonymous with the enterprise she fostered. Her role in the market was akin to that of parent, where her care in allowing a branded connection meant that the consumer could trust in the suitability of the goods for the purpose they were designed for, reinforcing ideas about the material characteristics of a home environment which a young child enjoys and perhaps 'needs' in order to thrive.

Still, throughout her professional life, when it suited her mood, Beatrix Potter maintained an intellectual distinction between literature, on the one hand, and toy books and side-shows on the other, referring to the latter with no affection. This was an outcome of her frustration at the tedium of needing to continue to refresh her own range across seasons, especially given that quality wares should remain serviceable for some time. But, taking into account her strong nationalistic views about supporting quality trade, it may also have been a result of her experience of family businesses, as these struggled with the production demands of mass manufacturing in what had become an international market. To Potter, quality was not simply an inherent characteristic of manufactured goods. It was the product of a process where she was involved, on some level, in authorising the aesthetics of the wares. To Potter, regardless of protection afforded under copyright or design law, unauthorised goods were, by definition, inferior product: they were imitations or piracies. Within Britain, working with company structures where the head of the firm's door could be opened and, perhaps, also influenced by the opinion of others in trade and professional networks, it was possible for an individual creator to directly negotiate – to assert parental care and control – over her commercial offspring. This could turn unauthorised wares into authorised product. But what she had observed and experienced with the development of the Peter Rabbit enterprise was the impossibility of herself, or any individual firm, maintaining control. As inspiration for commodity production in a global marketplace for cultural goods, *Peter* had developed a life of his own. The appearance of a direct family connection with her still carried a premium, but the meaning of this 'family' had been transformed.

3

Instructions for a Successful Boy

In January 1929, Antonio Gramsci wrote a letter to his wife asking how their son, Delio, was getting on with the Meccano set he had sent him for his birthday.[1] His letter illustrated far more than a concern about a personal gift and whether or not it would be suitable for his son. Gramsci was particularly interested in knowing if the toy deprived a child of his inventiveness. Meccano was a building construction kit made up of metal components, nuts, bolts and gears that could be assembled into a range of mechanical models as suggested by the picture on the box and sets of instructions, although the components could also be used in free play. From his prison cell, Gramsci had been requesting toy catalogues to select the Meccano set that seemed most appropriate for his child.[2] And a year later he was still amused by 'the very invention of Meccano [which] shows how quickly the child [was] intellectualised'.[3] Gramsci's ambivalent reaction towards Meccano echoes some of Charles Dodgson's earlier concerns about the importance of fostering the child's imagination discussed in Chapter 1. However, Gramsci was far more interested in thinking about the particular kind of engagement promoted by this kind of toy. Meccano epitomised an ongoing twentieth-century preoccupation with children and the effect of toys on their education. As a mass-produced commodity, Meccano traded on a specific niche, exploiting parental desires for educational toys. One of its promises was that the toy would grow along with the child and accompany them into adulthood. Meccano was not just a toy. It was a toy to build toys, as well as a platform to recruit friends and socialise, supported by a brand programme that turned children into consumers.

1 Gramsci to Giulia, 14 January 1929 in Antonio Gramsci, *Letters from Prison*, vol. 1, Columbia University Press, 1994, 242; see also, for an insightful sociological account, Ruth Wainman, '"Engineering for boys": Meccano and the shaping of a technical vision of boyhood in twentieth-century Britain' (2017) 14(3) *Cultural and Social History* 381–96.

2 Gramsci to Tania, 19 April 1928, in Gramsci, above n 1, 195.

3 Gramsci to Giulia, 1 July 1929, in ibid, 276.

This chapter explores how a distinct understanding of play and subjectivity was embodied in Meccano and how this development was reflected in the ways intellectual properties were conceived and exploited. Meccano and other construction toys, like Erector and American Model Builder, became toys that challenged and transgressed imagined public and private dichotomies. On the one hand, here was a private firm selling what is often considered to be a public virtue: the practical education of the child. Educational instruction, rather than frivolous play, constituted one of the most important selling points of the toy. The marketing of Meccano configured the family as a site of production of masculine identities, where civic leadership was literally modelling through play with the company's toys, recruiting generations of boys into imagining their contributions to engineering and the mechanical infrastructure of factories, transportation and the city. Meccano demonstrated how ideas about the family and the market could be simultaneously performed and sold in a commercial product. This was not a deliberate corporate strategy designed from the outset. As we will note, some operations were triggered by ongoing adaptations and exchanges with the children who engaged with the toy. However, the commercial ambition generated many tensions and contradictions that needed to be diffused for the toy to become a global phenomenon. Intellectual property claims and disputes provided an avenue for managing and defraying these tensions. While we argue that patents, copyright and trademarks played an interesting role in this regard, this chapter does not set out in detail the intellectual property strategy surrounding Meccano in the conventional way – with reference to a portfolio of patent and trademark filings, copyright claims and litigation outcomes associated with merchandise. The use of intellectual property to enforce exclusive rights to Meccano might not have been especially noteworthy. Indeed, we explore some instances where Meccano's legal claims failed. What we are more interested in showing is how, through engaging in ordinary patent, copyright and trademark activity on a global scale, significant ideas about the qualities of the particular intangible properties of Meccano advanced. This included promoting the notion of Meccano as a suitable toy for children, as it possessed educational qualities, so that the market for the toy and the boy could grow together. Although girls could obviously play with Meccano, it was not marketed to them. It was the design of a consumption programme around the intangible properties of Meccano as a toy specifically for boys that contributed to the success of the toy. For this very reason, Meccano offers a useful point of departure for reconsidering how intellectual property connects to a history of consumption. Our history considers intellectual property not just as a protective mechanism based upon ownership of rights, but far more importantly as a constructive vehicle in which intangible properties underpinning the rights are reconfigured, enhanced and actualised through the manner of their circulation in the market and the family.

Meccano's creative play between manufacturing and advertising sheds light on the ways in which intellectual property operated in the twentieth century. We argue that the law had a far more elusive and oblique operation than has often been assumed. For instance, methods of doing business and the presentation and the evolution of the toy were shaped by intellectual property practices, in turn affecting the understanding of what an intangible property conveyed. The toy was converted into a business in which the importance of selling the toy focused on the promise of a future rather than just the promotion of an object of consumption. In order to unravel how relevant this horizon was in encouraging connections and relays between prospective audiences and the company, the chapter will focus on how this shift in commodity relations directly affected not only the manufacture of the toy but also its contexts of distribution and retail. Moreover, it shows how the productive features of the toy, such as standardisation, interchangeability and engagement, determined the making of a kind of consumer that did not exist before, who in advertising literature was referred to as the 'Meccano Boy'. By looking at how this type of child came into being, the chapter analyses the effect of intellectual property in creating its own subject of consumption. In other words, we argue that the toy and the boy resembled each other not only because they occurred at the very same historical juncture but also because their emergence was the effect of a creative connection between intellectual property and consumption. The techniques for creating Meccano Boys consisted of participatory endeavours such as model-making contests in which the self of the child and their place within a Meccano community, which spread across the British Empire and beyond, was constituted. Because of that special characteristic, Meccano anticipated exploitation programmes and social practices that would become ubiquitous in intellectual property throughout the second part of the twentieth century and which continue into the twenty-first century. The participation schemes became so successful because they also served to extract data not only from children who joined but also from those who could potentially be interested in participating. In so doing, they provided instructions for children to organise themselves into clubs and guilds which, if successful, would make those friendships visible enough to be monetised.

3.1 PROPERTIES IN PLAY

By the late nineteenth century, the incipient preoccupation with the development of the child, a tendency augured by Ellen Key,[4] was also perceived in the growth of inventions related to children's play, which began to reach patent offices around the world.[5] This increase in filing prompted some institutional changes at patent offices, like the creation of specific departments or divisions to examine toy inventiveness.[6]

[4] Ellen Key, *The Century of the Child*, G.P. Putnam's Sons, 1909.

[5] 'Perpetual motion' *Democrat and Chronicle*, 24 June 1889, 1; see also 'More queer inventions' *The Times*, Philadelphia, 29 July 1894, 24.

[6] 'Expert on toy patents' *Detroit Free Press*, 10 January 1915, 76; 'Mrs Santa Claus has been found' *New York Times*, 12 December 1915, 54.

One of the curious features of these toy patent applications was that, in aiming to provide solutions to overcome problems, they present us today with an understanding of how society was imagining and focusing on the child and its environment in the twentieth century. While it might be interesting for humanities scholars to investigate the different images of childhood underpinning these patented devices and their purported value, we would like to focus here on the history of Meccano's first patent application, which exemplified an appeal to the educational aspects of play in its claims. The British patent application number 587/1901 ('Improvements in Toy or Educational Devices for Children and Young People') is often flagged as the beginning of the constructional toy.[7] The application was filed on January 1901 by a butcher's clerk from Liverpool, Frank Hornby. While the invention initially used the slogan 'Mechanics Made Easy' to commercialise the invention, the toy was later labelled and became well known as 'Meccano'.[8]

If we consider the specificity of patents as legal documents, the original patent application lodged by Hornby displayed several interesting features. It should be noted that patent applications are subjected to searching scrutiny by an expert reader, the patent office examiner. So, patent drafting was often carried out by agents who took the utmost care in trying to achieve the widest protection for their clients while, at the same time safeguarding the application against objections by the examiner and oppositions from third parties. In other words, patent drafting aimed to maintain a delicate balance between disclosing the invention sufficiently to pass the technical legal tests (novelty, sufficiency and utility) and avoid unnecessary details that could reveal too much to commercial competitors or make the specific patent claims too broad to be valid.

The patent application lodged by Hornby was drafted by a specialist patent agency, W. P. Thompson & Co, which introduced content that looks, at first glance, unusual. Firstly, there was a significant emphasis on the role of the toy as an educational medium, as the 'means whereby the interest in mechanical construction from an elementary point of view, [was] enhanced in addition to providing an interesting means of mechanical education'.[9] In fact, three out of the four patent claims included the educational character of the toy.[10] Secondly, the industrial concept embodied in the application was the manufacturing of a specific device

7 British Patent 587/1901 ('Improvements in toy or educational devices for children and young people'); see Kenneth D. Brown, *Factory of Dreams: A History of Meccano Ltd*, Crucible Books, 2007, 31.

8 'A charming Christmas present for boys: mechanics made easy' *Bournemouth Daily Echo*, 20 December 1902, 3; 'Boys with a constructive mind', *Shipley Times and Express*, 15 December 1905, 7; 'New and strange: mechanics made easy' *Pearson's Weekly*, 6 May 1909, 911.

9 'Complete specification' British Patent 587/1901 ('Improvements in Toy or Educational Devices for Children and Young People') 2.

10 Ibid, 4.

with interchangeable pieces, which had the capacity to be assembled and fastened together to make mechanical objects.[11]

One explanation for this detailed drafting comes from the special character of toy patents. As mentioned above, this kind of patent application presented some challenges to patent offices' examination procedures, which prompted the appointment of toy specialists. The main difficulty in getting toys recognised as patentable inventions was not so much the criteria of novelty but rather the second legal requirement of utility. Toy patent applications were occasionally rejected or invalidated for failing to address the question of the purpose of the invention and, as a result, for not having sufficiently fleshed out the invention in the claims. In drafting the specification it was important to avoid the assessment by the examiner or the judge that such a claim was 'ridiculous'.[12] In *Cole v Saqui* (1888), Kekewich J was confronted with this specific issue and clarified that 'although it is a small matter, still the amusement of children of all ages is after all a useful thing, and I see no reason why a toy should not be regarded as having utility for the purposes of a patent as much as a steam engine or any other more important machine'.[13] Although doubts regarding toy patents appeared to have been dissipated by this decision, some uncertainty remained at the level of practice, specifically when patent applications failed to specify or expand on the utility of the toy.[14] As one patent agent observed, defective or imperfect claims were those like a toy horse patent application which ended up saying, 'The child can hold to the handle while Nurse, little Willie, or Polly can push the horse for him'.[15]

It is no surprise that the Meccano specification placed special emphasis on the educational potential of the device in order to explain the sufficient utility of the invention. What made it remarkable was not the reference to the educational device but the way in which its description blended with the qualities expected from the child to make it useful, entertaining and instructive. The invention was a distinct toy designed to make more and more toys. This functional feature was described in the specification as accomplished through the exercise of 'inventive ingenuity'.[16] The sort of ingenuity described had a social dimension. It did not refer to the maker of the invention who supplied the ingenuity but shifted focus to the end consumer of

[11] Ibid.

[12] See *Britain v Hirsch* (1887) 5 RPC 74, 76.

[13] *Cole v Saqui* (1888) 5 RPC 489; 495; see also Roger William Wallace and John Bruce Williamson, *The Law and Practice Relating to Letters Patent for Inventions*, William Clowes & Sons, 1900, 122.

[14] The decision by Kekewich J was reversed on appeal, but the patent was held void not for lack of utility but for want of novelty and invention; see *Cole v Saqui* (1889) 6 RPC 41.

[15] 'Imperfect specifications and defective claims' (1884–1885) *Transactions of the Chartered Institute of Patent Agents* 210, 211.

[16] The specification described 'a child of ordinary ingenuity' as the one expected to play with the toy; see 'Complete specification' British Patent 587/1901 ('Improvements in Toy or Educational Devices for Children and Young People') 3.

the patented product – the child for whom it was bought. The invention ingenuity described in the patent specification appealed to a faculty inherent in all children, but it suggested that this potential was unleashed through the invention. In doing so, highlighting the relationship between the invention and the child in the patent specification transformed the invention from a number of simple perforated metal strips, nuts and screws into a toy, as well as an educational device. The mechanical education claimed by the invention undoubtedly called for imagination, particularly when the assembly of the perforated metal strips was unscripted. However, as discussed below, the structures pictured on the boxes, the advertising literature and in the instructions might be construed as a constraint on the child's imagination, while suggesting a scope for future ingenuity sufficient to satisfy the patent examiner's utility requirement.

The historical significance of Meccano lies not just in the novelty of the invention, but in the way in which it managed and actualised legal and commercial information, from the patent office to the department store. For instance, the different perforated metal strips of the device claimed in the patent specification allowed connection and rotation, hence enabling the possibility of constructing movable artefacts, such as miniature cranes. The drawings attached to the patent application already illustrated the potential of the toy to represent mechanical things and hence the utility of the toy being that the boy could become an inventor (see Figure 3.1). The fact that the device was simultaneously a system of representation for mechanical things and an object of consumption troubled those who believed that the imagination of children was not fostered but adjusted to specific modern lines and expectations. This was Gramsci's initial concern about the role of imagination and education promoted by this toy. His interest in Meccano lay precisely here because, as he wrote: 'I've never been able to decide whether, since it deprives the child of his inventive spirit, Meccano is the modern toy that one ought to recommend the most. … In general, I think that modern culture (of the American type) of which Meccano is the expression, makes people somewhat dry, mechanical, bureaucratic'.[17]

Following the advice of the patent agency, W. P. Thompson & Co, Hornby tried to extend his patenting activity to the United States, Canada, Australia and New Zealand.[18] Somewhat oddly, this patenting route was not simply to secure patent rights in these jurisdictions. Patents were taken out because they were the likely source of agency contracts and franchises abroad.[19] The dynamism seen in rapid patent writing and international filing of applications shows Meccano as a modern

[17] Gramsci to Giulia, 14 January 1929, Gramsci, above n 1, 242.

[18] The list of the first Meccano patents is included in some of the instruction manuals published by Meccano; see *Instructions for the Whole Series of Models and Thirteen Progressive Outfits*, Meccano, 1914, 2.

[19] Meccano branch offices often coincided with the territories where the patent had been secured; see 'In the Factories', *Toy and Fancy Goods Trader*, 3 May 1915, 26.

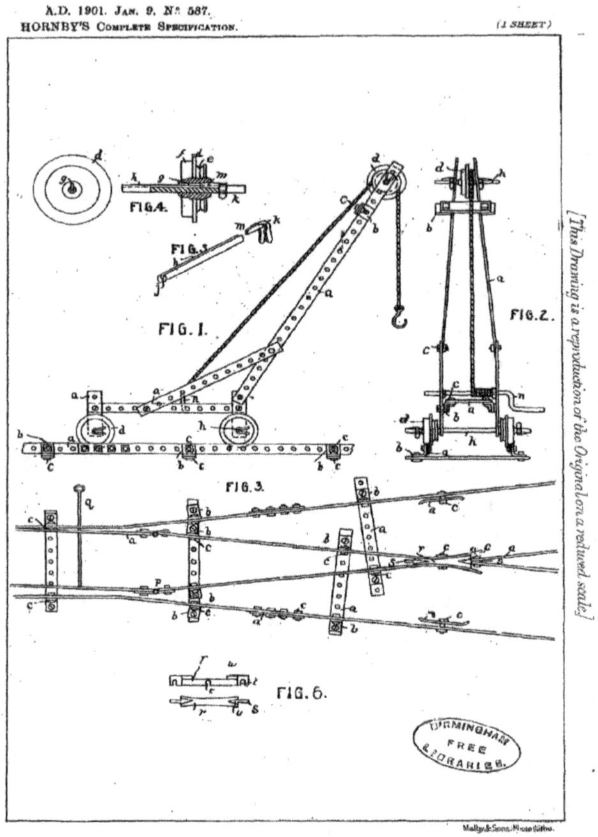

FIGURE 3.1 British Patent 587/1901 ('Improvements in Toy or Educational Devices for Children and Young People')
Crown Copyright

business pursuing a global network. W. P. Thompson & Co. used its international contacts to file Hornby's toy application overseas. After the patent application in Britain, Griffith Allen & Watson in Australia, Henry Hughes Ltd in New Zealand, Marion & Marion in Canada and Dodge & Sons in the United States began acting for Hornby when trying to obtain overseas patents.[20] More than the invention itself, this legal strategy of having local agencies lodge patent applications in other countries was the springboard towards establishing the worldwide reach of the toy.

Despite the legal expertise employed to enlarge the patent portfolio, not all filings were equally successful. While the examination of the application went smoothly in

[20] Australian Patent 18850/1902 ('Improvements in Toy or Educational Devices for Children and Young People'); NAA: A4617, 11649; New Zealand Patent 14407/1902 ('Improvements in Toy or Educational Devices for Children and Young People'); Canadian Patent 78564/1901 ('Educational Toy/Jouet'); US Patent 69,311/1901 ('Toy or Educational Device').

Britain, it did not follow a similar pattern in the United States.[21] This difference is a reminder that the two patent offices operated under different premises and bureaucratic habits, which in turn reflected the different drafting of patent applications performed by local agents. Instead of having an unopposed and easy route to the patent grant, the US application faced several obstacles from the outset. Curiously, the difficulty did not stem from the need to show that the toy was useful, as it was established practice in the patent office at Washington, DC, to consider play as a utility purpose.[22] However, the British application had emphasised this point so strongly in order to highlight the educational qualities of the invention that the claims had become unsatisfactory and unclear to the American patent examiner.[23] This caused a significant delay between the application and the grant. The US patent office rejected some of the claims for lack of novelty or for being too indeterminate.[24] After different drafts of the patent application, the scope of the claims was revised and narrowed from four to two claims for the patent to be allowed and granted.[25] Interestingly, the claims erased were those that blended the toy and the 'inventive ingenuity' of the child.[26] This meant that the revised application ended up being more vulnerable than the initial application. Ultimately, these bureaucratic problems and contingencies contributed to difficulties Meccano had in positioning its toy in the United States. The weakness of the patent was leveraged against Meccano when it tried to defend its toy against imitations.[27]

[21] Although the Paris Convention for the Protection of Industrial Property (1883) improved foreign patent filing, the patent examination procedures across jurisdictions were different. The UK Parliament and US Congress permitted foreign patent applicants to apply for a patent in each other's jurisdiction within seven months of the original filing (later extended to twelve months) with the patent taking effect at the date of the first filing. Patent duration was limited to the term of the inventor's shortest-running foreign counterpart. The patent term was fourteen years in the UK, seventeen in the United States. See section 103, The Patents, Designs, and Trade Marks Act 1883; Revised Statutes of the United States, Section 4487.

[22] This point of practice appeared settled, but some problems resurfaced in the 1940s when toys and dolls were not only appreciated for their 'play' features but also for their 'display' qualities; see the exchanges in George Benjamin, 'Protection for dolls' (1943) 25(5) May *Journal of the Patent Office Society* 352; Herbert W. Gediman, 'Design patents for dolls' (1943) 25(7) July *Journal of the Patent Office Society* 525; George Benjamin, 'Protection for dolls' (1943) 25(9) September *Journal of the Patent Office Society* 679. It is not a coincidence that a similar doctrinal discussion had emerged in copyright to define the artistic works; see *Lucasfilm Ltd v Ainsworth* [2011] UKSC 39.

[23] Alan M. Johnson, Assistant Examiner in Charge to Hornby (cc Dodge & Sons); 12 August 1901; US Patent 810148 RG 241; NAID 302050; NARA, Kansas: Series: Patent Case Files, 1836–1978.

[24] Charles C. Stauffer, Examining Division VII (Velocipedes, Games, Toys) to Hornby (cc Dodge & Sons); 5 September 1902; US Patent 810148 RG 241; NAID 302050; NARA, Kansas: Series: Patent Case Files, 1836–1978.

[25] Frederick J. Allen (Commissioner of Patents) to Hornby (cc Dodge & Sons); 26 December 1905; US Patent 810148 RG 241; NAID 302050; NARA, Kansas Series: Patent Case Files, 1836–1978.

[26] The claims were also held to be problematic and erased in the Canadian patent for the same invention; see Canadian Patent 78564/1901 ('Educational Toy/Jouet').

[27] The examiner's citations to previous patents (No 604,708; 305,879) were used by Wagner in his appeal against Meccano; *Wagner v Meccano Ltd* 246 F 603, (6th Cir 1917).

These controversies highlight the elusive nature and exploitation of constructional toys and the problems with describing the invention in terms recognisable to patent jurisprudence. One of the most interesting disputes was the protracted confrontation between Meccano and a toy called American Model Builder. This dispute involved a series of legal cases tried in the United States, France and Australia.[28] Such worldwide litigation might be considered as part of a tactic, at a symbolic level, of pursuing legal cases against specific competitors across different jurisdictions to position Meccano as a global toy. As discussed in Chapter 4, this entrepreneurial legal strategy was not unique as similar approaches would also be followed by other multinational corporations, such as Disney. However, this would become a defining feature of Meccano, whose willingness to litigate was selective and strategic. Indeed, this transnational litigation developed despite the difficulties (and expense) taken on by Meccano Ltd in its efforts to stop the circulation of the American toy.

The first action brought by Meccano was in 1913 at the District Court in Ohio to try to stop the manufacture and distribution of the American Model Builder.[29] The American toy was a constructive toy like Meccano composed of metal parts by means of which different engineering models could be built from component parts. Although the litigation looked like a typical case of imitation, the courtroom exchanges revealed an unexpected and profound problem. The defendant was supported by local department stores, including one of the most significant quality traders, John Wanamaker, in Philadelphia and New York.[30] A similar pattern took place in Australia, where the Sydney department store, Anthony Hordern & Sons, had found the terms and conditions of the American toy more favourable, as discussed further below. Although the outcome of these cases varied, Meccano insisted on fighting against global sales of the American toy specifically because it was the one which most threatened building direct relationships with retailers and hence with their consumers. The American toy began to reproduce the commercial methods that had made Meccano successful. Rather than just having manufactured a similar toy, what preoccupied Meccano was that American Model Builder also followed an analogous system to capture and connect to consumers. The point was that it had grasped the distinct ways in which some of the marketing arrangements devised by Meccano worked. One of the most innovative business strategies developed by Meccano was to eschew wholesalers, instead selling the toy directly to retailers. By simplifying the distribution network and broadening the margin of profit for retailers, Meccano had in turn secured a space for the toy in department

[28] 'Meccano takes action' (1914) March *Toy and Fancy Goods Trader* 25; 'Litigation about toys' *The Sun*, 10 September 1918, 5.
[29] 'Christmas toys subject of suit', *Cincinnati Enquirer*, 25 December 1913, 15.
[30] 'Wanamakers move' (1914) May *Toy and Fancy Goods Trader* 92.

stores.[31] This franchise arrangement was especially advantageous as the appeal to consumers lay not only in the display of the toy and advertising but more importantly in its public demonstration.[32] These demonstrations allowed potential customers to see the toy in operation and learn how different pieces could be assembled to construct different toys. In so doing, the public demonstrator could conjure up precisely what the patent application claimed, the exercise of 'inventive ingenuity', a kind of magic made visible to those children and parents who came to the department store. As a commentator recalled about the success of Meccano, 'these articles met a popular demand, but no such demand existed until they were demonstrated'.[33] The problem with American Model Builder was that it had started to occupy the space of wonder previously reserved in the store for Meccano.[34] This contextualisation of Meccano was influential within the US courts. One of the judges who tried these cases, the Honourable Howard C. Hollister, referred to Meccano as a 'toy of great utility and educational value, stimulating the imagination, appealing to a boy's creative faculties, that not only gives enjoyment, but is highly instructive'.[35] That judicial description was one of the greatest successes of the protracted litigation, since Meccano repeated it verbatim in the promotional stories highlighting its importance and testament of goodwill.[36]

3.2 SELLING EDUCATION

Given that educational appeal was already included in its patent claims, one of the most attractive aspects of Meccano was how its educational potential unfolded into a lucrative business. What the invention produced was not just 'education', but the strategic selling of 'education'. Such commercial proposition went beyond the patent filings and unfolded from the very first slogans and endorsements to seed the toy in the marketplace.[37] While these early testimonials could be interpreted as

31 This space was often the shop window, but there were instances in which the demonstrations took place in other portions of the shop devoted to Meccano; see 'Meccano: All spare parts kept in the stock. See models in Window. Mason's Photo Stores, Bradford' *Shipley Times and Express*, 19 December 1913, 10; 'James A. Pollock' *Northern Whig*, 11 December 1911, 10; 'Frank Wiseman's' *Auckland Star*, 16 December 1927, 11.

32 'Meccano Ltd' (1920) March *Toy and Fancy Goods Trader* 170; 'Meccano demonstrators wanted' *Sheffield Daily Telegraph*, 6 December 1913, 2; 'Meccano demonstration' *Wanganui Herald*, 14 April 1914, 2.

33 'The Demonstration Method of Selling' (1914) December *Toy and Fancy Goods Trader* 161.

34 'Kids attention! American model builder prize contest' *Santa Ana Register*, 15 December 1914, 6.

35 *Meccano Ltd v Wagner*, 234 F 912, 915 (SD Ohio 1916).

36 Frank Hornby, 'Life story of Meccano' (1922) January–February *Meccano Magazine* 2; Frank Hornby, 'The life story of Meccano' (1932) February *Meccano Magazine* 92.

37 'Modern professors recommend mechanics made easy' *Sheffield Evening Telegraph*, 13 December 1907, 1; *Sheffield Evening Telegraph*, 20 December 1907, 1; *Sheffield Evening Telegraph*, 27 December 1907, 1.

congratulatory sanctions for the invention, their reiteration in the promotional literature of the toy indicated a remarkable interest in the publicity value of these associations. The initial strategy was not only to demonstrate the educational merit of the toy but to show its market potential. The endorsement of the toy provided a marketing tool – 'an academic credibility' which could be turned into a crucial selling point.[38] Despite some incidental references to film celebrities and an attempt to get the toy officially used in public institutions, Meccano was sold primarily through commerce and less through sponsorship, academic or otherwise.

As has been noted by many historians, advertising occupied a pivotal role in the development of Meccano as a toy business enterprise.[39] In the attempt to gain differentiation and set the toy apart from other competitive novelties, Meccano gave itself a corporate identity. In 1907, the name 'Meccano' was registered as a trademark and, one year later, Hornby found the necessary capital for the establishment of a new private company, Meccano Ltd.[40] It is important to highlight that the toy and the legal constitution of the relevant trading corporation advanced together such that it was the toy itself that took on a corporate form. In fact, the worldwide exploitation of the toy, and the litigations and controversies mentioned above, only took place following the setting up of new management and corporate structures abroad. In 1912, Meccano France was incorporated.[41] One year later, the Meccano Company Inc was established in New York.[42] The more the toy advanced in corporate form, the more reliance it had on trademarks and advertising. When 'Mechanics made Easy' was shortened to the marketing-friendly 'Meccano', the company increased its focus on the distinctive material features that surrounded the toy, such as the advertising services provided to retailers, the outfits, the box and the manuals of instructions included therein. Such development of a corporate personhood tied to a brand was not only based on a worldwide programme of trademark registration but also on the subscription to a system of trademark watching.[43] To give an example, after being notified of problematic applications, such as attempts to register the trademark Meccano for soaps and perfumery in Spain, Meccano Ltd asked for legal advice and opposed those registrations.[44]

38 Brown, above n 7, 198.

39 Roger Marriott, *Meccano*, Shire Publications, 2012, 21; Kenneth D. Brown, *The British Toy Business: A History since 1700*, Hambledon Press, 1996, 121.

40 'Memorandum and Articles of Association, Meccano Ltd, incorporated June 4, 1908', Box D, Items 1–2, MAL: B/ME.

41 'Articles of Association of Meccano (France) Ltd', 7 August 1912, Box D, Item 6, MAL: B/ME.

42 'Meccano methods' (1915) November *Toy and Fancy Goods Trader* 10.

43 'Vigilance to protect trade marks abroad' (1928) 23(6) *Bulletin of the United States Trade Mark Association*, 128; *Trade Marks Directory Service*, London, 1950, 32; see Jose Bellido, 'Toward a history of trade mark watching' (2015) 2 *Intellectual Property Quarterly* 130, 141.

44 'Opinion by Kew Shelley regarding the opposition of Trade Mark Meccano No 625968', 3 March 1944; Box 22, Item No. 1, MAL: B/ME.

As already mentioned, unlike traditional toys such as dolls or rattles, the marketing of Meccano required the toy to enact and attract two main cultural qualities – education and entertainment. These were often considered to be contradictory activities. The best way to connect them and to make the toy a marketable commodity was to frame its destiny as a family affair. Such advertising operations also served to solve the classic problem associated with selling toys: the split between purchaser and consumer. That is, the one who would buy the toy was not the child but his parents. Meccano needed to sufficiently captivate both parents and children. Although there are similarities to the issues mentioned in previous chapters, it is important to highlight some differences. Charles Dodgson had used the conception of a personal gift to elide Victorian concerns about exploitation and profiting from the child. Beatrix Potter's toy books and sideshows carried on this tradition, but the primary market was the family and friends of the younger child, whereby play with her product, whether it be a toy book or a doll, was an activity undertaken in intimate settings. Meccano sought to position its toy in the market differently. While an appeal to the standard, white middle-class family template was axiomatic, there were other engagements with the toy that expanded its allure. Perhaps the most attractive feature to entice both parents and children was that the education promised by Meccano was imagined in terms of the future roles of the children as leaders of industry and business. This framing helped stabilise a narrative of the device as 'a toy and educator in one'.[45] Advertising functioned then as a legitimatising force, overcoming traditional views which could have limited commercial prospects if Meccano had remained tied to traditional sources of education, institutions such as the school or the state. By challenging the habitual ways of imagining instruction and amusement as conflicting activities and initially shifting the focus towards indoor-family scenarios for the pedagogy of the child, Meccano carved out an appealing commercial space for the toy. Meccano was first assigned the domestic role of affectively connecting parents with children in the task of building an education. One of the ways that Meccano nurtured that domestic space was by forging a brand infused with a 'personal touch'.[46] The intertwining between personal and family features manifested itself in the advertising literature.[47] On the one hand, printed publications offered the family an advertising bildungsroman, a vehicle to be involved in the Meccano story. The biography of the business founder, Frank Hornby, served as an inspiring story for children to identify with a triumphal

[45] 'Meccano: a toy and educator in one' *Oregon Daily Journal*, 11 November 1913, 20.

[46] See, for instance, 'Essay competition: what Meccano has done for me' (1919) May *Meccano Magazine* 3; 'Which would you choose?' (1921) July–August *Meccano Magazine* 1.

[47] 'Give your boy Meccano this Christmas' *Daily Mail*, 4 December 1913 10; 'Give your boy Meccano and he too will build this model' *Daily Mail*, 10 December 1913, 8; 'Give your boy Meccano' *Daily Mail*, 3 December 1921, 1.

narrative of success and achievement.[48] It served to captivate parents too, particularly those who saw their children's education as a future investment. On the other hand, desires and projections of children and families were also turned into promotional forays. There is no better example of this than *Adventures in Meccanoland*, a story issued by Meccano in 1928 which drew from the imaginative letters and models of children who had written to the corporation.[49]

Keeping in mind the initial interest in international patent filing and agency arrangements behind Meccano Ltd, one thing that stands out in the approach taken is that the selected trademark ('Meccano') envisaged a world project: a newly coined, standardised word that could be pronounced and read everywhere.[50] Although the name was conceived as a universal token facilitating the free circulation of commodities, it faced a number of difficulties in practice. Ironically, this universal word triggered creative lexical inflections. Alternative locally made construction toys, such as 'Mekano', 'Mechano', 'Mecanic', 'Mekanik', 'Meccaniky', 'Supermeccano', 'Meccanometal', 'Meccastar' and 'Electromeccano', mushroomed in remote countries, from Uruguay to Iran.[51] Similarly, Meccano found material challenges at national borders with the imposition of national tariffs on foreign goods, where local manufacturers of lookalike products were exempt.[52] Juxtaposing these two challenges highlights how resourceful Meccano was in arguing for or against imitations abroad.[53] Put simply, strategies to protect and police Meccano efficiently shifted from claims based on the intangible to the material qualities of the toy, depending on the circumstances. On the one hand, a tabulated list of legally enforceable trademarks was repeatedly used, together with a surveillance system at the level of trademark registries and markets.[54] This method was accompanied by

48 Maurice Philip Gould, *Frank Hornby: The Boy Who Made $1,000,000 with a Toy*, Meccano Company, 1915.

49 *Adventures in Meccanoland*, Meccano, 1928; see also Hubert Lansley, *My Meccano Days: The Story of Meccano in its Heyday, 1924–1930*, *Constructor Quarterly*, 1994, 18.

50 Advertisers and branding agencies observed that 'for children, the name must be simple, and either indirectly descriptive, concrete or very short'; see A. H. Cousins, and H. E. Wadsworth, *Trade Names: A Guide to their Invention, Protection and Use*, Harlequin Press, 1934, 13.

51 See the bundle of correspondence on the infringement of patented name (sic) 'Meccano' in Spain, Norway, Iran, India, Sweden, South Africa, Canada, Denmark, Germany, Holland, Austria, Iceland, Belgium, Switzerland, and USA, Box 22, Item No 1, MAL: B/ME.

52 Meccano sought a tariff reduction in Australia which included highlighting complaints by Australian children about cost disparities compared to New Zealand. The agent, E. G. Page & Co. attributed the situation to unfair tax classifications and denied there were any local comparators hence tariff protection. 'Tariff Board; Request for reduction of duty'; 2 May1933, NAA: A1732, 688 (Part 1); see also 'Tariff Board: mechanical toys' *The Age*, Australia, 17 May 1933, 10.

53 'Action by Meccano Ltd in French Courts' (1923) February *Games and Toys* 296.

54 In the early 1930s, the list already contained more than forty different Meccano trademarks registered around the world, showing how specific registration patterns had followed the appointment of agents, for instance, in Latin America. Among others, the list included the following registrations: Great Britain (296321) registered 14 September 1907; France (16043) registered 1 June 1908; Belgium (44396) registered 2 June 1908; Spain (22826) registered 14 May

forensic investigations reporting similarities between local toys and Meccano, sent by post or telegram to decide whether an action should follow. For instance, the agent in South Africa did not hesitate to send the specimen of a product called 'Boys Mechanic Set' which, according to him, 'closely resemble[d] Meccano outfits' and began investigating its sales, distribution methods and other details which were going to be cabled to Meccano for the corporation to decide whether to litigate or not after receiving the local toy.[55] On the other hand, the tariff discussion led Meccano's agencies to argue for differences in local production in order to praise the distinctiveness of their toy and the need for a tariff exemption. For instance, E. G. Page, the Australian Meccano agent, emphasised before the Tariff Board how local toys such as 'Ezybilt' or 'Buz Builder' could not be compared to Meccano and claimed that 'the Meccano system comprises parts which will never be made in Australia'.[56] Markets, and not just specific companies, were the subject of surveillance by agents. As Meccano wrote to its South African agent in 1945, 'your vigilance and attention are appreciated, and we know that you will continue to collaborate, letting us know immediately of anything that calls for our intervention, advice or comment'.[57]

Perhaps Meccano's most interesting invention was not the toy itself but the assembling of a media infrastructure to forecast commercial risks. We can get a sense of this predictive policing by looking at how the firm decided whether a dispute was worth the trouble of a legal or policy intervention. The decision to act against competitors, and to what degree, did not depend simply on the flagrancy of the infringement, or even on what evidence Meccano could rely upon, but also on the extent to which competitors' toys could pre-emptively challenge Meccano's success.[58] The range of data routinely exchanged between Meccano and its agencies went from product and package similarities to pricing, promotional advertising, timing and relationships with retailers. But this was also contrasted with other

1913; United States (157149) registered 21 October 1920; Argentina (27,754) registered 11 December 1911; Bolivia (2692) registered 28 January 1928; Chile (41,812) registered 19 January 1928; Peru (41,812) registered 8 February 1928; Brazil (26,877) registered 30 January 1928; Venezuela (6596) registered 8 February 1928; Colombia (6290) registered 30 March 1928, see Box 22; Item No 1; B/ME; MAL.

55 Arthur H. Harris, Johannesburg, to Meccano Ltd, 22 November 1944; Box 22, Item No 1; B/ME; MAL.

56 'Tariff Board's Report on Toys classified under Tariff Item 310 (B), 29 June 1955, 1867, Australia Parliamentary Papers, SLNSW: NQ 328-9401/4.

57 Meccano Ltd to Arthur E. Harris, Johannesburg, 28 February 1945, Box 22, Item No 1, B/ME: MAL.

58 This scrutiny and meticulous analysis of locality, materiality and business methods can be seen in many different exchanges between Meccano and its agents. For instance, Meccano's agent in Argentina, sent a memorandum explaining how 'El Inventor', a local constructional toy, did not appear to be fixing retail prices and did not undertake much advertising. Moreover, the toy missed the advantage of contacting the retailers and its manuals, box, labels were very poor and the swing in of the parts bad; see J. F. Macadam & Co. to Meccano Ltd, 1 October 1942, Box 22, Item No 1, B/ME: MAL.

factors, such as the availability and circulation of Meccano and its parts across that country, a consideration incidentally affected by war shortages.[59] Supply chain disruptions even led some agents to recommend that the best way to defeat rivals was to manufacture Meccano locally. One of these was Meccano's distributor in Argentina, J. F. Macadam & Co, which suggested that the best way to defeat a competitor was 'to manufacture here under the Meccano name and keep prices as low as possible'.[60] Interestingly, the response from Meccano was not to enhance manufacturing capacities but to outsource them with the enrolment of those who had been previously identified as rivals, presumably infringers.[61] Having them manufacture or box Meccano mitigated three challenges at once: tariffs, distribution and piracy.[62] As a result, Meccano avoided getting bogged down in protracted legal cases like those that characterised its first two decades of existence. In doing so, disruptions in the distribution chain were regularly absorbed by the use of trademark. It is here where we see that the trademark and its advertising became the main vehicle by which Meccano stayed close to its prospective customers. The decision whether or not to escalate a matter and take action centred on assessment of the impact on the supply of Meccano to children. By the late 1940s, Meccano saw settlement as a preferable way of dealing with competitors to the previous policy of recourse to courts. It was seen as more productive to settle either via an undertaking or by entering into a negotiated agreement by which competitors ceased trading.[63]

3.3 THE LOGIC OF THE ACCESSORY

As early as 1914, one of the main toy trade journals observed that 'the great aim of all those who understand the bringing-up of children is to keep them constantly engaged, and at the same time though, encouraging them to play as long as possible with one toy'.[64] Meccano tried to capitalise on that cycle by offering a system of different-sized building outfits, sold at progressive prices.[65] In a sense we could say that the toy mirrored a standardised view of childhood, a vision of an education along mechanical lines. The outfits were designated progressively from zero to six, reflecting the transformation of a child into a boy. The outfits were complemented with adjustable and interchangeable parts which enabled them to be updated as a

59 'Meccano, owing to war conditions, is unobtainable today in this country and the consultant fears that the public will be deceived into thinking that the local product is a wartime substitute for the well-known Meccano'; Arthur E. Harris to Meccano Ltd, 5 December 1944, Box 22, Item No 1, B/ME: MAL.

60 J. F. Macadam & Co. to Meccano Ltd, 15 January 1942, Box 22, Item No 1, B/ME: MAL.

61 A similar strategy was also adopted by other corporations such as Disney; on this see Chapter 4, 134.

62 For instance, Meccano pursued that strategy with the Spanish toy 'Metaling'; see Meccano (Secretary) to José Palouzié, 30 December 1931: AP.

63 Agreement between Meccano and Novedades Poch ('Metaling'); January 1932: AP.

64 'Toys as teachers' (1914) February *Toy and Fancy Goods Traders* 272.

65 'Meccano Methods' (1915) November *Toy and Fancy Goods Trader* 9.

chain of buying. These additional pieces also served as the means through which to acquire or complete an outfit.[66]

While the possibility of continuously adding parts resembled a learning process and a consumption trajectory, the interchangeability, however, problematised the very definition of the toy. What emerged from the ability to continually add accessories was the possibility of converting Meccano into a 'system'.[67] Although this method helped Meccano avoid the persistent shortcoming of all toys, namely, ageing and obsolescence, interchangeability presented its own vulnerabilities. For the strength of the system of expandable outfits was also its weakness. The most significant aspect of this was that it opened up the possibility of hacking. There was no better way of replacing Meccano than interfering in its ongoing process of adjustment and upgrade. This could be done by first providing interchangeable parts that children could use together with their Meccano outfits. In fact, the most dangerous competitors for Meccano had been precisely those who understood this mode of market attachment between outfits and parts.[68] The American Model Builder became such a strong competitor precisely because it had decoded Meccano's business methods.[69] It made its toy with holes in perforated strips the same distance apart as in Meccano, so that it could benefit from their interchangeability.[70] More generally, the two systems became compatible as the properties of the toy were made exchangeable. Similarly, the main threat arising from Mecanic, a toy briefly circulating in France in the early 1920s, came from its interchangeability with Meccano parts.[71] The problems of interchangeability intensified in the retail environment because pieces were incidentally sold behind the counter or ordered through a catalogue, which explains why Meccano was particularly concerned with the way its products were handled and promoted in department stores such as Wanamaker's in the United States or Anthony Hordern's in Australia.

Ultimately, these legal controversies triggered a material reaction in Meccano products, as pieces began to be stamped with the brand, reinforcing the trademark recognition of the system. But, more importantly, they further demonstrated that the market for construction toys best realised its potential when the child was hooked on the brand through its accessories.[72] According to one contemporary observer, 'when a purchaser buys a Meccano outfit, he comes again and again to buy more outfits

66 'Meccano: the instructive toy' *Philadelphia Inquirer*, 6 December 1913, 18.

67 *Meccano v Wanamaker*, Bill of Complaint, Southern District of New York, 9 December 1916 SDNY E14–43; NARA, New York.

68 'Meccano v Wagner' (1916) 6 *Trade-Mark Reporter* 487, 490.

69 Frank Hornby, 'The life story of Meccano' 1921 May–June *Meccano Magazine* 2.

70 'Imitation of a mechanical toy' (1916) 12(11) *Bulletin of the United States Trade Mark Association* 276.

71 'Action by Meccano Ltd in French courts' (1923) February *Games and Toys* 296.

72 'Meccano Ltd v Wagner et al. US District Court; Southern District of Ohio, 12 June 1916' (1916) 6 *Trade-Mark Reporter* 487, 490.

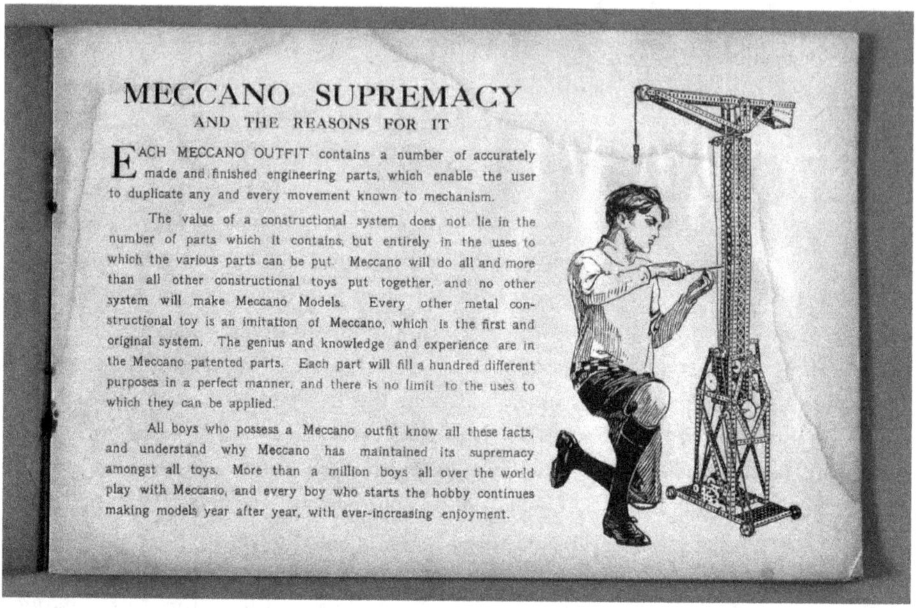

FIGURE 3.2 Meccano instruction book, 1916
Courtesy of Powerhouse/Museum of Applied Arts and Sciences, Australia

and parts . . . Of no other system can this be said'.[73] While the introduction of new parts arguably improved the system, their importance was increasingly recognised from their presumed effect of 'intensifying the enthusiasm among the boys'.[74] Here, we can see how the role attached to accessories and interchangeable parts as a breeder of further sales enacted the gradual transformation of the initial purchase into a habit of consumption.[75] The connection with young enthusiasts was strengthened when Meccano owners were able to convert their sets into larger ones.[76] In doing so, construction toys such as Meccano could claim that play was inexhaustible, or at least that play could last until the child had outgrown toys of that kind in general.[77]

3.4 THE MECCANO BOY

By constantly emphasising the educational value of the invention, carefully setting up a system for the registration and surveillance of trademarks, and consistently

73 'It pays best to sell Meccano' (1915) 31 May *Toy and Fancy Goods Trader* 9.
74 'Meccano: engineering for toys' (1920) February *Toy and Fancy Goods Trader* 7.
75 'Meccano products' (1923) November *Toy Trader* 50; see also 'Meccano: Advertising and Marketing Policy; 19 Jan 1960'; J. Walter Thompson Company; London, HAT50/1/108/2/2/7.
76 'Meccano' (1921) February *Toy and Fancy Goods Trader* 18.
77 'Minibrix offers you a life-time of business!' (1937) June *Games and Toys* 9.

trying to keep children engaged through outfits and accessories, Meccano embodied an industrial vision of childhood. The culture of standardisation and industrialisation determined the ways in which its addressee, the child, was imagined. The packaging and the labelling of the toy often reproduced an image of a boy successfully building a crane or another model. The image of that boy was repetitively imprinted upon the commodity. So inseparable were these representations from the toy that even its imitators followed suit. One might say that the ultimate success in branding practices was the construction of that positive image labelled as the 'Meccano Boy'. The advertising highlighted emotional virtues of the play. As one advertisement described, the Meccano Boy was a 'sturdy, happy-faced young man, with joy and fun oozing from every feature and limb. He is always dressed in the same way in the characteristic Meccano jersey, and is always enjoying himself'.[78] The connotations the toy had actively tried to convey, such as happiness, inventorship and success, were thus embodied by that specific image. The Meccano Boy worked as a mass-produced aspirational template for children to identify with and become a consumer. In other words, the child as a consumer was created precisely by the branding practices through which Meccano constituted itself. As already stated, Meccano's advertising strategies fluctuated between the appeal to parents and to children due to the special character of toys as a commodity. On the one hand, advertisements repeated how 'your boy will be as bright and happy as those Meccano boys who have built fine working models'.[79] On the other, children were promised a land of perpetual fun.[80] Meccano embodied intellectual properties that readily transcended the specifics of patent, trademark registrations and copyrights. Meccano became what it was through the strategic work of connecting the product to its prospective consumers, whether parents or friends of the child, or the children themselves. What we would like to highlight is not just how the deployment of company intellectual properties identified happiness or pleasure as the main objective. Their more important underlying presumption was that boys themselves could be made. The child as a consumer could be profitably stimulated (or constrained) and set on a constructive path by a set of Meccano instructions, pieces and rituals.

The figure of the Meccano Boy embodied a sort of Taylorisation of consumption: that is, Meccano broke down the labour of education and play to optimise the recruitment of participants and efficiently channel the child's imaginative and social impulses towards further consuming and promoting the product. The Meccano template contributed to the universality claimed for the toy. However, Meccano also introduced several advertising techniques aimed at helping consumers to stand out

78 *Meccano News* (1920) No 1, November, 9; see also 'Meccano boys' *Timaru Herald*, 26 December 1921, 2.

79 'Glorious times for your boy with Meccano', *Indiana Gazette*, 18 December 1914, 7; 'Give your boy Meccano', *Morpeth Herald*, 11 December 1914, 12.

80 'The big toy store offers: toys for the boy with a mechanical turn', *Allentown Leader*, 8 December 1913, 8.

from the crowd and feel personally connected to the system. Perhaps the most critical of these was the organisation of model competitions and prizes. These competitions appealed to Meccano for obvious promotional reasons. As is discussed below, they also provided source material for the development of new product lines. Competitions were especially attractive to toy department stores, since they served as a vehicle 'to stimulate sales, additional traffic, goodwill and valuable newspaper publicity for the department'.[81] According to Hornby, the success of these competitions was due to 'the patented interchangeable parts which enable the user to make any mechanical movement he desires'.[82] As such, the contests also provided an arena for children to demonstrate their modelling skills and achieve recognition.

However, their greatest significance resided in their ability to attract children by making them participants in the development of the 'uniqueness' of Meccano. The events functioned both as a device to capture interest and as a social marker, enabling children to overcome the standardisation process implicit in the toy. In entering a competition, the child could separate himself from the mass and could inscribe his name in a projective narrative, merging Meccano's success story with his achievement. Winners were rewarded not just with prizes but with self-promotion for having won the race to become the real 'Meccano Boy'. Their names, models and photographs were often published in Meccano literature and exhibited at department stores.[83] These pursuits constituted one of the ways in which children were being newly framed as consumers.

Photographs with their sets evoke the blending properties of the toy and the boy, published because of their display abilities and marked as investment prospects for the family and the market. Their stance, sense of longing and happy expressions illustrate how the children portrayed were not merely advertising vehicles. Rather, they became a commercial subject being promoted, displayed and fabricated through modelling practices and contests.

3.5 INSTRUCTIONAL MODELS

Meccano models showcased the peculiarities of the toy. Like the scale models described by Alain Pottage and Brad Sherman that were once submitted to help make patent machinery claims comprehensible, these representations of the toys were constituted as one of the 'means of communicating the invention'.[84] Their mechanical framing also indicated the forging of a distinct relationship between

[81] 'About clubs: sales promotions for October', (1934) September *Playthings* 56.

[82] *Meccano Prize Models*, New York, 1915, 2.

[83] 'Our mail bag (T.W.R. from Shrewsbury)' (1917) March *Meccano Magazine* 4.

[84] These scale models were used in litigation as the means to make machines comprehensible (or visible) to jurors and judges. Patent examiners also required models until 1880; see Alain Pottage and Brad Sherman, *Figures of Invention: A History of Modern Patent Law*, Oxford University Press, 2010, 16–17.

FIGURE 3.3 Boy with Meccano, George Garland Collection, 1953
Courtesy of West Sussex Record Office.

engineering and subjectivity, broadly paralleling the age of mechanical invention and the discourse of achievement. However, it is necessary to highlight several differences between those earlier nineteenth-century patent models and the Meccano miniatures. The latter were shaped by the distinct way in which their properties as toys circulated in the marketplace. Unlike patent models, their examination, registration and communication did not usually take place in workshops, patent offices and courtrooms but rather in family homes, clubs and department stores.

Interestingly, Meccano began to request that actual models for contests should not be sent.[85] Instead, the submission was reduced from a three-dimensional model to two dimensions, as a photograph or a good drawing, together with a detailed explanation of the mechanical model.[86] While these changes risked turning model contests into photo contests, the noteworthy point here is that this shift in practice raised concerns about the fairness of the competition and the authorship of the models. In the 1930s, Meccano tried to stop fraudulent participation, such as models made by parents who felt that irresistible urge to construct the models themselves to increase their child's chances of winning. In order to warn against this type of parental 'help', Meccano explicitly stated that the submission ought to be the product of unaided work.[87]

[85] 'Meccano model-building competition', (1932) January *Meccano Magazine* 48.

[86] Ibid; 'Meccano model-building competition', (1932) February *Meccano Magazine* 122; 'Model building competition' (1923) March *Meccano Magazine* 210.

[87] 'Machine tool competition', (1926) May *Meccano Magazine* 329; 'A novel model-building competition' (1926) May *Meccano Magazine* 333; 'Model-building competition', (1932) April

The possibility of submitting drawings instead of actual models also established another interesting promotional layer for the toy. It created a way of including boys who lacked purchasing power at the relevant time. Participants who did not actually own a Meccano outfit were able to submit their model by drawing it. The paradox triggered here was that you could be a Meccano Boy without owning a set. This blurring of the distinction between ownership and participation was crucial for the success of the brand since it increased its aspirational nature. With contests garnering about 10,000 entries annually, Meccano further exploited these events by using them as opportunities to get more and more information about potential customers. Firstly, these schemes enabled Meccano to extract data about consumption since entry forms had already segmented the market by age and demographics.[88] Secondly, because children from across the British Empire and beyond could participate in competitions, whether or not they possessed any or every set, this helped represent the Meccano notions of modernity, progress and civic participation as universal and generally accessible to all educated people. Thirdly, the application process consistently requested that participants include the names and addresses of three of your 'chums' and 'friends', which in turn could be converted into data to further expand the commercial reach of the toy.[89] As such, creating a database became part of Meccano's logistics, offering pointers for marketing and distribution angles. And, most importantly, this data had been voluntarily (and happily) provided by the children and their parents.[90] Another notable consequence made possible through these model-building competitions was their effect on the development of the toy. As they were organised to receive the newest, most ingenious and original models, the competitions became a rich source of model plans. The best models were included in Meccano's instruction books.[91] Again, interestingly, children and their parents had voluntarily given away photographs and drawings of model designs in toto as they had been previously asked to waive their copyright in the images to participate in the contest.[92]

Meccano Magazine 296; 'New year model building contest', (1933) January *Meccano Magazine* 51; 'Meccano model building contest' (1934) January *Meccano Magazine* 57; 'Model-building competition' (1934) April *Meccano Magazine* 319; 'Grand model-building contest' (1934) May *Meccano Magazine* 411.

88 Anthony McReavy, *The Toy Story: The Life and Times of Inventor Frank Hornby*, Random House, 2002, 113.

89 'This is Meccano week!' *The Sketch*, 4 December 1929, 8; 'Meccano: the toy that made engineering famous', *Sydney Morning Herald*, 10 December 1929, 15.

90 'The new Meccano', (1926) September *Meccano Magazine* 603; 'The new Meccano', (1926) October *Meccano Magazine* 626.

91 'Special summer model-building competition', (1927) July *Meccano Magazine* 643; 'Grand Christmas model-building competition', (1927) December *Meccano Magazine* 1901.

92 Although unsuccessful photographs and drawings were returned, the photographs of the prize-winning models became 'the property of Meccano Ltd'; see 'Meccano building contest', (1926) June *Meccano Magazine* 389.

These instruction books (or manuals) became one of the key components of the Meccano system. The initial purpose of these manuals was to explain the uses of the construction set for making toys by showing pictures and photographs illustrating its scope and range of possibilities. Furthermore, they continued to be published, incorporating suggestions for improvements to previous models. As a result, their publication went hand in hand with the worldwide expansion of the Meccano business as part of the kit that exploited and explained the fun, pleasure and instruction provided by the toy. 'No Meccano boy is properly equipped unless he has them' – it was repeatedly claimed.[93] By the mid-1930s, these manuals were printed in seventeen languages, from Spanish to Chinese.[94] If we look closely at these peculiar publications, it is possible to see that the invention's appeal derived from its ingenious nature, converting the toy into a sort of programmable assemblage device or, as suggested above, a toy to make toys, exemplifying the internationalist promise of modernity. Since the litigation proceedings against the American Model Builder, the instruction manuals specifically began to acquire a pivotal role in protecting the toy against competitors. When patent or trademark protection failed or were put in doubt, the manuals constituted the starting point from which Meccano could defend its property in copyright to frustrate competitors.[95]

At first glance it might be thought that copyright protection would have been limited by the functional nature of Meccano instructions, given literary works were required to demonstrate originality and much of the text of the instructions was factual, with modest literary and informational content. In the Australian litigation, Meccano Ltd sought to restrain the retailer Anthony Hordern & Sons from selling American Model Builder on the basis that importation of the sets infringed the literary and artistic copyright in the UK models. Here, the images in the Meccano manual proved quite helpful. Such was the unexpected importance of the drawings in the manuals that in the middle of those legal proceedings Hornby himself announced how anxious he was 'to secure copies of early editions of Meccano Manuals', offering to pay children for them or replace them with one of the latest books.[96] In determining if copyright subsisted in the Meccano manuals, the court found that

> the book is really complete in itself. The pictures coupled with the letterpress, convey a full idea of what can be done with the toy, and can be read and understood by a boy who has never seen the toy .... In the present case, from a

93 'Meccano manuals of instructions' (1920) June–July *Meccano Magazine* 1920, 4; 'Meccano manuals of instructions' (1921) July–August *Meccano Magazine* 8.

94 'Romance of Meccano: a wonderful toy' *The Observer*, 27 September 1936, 29.

95 There were also actions in passing-off, but the distinctive nature of the Meccano trademarks, consumer awareness of them, and the absence of this branding on substitute products posed an impenetrable defence. See *Meccano Ltd v Antony Hordern & Sons Ltd* [1918] 18 SR (NSW) 606, 608–10.

96 'Old Meccano manuals' (1918) February–March *Meccano Magazine* 1918, 3.

> comparison of the manuals, there can be no doubt, and it is not in fact disputed, that the compiler of the American Model Builder manual did use, for the purpose of preparing his manual, many of the designs contained in the plaintiff's manual.[97]

Some designs were considered slavish copies, others were original drawings made by a skilled draughtsman from a different angle. While making models based upon the Meccano manuals was not considered infringement, to reproduce the lookalike models in a book was held to constitute a copyright infringement even when reflecting a different angle by the draughtsman. Although differences between the manuals existed, precisely because the draughtsman had intervened, the court felt they were still copies of Meccano's original designs.[98] Incidentally, the court further noted that the Australian retailer had received letters from the plaintiff's solicitors, alleging patent and copyright infringement and passing-off and asking the rival to meet with them to discuss this matter.[99] As the department store had persisted in its right to sell the American sets to service local demand, there was an order for delivery-up of all infringing manuals left in the store's possession.[100]

Meccano manuals functioned as a publication record that could be used as evidence of direct or indirect copying of illustrations. Despite the fact that, or precisely because, the models depicted in the Meccano manuals were not intended to limit the possibilities of the outfits, the comparison between Meccano and allegedly infringing instruction manuals enabled questions about labour, thought and originality to arise. As such, the types of evidential logic typically underpinning copyright cases could be brought to bear. Namely, that it was possible to conclude the high improbability of a great number of similarities between the models depicted in the manuals being the result of coincidence, and thus similarity inferred indirect copying of the designs, rather than reflecting the limited ways in which one might draw a tractor made out of perforated metal strips, for example.

Much more can be said about the way copyright was strategically used in relation to manuals for instructions. For instance, Meccano began registering its copyright in relevant jurisdictions after realising how significant ownership of literary and artistic copyright attached to models had turned out to be in the Australian litigation.[101] Manuals not only enabled comparison with individual models; they also aided

[97] *Meccano v Hordern*, above n 95, 611.

[98] Ibid, 613. Meccano introduced the testimony of an engineer who acted as an expert witness showing the similarity between the manuals; see George Alfred Julius in '*Meccano v Hordern* (1918)' 697–716 (examination); 717–25 (further examination); 726–9 (cross-examination); SRO (NSW): NRS-2713-1 (6/2823).

[99] The letters threatening proceedings were acknowledged by Meccano's Australian agent, Emerson George Page in '*Meccano v Hordern* (1918)' 627–46, 639 (examination); SRO (NSW): NRS-2713-1 (6/2823). However, Meccano failed to prove the 'passing-off' point, arguably the claim more directly connected to the retailer; see *Meccano v Hordern*, above n 95, 614.

[100] 'A mechanical toy' *Sydney Morning Herald*, 18 September 1918, 9.

[101] 'Application for the registration of copyright in a literary work: Meccano Instructions for the No 0 outfit, 15 September 1921; NAA: A1336, 9727.

comparison of the ways in which those models had been enumerated, classified and described. In a sense, models depicted in manuals helped further demonstrate the wonders of the invention, illustrating ingenuity occurring within the system from oscillation between play and constraint that characterised it. One of the ways in which presumed infringers were found was by isolating the models in their manuals which could only be actually assembled with Meccano and not with other constructional toys.[102] Although the possibilities of Meccano were claimed to be unlimited, a certain abstraction was required to build things out of its prefabricated components. For that very reason, the printed matter with its models and explanatory notes offered the possibility of pinning down and creating boundaries around the kind of intangible properties which lay behind the invention. Above all, Meccano was a modular system, since the components and pieces that could be assembled followed certain basic rules to obtain a variety of figures. As Pottage has observed, 'the modularising connectivity turns out to have a cultural, ethical and affective significance that is capitalised in the [Lego] brand'.[103] Similarly, Meccano embraced that connectivity via different socio-technical arrangements, from the development of guilds to the publication of a magazine, as discussed below. Those arrangements were important not only to feed the manuals with new models but also because they produced the enthusiasm necessary for the Meccano brand to position itself as the main constructional toy in the market.

3.6 BUILDING A MOVEMENT

The most important factory for the production of Meccano Boys was a publication: the *Meccano Magazine*. It began in 1916 as a four-page sheet, 'to help Meccano Boys to have more fun than other boys'.[104] It grew progressively in size and content, and a few years later it changed its slogan to a magazine 'published in the interest of Meccano boys'.[105] The remarkable aspect of the magazine was that it connected all the pieces mentioned so far: the manuals, the competitions, the prizes, the photographs, the children and the brand behind the various linked corporations. In other words, the magazine was a typeset version of Meccano, not just as a toy, but a system selling education and entertainment that also constructed the boy as a builder and architect of a world of mechanical things. It brought parts and models into the same pages, showing their interchangeability, and demonstrated possibilities for the toy and the boy to converge.

[102] Crawfords to Meccano Ltd, 18 March 1946 (Indications of direct copying of our illustrations: 'Meccastar'); Box 22; Item No 1, MAL: B/ME.

[103] Alain Pottage, 'Lego v OHIM' in Jose Bellido (ed.), *Landmark Cases in Intellectual Property Law*, Hart, 2017, 346.

[104] (1916) September–October *Meccano Magazine* 1.

[105] (1922) March–April *Meccano Magazine* 1; see Lynne Vallone, *Big and Small. A Cultural History of Extraordinary Bodies*, Yale University Press, 2017, 210.

To a certain extent, the Meccano system was laid bare by and through the magazine. On the one hand, it functioned as a record of the way in which the toy was evolving from educational activity into a hobby. On the other hand, the magazine became an important accompaniment marking the passage into adolescence for many interwar and post-war children. While the magazine included a serialised 'life-story' by Frank Hornby of the period from the moment in which he 'took patents' to the first eventful fifteen years of Meccano,[106] it was mainly composed of material orientated towards children. As the first issue announced, its aim was to go ahead publishing new models, new ideas and new fun for 'you'.[107] Initially hampered by wartime paper shortages, this personalised yet corporate desire to connect with children was deemed so crucial that Meccano promised to continue publishing it even 'if we have to use tissue paper'.[108] This reassuring answer was given to a child from Beckenham, a small town in Greater London, who wrote to the 'mail bag' column worried about the future of the publication.[109] The mailbag was included in the magazine from the outset, first conceived to promote and improve Meccano products by gathering feedback from children – 'if your letters ... are interesting enough, you will probably find them printed in the Meccano Magazine'.[110] However, it also had an advertising function. For instance, publishing invented letters promoting the toy for sales purposes. Letters, real and invented, generated a printed space for the community of toy enthusiasts. Like other trade magazines, one of the advantages of printing these testimonials and epistolary exchanges came from the way they could increase public goodwill towards the brand and stimulate sales. For instance, the toy dealer could fully explain the uses of Meccano to prospective buyers through the magazine, a complimentary copy of which was sent to each dealer.[111] A claim emphasised in Meccano's patents – that is, the inventive ingenuity that the toy fostered – was particularly enhanced through this correspondence. Not surprisingly, the magazine's editor asked its readers 'who know of any strange or useful purposes to which Meccano has been applied, to write me'.[112] By publishing these new uses, the invention was further expanded, adjusted and adapted to and indirectly by children.

As mentioned before, advertising of Meccano frequently depicted the toy as a family affair to confront the question of consumption, as the actual purchaser of the toy was not the child but his parents. One of the ways to fabricate that specific double address to children and parents was to incorporate the family connection in

[106] Frank Hornby, 'Life story of Meccano' (1921) July–August *Meccano Magazine* 2; (1921) November–December 2; (1922) January–February 2.

[107] 'Our first number' (1916) September–October *Meccano Magazine* 1.

[108] 'Out mail bag' (1916) November–December *Meccano Magazine* 4.

[109] Ibid.

[110] 'Our First Number', above n 107.

[111] 'Meccano: engineering for boys' (1922) February *Toy and Fancy Goods Trader* 56.

[112] 'Novel uses for Meccano' (1916) November–December *Meccano Magazine* 1.

the magazine. For instance, the 'mail bag' began publishing letters from parents proud of their sons and their outfits.[113] And the magazine incorporated sections specifically addressed to parents, praising the endless qualities of the invention that 'only becomes a toy when it is being played with'.[114] It was not only the constitution of boys that Meccano was interested in. One of the advertising angles used by Meccano consisted of emphasising the utility of the toy as an invention that strengthened family bonds and modernised domestic role models. 'Dad' was explicitly described in the magazine as the one who 'buys us Meccano and gives us a hand with the models till his fingers ache with screwing up the bolts'.[115] When it announced that 'Dad and the boys [had] built this'[116] or depicted the Meccano Boy asking his father to come and see the model he had made, it reinforced the ideal family as one led by the company's example, where family engagement in consumption was central to the communication of paternal love and guidance.

In addition to these specific appeals to the family, the magazine gradually concentrated on enabling the sharing of the children's own letters, relaying their experiences of how to make the most of the toy. This focus underlined the vision of the child as a subject in the making and served to situate the toy as an educational facilitator that fostered development. The social dimension of becoming a Meccano Boy made consumption of the toy a collective and outward experience that facilitated taking one's place among like-minded others. As such, the emphasis on child development involved shifting the expectations of play from the family environment to the outside world.

Meccano capitalised on this external path to boyhood and endorsed the 'groups' and 'clubs' children had formed to play with the toy. Much of the content of the magazine moved towards the encouragement and representation of this form of collective consumption outside the home. Meccano encouraged boys to establish clubs in their towns and recommended they 'write to us, and we will help them to overcome their difficulties'.[117] The emergence of a distinct Meccano literature trying to help children with these formative endeavours ('How to run a Meccano Club') coincided with the advertising material distributed to retailers ('How to sell more Meccano') and the growing importance Meccano attached to the protection of all its trademarks.[118] Although Meccano reiterated that local groups proliferated

[113] 'Meccano: gems from our mail bag' (1916) September–October *Meccano Magazine* 4.

[114] 'To parents' (1918) February–March *Meccano Magazine* 3.

[115] 'Dad' (1916) September–October *Meccano Magazine* 2.

[116] 'The new Meccano', *Winnipeg Tribune*, 3 December 1926, 9; see also 'The boys built it – in colours – and dad helped', *The Sketch*, 8 December 1926, 47.

[117] 'Meccano clubs' (1919) December–January *Meccano Magazine* 2. Clubs also increased pass-on readership of the magazine as one copy circulated among its members; see 'Minutes' of the meeting held 26 March 1929; Meccano Club Minutes (1927–1932), WYAS: C678/11/8/5/3.

[118] 'Meccano help' (1920) October *Toy and Fancy Goods Trader* 130; 'Meccano sales help' (1921) September *Toy and Fancy Goods Trader* 118; 'Meccano publicity' (1921) October *Toy and Fancy Goods Trader* 90; see also *How to Run a Meccano Club*, Liverpool, 1928, 3: AP.

spontaneously, the fact is that it gave them a sense of direction and belonging while at the same time viewed them as marketing opportunities, as the groups yielded a good deal of valuable information about Meccano Boys. Perhaps the clearest example of the way in which Meccano handled these opportunities was the creation of a special association to steer and aid clubs: the Meccano Guild. This form of association reinforced the civic aspirations of the Meccano system. Consistent with the original patent claims, Meccano Guild membership provided more than mere entertainment or a way of defraying concern for idle youth. The Meccano Guild resembled the Boy Scout movement in a number of ways. Its proselytising and organisational features were sites of gender and racial formation, which served to enrol children and provide them with initiative and purpose. However, the main difference between the two was that the Meccano Guild was directly connected to the promotion and consumption of a toy. Insofar as the guild was a template for club activities, it served as a cast for producing Meccano Boys.[119]

It is important to note that the guild would have been impossible without the *Meccano Magazine*, particularly without the epistolary exchanges and the discourse around the toy that the magazine generated. Alongside the 'mail bag', the magazine started publicising the guild's objectives and the ways to become a member.[120] Whereas the aim of the guild seemed straightforwardly the encouragement of learning mechanical and engineering principles, its formation was, in turn, advertised as an additional selling point.[121] The guild created a framework for clubs to be replicated while fostering activities that could feed back to the magazine. By emphasising the organisational qualities and the guidelines on which these clubs could be modelled, the guild secured content for the magazine and promotions such as tie-in competitions and club activities organised in co-operation with local retailers. Meccano emphasised that the guild was run separately from the commercial side of the company. However, these clubs also offered an additional avenue to regulate play. By making children members of the guild, the possibility of brand substitution at the retailing level was reduced because consumers had already made up their minds about precisely what they desired before the act of purchase.

Among the most interesting strategies applied to collectivising play and making consumption of Meccano ubiquitous was the individualisation and gratification of those enthusiasts who had helped build up goodwill towards the brand, which in turn brought more children into the guild. Meccano came to rely on certificates, medals and badges to motivate children to join and convince others to join the

[119] See, e.g., the applications for guild membership in 'Names wanted' (1922) March–April *Meccano Magazine* 5.

[120] 'How to join the guild' (1919) September–October *Meccano Magazine* 3; 'Message to members of the Meccano Guild' (1919) November–December *Meccano Magazine* 3.

[121] 'The Meccano Guild' (1919) October *Toy and Fancy Goods Trader* 1919, 54; 'The Meccano Guild' (1919) November *Toy and Fancy Goods Trader* 118; 'A Meccano Guild for France' (1922) October *Meccano Magazine* 1922, 9.

guild. In exchange for membership, the children got blue triangular badges described as 'signs of fellowship'.[122] Those guild members who were particularly active received recruiting medals and merit awards after showing particular ability or aptitude for club work.[123]

While these items acted as badges of affiliation, echoing recent controversies about the legal meaning of trademark use,[124] the identity nurtured by the toy was built up in the promotional strategies used by Meccano. Meccano marked not only its products but also its consumers, as the brand itself was a product of their making. In other words, the commodity and the identity sought after by children, the Meccano Boy, mutually coalesced. The guild built a bridge for children from different countries to connect by enacting an imaginary space where the Meccano invention could expand. From its very beginning, the magazine featured letters from children from Canada, Australia, New Zealand and South Africa 'where we have Meccano depots, and in India and all the smaller colonies [where] Meccano fires the mind and brightens the play hours of thousands of boys'.[125] Although the panoramic gaze described here played upon a vision of connectivity associated with the British Empire, the adaptability of the toy and the communication circuit enabled by the magazine meant that Meccano could adapt itself to many different national and local narratives. While capitalising on the thirst for knowledge, contact and information, the guild served to signal the attributes ascribed to Meccano Boys: civic leadership, entrepreneurship, and friendship. Above all, it pointed out that organisation was the key to success. It provided children with policies and tools for the clubs: how to lead a club, how to become treasurers, how to organise activities and how to discipline members. By the early 1930s, membership of the guild had grown to over 100,000. When Meccano expanded into France, Spain and many other countries, the same advertising literature was translated. One of the factors that contributed to the internationalisation of Meccano as a brand came from the meticulous translation and distribution of this advertising literature to foreign agents or subsidiaries. The leaflets about setting up clubs, the prizes and competitions, the instruction manuals and displays were all translated and standardised, but their content was filled out abroad. That is, the contests, the children who participated in those events and the purchases they made were local.[126] Similarly, versions of the magazine were published in Spanish and French, repeating the format that had already proved successful. It might be argued that standardisation was key for the circulation of Meccano and that the value of the brand was derived from practices

[122] 'To our Meccano boys' (1920) March–April *Meccano Magazine* 1.

[123] 'Special Merit Medallions' (1922) May–June *Meccano Magazine* 4.

[124] *Arsenal v Reed* [2003] EWCA Civ 696; see also the opinion of the Advocate-General Ruiz Jarabo Colomer in Case C-206/01 point 81 (linking the football badges to merchandising operations).

[125] 'Meccano in other lands' (1916) November–December *Meccano Magazine* 2.

[126] 'Display of models: meeting of Meccano club' *New Zealand Herald*, 16 May 1925, 14.

that allowed children to be directly involved in the performance of the invention and the reading of the magazine. Seen from this perspective, the Meccano Boy might also be considered both a graphic standard and a selling point, as he served as a template to absorb local peculiarities.

In 1921, the magazine's editorial work was taken over by Ellison Hawks, a popular science writer who worked in Meccano's advertising department.[127] Hawks expanded the magazine's content by using imaginative writing prompts, such as asking children what they would do 'if they were the editor' of the magazine.[128] However, the most remarkable and creative strategy for reaching a juvenile audience was the enrolment of a teenager to the Meccano staff: Hubert Lansley.

Lansley was the prototype of the Meccano Boy, an aficionado who had begun publishing his own magazine devoted to the toy.[129] His handmade magazine was so successful that it caught the company's attention. Indeed, they had determined to ask him to refrain from the unlawful use of the trademark. However, after a meeting, they decided instead to hire Lansley. He started making models of the toy at the factory and continued contributing to the magazine's editorial work. The pseudonym under which he wrote, 'Spanner', says it all.[130] Lansley became an important 'tool' for improving the Meccano system. The magazine's most memorable decade coincided with the work he carried out with Hawks. No one could better identify child-related trends and tastes than a boy. No one could develop a more personal and constructive relationship with child consumers than one of their own peers.[131] Under this editorial input, the magazine's circulation reached its peak. And it did so by incorporating material such as stories, book reviews and advertisements that went beyond the toy itself. This meant widening the appeal of the magazine and moulding the visuals so as to entice children who were not yet Meccano Boys. Significantly, the magazine repeated this strategy on several occasions, not just hiring a teenager as a contributing editor but also commissioning children to act as writers and artists. For instance, a thirteen-year-old child, Frank Hampson, who would later become a well-known British comic illustrator, had his first ever commission and publication in the *Meccano Magazine*.[132]

Taking a prominent place among regular children's publications, the magazine had a particular kind of material and social agency, working as a vicarious and peripheral proxy for the Meccano brand. In that sense, the *Meccano Magazine* can

[127] Peter J. Bowler, '*Meccano Magazine*: boys' toys and the popularization of science in early twentieth-century Britain' (2018) 3 *British Journal for the History of Science: Themes* 129.

[128] 'New essay competition' (1921) January–February *Meccano Magazine* 1921, 5.

[129] 'An amateur editor who publishes, edits and prints' (1922) September *Meccano Magazine* 11.

[130] 'Obituaries: Hubert Lansley. Spanner who was nuts about Meccano' *The Guardian*, 16 August 1997, 17; 'Hubert Lansley' *The Times*, 16 August 1997, 21; Keith Waterhouse, 'The Ugs again, as good cooks go' *Daily Mail*, 14 August 1997, 14.

[131] Lansley, above n 49, 15.

[132] Sally Morris, *Living with Eagles: Marcus Morris, Priest and Publisher*, Lutterworth Press, 1998, 98.

be viewed as a merchandising operation anticipating what other British children's publications, such as *Eagle*, pursued in the 1950s. That is, using a magazine to build up a commercial strategy to sell related commodities.[133] Print media offered a serial method to regularly expose children to the toy and its accessories. It also functioned as a vehicle to introduce them to what other children were doing and a guide on how to become a Meccano Boy.[134] The great advantage of a children's publication over other forms of enterprise lay in its modalities of distribution and consumption.

FIGURE 3.4 Shopfront for J. Parker, newsagents, *c.* 1949–1956
Courtesy of Tate Gallery. © Nigel Henderson Estate

133 John B. Myers, 'A preliminary survey on merchandising and large-scale exploitation to be built-up on the regular publication of a juvenile paper, March 1950'; Box 13; Item 7: MM/CUA.
134 'Meccano boys as editors' (1921) May–June *Meccano Magazine* 1.

Whereas films were exhibited in the cinema circuit and animated film merchandise was distributed elsewhere, the benefit of a magazine was its capacity to easily circulate from the newsstand to the home, establishing Meccano in children's minds beforehand, making them pre-sold consumers.[135]

The magazine publicised the qualities of the toy and the excitement of being a Meccano Boy. It did so together with other selected content, establishing an implicit association and relationship difficult to achieve at the toyshop or at the retailer.[136] Its content and circulation were so popular that other juvenile publications asked Meccano for a licence to integrate it into their magazines with other material and redistribute it so 'you would be able to communicate more frequently with the Spanish buyers of your articles than you are doing now. And this not only in Spain, but in all Spanish speaking countries, a wide field indeed, as we are able to reach all parts of Spanish America through our bookseller friends'.[137]

By placing Meccano side by side with things that interested children, the magazine became one of Meccano's most important branding strategies. Significantly, its function resembled a mass consumption device: the shop window.[138] The magazine presented not only the activities of Meccano clubs but also showcased children's interests and advertisements, projecting liveliness and enticement on every page. It provided the imaginative travel that some journalists had already observed in relation to children's magazines, which served as 'the magic carpet by means of which a speeding of transfer of goods from factory to user [was] effected'.[139] This strategy was again an attempt to control the distribution system of the toy by positioning the Meccano brand beyond wholesalers and retailers and directly connecting it to children. One can observe the application and effect of this technique by looking at one of its covers, published in the commercially most important month, December, of 1954.

It showed Meccano Boys and other children staring at the toys and goods arranged in a shop window. The window displayed in the forefront the most famous model that could be made with the toy, a replica of the Eiffel Tower, together with other merchandise in the background. Although the magazine cover page was great in capturing the way in which such a display could arouse the interest of passers-by,

[135] The arrangements by which the magazine was able to be ordered at any newsagent or bookstall were announced in 'Surprises at the store' (1923) August *Meccano Magazine* 2.

[136] Images were so fundamental to the magazine that even book reviews began to include them; see, for instance, W. H. McCormick to George Routledge & Son, 3 April 1937 (sending the electro of Vickers Wellesley Bomber to illustrate the review of *Boys' Book of Flying* by Charles Boff); UoR RKP: RKP 64/2.

[137] Editorial Juventud to *Meccano Magazine*, 8 March 1933; Box 201 (Correspondencia), ANC: Sig. 361.

[138] Cochoy describes the window shop as a "captation device", an operation to arouse curiosity; see Frank Cochoy, *On Curiosity: The Art of Market Seduction*, Mattering Press, 2016, 54.

[139] O. Rivington, 'The magic carpet of commerce' (1919) December *Toy and Fancy Goods Trader* 128; see also *The Magic Carpet*, Meccano Ltd, 1925.

FIGURE 3.5 Cover of *Meccano Magazine*, December 1954
Photograph © British Library Board. LOU.EW 7 [1954]

the most interesting feature to note is that the magazine itself functioned as a shop window. Nobody expressed this better than Keith Waterhouse, who wrote:

> It was not Meccano mag's editorial comments I craved on my monthly fix but its advertisements. There was page after page of them. It was like a Christmas catalogue appearing all year, a Santa's Workshop in photogravure …. It was like pressing your nose to a toyshop window without your cold breath steaming up the pane and spoiling the view.[140]

[140] Keith Waterhouse, 'Parts we couldn't reach' *Daily Mail*, 26 November 1987, 8.

3.7 OUTDATED

During the early 1960s, Meccano hired a well-known advertising agency, J. Walter Thompson, in a desperate attempt to rejuvenate its brand and increase its diminished sales.[141] Although the agency praised some of the toy's features, it identified several possible explanations for why it was failing to keep pace with the tastes and interests of a new generation of children. Firstly, Meccano had been superseded by toys made from different materials and with different design values, such as Lego. Secondly, the shop-window space represented by the magazine was also no longer as effective and attractive, as it had been taken over by another more domestic medium: the television set.[142] Lastly, the images that the brand projected, for instance, the connection between father and child or the building up of a new generation, had become too old-fashioned. In other words, the children who had been 'brought up' on Meccano had already grown up.

While the impact of television on merchandising and the legal controversies it generated are explored in subsequent chapters, the Meccano system was very innovative in a number of ways. It incorporated several enduring socio-technical features and standardising procedures to connect to children on a mass scale. Although it registered trademarks and filed patents, the intellectual property aspects the corporation focused upon shifted from the rights themselves to an array of peripheral commercial and legal practices enacted to protect and project the Meccano system. For instance, copyrights ended up being an important mechanism to protect the invention against competitors. Furthermore, trademarks became useful for the establishment of a guild which helped to reduce the problem of brand substitution. Additionally, exchanges with children occasionally led to patent improvements. Further, one of the most interesting inventions that Meccano produced was, as highlighted in the chapter, the magazine. Both attractive and educative, the magazine shaped the passage from childhood to boyhood as promised by the invention. For a while, it held a unique position as a window to the world. It introduced children to new interests beyond Meccano and broadened their horizons and knowledge of the world. At the same time, it served to position the Meccano brand as the means to engage with these wider concerns, making private consumption a matter of public importance. Alongside this, it functioned as a device to encourage Meccano Boys and other children to become consumers. As a communication medium, the magazine highlighted the importance of print, correspondence and advertisements as key instruments through which corporate and personal identities could be forged. Although its imagery and values had

[141] 'Meccano limited: future prospects. A framework for discussion', J. Walter Thompson Company, London, Nov 1961, HAT50/1/108/3/2/8.

[142] For an insightful analysis of the demise of the company from a business point of view, see Kenneth Brown, 'Death of a dinosaur, Meccano of Liverpool, 1908–1979' (1993) 66 November *Business Archives Sources and History* 22, 27.

become outdated by the 1960s, such innovative commercial and legal practices blurred the boundaries between content and advertising, between editorial work and children's participation, and between the family and the market. As they anticipated merchandising practices to come, it is no surprise that legal authorities found it difficult to classify the magazine for tariff purposes. Was it an advertising booklet? Was it an independent magazine designed for children? These questions were addressed when Meccano was trying to reach Australian children. The answer given by Meccano agents was particularly interesting as it indicated how pivotal the *Meccano Magazine* had become for the toy. Even though some advertisers did not like to pay for circulation outside Britain, the view submitted by the agents was that the magazine constituted a crucial part of the Meccano system – that is, a part of a progressive system which educated and instructed the young mind.[143] Such was the importance of the matter to the company that it was raised over and over again with officials.[144]

Although some commentators have referred to Meccano as the British Disneyland,[145] and indeed there were certain similarities, the two companies operated under different postulates which in turn reflected their different social and economic ambitions and corporate values. While they both set up company structures to reach child audiences and their respective brands were built on activities that promoted child participation and engagement, the two enterprises had different media and communications practices. The next chapter focuses on the ways in which cartoon and film animation successfully captured the child's interest and, in so doing, further transformed the configuration of children as consumers. Disney embraced character merchandising as a crucial component to rejuvenate its brand so as to avoid the old-fashioned ascription that diminished the appeal of brands such as Meccano. Whereas Meccano emphasised civic character formation as a regulatory value to model and practise in its boyhood constructs, Disney used animated characters for the sake of entertainment. Instead of exploiting the passage from childhood to boyhood, Disney concentrated its focus on childhood itself, freezing it as the main site of consumption. Once childhood was conceived as a site and not as a developmental stage, the possibility for a brand to survive and be rejuvenated increased, alongside innovations in intellectual property practice. The next few chapters address this point, which is, in our view, one of the key features that shaped intellectual property in the twentieth century.

143 'Tariff Board: request for reduction of duty', 2 May 1933, NAA: AA1732, 638.

144 'Sales Tax Assessment Acts 1930–1936/Meccano Magazine', NAA: D596, 1939/704; 'Hobbies and Meccano Manual-classification', NAA: A425, 1965/4521.

145 David Veart, *Hello Girls and Boys! A New Zealand Toy Story*, Auckland University Press, 2014, 71–2.

4

Animated Properties

We previously explored the conception of the child as envisaged by Charles Dodgson, highlighting his investment in the nineteenth-century distinction between productive and reproductive spheres. Childhood was romanticised as a precious time for imaginative and creative exploration, a state of play this author sought to indulge in private settings, free from the confinement of purposeful activity and the corrupting influence of commerce. In comparison, Beatrix Potter was far less sentimental about children. Her toy books and sideshows directly targeted the home as an important site of consumption. However, notwithstanding a much greater engagement with manufacturing and retailing, Potter too remained a *children's* author, interested in the character formation of the child. And, like Dodgson, she used intellectual property rights and licences conservatively – to protect the quality of a childhood experienced through the Peter Rabbit wares that bore an association with her name. Both children's authors approached the state of childhood as a time for being nurtured, curious and at rest, not as a site for industrially productive activity. Chapter 3 traced a change in the approach to the market for children. Meccano was a social toy, a toy to make toys, where playful activity was inflected with the virtue of preparing youth for service within the industrial base of modernity. The deeper penetration of commodity relations within the family and associated transformations in forms of social reproduction generated anxieties and hesitations. Ideas of authorship, intellectual property claims, disputes and novel constructs, such as the Meccano Boy, helped defray concerns surrounding changes to the life experience of children flowing from commodification within the domestic sphere. Chapter 4 continues with this exploration, looking at the highly energetic spirited engagement in exploitation opportunities that accompanied film-going in the 1920s and early 1930s.

Multiple ideas of 'animated property' are explored in this chapter. The distinctive properties of film animation are first considered. This discussion draws upon film theory and history, where film is not discussed as simply a technology for recording the world. Film is a technology of animation, engaging spectators in new ways of interacting with and understanding their place in the world. It creates the foundation for an array of new kinds of interactions – building new worlds of experience that connect the screen and the material world. From this perspective, character animation involves more than making a fictional expression appear lifelike. Fictional personalities come to life on and well beyond the screen, grounded in new experiences and play with manufactured goods that revolve around visual representations of featured characters.

The material life of animated film characters is explored in view of the property relations and social interactions enlivened by Felix the Movie Cat. The character was recognised because of his highly stylised animalistic characteristics, expressed through a stark black shape against a white background, with an outline that stretched and flexed to reveal a very distinctive personality, filled with curiosity and other recognisable human emotions and antics. Felix was a film character without parallel in the 1920s, supplanted by 'Mickey Mouse' in the early 1930s. Both film stars stimulated a frenzy of play across the globe – spontaneous, authentic and essentially commercially non-productive play such as dressing up in character-inspired home-made costumes; fan tributes and encounters that 'coincidentally' promoted interest in the films; film exploitation cross-promotions; and interactions with an enormous range of authorised and unauthorised merchandise. Many parties laid claim to the fictional characters, but in some regards, they spoke for themselves. For example, the tables could be turned where the 'lowdown' on Walt Disney was provided by 'his pal and intimate, Mickey Mouse'. Pat Sullivan also called Felix his child.[1] Their respective studios marketed these personalities as if they were real living film stars. Film agencies negotiated over access rights, not just to the films but to exclusive relationships of all kinds. Exhibitors, manufacturers and advertisers in diverse fields of activity appropriated these characters too. And of course, so did their adult and child fans. This challenged distinctions between a spectacle and performance; participation in cultural activity and recruitment into new forms of consumption; and fantasy and real life.

Felix and Mickey Mouse were far from unique in stimulating emotional connections and responses from viewers. In addition to the celebrity afforded to characters from advertising campaigns such as Sunny Jim (1902) (discussed in Chapter 2), the British Empire Exhibition (1913) featured living tableaus with actors appearing as 'Johnny Walker', the 'Kodak Girl', the 'Michelin Man', 'Dirty Dick' and the Pears' 'Soap Tramp'. In London in 1920 there was a mile-long publicity parade with floats of characters, many of whom featured advertising constructs.[2] The Wembley

1 'The personalities behind the laughs' *Motion Picture Daily*, 20 June 1931, 9; John Canemaker, *Felix: The Twisted Tale of the World's Most Famous Cat*, Da Capo Press, 1996, 131.

2 John Taylor, '"A fascinating show for John Citizen and his Wife": advertising exhibitions in early twentieth-century London' (2018) 51(4) *Journal of Social History* 899, 906.

FIGURE 4.1 Felix Wembley Empire exhibition postcard, 1924
Fleetway Press Ltd, 1924.

Empire Exhibition (1924) featured special edition Felix postcards and a pavilion, the Pears' Palace of Beauty, which presented a pageant of Beauty through the Ages, from Helen of Troy to Miss 1924.[3] The visual appeal of these public events and their promotion directly solicited further public participation in fantasies about the characters represented, creating a wide range of new commercial opportunities. The attractiveness of these kinds of associations could generate so many different versions and themes circulating in the media and across diverse ranges of manufactures that 'crazes' followed. These cultural exchanges augmented reputations in ways that confounded recognition of exclusive intellectual property ownership.

[3] *Pears' Palace of Beauty*, A.&F. Pears Ltd, 1924.

Contrary to what is often assumed by media historians and lawyers, copyright, design and trademark laws were not particularly useful in resolving claims between traders. Sullivan and Disney both faced considerable challenges in enforcing asserted rights in the 1920s and early 1930s. In comparing the two studio's responses to this problem this chapter explores how the perceived solidity of Walt Disney's right to Mickey Mouse emerged. We need to set aside assumptions about the inherent potency of intellectual property rights to consider more closely the sociality of intellectual property relations and the emergence of protocols of consumption as these came to be expressed in the 1930s, promoted by film exploitation and rights management expertise. After 1930, alongside Walt Disney Productions, Disney Enterprises established teams of licensing agents who co-operated with exhibitors and toy manufacturers to develop an international infrastructure that sponsored authorised forms of play. Competing and conflicting commercial claims to the 'Disney universe' were unknotted and massaged into compliance, in the context where agents could sweeten their overtures with the promise of preferential access to new studio fabrications, marketing material and tighter brand management. Coherence and stability in the narration and visual identity of Disney characters that formed a Disney universe were effected, not, as has been assumed by film historians, by Walt's expansive creative vision and control over Disney studio production coupled with enforcement of Disney intellectual property rights, but by the effectiveness of intellectual property licensing strategies and idealisations of the value of exclusive rights that propelled cultural uniformisation and commodification. This shift was signified by the promotion of a new legal imaginary, the fantasy of 'world rights'.

4.1 CINEMA AND ANIMATION

Film historians link the visual experience of film with the secular magic of the modern city, its lights, novelties, shopping arcades and toys.[4] Regardless of the subject matter caught on film, the early medium was one that directly solicited spectator attention, pleasure-seeking and viewer curiosity. Film was world-building, reflecting and amplifying a sensual experience of modernity that could be collectively shared and appreciated through, and well beyond, the screen. In this regard, all film can be addressed as animation, the creation of 'a world *that has been animated,*

[4] Tom Gunning, 'The cinema of attractions: early cinema, its spectator and the avant-garde' in Thomas Elsaesser (ed.), *Early Cinema: Space Frame Narrative*, British Film Institute, 1990, 56–62; Dana Cooley, 'Walter Benjamin's play room: where the future so eloquently nests, or: what is cinema again?' in Santiago Hidalgo (ed.), *Technology and Film Scholarship*, Amsterdam University Press, 2018, 116.

rather than … [merely] a world whose movement has been recorded and reproduced'.[5]

Films that featured fictional animated characters heightened this experience. A continuous transformation of the contour line played with time, space, bodies and the ways these connected:

> What a magic of reconstructing the world according to one's fantasy and will! A fictitious world. A world of lines and colours which subjugates and alters itself to your command. You tell a mountain: move, and it moves. You tell an octopus: be an elephant and the octopus becomes an elephant. You tell the sun: 'Stop!' – and it stops.[6]

Early bendy-line 'rubber-hose' animations, such as Felix the Cat and Mickey Mouse, were not films made for children but, like *Alice in Wonderland*, visually represented liberation from the confinement of the adult experience, expressing the possibility that anything can arise.[7] The elasticity of the cel-animated form was of a different order to that represented in Dodgson's engaging *Alice* line drawings because of the centrality of movement to the expression of character. Donald Crafton argues that animation shares more with performance than reading. It is not a sender–reader communication model. Rather, animation produces 'a galaxy of relationships, many of which remain unknowable'.[8] This interactivity generates new forms of imagined claims to intangible property rights centred on film productions and, also, social and economic dynamics that disrupt these claims as spectators explore an expanding universe and commercial products that comprise it, suggesting further possibilities for understanding their subjectivity, taste and social connections.

From a utopian perspective, film animation 'speaks to life, autonomy, movement, freedom'.[9] This can be contrasted with the conditions of its production: the dependency upon 'division of labor, precision of control, abundances of preplanning, the preclusion of the random'.[10] Whether the promise of early animation ever illustrated sufficient openness that it housed revolutionary or utopian potential, or whether it only ever represented a fictitious freedom from industrialisation and urbanisation – a diversion from the oppression of Fordism and Taylorism – was debated in the

[5] Karen Redrobe, 'The worries of the world(s): cartoons and cinema' in Marta Boni (ed.), *World-Building: Transmedia, Fans, Industry*, Amsterdam University Press, 2017, 254. Emphasis in original.

[6] Jay Leyda (ed.), *Eisenstein on Disney*, Seagull Books, 1986, 3.

[7] *Alice* is also discussed in ibid. 11–13.

[8] Donald Crafton, *Shadow of a Mouse: Performance, Belief, and World-Making in Animation*, University of California Press, 2013, 18.

[9] Hannah Frank, *Frame by Frame: A Materialist Aesthetics of Animated Cartoons*, University of California Press, 2019, xxv.

[10] Ibid.

1930s.[11] It is still debated today.[12] The rise of Mickey Mouse and the cinematic demise of Felix is often explained with reference to the personal attributes and managerial styles of the founders of the respective studios. Felix's instigator, Sullivan, was afflicted by alcoholism, lacked attention to business detail and, rather than invest in new technologies, he remained committed to a two-dimensional irrational black-and-white animated world. His studio was also late to incorporate sound on film.[13] This can be contrasted with Walt Disney's strong personal, creative vision and business acumen, securing a high degree of control over labour and production processes, supported by brother Roy managing general business and finance. They invested in innovations with sound and colour and recruited expertise as they identified a need for it. As the size and scale of the Disney studio expanded, cel animation was implemented with a high degree of rationalisation in managing the labour of employees, fusing humans and machines, industrialising the act of creativity.[14] Film historians note that a Disney genre of authorship[15] emerges from these conditions. Safer, tamer narratives start to predominate, transforming audiences into passive consumers of all the commodities that comprise the Disney universe. This incorporates individual films, but also licensed print cartoons, fashion, Mickey Mouse Clubs and merchandise.[16] But how the initial 'frenzy of the visible'[17] – unleashed by film and precursor visual displays and technologies of representation – was controlled beyond the studio, as well as the key role of distributors in managing the film trade, is skimmed over in animation history. It was not only film narratives that changed. Somehow freewheeling commodification practices and spectator engagement also became more orderly and disciplined and distributors lost direct control over character merchandising. Once both angles were better contained, the name Walt Disney came to personify 'family entertainment'.

Felix was a global phenomenon throughout the 1920s, a playful companion to former vaudeville performers and film stars like Charlie Chaplin and Buster Keaton. The character debuted in 1919. He was not originally named, though he sometimes was referred to generically as tomcat. By 1921 Felix was promoted as a distinctive film personality and as a form of studio property, represented by his own agent, M. J. Winkler. Who or what was Felix?

11 Walter Benjamin [and Michael W. Jennings], 'The work of art in the age of its technological reproducibility [first version]' 2010 (39) *Grey Room* 11–38; Henri Lonitz (ed.), *Theodor Adorno and Walter Benjamin: The Complete Correspondence 1928–1940*, Polity Press, 1999.

12 For an overview, see Redrobe, above n 5, 253–70.

13 Canemaker, above n 1, 129.

14 Kirsten Thompson, 'Implications of the cel animation technique' in Teresa de Laurentis and Stephen Heath (eds.), *The Cinematic Apparatus*, St Martin's Press, 1980, 106.

15 Paul Wells, *Animation. Genre and Authorship*, Wallflower, 2002, 77–90.

16 Colin Williamson, 'Walter Benjamin: afterimages of the aura' in Murray Pomerance and R. Barton Palmer (eds.), *Thinking in the Dark: Cinema, Theory, Practice*, Rutgers University Press, 2015, 55.

17 Jean-Louis Comolli, 'Machines of the visible' in de Laurentis and Heath, above n 14, 122.

4.2 WHAT IS FELIX?

Patriarchal intellectual property constructs are so dominant in our culture that explanations of who or what Felix is normally fixated on accounts of his paternity assessed with reference to attribution of authorship. Film historians and animation buffs are quick to point out that it was Otto Messmer, not studio owner, Sullivan, who drew the cat character and should rightly be identified as the creator of Felix.[18] This attribution of authorship is determined without consideration of copyright ownership. In addition, as commercial interest in cartoon characters developed, trademark and unfair competition law did too, leading to additional new kinds of property claims to the fictional creations.

In the early twentieth century, copyright law struggled with the legal classification of film.[19] The medium's fluid form of creative expression and technological manifestation defied ready identification of merely one author. Narrative films were considered performative in character, a kind of dramatic work that protected plot and character as set out in the script or scenario, but also captured as a sequence of photographs. A series of photographic negatives might also be individually considered artistic works under copyright law. However, an individual drawing or photograph was not the true origin of the animated cartoon personality because of the distinctive processes utilised to produce cel animation.

Cel animation emerged alongside the development of film.[20] The main techniques involved using translucent sheets of celluloid (Bray–Hurd patented method) or paper sheets (Barré 'slash' method) to separate the drawing of the cel space where the figure moved from that of the background space. Cel animation is widely credited with allowing new specialisations of labour: 'one person may do the background, while another does certain main poses of the character, and yet another fills in the phases between these major poses'.[21] An animation 'studio' comprised specialised tasks and work hierarchies: scripting and planning, chief animator, assistant animators, tracers, inkers, inbetweeners, colourists, photographers, and so on. Divisions of labour created efficiencies that greatly improved production capacity. This was key to servicing the strong demand of film distributors for this kind of content.

[18] Canemaker, above n 1, 155–60.

[19] See Oren Bracha, 'How did film become property? Copyright and the early American film industry' in Brad Sherman and Leanne Wiseman (eds.), *Copyright and the Challenge of the New*, Kluwer Law International, 2012, 141; Peter Decherney, *Hollywood's Copyright Wars: From Edison to the Internet*, Columbia University Press, 2013; Kathy Bowrey, *Copyright, Creativity, Big Media and Cultural Value*, Routledge, 2021, 115.

[20] Donald Crafton, *Before Mickey: The Animated Film 1898–1928*, MIT Press, 1982; E.G. Lutz, *Animated Cartoons: How They Are Made, Their Origin and Development*, Charles Scribner's Sons 1920, 57–79.

[21] Thompson, above n 14, 107.

Sullivan had learnt the art of cel animation from working for Raoul Barré. The first Sullivan cat film, *Feline Follies*, was a four-minute, ten-second clip produced for Paramount Studios using the Barré technique of inking on paper.[22] Otto Messmer drew the cat and continued to develop this character in later animations he directed. There were many popular similar black-and-white cartoon cats appearing at the time in comic strips and in animated films, such as George Herriman's *Krazy Kat*.[23] Messmer designed this particular black male cat's 'plastic' nature: alternating between animal and human behaviour as he explored the world, as well as creating gags which often drove the story. Messmer identified the centrality of gags as a defining feature of Felix stories.[24] He drew Felix's walk based on earlier animated cartoons he had done of Charlie Chaplin for Sullivan's studio, where the comedian had assisted by providing photographs in different poses. Still, Felix had his own walk:

> Walking up and down – looking for a solution for something. He represents the thoughts of any child, wondering what things are all about – what's up in the sky, under the sea and so forth .... He'd often use a question mark for a hook, and an exclamation mark for a ball and bat.[25]

A popular licensed British commodity that emerged was sheet music for a song called 'Felix Kept on Walking' (1923).[26] Felix was represented with human emotions and desires:

> Also, outside of bringing good luck to things, we tried as much as possible to show a little lesson for children. In other words, 'Kindness'... I made one once with *Felix is Fishing*. He catches a cute little fish, y'know very cute. In a close up, he's looking at it. The fish is sad and Felix starts to cry, y'know (Chuckles). That's what got Felix Famous. He's showing emotions, when the others, though they were well done, just looked like dolls moving around.[27]

Though Messmer directed most of the Felix stories, it is not clear who was responsible for the initial unsentimental cat-love story in *Feline Follies*. On 'hearing' a meow, a house-cat kept as a mouser begins a pursuit that leads to a tryst with Miss Kitty White. This relationship results in him being thrown out of home because the

22 Mark Newgarden and John Mariano, Interview with Otto Messmer, 7 March 1980, JCAC: Box 18; Folder 203. This process was later changed with the use of cels for backgrounds.

23 The 1916 film representation of *Krazy Kat* by Frank Moser bore little resemblance to the original Herriman drawings. Jeff Lenburg, *The Encyclopedia of Animated Cartoons*, Facts on File Inc., 2nd edn, 1999, 96.

24 Newgarden and Mariano, above n 22; Canemaker, above n 1, 34–6, 53.

25 'Otto Messmer and Felix the Cat: interview with John Canemaker' (1978) 37 March *Cartoonist Profiles* 21.

26 Lyrics by E. E. Bryant, music by Hubert W. David, published by Lawrence Wright Music Co. Ltd, London, 1923. The music was 'issued in conjunction with "FELIX the CAT" cartoons, appearing exclusively in Pathé's "Eve's and Everybody's Film Review"'.

27 Newgarden and John, above n 22.

mice make merry while he is dreaming, courting and having fun. Out on his own, he is, at first, pleased to find Miss Kitty. But he runs far away once confronted by a clamour of demanding, mewing kittens. The cartoon ends when the downcast cat wanders into a gas plant and gasses himself.

Sullivan's role was largely an entrepreneurial one – employing staff to fulfil contracts with increasingly larger, vertically integrated film studios.[28] Studios distributed films in bundles. They were booked a year in advance in blocs, often with minimal information provided to assess the suitability of the bundled content: 'A' (features), 'B' (supporting and shorter films) and 'C' (actualities and topical fare). It was the regional distributors who handled the logistics of supplying films to exhibitors.

The cat figure was revived when *Paramount Magazine* was launched in 1919. Film studio magazines featuring topical news and fashion were a popular entertainment feature. While *Felix* animations may have been produced as 'B' short films, cartoons were popular fare that often appeared at the end of a news magazine reel, mirroring the lure of newspaper cartoons that drove newspaper syndication.[29] After *Feline Follies* and a follow-up – *Musical Mews* – a contract was signed for a whole series. About thirty more short films were produced for *Paramount Magazine*. During this period, the cat's popularity grew. He was named by a *Paramount Magazine* film editor as 'Felix', a cross between a feline and felicity, a good luck cat. Under the terms of the agreement the copyright was owned by Paramount Studios/Famous Players-Lasky.[30] As will be explained below, it is not very clear what this meant for the creator and his studio.

Messmer never formally claimed to 'own' Felix and had no credit as director of the films. When pushed about this in interviews he always first noted his status as an employee, where his employer owned the copyright. He was paid a dollar a foot for a 650-foot film.[31] Secondarily, he spoke of his learning a lot from Sullivan in the early days about the cel-animation process. Commonly described by interviewers as modest and shy, Messmer always acknowledged the collective effort required to make animated films. The studio was often hectic, working contract to contract, struggling to meet deadlines. This was the case even when Sullivan was more financially secure. Longer-term issues of credit or ownership of the characters was not initially a big consideration for those engaged day to day and into the early morning producing *Felix* films.

Sullivan conformed to a hard-drinking, hard-living stereotype, opportunistically pursuing business deals whenever he could scent that money was on offer. He

[28] Janet Staiger, 'Combination and litigation: structures of US film distribution, 1896–1917' (1983) 23(2) *Cinema Journal* 41.

[29] See Jose Bellido, 'King Features Syndicate, Inc. and Betts v O.&M. Kleeman Ltd' (1940) in Jose Bellido, (ed.), *Landmark Cases in Intellectual Property Law*, Hart, 2017, 205.

[30] Canemaker, above n 1, 56, 59, 169.

[31] David Weinstein, Interview with Otto Messmer (undated), JCAC: Box 18, Folder 203.

vigorously asserted rights to Felix. Ownership was signalled by centre billing in opening credits in films, which notified audiences that the film was 'by Pat Sullivan'. Omitting reference to 'Pat Sullivan studios' in the early films did imply Sullivan personally drew and directed these. In addition, *Paramount Magazine* was given credit at the top of the opening screen, with a credit to Famous Players-Lasky Corporation at the bottom. A credit to *Paramount Magazine* also featured at the bottom of the black-and-white title cards, which, in the silent era, progressed the story.

The closure of *Paramount Magazine* in 1921 presented Sullivan's studio with a huge problem – due to the assignment of intellectual property rights there was a potential loss of the right to produce *Felix* films altogether. Through boorish behaviour, perhaps including urinating on Paramount studio head Adolph Zukor's desk and refusing to leave, Sullivan was given back the rights to Felix.[32] But what kind of property had Felix now become?

From Sullivan's perspective, Felix was a cultural phenomenon and legal object to be redrawn according to his personal will – a right to the personality and look of a distinctive fictional subject inked by Messmer and his team, also a 'plasmatic' business opportunity that emerged from the character's fame. There was, however, a body of law that could have supported Sullivan's claim here. A creator's right to fictional cartoon characters was recognised under US unfair competition law in a series of related cases from 1915 to 1921, with the validity of the concept supported by the Supreme Court decision in *International News Service v Associated Press* (1918).[33]

The cartoon cases concerned rights to the newspaper characters 'Mutt' and 'Jeff'. Harry C. 'Bud' Fisher first drew the 'Mutt' character, and it was published in the *San Francisco Chronicle* in February 1907, and from December 1907 in the Hearst newspaper, the *San Francisco Examiner*. The following year Fisher became a newspaper employee and created 'Jeff'. In 1909 he entered into the first of what would become sequential contracts with Star Company (part of the Hearst newspaper syndicate) to exclusively produce a cartoon strip featuring both characters for 'publications and newspaper enterprises that William R Hearst is or may be interested'. It was during this period that the strip was first published with the title 'Mutt and Jeff' accompanied by the tagline '—by "Bud" Fisher'. Under his first contract with the Hearst Syndicate, Fisher's fee was $50 a week, increasing to $60, $75, $200 and $250. Under his final contract, Fisher received $300 a week. Once free of his obligation to Hearst Syndicate, Fisher signed with the rival Wheeler newspaper syndicate in December 1914 for $1000 a week. However, Hearst/Star Company asserted a right to a trademark in the names Mutt and Jeff and their representations, arguing that only they could use the title on new drawings of the characters. Star

32 Canemaker, above n 1, 59.

33 248 US 215.

Company's entitlement to registration was based on the claim to be the first to use the title 'Mutt and Jeff' in trade. Trademark law does not favour the right of the creator but the first to use the trademark in commerce. Trademark law favoured the newspaper syndicate, so Fisher sought to resolve the conflict by arguing that Star Company was engaging in unfair competition, a body of law created to protect the public from deception and unfair business practice.[34]

It was argued that if someone other than Fisher featured the antics of Mutt and Jeff, this would deceive the public who would assume there was an association with the original artist. Further, Fisher would be unfairly restrained in exercising his rights as an artist. Judgment was in Fisher's favour: 'The cartoons, in effect the products of Fisher's hand and brain, are to be treated as a commodity of barter and sale, the same as tangible goods and merchandise'.[35] The Court of Appeal affirmed this view, noting the characters 'have been so connected with the plaintiff as their originator and author that the use by another of new cartoons exploiting the characters "Mutt and Jeff" would be unfair to the public and to the plaintiff'.[36] Fisher's position was not affected by periods he served as an employee or under contract because the court found that the characters had acquired a reputation prior to and independent of the use of the names Mutt and Jeff by the newspaper syndicate.

Fisher's and Sullivan's situations were somewhat similar. A relatively precarious commercial existence led to contracts with distributors, where the right to the next series was renegotiated in a climate where the respective characters were growing in popularity and driving syndicated distribution in newspapers and films. *Mutt and Jeff's* fame was also assisted by film animation produced by the Mutt and Jeff Film Exchange from 1917. This was set up by animation pioneer Raoul Barré with Charles Bowers, while Fisher was serving in the Canadian army. On his return Fisher continued this line of films, produced by a new entity, the Bud Fisher Films Corporation.[37] Similar to suppression of Messmer's claim to Felix, the *Mutt and Jeff* film animators were never credited because 'Fisher denied them credit, wanting only his name to appear in connection with the characters'.[38]

Like Sullivan, Fisher's uncertain legal claim to own the names and general representations of the cartoon characters was bolstered by insistence upon public credit as 'creator' at point of distribution. Fisher had also demanded approval over titling. These actions were not just egoistic claims to paternity or copyright assertions to secure a desired attribution of authorship. Continuity in signalling the creator's

[34] 'Star Co. v Wheeler Syndicate, Inc. (1916)' *NY Law Journal*, 15 August 1916, republished in Louis D. Frolich and Charles Schwartz, *The Law of Motion Pictures*, Baker, Voorhis & Co., 1918, 474.

[35] Ibid.

[36] *Fisher v Star Co.* (1921) 231 NY 414, 132 NE 133, 139.

[37] Crafton, above n 20, 197.

[38] Lenburg, above n 23, 37.

personal attachment to the characters helped maintain a commercial connection to any intangible property that might exist outside of the specific terms of any intellectual property assignments or licences. It was personal goodwill, not the copyright in drawings ghosted by Sullivan and Fisher employees, that underpinned the syndication market. It is likely Sullivan was aware of the Mutt and Jeff litigation given the personal and social connections between animators in New York and, in particular, the history between Barré and Sullivan. Barré ended up working for Sullivan in the late 1920s and even drew Felix for a time.[39]

Sullivan was not intimidated by Zukor and did not fear the consequences of falling out with him. He had a lawyer, Harry Kopp, whom he retained for personal and business needs. Although the Mutt and Jeff litigation was ongoing in 1919, an action under unfair competition law was an option if Sullivan could have afforded the risk of litigation. In his favour, the original animation of the cat in *Feline Follies* preceded any contract with Paramount/Famous Players-Lasky for a series of films. The cat was a Sullivan creation, produced in his studio where he was clearly first owner of the copyright, even though, after signing a contract for the series, copyright was assigned to the film distributor. However, Fisher was indisputably the creator of Mutt and Jeff and he alone named the characters. While the original tomcat came from Messmer's hand and brain, the name Felix came from a Paramount employee. There were two potential claims to creation here, both interrelated. While the animation studio created the first imaginative expression of the character – which could be considered a commodity in itself in the same manner that Mutt was attributed as Fisher's creation – it was the distributor's involvement that created the name by which the character became known to the audience. Both the distinctive representation and distinctive name needed to combine for Felix to generate a reputation. In the Mutt and Jeff litigation the court prioritised the rights of the animator as creator of an antecedent property, considering that the syndicate simply disseminated the work, which any newspaper could have done. But, in Sullivan's case, Paramount studio did more than this. Their investment in the series and naming the character, which reinforced the 'good luck' cat motif, was essential to the emergence of the Felix character. It was the relationship with Paramount that provided impetus for Felix to become a commodity, a subject instantly recognisable to fans, an intangible property that drew custom to the products that bore his name and likeness.

It is interesting to note that the first film made on leaving Paramount, *Felix Saves the Day* (1922) begins with an animated title credit. A cat head, body, arms and legs, individual letters spelling out 'Felix' and lastly a tail are formed of black ink climbing out of the end of a pen which is held completely still by an anonymous white hand. Here, Felix is not really drawn so much as he is presented as being in control of his own manifestation, with a bendy-line umbilical cord of ink connecting to the artist's

[39] Crafton, above n 20, 313.

hand. The character then stands to one side to make way for the notice 'A Pat Sullivan Cartoon', which takes centre stage. An additional credit of Sullivan as 'Artist-Originator' also adorns the screen.[40] Following the experience with Paramount, in interviews Sullivan also took to perpetuating an entirely new, fictional origin story for Felix, attributing inspiration for 'his' drawing to a New York alley-cat picked up by his wife and brought to show him in their home.[41] The account is usually recited by film historians as an example of Sullivan's hubris and moral turpitude in side-lining Messmer. However, an exclusive legal claim to Felix under US unfair competition law was strengthened precisely by this type of solitary 'artist-originator' story. With his eye for a deal and advancing self-interest, Sullivan would have noticed the convention and may well have been aware of its legal relevance.

Disney also told an origin story for his studio – 'It was all started by a mouse' – and, from 1931 publicly celebrated Mickey's 'birthday' dated to the first screening of *Steamboat Willie* in 1928.[42] Like that of Felix, this narrative slid over the reality of significant contributions to the mouse's manifestations and the foundation of Disney studio.[43] Some critics delight in reminding readers that not only did Ub Iwerks first draw Mickey, it is possible that Disney could not successfully draw the character or his trademark 'Walt Disney' signature.[44] David McGowan notes, the attempt to create a narrative fixity to the character became even more prominent over time, erasing the changing representations of Mickey Mouse across the twentieth century. These include significant changes in Disney narratives, especially following the Ohio censorship board banning *The Shindig* (1930), due to the udders adorning an 'implicitly "naked"' Clarabelle Cow, reading Elinor Glyn's erotic novel *Three Weeks*.[45] While Iwerks originally achieved a screen credit for his drawing of *Mickey Mouse*, he was also a part-owner of the Walt Disney Studio. This company was replaced by a tripartite structure, Walt Disney Productions Ltd, Walt Disney Enterprises and the Disney Film Recording Company in 1929. Carl Stalling, a composer and music director, also invested $2,000 in the Disney Film Recording Company. Paul Wells argues it was only after Iwerks and Stalling departed that Walt Disney could establish a more hierarchical management infrastructure where he:

> moved onto a plane in which his role may be understood extra-textually. For example, by the late 1920s, it is possible to suggest that he had become 'a figure

[40] 'Felix the Movie Cat for Gund MFG Co'. *Playthings*, May 1922, 54.

[41] Canemaker, above n 1, 85.

[42] David McGowan, 'Monochrome Mickey: modern nostalgia texts and the animated star image' (2018) 46(4) *Journal of Popular Film and Television* 219.

[43] In trade press, Disney did, however, acknowledge other technical contributions. See 'The personalities behind the laughs' *Motion Picture Daily*, 20 June 1931, 9.

[44] Richard Schickel, *The Disney Version: The Life, Times, Art, and Commerce of Walt Disney*, Simon & Shuster, 1968, 33.

[45] McGowan, above n 42, 222.

> who embodies a coherent position about a film which makes complex production processes invisible, and obscures or inhibits an alternative view about the authorially determined claims of others in the execution of a film'.[46]

Artist-origination narratives, fictional and factual, are a form of extra-textual branding that generates goodwill. In the context of animation, these provide a convenient shorthand that helps gloss over not only labour relations within studios, but also the legal difficulties of asserting exclusive ownership to an ethereal industrial property distributed across time and space. These stories strengthen the hand of the animation studio when it is particularly vulnerable, such as when the studio is negotiating new terms and conditions of distribution needed to finance further production, and where, if contracts are successfully concluded, this may lead to further changes to the star's features and cultural properties.

Once Zukor's interest in Felix was exhausted, Sullivan pitched a series of Felix films to Warner Brothers. This offer was rejected, but the opportunity was picked up by Harry Warner's secretary, Margaret Winkler. She became the first woman film distributor handling independent film productions in the United States. This business relationship was very successful in growing Felix's brand, but it also produced multiple new rounds of conflicting claims to Felix, the most significant dispute being one that ended their relationship in 1925.

4.3 FELIX STRETCHED IN ALL DIRECTIONS

When Sullivan came to M. J. Winkler in 1921, he was only able to produce further Felix films by her underwriting them. She financed two films on the understanding that if they were satisfactory, she would fund another ten. Winkler obtained 'an exclusive right to use, lease, distribute and otherwise exploit throughout the entire world motion pictures and prints from the negatives' for a fee of $1,000 for the first six, $1200 for the next six and 50 per cent of foreign sales. There was no intellectual property clause. There was also no mention of merchandising rights: however, her advertisements in film trade magazines represent that she acted as agent for merchandising deals.[47] In the early 1920s the art of film exploitation was itself a subject of much discussion in film trade magazines, with special features such as 'How Pathé helps the exhibitor',[48] 'A tie-up explained',[49] 'Selling the picture to the public' and 'Index to exploitation suggestions'.[50]

46 Paul Wells, *Animation: Genre and Authorship*, Wallflower, 2002, 80. Note omitted.

47 *Margaret J. Winkler v Patrick Sullivan, Harry Kopp, Earl Hammons and Educational Films Corporation of America*, Supreme Court (NY): Exhibit A, papers on appeal filed 5 September 1925, JCAC: Box 13; Folder 123 (Harry Kopp).

48 *Bioscope*, 20 October 1921, 22.

49 *Bioscope*, 10 May 1923, 47.

50 Special lift-out feature, *Bioscope*, June–September 1923.

Winkler entered into an agreement with British Pathé to distribute the first series of new Felix films overseas. Perhaps due to Pathé's market dominance and promotion expertise,[51] Felix ended up being far more popular in the UK.[52] Pathé launched *Eve's and Everybody's Film Review* in June 1921, a light entertainment news magazine designed to bring in women audiences. During World War I, women had emerged as the largest and most loyal film constituency. This continued into the 1920s, with estimates that three-quarters of the audience were women, where women were also identified as choosing entertainment for the whole family. Newsreels and cartoons were considered as a way of creating a perception of value for money. From June 1922 to January 1926 Felix was exclusively screened as part of *Eve's Film Review*.[53] Though Sullivan was not aware of it till he visited London in 1924, the Felix cartoons were often 'mutilated', being shown in chapter format rather than, as he intended, full reels.[54]

For an entirely new independent film business, and one run by a woman, Winkler was astonishingly effective in building relationships with US distributors, creating further buzz by announcing her own success in trade newspapers, accompanied by eye-catching illustrated cartoons and endorsements by Felix drawn by Sullivan's studio. In 1922 there was a second agreement for a further twenty-four Felix cartoons, no less than 650 feet in length, for $1,750 per film. The studio was also required to produce posters to promote these. It contained a clause creating a first option on additional series for the same price.[55] Due to production pressures created by a two-week turnaround, the character's look was transformed from what Messmer described as the original more dog-like Felix to a character that was rounder. With less angular lines it was quicker to draw his transformation into other shapes.[56]

In 1923 Sullivan rejected Winkler's offer for another series. He wanted to produce more films and of a longer length. He entered into a contract with Joe Brandt (who, along with Harry Cohn, built Columbia Pictures), for thirty-two films at $3,500 each of at least 700 feet.[57] Winkler retaliated. She advertised in film trade magazines that she was aware that Sullivan was offering rights to a new series and, as distributor of the first two, she had first option and would take 'extreme legal measures' to protect her interest.[58]

[51] Jon Silver, 'The first global entertainment company: explaining Pathé's dominance in the pre-Hollywood film industry' (2010) 24(6) *Continuum* 877.

[52] Lenburg, above n 23, 27.

[53] Jenny Hammerton, *For Ladies Only? Eve's Film Review: Pathe Cinemagazine 1921–1933*, The Projection Box, 2001, 11.

[54] Canemaker, above n 1, 89.

[55] Supreme Court (NY), above n 47, Exhibit B.

[56] Newgarden and Mariano, above n 22.

[57] Supreme Court (NY), above n 47, Affidavit of Harry Kopp.

[58] Ibid. Affidavit of Pat Sullivan.

FIGURE 4.2 Advertisement, 'The Five Senses of Felix the Movie Cat', 1922
Gund MFG. Co. Advertisement, Playthings, May 1922. Courtesy of The Strong, Rochester, New York

At the same time Winkler began to advertise a series by relative newcomer, Walt Disney, the *Alice Comedies*. These featured an *Alice in Wonderland*–inspired actor dancing with animated characters, a principal one being a cat, Julius. This was inflammatory. Even Disney commented to his animators that it looked 'too much like Felix'[59] and this was likely to pose copyright problems. It was not the first Felix-lookalike film character in this period, but usually Winkler, her husband lawyer Charles Mintz, Sullivan and his lawyer Harry Kopp, worked together to prevent these appearances surviving.[60] Felix products and Felix lookalikes were becoming increasingly difficult to control.

Winkler had advertised Felix the Movie Cat as a living creature, full of possibilities. He was presented as teen-like, with a personality of his own but still in need of the watchful eye of his family – Sullivan as parent, Winkler as guardian. In a doll 'tie-up' in 1922, Felix is described as 'a cartoon character *introduced by* Pat Sullivan, creator of *Felix* cartoons which are *controlled by* Miss MJ Winkler'.[61] The commercial versatility of the 'actor' was demonstrated by alerting readers to the character's five senses: 'Felix. The Movie Cat: Seeing. Hearing. Smelling. Tasting. Feeling'.

This ad also advises that Felix 'by Pat Sullivan studios' is now available in doll form to service a 'craze' initiated when 'scores of bathing beauties and boardwalk strollers carried the little cats along the ocean front'. Spectacles of this sort became common. Film cross-promotions emerged in the UK, with the Pathé news teams capturing 'spontaneous' spectacles, such as a Felix parade where cinematographers happened to be on hand to capture an enormous Felix float and characters in home-made dress-ups parading the streets in advance of the 1922 Chelsea Art Ball. Many news clips promoted a manufacturing tie-in arranged by Pathé with toy company J. K. Farnell & Co. Film footage captured dolls appearing in public spaces and at functions with celebrities, joining expeditions of discovery to far-flung places and carried by cute members of the public. A 1924 clip displays three-foot-high Felix dolls leaving the toy factory, the bodies arranged in lifelike poses strapped in by

59 Canemaker, above n 1, 90–1.
60 Ibid.
61 'Felix the Movie Cat', above n 40 (our emphasis).

FIGURE 4.3 Felix-lookalike dolls, 1924
Games & Toys, July 1924, 73; Sept 1924, 59; 73; 98. © British Library Board. Courtesy of the British Toy and Hobby Association.

ropes, looking out at the passing public from the open truck gate.[62] King Features Syndicate, a Hearst company formed in 1915 dedicated to promoting comics to push newspaper syndication,[63] obtained the rights to the Sunday page and daily *Felix* newspaper cartoons. The Sunday pages were largely drawn by Messmer, who would later complain about having to 'forge' Sullivan's signature on every page.[64] Other commercial arrangements included postcards, combs, tie pins, silver spoons,

[62] British Pathé newsclips, 'Chelsea Art Ball, AKA our famous Felix the Cat' (1922); 'And Felix goes to (the Arctic)' (1924); 'Felix the Cat meets "Royalty"' (1923); 'Felix goes to India' (1924), *Pathé Gazette/Yorkshire Evening News* cross-promotion; 'Everybody Loves "Felix"' (1924).

[63] Bellido, above n 29, 209.

[64] Newgarden and Mariano, above n 22.

candles, blankets, pins, radiator caps, handkerchiefs, toys and china and a Felix actor-impersonator. In addition, there were many unauthorised representations, sometimes with a very weak resemblance, and, usually, presumably for legal reasons, they dared not use his name (see Figure 4.3).

However, as Winkler, Pathé and Pat Sullivan Studios all authorised deals without reference to each other, distinguishing an authorised from an unauthorised production is practically impossible. For example, the Wembley British Empire Exhibition (1924) featured Woolstone Brother postcards marked 'Felix the Film Cat, which appears exclusively in Pathé's "Eve's and Everyone's Film Review"'. 'Fleetway Press sole concessionary' postcards printed the notice 'UNIVERSAL COPYRIGHT BY PAT SULLIVAN. ALL RIGHTS RESERVED'. Suggestions of exclusivity with regard to this character were simply misleading. However, these claims were commercially meaningful as devices that promoted licensing.

Sullivan particularly objected to Pathé asserting merchandising rights independently of him. Legally he was on weak ground. He had no trademark or design registrations. It was not thought to be copyright infringement to use the character in manufacturing.[65] A near equivalent to US unfair competition law, an action for passing-off, did protect the British public and traders against deception and trade misrepresentation. However, this action could not succeed because Pathé was just as well recognised as Sullivan's studio for having an exclusive connection to Felix the Movie Cat in the UK. Many advertisements referred to Felix as 'the cinema favourite'. Advertisements for the Dean's Rag Book Company velvet doll included the description: 'FELIX, The film cat that appears exclusively in "Pathé's Eve and Everybody's Film Review". *The only models that are really like Felix on the Film*'.[66] Sullivan may have originated Felix in the United States, but Pathé made him famous in the UK.

Brandt abandoned the contract with Sullivan as Winkler began a legal action seeking to enforce her option for a new series under the second contract. With production uncertain for 1924, the parties reconciled sufficiently to enter into a new contract for a *Felix* series on the first day of the hearing, leaving the issue as to whether Winkler had a valid renewal option unresolved.[67] Sullivan also entered into a tripartite agreement with Winkler and Pathé to share merchandising revenue.[68] It is clear that these arrangements were merely an interim step to Sullivan leaving Winkler and independently asserting control over Felix's future.

In December 1924, a notice appeared in the trade journal *Games and Toys*, advising the appointment of a Birmingham patent agent with power of attorney who would be collecting money due under old licences and who had power to both

65 This is discussed further below.
66 'Dean's A1 dolls and toys' (1924) September *Games and Toys*, 55 (emphasis in original).
67 Supreme Court (NY), above n 47, Exhibit E.
68 Canemaker, above n 1, 89.

enter into new agreements and cancel them. It also threatened: 'We understand that proceedings will be commenced against unauthorised users of the copyright, and anyone desiring to make use of it should communicate with Mr Forrester'.[69] An unsuccessful copyright action was brought against a manufacturer of a Felix-lookalike doll. The court found that copyright in the 2D picture of Felix was not infringed by making an article in 3D.[70] Design law, not copyright, regulated the visual appearance of manufactures.[71] A member of the bar later acknowledged this case, noting that Felix had retained an independent commercial life, informing the judge that as no injunction was granted to protect the copyright 'they might assume that *Felix* was still walking'.[72]

However, members of the profession also fostered confusion about when a licence was needed. The copyright–design interface was discussed in the *Transactions of the Chartered Institute of Patent Attorneys* in 1924. Most present supported the view that design registration was the relevant form of protection for manufactured articles whenever a design was capable of being registered. However, Mr Armstrong reported the advice he had given:

> Another client has asked if he was free to sell models of Felix the Cat, and the reply was, 'No' because he noticed some were already on sale that had been labelled indicating a licence from Pathé Frères to manufacture such models.[73]

Pathé Frères had no registered designs and, even assuming they had a relevant assignment of copyright, it would not have been of assistance. However, it was in the commercial interest of these attorneys to promote design registration and licensing, regardless of the legal need for them.

In February 1925, Kopp also set up a new production company under his control, Bijou Films, to produce future *Felix* films. The company entered into a contract with an established British firm, Ideal Films Company, to distribute these. After Winkler's legal action was dismissed, she advertised in *Film Daily* that she had obtained the services of a former Sullivan employee, Bill Nolan, to produce *Krazy Kat* cartoons that would be distributed by Pathé. *Krazy Kat* replaced *Felix* cartoons in *Eve's Film Review*. However, Winkler also lodged an appeal. New warning notices appeared in *Film Daily*, notifying that the action remained unresolved.

69 'Felix novelties' (1924) December *Games and Toys*, 40.

70 *Ware v Anglo-Italian Commercial Agency Ltd* (1907–1923) MacG Cop Cas 346 determined that, while copyright protection extended to materials of all kinds, if an article could be repeated in fifty copies, a man had the option of design protection. If he relied on copyright in a photograph of the object, this did not extend to preventing another constructing the object.

71 There still remained attempts to use copyright expansively to regulate character merchandise for decades to come. See *King Features Syndicate, Inc. v Betts v O.&M. Kleeman Ltd* [1940] Ch 806.

72 The *Felix* case was unreported. 'Chancery Division', *The Times*, 18 July 1930, 5.

73 'Discussion of Mr Byrnes Paper' Ordinary Meeting, *Transactions of the Chartered Institute of Patent Attorneys*, 14 May 1924, 224.

Winkler's legal action was finally thrown out in August 1925, the court accepting that Sullivan had not sought to exercise an option under the second contract to make a further series for the same price, as he had offered to make longer films for a different price. If this interpretation was wrong, the 1924 contract would be treated as an exercise of that option, which then merged with the second contract. Winkler had no additional contractual right to an option on a new series.[74]

In the UK, a suite of British Felix character trademarks were registered in Sullivan's name in 1925 covering an extraordinary range of classes: films, metal goods, porcelain, paper products, games, jewellery, brushes, food ingredients and Indian rubber.[75] Kopp also started to license goods in the United States, including a crystal radio set encased in a Felix-shaped body. However, as became apparent after Sullivan's death in 1933, there was no following-up of assignments of Felix trademarks or tracing of royalty agreements that had been entered into by Winkler and her licensees, including the most lucrative and long-lasting arrangement with plush toy-maker George Borgfeldt & Co. Throughout the 1920s Sullivan also continued to enter into oral agreements with all kinds of traders in the United States without leaving any trace of the details and making payment of licence fees essentially voluntary. Most problematically, at some point he also entered into a contract with King Features Syndicate for further cartoons on terms which described him as an employee. Kopp claimed to have no knowledge of this. If so, it suggests that no one was really managing the merchandising side of the business at a time of peak Felix interest in the United States. As Sullivan's executor, Kopp advised the court that the contract with Kings Features Syndicate left Sullivan's estate with no republication rights to *Felix* newspaper comics or royalties, with future payments only due if Messmer and others drew new, original cartoons. Following the Mutt and Jeff litigation, perhaps unfair competition law could have supported a claim by the Sullivan studio. However, the newspaper syndicate relied on its entitlement to copyright under the agreement and threatened to cease running new cartoons altogether. As film production had ceased in 1930, no new print cartoons had flow-on consequences for licence renewals and would severely restrict interest in licences for new merchandise. In 1934, King Features Syndicate claimed it offered 'the greatest combination operation on earth'.[76] It was not easy to break with the company or publish cartoons with independents and achieve the same level of distribution. At a time of increasing newspaper circulation and population growth, the number of daily newspapers in the United States had dropped by 10 per cent every decade since 1909, with increasing numbers under single control. Syndicated comics were sold like films, promising territorial exclusivity, not only in hometowns

[74] Supreme Court (NY), n 47 above, 'Opinion of the Court' 3 August 1925.

[75] Pat Sullivan, UK TM 460,381-9. Felix Character Mark Filed 7 July 1925. Classes 8, 13, 14, 16, 39, 40, 42, 49, 50; TNA: BT82/1133.

[76] Bellido, above n 29, 209.

but also stretching into neighbouring ones. When exclusive contracts with syndicates expired, features did not often change hands.[77] Pressed to identify surviving Sullivan assets and meet the expectations of Sullivan's beneficiaries, Kopp bought back 'any interest' King Features Syndicate might have in use of the character Felix beyond publication of the comic strip for $2,000.[78]

Throughout the 1920s, attractive fictional film characters animated the production of reams of licensing agreements on many continents. These stretched the ways audiences could connect with the characters. 'Rights' were licensed without parties being able to really define the intangible property concerned with precision or certainty. Contractual arrangements multiplied not only iterations of the characters but also suggested commercial connections. In practice, Felix was represented by myriad commercial uses to which his likeness was put. This encompassed businesses that claimed 'exclusive' rights, others that did not, some attributing a connection with Sullivan's studio, others with film distributors and agents, and others simply relying on visual similarities to attract custom. Agreements with licensees fragmented the associated intangible property across space and time. Territorial arrangements carved out space with reference to broadly defined areas of the globe such as North America, British Isles, Australasia, South Africa and Latin America. These terms did not neatly map onto jurisdiction. Registration requirements were specified in domestic laws and regulations. As is discussed below, in many cases local traders had already appropriated cartoon characters and had registered trademarks that conflicted with the 'exclusive' licence terms claimed by the artist-originator. Time was usually addressed in terms of requirements to bring goods and services to market within particular timeframes, in the renewal dates of arrangements, and requirement of payment of royalties at specified times. The scope of authorised product lines was further delineated with reference to their fabrication, for example, manufacture of dolls, or the narrower specifics of these materialisations, such as dolls made of paper, plush or wood. These demarcations did not neatly correspond with the classifications set out in design and trademark registers.

While Sullivan and Kopp's management of licensing was negligent, it was the ongoing film and newspaper cartoon appearances that kept characters and reputations 'alive', propelling the extended animated universe. Regardless of artist-origination stories, animation studios had limited control over the life of this industrial property. Agents and distributors had considerable industrial clout because most animation studios were dependent upon renewal of licensing agreements to finance ongoing production and to have their films seen by the public. Disney was also challenged by these dynamics.

77 Anonymous, 'Local monopoly in the newspaper industry' (1952) 61(6) *Yale Law Review* 948, 949, 967.

78 Harry Kopp, Affidavit of Legal Services Rendered Filed in Settlement of the Estate of Pat Sullivan, Surrogate's Court, New York County, 14 June 1934: JCAC: Box 18. Harry Kopp Folder.

4.4 THE ORIGINS OF MICKEY MOUSE

Following the successful release of Disney studio's *Alice Comedies*, Winkler Productions and Universal Studios entered into an agreement for twenty-six cartoons featuring a character, *Oswald the Lucky Rabbit* (1927), with the animation services provided by Disney studios. Oswald was described by Universal as 'an exclusive creation of the artist' – Walt Disney.[79] Iwerks played a central role in the production of the new cartoon, with Oswald described as 'even more of a Felix clone than Julius'.[80] Oswald was a hit. When it came to renegotiation over the next series, Winkler Productions sought to take effective control over the Disney Studio, offering Disney a fee for production services that would make it difficult to make any profit. Mintz claimed that, under the terms of the agreement between Disney studio and Winkler Productions, Oswald was Winkler Productions' intellectual property. Mintz had signed a new agreement with Universal and began hiring away Disney Studio staff. Disney complained to Universal, but the firm was reluctant to break its agreement with Mintz, advising Walt Disney to work with him in the short term. Once the contract with Winkler Productions expired, Universal set up its own studio to produce *Oswald* films. Disney recognised that it was pointless to persist in a claim to wrestle back rights to Oswald against either company, regardless of the credit both gave him as the character's originator and his studio's claim as first owner of the copyright.[81]

Mickey Mouse, drawn by Iwerks, emerged in *Plane Crazy* and *The Gallopin' Gaucho* in 1928 out of necessity for the Disney studio to create a new cartoon series. The development of the character took place offsite to avoid it coming to the attention of staff loyal to Mintz, as the studio continued to finish outstanding *Oswald* cartoons.[82] However, as an independent production studio, Disney could not attract a distributor for these films and, unable to secure new distribution arrangements, the studio could not finance further productions. This motivated Disney to join 'the sound revolution' with *Steamboat Willie* in 1928.[83] The film was financed and distributed by Celebrity Productions, controlled by Pat Powers, a businessman who essentially created a clone of De Forest sound technology, the Cinephone Sound system. The Broadway release of *Steamboat Willie* was heralded as a test of the will of the ERPI/RCA/Western Electric sound cartel, whose clauses with exhibitors sought to prevent the use of 'interchangeable' technology in theatres.[84] *Mickey*

79 Crafton, above n 20, 209.

80 Canemaker, above n 1, 95.

81 Timothy S. Susanin, *Walt before Mickey: Disney's Early Years, 1919–1928*, University Press of Mississippi, 2011, 165–77.

82 Bob Thomas, *Building a Company, Roy O. Disney and the Creation of an Entertainment Empire*, Hyperion, 1998, 58.

83 Crafton, above n 20, 211.

84 Edward W. Kellogg, 'History of sound motion pictures: second instalment' (1955) (63) July *Journal of the Society of Motion Picture and Television Engineers* 356, 357.

Mouse films were an effective vehicle for promoting the Cinephone Sound system, but Powers lacked the contacts and ability to sell the film. A Broadway theatre manager and promoter, Harry Reichenbach, booked *Steamboat Willie* for a two-week run, where it was well reviewed, which in turn attracted the interest of distributors.[85] Like Mintz, Powers was unscrupulous, hiring away Iwerks to produce his own series when the contract with Disney was up for renegotiation in 1930. Powers pressured MGM to not deal with Disney, claiming he owned the rights to the series. There was also a dispute about accounting practices. However, Columbia Picture's Cohn was not scared off by Powers. As well as investing in future Disney productions, he agreed to provide US $25,000 to defend a lawsuit. Columbia also picked up the North American distribution rights to a new Disney venture *Silly Symphonies* in 1929, and world rights in 1931. In this period, Columbia also licensed rights to new rival sound cartoon series featuring *Krazy Kat*, produced by Winkler Productions, and *Oswald*, produced by Universal.[86] But the problem remained that the Columbia Pictures contracts also made it hard to turn a profit. Roy Disney explained:

> We made pictures there on a basis of $7,000, $9,000, and finally $11,000 advance when we delivered, against a contract that was sixty-forty-forty-sixty. In other words, 40 percent for distribution, 60 percent goes to pay for those advances plus prints and advertising, and when they were all paid, we got 40 percent and they got 60 percent. We saw very, very little over-ages.[87]

A slightly better deal was arranged with Universal Artists in 1931, but with Roy Disney trying to retain control by limiting direct investment by distributors and Walt Disney continuing to grow the studio and innovate with film production techniques there remained an ongoing problem of undercapitalisation. This left the Disney studio continually vulnerable to 'squeeze plays' from distributors.[88] Eventually, this led to a reconsideration of the role of character merchandise and the value of intellectual property rights.

4.5 INTELLECTUAL PROPERTY LIMITS

The effective combination of sound and animation in *Steamboat Willie* created a 'hit' cartoon. Many manufacturers were keen to produce Mickey Mouse merchandise, and some sought out licensing arrangements with Disney. This led to registered design and trademark rights, but not only by Disney. Artist-originator ownership claims to characters were relevant in copyright, but far less relevant to proprietorship of design and trademark registration. Further, even when registrations

85 Thomas, above n 82, 62.
86 Ibid. 66; Donald Crafton, *The Talkies: America's Transition to Sound, 1926–1931. History of American Film* vol. 4, Charles Scribner's Sons, 1997, 393–5.
87 Thomas, above n 82, 70.
88 Ibid. 95–8.

were achieved, the exclusive legal benefits conferred by these regimes could be very limited.

The right of manufacturers to an exclusive design right over the Mickey Mouse character was tested very early. In 1930 an action was brought in the UK by Mickey Mouse doll-maker Dean's Rag Book Co. against an importer of a lookalike 'Squeakie' mouse, Pomerantz & Sons, trading as Pomson's. Disney was not party to the proceedings. Dean's' designer, Richard Ellett, was a theatre designer and lover of films. As company secretary, then chief designer, for Dean's, he used his theatrical contacts to create character merchandise for the company, including the Peter Rabbit doll (1915) (discussed in Chapter 2), Charlie Chaplin (1916) and Felix the Cat (1924).

Steamboat Willie was distributed overseas by Ideal Films Ltd. Ellett attended the London opening in 1928, meeting Iwerks and Walt Disney. He tried to enthuse them in licensing the right to a Mickey Mouse doll. Disney was shown examples, but Ellett reports that he doubted the idea of the venture.[89] As discussed above, in this period Walt and Roy Disney's main priority was managing film production and securing film distribution.[90] However, Walter E. Disney registered a design right for a Mickey Mouse toy in the United States in October 1929.[91] The problem was that the studio lacked any independent capacity to conduct business outside the United States.

Dean's Rag Book Co. registered a design right for a Mickey Mouse doll and a related trademark in 1929 (see Figure 4.4).[92] The doll swing tag made no mention of a Disney connection. It acknowledged, 'By Exclusive arrangement with Ideal Films Ltd. All rights reserved. Reg'd design 750611'. A German wind-up tin motorcycle driven by 'Mickey-Maus' was also licensed by Ideal Films.[93] No written agreement with Disney appears to have been entered into until December 1930.[94] It is possible that the distribution contract with Ideal Films permitted the distributor to enter into

89 Dawn Cope and Peter Cope, *Dean's Rag Books and Rag Dolls*, New Cavendish Books, 2009, 48–9.

90 US TM 266,717 was registered for 'Motion Pictures reproduced for copies for sale' on 21 May 1928, but no registrations appeared in relation to other classes of goods at this time.

91 Walter E. Disney, Design for a Toy, US design 33,219, 30 October 1929.

92 Dean's Rag Book Co., UK design 750,611, 16 December 1929; TNA: BT82/1229; UK design 751,887; 31 January 1930; TNA: BT52/1435, UK TM 508,041, 21 November 1929, Class 4, Games and Sporting Articles.

93 David Gerstein, 'Mickey Mouse Annual: William Haughton in the British golden age – part one' (2008) (72) *Tomart's Disneyana Update* 48.

94 It was not possible to access the full Dean's Rag Book archive or the Disney studio archive. The 1930 contract created an exclusive option to use such comic cartoon characters 'other than Mickey Mouse and Minnie Mouse' for five years. Dean's would be notified of the characters and then have thirty days to exercise the option and use the representations upon utilities, goods, wares and merchandise that were approximately the same as being currently used: contract between Dean's Rag Book Co. and Walt Disney, signed by agent, William B. Levy, 23 December 1930.

FIGURE 4.4 Dean's Mickey Mouse doll design registration, 1929
Courtesy of National Archives, UK

merchandising agreements, and the Disney studio received a share of royalties. Whatever the case, it was the film distributor, not the animation studio, which sought to control intellectual property rights associated with the film character trade. Dean's also printed a British children's annual featuring Mickey Mouse on the cover for Christmas 1930. It has been described as

> a grotesque approximation of Mickey seated at a drawing table, brandishing a quill. One has to wonder if he drew his own picture; the rodent had beady eyes, five-fingered hands, and unusually human proportions.[95]

[95] Gerstein, above n 93, 49.

The artists who produced the early editions had limited source material available to work with. Mickey Mouse was not presented in coherent stories and cultural references were anglicised, with Mickey eating British food and talking about the British colonies.[96] There were similar issues with the quality of the representations and stories with the first *Mickey Mouse Magazine* launched in the United States in 1933.[97]

When Dean's sought to enforce its registered design right, this proved very difficult. Section 49 of the Patents and Designs Act 1907 allowed for registration of 'a new and original design, not previously published in the United Kingdom'. Registration required the applicant to nominate a specified class or classes of manufactured good to which it proposed to apply the design, and visual representations defined the monopoly.[98] Design protection, called 'copyright in the design', was for five years, extended to fifteen years by optional renewal.[99] Any fraudulent or obvious imitation of the design was a piracy.[100] That rights to a fictional film character were considered worthy of litigation was commented upon as a sign of times: 'American is every day becoming a more and more necessary language for the legal profession to know'.[101]

Pomerantz argued that the three *Mickey Mouse* films that had been screened in the UK deprived any originality in the design. This led to a factual inquiry into the design process. Ellett defended the originality of his design, explaining he immersed himself in the films, then drew from memory. He stressed the introduction of features which do not appear in the film, such as his decision to put neckwear, teeth and whiskers on the doll. His contribution was drily reported in the Australian press with the byline, 'Inventor of whiskers'.[102] Copying of Dean's design was suggested because of similarities in the feet which also differed from those in the films.

The head of the British Toy Manufacturers Association gave evidence that it takes considerable 'artistic skill, craftsmanship and technical experience' to make a 3D version from the 2D concept. The association was a partisan body that advocated as witnesses in the court for enlarged design and trademark rights, largely on the basis that it felt that these might assist in trade protection by preventing German and Japanese imports. The association was more neutral with respect to patents. Through its journal *Games and Toys*, the association created an awareness of the extent of rights by listing new registration details each month. Some descriptions of

[96] Ibid.
[97] Michael Barrier, *Funnybooks: The Improbable Glories of the Best American Comic Books*, University of California Press, 2014, 16.
[98] Patents and Designs Act 1907, s50.
[99] Patents and Designs Act 1907, s53.
[100] Patents and Designs Act 1907, s60.
[101] 'Chancery Division: "Mickey Mouse" in court – Dean's Rag Book Company Limited v Pomerantz and Sons', *The Times*, 18 July 1930, 5.
[102] 'Mickey Mouse. Inventor of whiskers', *Brisbane Courier*, 24 November 1930, 15.

new patents could be read as a 'how to' guide for informed readers of the journal. However, when it comes to copyright, design and trademark, advertisements frequently stress that a toy is exclusively licensed, made with approval of the artist or distributor or supported by a 'Universal Copyright'. These notices helped further promote licensing practice. The trade association also provided a remedy to those who asserted themselves as owners, publishing apology advertisements for perceived transgressions, possibly in lieu of going to court.

In Squeakie's defence it was argued that the films had caused a 'riot' and

> if two persons wished to register designs of Mickey Mouse toys which they wished to be recognised by the public as Mickey Mouse, the two toys of necessity would have very strong features of resemblance.[103]

Pomerantz gave evidence that he drew Squeakie after seeing the film, but he had not seen the Dean's doll at that time. He suggested that because of visual differences the two dolls were not 'in the same product line'.

The court found that, even though toys often have ribbons, mice always have whiskers, and Mickey Mouse was well-known subject matter, a particular 3D representation of a film character would be a valid design. However, Luxmoore J accepted that the two designs were independently derived from the films. Without copying of the original design, there was no piracy.[104] Both parties claimed victory in the same edition in *Games and Toys* (see Figures 4.5 & 4.6).

In reproducing the layout from *The Times* law reports and celebrating its victory over the German-origin trader on page one, Dean's advised that 'to spare others from any embarrassment of an infringement action', traders should make sure they only purchase toys bearing registered designs and trademarks.[105] In doing so, the account misappropriates the symbolic power of legal authority in support of a baseless claim of the need for a licence. The Pomerantz advertisement appearing later in the edition sets the record straight:

> An action in the High Courts of Justice to restrain sales of Squeakie as being an alleged infringement of a registered design of MICKEY MOUSE was dismissed by Mr. Justice Luxmoore on 22nd July 1930.[106]

The narrowness of registered design rights in the UK frustrated attempts by artist-originators to control manufacturing of animated characters and grant meaningful exclusive licences.

[103] 'High Court of Justice: Chancery Division, "Mickey Mouse" in court – Dean's Rag Book Company Limited v Pomerantz and Sons', *The Times*, 19 July 1930, 4.

[104] 'High Court of Justice: Chancery Division, "Mickey Mouse" in court – Dean's Rag Book Company Limited v Pomerantz and Sons', *The Times*, 23 July 1930, 5; see also *Dean's Rag Book Co v Pomerantz* [1930] RPC 485.

[105] 'Mickey Mouse' (1930) August *Games and Toys* 1.

[106] 'Pomson's Squeakie goes to court and wins' (1930) August *Games and Toys* 71.

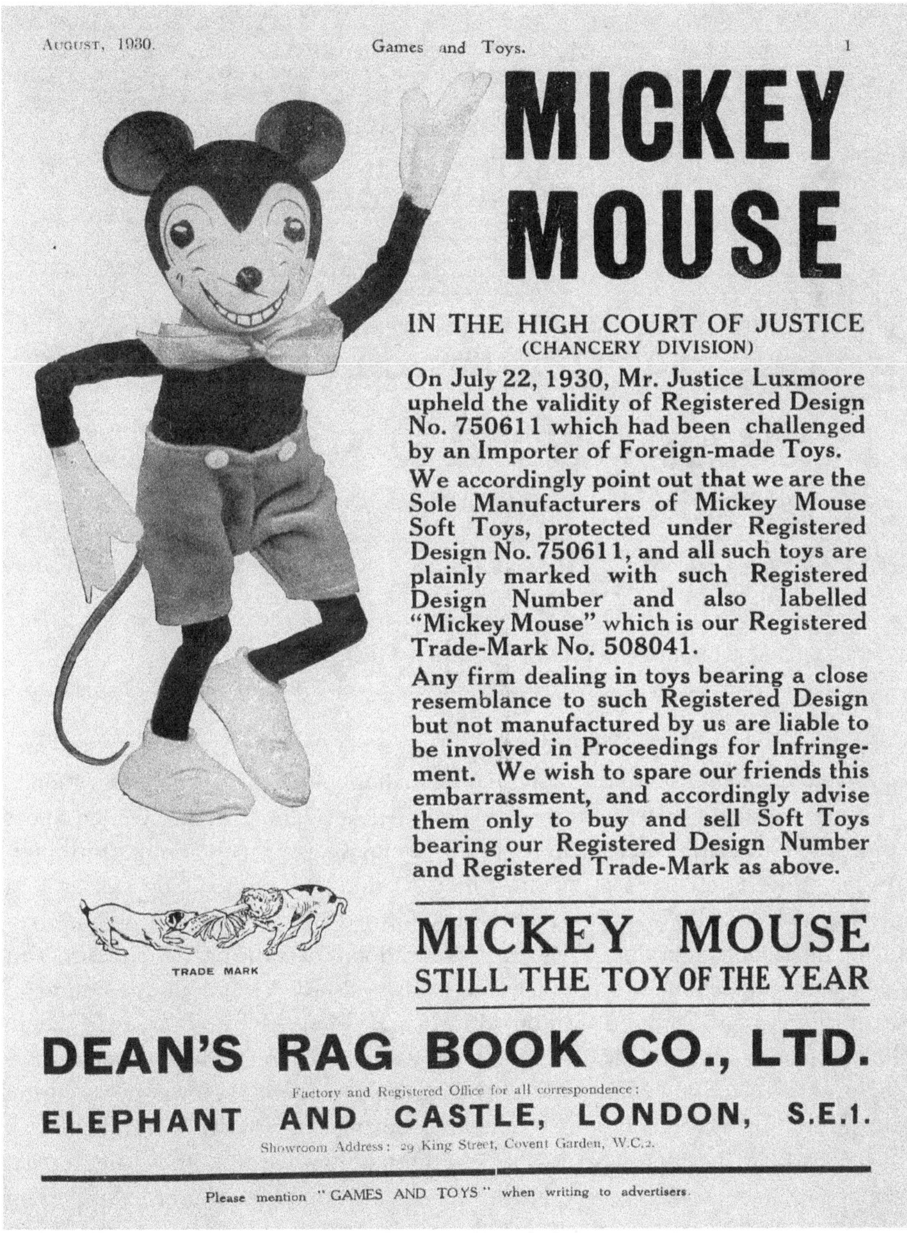

FIGURE 4.5 Advertisement, 'Mickey Mouse in the High Court', 1930
Games & Toys, August 1930, 1. © British Library Board. Courtesy of the British Toy and Hobby Association.

FIGURE 4.6 Advertisement, 'Pomson's Squeakie Goes to Court', 1930
Games & Toys, August 1930, 71. © British Library Board. Courtesy of the British Toy and Hobby Association.

Trademark law also produced mixed results, depending on jurisdiction and registration strategies such as timing, representation and width of the application.

Disney registered trademarks for the words 'Mickey Mouse' in the United States in 1928.[107] The significance of this right was soon tested, again by a film distributor. In 1930 Pathé Exchange's president, Alfred Manon, summoned Roy Disney to a meeting with Amedee Van Bueren, who had formed a new studio in 1928, purchasing the unit that had produced *Aesop's Fables* cartoons over the past seven years. Van Bueren announced he would make cartoons with RCA Photophone sound.[108] *Aesop's Fables* had featured 'Milton Mouse' and 'Mary Mouse' from 1921. These characters bore some similarities to the Disney representations. The characters wore gloves and clothes, and Mary wore a skirt, similar to Minnie's. However, they were also quite pointy-nosed and more rodent like, looking closer to the Dean's Rag Book Co's dolls than the representations in the Disney films. Roy Disney alleged that Manon told him: 'You fellows had better get together with Van Beuren. Van Beuren is going to produce more cartoons whether you get together with him or not. If you don't get together with him, he will run you out of business'.[109] Key Disney staff

[107] Walter E. Disney, word 'Mickey Mouse', US TM 247,156, 18 September 1928, Class 26, for Motion Pictures Reproduced in Copies for Sale.
[108] Crafton, above n 86, 390.
[109] Affidavit of Roy O. Disney, *Pathé Exchange and the Van Beuren Corporation v Walt Disney Productions*, Transcript of Record, US Circuit Court of Appeals, Ninth Cir 1931, 24; Equity

were lured away to Van Bueren's studio. This predatory competition prompted further Disney registrations of new character trademarks, pictorial representations of Mickey Mouse and Minnie Mouse for use in films.[110] This was a prudent move. New Van Beuren releases distributed by Pathé Exchange – *Stone Age Stuff*, *The Office Boy*, *The Big Cheese* and *Circus Capers* (1931) – featured mouse characters, but Milton and Mary were not the same mice as depicted in *Aesop's Fables*. The body, ears and shoes were now rounder; Milton's vest was gone; and he had adopted Mickey's trousers and buttons. Disney successfully sued for trademark infringement and unfair competition, with the court agreeing that the Van Beuren/Pathé films featured crudely drawn imitations of Mickey and Minnie.[111] However, the litigation dragged on. Roy Disney noted that the eventual outcome was that Van Beuren/Pathé had to pay into court a $50,000 bond but could continue to distribute the existing films subject to the undertaking to make no more using these characters.[112]

In the United States, trademark and unfair competition proved useful in protecting the interest of the artist-originator of cartoon character names and likenesses that first appeared in film, as in syndicated newspapers. However, the assertion of a trademark required a managerial infrastructure to facilitate licensing and to forestall predatory claims by film distributors and other traders. This planning was difficult but not impossible to do within the United States. It proved far more difficult to manage abroad.

Trademark is an industrial property right, where proprietorship comes from local use and local registration of the sign in a particular class of commerce. The Paris Convention for the Protection of Industrial Property (1883) afforded protection to patents, trademarks and industrial designs of nationals of convention countries, on the same terms as available to their own citizens.[113] The United States joined the convention in 1887. This meant that North American firms could apply for patent, design and trademark registration in accordance with the laws that applied in the jurisdiction where they sought protection.[114] However, in the UK it was Dean's Rag Books Co. which first registered a trademark for Mickey Mouse in 1929 and Minnie Mouse for dolls in 1930.[115] Dean's only entered into an agreement with Disney relating to the making of toy models 'other than' Mickey Mouse and Minnie Mouse

T-87, US District Court, Southern District of California. NARA, Pacific Region: Record Group 21.

110 Walter E. Disney, Pictorial representation 'Mickey Mouse', Trademark Number 273,816, Pictorial representation 'Minnie Mouse', Trademark Number 273,817, 12 August 1930, Class 26, for Motion Pictures Reproduced in Copies for Sale.

111 *Pathé Exchange and the Van Beuren Corporation v Walt Disney Productions* 51 F2d 1082 (1931).

112 Thomas, above n 82, 89.

113 Article 2 of the Paris Convention (1883).

114 F.A. Seely, *History of the International Union for the Protection of Industrial Property*, Government Printing Office, 1887, 7.

115 Dean's Rag Book Co., UK TM 508,041, 'Mickey Mouse' word mark, 21 November 1929; TNA: BT82/1229; UK TM 508,679 'Minnie Mouse' word mark, 11 December 1931, Class 49, Games and Sporting Articles TNA: BT82/1230.

the following year. In 1930, Disney Productions secured a UK registration for a Mickey Mouse character mark, specifically limited to film.[116]

The popularity of film cartoon characters meant that in many jurisdictions other companies sought to register the characters' names and representations for use as a trademark on all sorts of products. In some jurisdictions, the courts were sympathetic to Disney. In 1933, the Australian trademark registrar refused to allow Radio Corporation a trademark involving use of the words Mickey Mouse and Minnie Mouse on Astor Mickey Mouse Midget wireless sets. Radio Corporation appealed to the High Court where it was explicitly noted that the case did not concern enforcement of a copyright and that there was no trademark registration or indeed any exclusive rights held by Disney in the names or characters. However, section 114 of the Trade Mark Act 1905-34 (Cth) set out grounds for opposition to registration where the use would be likely to deceive. Such was the fame of the characters that C. J. Latham found

> the names and the figures are so closely associated in the public mind, in Australia and elsewhere, with Walter E. Disney and his activities, that the use of either the names of the figures in connection with any goods, at once suggests that the goods are 'in some way or other connected' with Walter E. Disney.[117]

Although the Astor radios were found to be infringing products, these were not removed from sale. Thereafter they were sold with a licence from Disney Corporation's Australian agent, a publisher, John Sands Ltd, appointed after the commencement of legal proceedings.[118] This kind of strategy of working with former 'pirates' also came to feature in other jurisdictions.

In 1930s Spain there were many beautiful Mickey Mouse–inspired trademarks in the market, where the story of the character merged with local folktales, stories and myths about mice already in place. Contemporary cultural studies and intellectual property scholars often criticise Disney as housing corporate plans to appropriate and homogenise national folklore, particularly after the success of the film *Snow White and the Seven Dwarfs* (1937) (discussed further in Chapter 5). However, the dynamic in Spain was precisely the opposite. Local playful activity actually helped develop a Disney brand presence in Spain in advance of interest in licensing activity by the company. Local Spanish traders successfully registered and enforced Mickey Mouse–inspired trademarks independently of Disney. However, sometimes new local registrations were opposed, including one in 1935 where Walt Disney, on

[116] Disney Productions, UK TM 514,147, 'Mickey Mouse', 30 June 1930; TNA: BT82/1241; UK TM 530,499, 20 July 1932, Class 8, Philosophical and Instruments (Motion Picture Films); TNA: BT82/1281.

[117] *Radio Corporation Pty Ltd v Disney and Others* (1937) 57 CLR 448, 453.

[118] George G. Turri, 'Mickey Mouse in Australian High Court' (1937) 32(10) *Bulletin of the United States Trade Association* 297, 305; Power of Attorney granted by Walter E. Disney on behalf of Walt Disney Productions, and Roy Disney on behalf of Walt Disney Enterprises to John Sands Ltd, 21 May 1934, NAA: A1861, 6703.

holiday in Europe, is astonishingly described as a subject domiciled in Barcelona.[119] The Disney case was supported by producing evidence of Walt Disney as artist-originator using marketing material related to the films. This was not successful on the predictable grounds that copyright was not relevant, and Disney was not the first to use the characters on the relevant products in Spain. A more productive pragmatic legal strategy ensued. This entailed negotiating with 'pirates' if they were judged to be industrially important, threatening them with an infringement action, then offering them exclusive licences, sweetened by Disney assistance in suing rivals who were also producing Mickey Mouse wares.[120] In this way the artist-origination mythology comes to be affirmed through a negotiated outcome with pirates. Over time, the original presence of a rival rights holder is forgotten, and only the Disney association endures.

4.6 PROTOCOLS OF CONSUMPTION

In Middle-French usage the term 'protocol' denotes the 'original record or minutes of a transaction, negotiation, examination, etc.; esp. such a document drawn up by a notary or other recognised official, forming the legal authority for any subsequent agreement based on it'. In contemporary usage a protocol is also a 'set of rules governing the exchange of data between given devices, or the transmission of data via a given communications channel'.[121] Reining in the unruly and somewhat chaotic adoption of Mickey Mouse and other cartoon creations by film distributors, agents and manufacturers was not achieved by law. It required the global establishment of protocols of consumption in both of the above senses. There needed to be a far more detailed and rigorous documentation of precisely what had been envisaged and agreed between the diverse parties seeking to associate with 'studio property' than had previously been captured in licence agreements. And there needed to be significant trader participation in communications channels and information flows controlled by Disney. The Disney studio was restructured in 1929/1930 to facilitate these goals. The restructure created much more specialised and co-ordinated management, with four separate interrelated business concerns: Walt Disney Productions and the Disney Film Recording Company, which created animated cartoons, Walt Disney Enterprises, in charge of 'ancillary activities', and Liled Realty and Investment Company, which owned and managed the real estate used by the other companies.[122] These demarcations facilitated far greater clarity and discipline in communication practices and sharing of knowledge, with management activity

[119] Trademark Opposition, 15 June 1934; AHOEPM: File 98,076.

[120] See Thomas, above n 82, 83–4. The Spanish cases are discussed in detail in Jose Bellido and Kathy Bowrey, 'Disney in Spain (1930–1935)' (2017) 60(8) *Business History* 1277.

[121] 'protocol, n'. *OED Online*.

[122] Didier Ghez (ed.), 'O.B. Johnston (1901–1992)' *Walt's People: vol. 20 – Talking Disney with Artists Who Knew Him*, Theme Park Press, 2017, 37.

focused on distinctive domains of expertise, including managing relevant legal technicalities and associated commercial challenges.

Initially, merchandising activity was considered 'ancillary' because opportunities had arisen spontaneously, with Disney being reactive rather than seeking to tightly control the activity. For example, Disney permitted the making of handmade dolls supported by the studio in 1930 which were considered very high-quality goods, but these were unable to be manufactured in scale. Another agreement was entered into to produce dolls with Geo. Borgfeldt & Co., and, as sketched above, there were arrangements with Dean's Rag Book Co. and others. However, Roy and Walt Disney initially looked to marketing and character merchandise as vehicles to promote the films. This included the development of Mickey Mouse Clubs in 1930. As we have already seen with the Meccano Boy, the use of clubs to promote goodwill in children's markets had become common by the 1930s.[123] Marketing experts advised that the key elements included official membership cards, participation awards, centring interest on the fun and novelty of membership rather than direct product promotion and free giveaways.[124] Mickey Mouse Clubs developed out of a campaign aimed at exhibitors to attract Saturday matinee custom.

> 'We formed them ourselves by selling the theater men on the idea of having a kiddies club', Roy explained. 'You give them a little something on their birthday, and they all had to pay admission. They had a ritual of a club, and they all belonged. Then we got people to make pins for them and banners and so on. We used to charge the theater men $25 as a basic license fee, and they bought all the accessories. ... if he was on the ball he could make himself $100, $150 a week'.[125]

The accessories promoted through clubs were originally a 'tie-in' managed by exhibitors and salespeople designed to promote and sustain reliable theatre attendance. Manufacturing was not something that interested the brothers personally. The new revenue streams created were useful but incidental to the primary business, which was making films and growing audiences for them. However, if the appearance of the products disappointed or where merchandise was felt in poor taste or of bad quality, there were reputational risks to the studio.[126] Reining in undesirable associations required a far tighter legal and commercial infrastructure. Further establishing greater control over tie-ins would have helped cement studio authority and bargaining clout when dealing with film distributors and other agents by reducing the scope for unregulated spin-off activities that diluted Disney goodwill.

The creation of the company, Disney Enterprises, presented the possibility of dedicated management systems that allowed greater centralised control to emerge.

[123] See Chapter 3, 95–7.

[124] E. Evalyn Grumbine, 'How to conduct clubs and contests', *Reaching Juvenile Markets: How to Advertise, Sell, and Merchandise through Boys and Girls*, McGraw-Hill Book Co., 1938, 185.

[125] Thomas, above n 82, 69.

[126] Ghez, above n 122, 41.

A new licensing infrastructure was developed, not by the Disney brothers, but a Powers Cinephone salesman, Walter Banks Levy – who, from June 1930, oversaw development of UK and European markets, and an advertising company, Kay Kamen & Streeter Blair, led by Kay Kamen – who focused on developing US and Canadian trade. From 1933, Kay Kamen was appointed as the sole licensing agent for Disney creations worldwide. Kay's nephew, George Kamen, was appointed as managing director of Disney Enterprises (Europe).[127] Through associated companies, Walt Disney-Mickey Mouse Ltd (UK, 1931), Walt Disney-Mickey Mouse SA (France, 1934) and Mickey Mouse SA (Denmark, 1934) and independent agencies in other jurisdictions, Disney Enterprises licensed intellectual property rights attached to 'Disney creations' for use on 'Disney articles'. The terms often included an advance payment by the licensee and a royalty per article, typically 5 per cent, with income accounted to Disney Enterprises.[128]

George Kamen stressed that Disney Enterprises did not directly engage in advertising or 'selling' licences or solicit trade. However, this hides the fact that legally trademarks cannot be 'stockpiled'; they can only be registered by those who have the intention to use them on particular goods or services. This legal principle posed a significant impediment. In 1935, *Variety* reported that Helen Warner, employee of the French subsidiary, 'has a tough time expanding the business because policy forbids active selling and there are no toy or trade newspapers in the country which would aid word of mouth. She has to wait for customers to come in'.[129] However, excited by the commercial prospects raised by the films, many did come to Disney agents, and this created enough opportunities for Disney Enterprises to begin to standardise company agreements. Kamen also bought back rights to remove unwelcome associations, secured new agreements with the more important and influential regional manufacturers and importers, and local registrations of industrial property rights were effected on behalf of Disney Enterprises. This activity helped establish tighter and more lucrative 'exclusive' territorial arrangements. For example, they agreed not to license competitors in the same range. George Kamen explained: 'We promise to, say, a manufacturer of towels that we shall not deal with any other manufacturers of towels'. However, many licensed manufacturers also complained that the benefits were very one-sided.[130]

Export restrictions, local taxes on imports, commercial pressures to support local employment after the Depression and domestic legal technicalities encouraged

[127] Kamen Ltd (UK) was incorporated on 15 August 1934; Companies House Archives (London, UK).

[128] Didier Ghez, *Disney's Grand Tour*, Theme Park Press, 2013, 23–4; contract between Disney Enterprises (represented by Mr Pierre de Beneducci, General Agent for Spain, Portugal and Italy) and Messrs Rogelio Sanchís, Barcelona, 6 September 1934; Rogelio Sanchís Archives (Valencia, Spain).

[129] Quoted in ibid. 52.

[130] George Kamen, 'The application of an idea to merchandise' (1935) December *Marketing: Journal of the Advertising Managers Association* 194, 195–7.

reliance upon local knowledge and business networks. This led to arrangements with independent agencies, but these were also a source of worry. Independent agents, such as Johns Sands (Australia) or Pierre de Beneducci (Spain, Portugal and Italy), could legally act without the direct control of Disney Enterprises, signing any contracts they wanted in connection with the studio. The Italian situation proved very problematic with de Beneducci signing agreements that were considered unsuitable, taking advance royalties and not forwarding funds to Disney Enterprises. Legally, it proved difficult to remove him.[131] Standard contracts were drawn up with requirements for negotiations to stay within certain bounds and protect Disney goodwill. Standard clauses included that products were suitable for purpose, in good taste and that there was no increase in the ordinary unit price for that kind of article. Marked down or cut-price products could also only be sold with approval from Disney Enterprises.[132] In some circumstances price reductions in licensing fees could be negotiated in order to meet price competition. However, manufacturers more often complained about the 'grasping' and 'hard-boiled' character of negotiations with Disney Enterprises. Sometimes, this was because the need for multiple negotiations and separate licences disrupted multinational operations, multiplying licensing costs for the 'same' article depending upon where it was sold. Interestingly, George Kamen did not object to unflattering characterisations, noting, 'I have no objection to being called grasping. So far as the size of the advance is concerned, we try to get as much as we can .... We sell by creating what we believe to be very valuable, so valuable that people will come to us and buy it'.[133]

Maintaining the visibility and purity of the artist-originator narrative connected to film animations was facilitated by the decision not to permit use of Walt Disney's own name or likeness or any Disney creations to directly endorse another's product or company. Companies only had the right to use the likenesses as 'attention-grabbers'. George Kamen advised:

> 'We do not want to tell the Mickey Mouse public that they *must* buy Mickey Mouse products. We give it to the manufacturer'. He also noted that they often declined licences because 'the appeal of Mickey Mouse is primarily intended for child consumption .... We want children to think highly of Mickey Mouse and if they had to take some nasty medicine with a Mickey Mouse on the bottle, they would immediately take a dislike of Mickey Mouse'.[134]

Official drawings of Disney creations were provided to assist with production of authentic representations and sample products by new licensees had to be approved. Products also bore a notice: 'Authorised by Disney Enterprises Ltd'. In fields such as food, poor quality products carried stronger reputational risks. O. B. Johnston said that 'people

[131] Ghez, above n 122, 72–5.
[132] *Fortune Magazine*, October 1933.
[133] Ghez, above n 122, 66; Kamen, above n 130, 194, 195.
[134] Kamen, above n 130, 195–7 (original emphasis).

would not blame the XYZ Spilt Pea Company if the Donald Duck Pea Soup was spoiled, they would blame the studio'. This led to the appointment of a Disney food inspector in the United States, who operated independently of the merchandising office.[135]

By 1934 the Bulletin of the United States Trade-Mark Association observed:

> Mickey Mouse refuses to be nationalized: He has become a citizen of the world. In France he is Michel Souris; in Germany, Michael Maus; in Greece, Mikel Mus; in Italy Michele Jopolino; in Japan Miki Juchi; and in Spain, Miguel Ratonocito .... More than 600 manufactured articles, ranging from doormats to watches and jewelry, bear his Disneygraph.[136]

This same year, Kay Kamen launched an annual merchandising catalogue. It listed licensed products and manufacturers. This helped Disney Enterprises keep track of sub-licences. Notation of the European branches established to manage the rights available to facilitate further licensing and revenue streams was also included.[137] The production of an annual catalogue reinforced the idea that discrete products were connected through a chain of authorisation of 'rights' managed by Disney's agents, and that opportunities were to be constantly renewed. Over time, this coordination also made possible the idea of 'standardisation' of the Disney range.

Success in trader buy-in can be seen from the outcome of the first contract signed in 1930 with Kay Kamen and Streeter Blair. Kamen was entitled to 40 per cent of gross receipts, not including the first US$50,000, this figure being the estimated income received in the previous year by Disney from character merchandising in North America.[138] In 1935 Disney accountant O. B. Johnston noted that, with over 100 agreements with manufacturers, character merchandising earned Disney Enterprises US$35 million.[139] George Kamen reported that 'publicity' generated by 45 UK agreements was worth £65,000.[140]

[135] Ghez, above n 122, 46. A more extreme form of surveillance and control by private policing was instigated in the 1960s' theme park developments. See Alan Bryman, *The Disneyization of Society*, Sage, 2004, 138–40; Carl Hiaasen, *Team Rodent: How Disney Devours the World*, Random House, 1998, 25–37.

[136] Clowry Chapman, 'Mickey Mouse and other things' (1934) 29(11) *Bulletin of the United States Trade-Mark Association* 271.

[137] See Leonard Mosley, *The Real Walt Disney: A Biography*, Grafton, 1985, 148–50; David Bain and Bruce Harris, *Mickey Mouse: Fifty Happy Years*, Harmony Books, 1977, 150; M.C. Beezy, 'Good Marksmanship' (2006) 29(10) *Los Angeles Lawyer* 20, 22; Cecil Munsey, *Disneyana: Walt Disney Collectibles*, Hawthorn Books, 1974, 107–26; Tim Hollis, *Toons in Toyland: The Story of Cartoon Character Merchandise*, University Press of Mississippi, 2015, 11.

[138] Contract between Walt Disney Enterprises and Kay Kamen and Streeter Blair, 29 June 1930. Licensing Design right US 82802 and trademarks to characters entitled Mickey Mouse, Minnie Mouse, Silly Symphonies, Horace Horsecollar, Clarabelle Cow, and Pluto the Pup.

[139] Ghez, above n 122, 46.

[140] Kamen, above n 130, 195 (emphasis in original).

4.7 THE DISNEY FAMILY

From the point of view of the consuming public, the visible stewardship of Disney Enterprises created the impression that licensees were working 'with Disney', rather than working *for* Disney Enterprises. Alongside this, consumers were also encouraged to identify with Disney by affiliating with the film characters and the Disney studio in the animation of their daily lives.

Integral to this was encouraging the idea of the respectability of film-going at a time of significant larger debates about the dangers of film attendance and the industry's 'duty to youth' to prevent exposure to content that might corrupt their moral compass. As already mentioned, Disney had fallen foul of state censorship codes with early animations. The Motion Picture Producers and Distributors Association of America (MPPDA) produced self-regulatory production codes to stimy more serious government interventions. These encouraged adherence to general principles of censorship to protect the moral standards of the vulnerable, which included women, children, lower classes and those with 'susceptible minds'.[141] At the same time, the MPPDA promoted Saturday matinee clubs.[142] Disney cartoons were actively promoted as a reliably funny form of entertainment that featured appropriate role models. For example, a 1931 *Motion Picture Daily* editorial begins:

> Hi, Mickey!
> WE doff the editorial straw hat in your direction today:
> Because, in these times when crowned heads are not easy heads, you manage to make 'em giggle.
> Because you seem to have a perpetual good time, even if you don't, and because audiences everywhere feel that way about it too . . .
> Because you're model in your conduct, which most of us are not, and because you manage to forever keep your nose clean.
> Because you bring credit to the picture business and a constant supply of golf sweaters to Walt Disney.
> Because you're as minus in temperament as some stars we know are plus and that *is* something.[143]

The entire edition of the trade newspaper featured Mickey Mouse and the studio. It also included an article on the emergence of 375 licensed Mickey Mouse Clubs. The clubs were described as 'a movement' that had 'enlisted' 750,000 American

[141] Codes included 'The Formula' (1924); 'Don't and Be Careful' (1927); and the 'MPPDA Production Code' also known as the Hay's Code (1930). See Richard Maltby, 'The production code and the Hays Office' in Tino Balio (ed.), *Grand Design: Hollywood as a Modern Business Empire, 1930–1939*, University of California Press, 1996, 43.

[142] Nicholas Sammond, *Babes in Tomorrowland: Walt Disney and the Making of the American Child, 1930–1960*, Duke University Press, 2005, 47–60.

[143] 'Hi Mickey!', *Motion Picture Daily*, 20 June 1931, 3 (original emphasis).

children. The club creed linked Disney goodwill with good conduct at home, school, play and with training in civic responsibility:

> I will be a square-shooter in my home, in school, on the playground, wherever I may be. I will be truthful and honorable, and strive always to make myself a better and more useful little citizen. I will respect my elders, and help the aged, the helpless children smaller than myself. In short, I will be a good American.[144]

In the United States, Disney marketing was influenced by current theories and debates about childhood. Hagiographies of Walt Disney reinforced rags to riches narratives attractive to middle-American culture:

> Consuming a Disney product became a mystical ritual by which one could consume the essence of middle America. It formed an exact counter to the tropes of infection in which harmful movies were described as delivering the ethnic, urban, proletarian past of their producers, and of distracting youthful consumers from the efficient and productive utilization of their leisure time. Through the figures of Walt Disney and Mickey Mouse, the company offered up a means of communion with the 'human center' of an American culture attempting to locate itself in an ostensibly generic American landscape and set of practices.[145]

The idea that Disney could be relied upon to help parents care for their children was reinforced with company messaging sent to exhibitors suggesting promotions to local mothers who could use the clubs as a form of cheap, supervised Saturday child-minding – no doubt an attractive prospect to parents and children alike.[146] Large numbers of unlicensed clubs were reined in with the appointment of a centralised club administration. Membership grew with further promotion, including club radio programmes and the *Mickey Mouse Club Bulletin*. Somewhere between one and three million children were counted as members of 600 clubs, where club-sponsored activities and exhibitors were supported by Kamen's leadership and development of Disney Enterprises.[147]

As discussed in previous chapters, department stores also licensed toy promotions. De Cordova notes: 'Mickey Mouse became a kind of star of the toy department, around which could be assembled a large supporting cast of other dolls and toys'. The costumed character passed out presents and acted as 'master of ceremonies' – there was a Mickey Mouse booth at Bloomingdales – with many promotions initiated by the stores themselves. The traditional Christmas window for toy promotion was extended by the emphasis on the weekly ritual of film-going and the

[144] 'Mickey Mouse clubs cover nation', *Motion Picture Daily*, 20 June 1931, 8.
[145] Sammond, above n 142, 172.
[146] Ibid. 166.
[147] Crafton, above n 86, 258; Richard DeCordova, 'The Mickey in Macy's window: childhood, consumerism and Disney animation' in Eric Smoodin (ed.), *Disney Discourse: Producing the Magic Kingdom*, Routledge, 2013, 208.

emphasis on the child's birthday, Thanksgiving and Mother's Day as opportunities for Mickey Mouse–themed events.[148]

The shift from animated shorts to full feature films with the release of *Snow White and the Seven Dwarfs* (1937) shifted the narrative centre from the antics of Disney artist-originated creations to studio-origination narratives supporting character appropriations of collectively shared folklore stories and characters traditionally introduced to children in the home through books.[149] It was the legal and commercial protocols established in the early 1930s that allowed the Disney family to grow as both quintessentially American and universal, especially outside the United States. These protocols had significant implications for the modern construction of childhood. Established forms of film promotion by exhibitors within the cinema precinct and the interests of the toy manufacturers and department stores in expanding the toy-buying season converged with extended Disney corporate regulation after the 1930s. Regardless of whether or not one was a Disney fan, this legal and commercial infrastructure produced a philosophy of family entertainment that had to be negotiated, embraced, ignored or resisted everywhere a Disney brand presence was felt. Synergistic entrepreneurialism contributed to the projection of mutually reinforcing connections linking the child's emotional life, character development, the sociality of play and the experience of happiness to 'safe' channels of consumption. The Disney brand of family entertainment personified this aspiration, with familial affiliations promoted by the identity of 'Uncle Walt'.[150]

[148] DeCordova, above n 147, 206; Sammond, above, n 142, 172.

[149] The cultural and commercial impact of this and related appropriative activities are explored in Chapter 5.

[150] The technique of 'Uncling' is taken up in Chapter 7.

5

Licensing Gone Wrong

In the 1960s, a *Peter Pan* movie to be directed by George Cukor, with Audrey Hepburn playing the main role, was never made because of a bitter copyright battle that developed between Great Ormond Street Hospital and the Disney Corporation over the classic J. M. Barrie text. The disagreement resulted in a legal dispute that went all the way to the Court of Appeal, and, although the controversy is not considered a landmark intellectual property case, the dispute is significant because it hides more than it reveals.

On the surface, it is a typical contractual wrangle about the extent of intellectual property rights transacted, but, beneath that, one can see a clash between competing visions of the specific relationship between childhood and the law. As detailed in previous chapters, it might be difficult to disentangle these concepts because thinking about and managing intellectual property always embodies an assumption about its limits, or the lack thereof, particularly in relation to children as consumers. Although one of the judges criticised Disney for subjecting a charitable institution to the ordeal of going to the courts, our point here is both more obvious and more subtle. The very fact that the hospital went to court shows how successful Disney had been in its commercial operations in Britain. The dispute is especially interesting not because Disney scuppered licensing opportunities envisaged by the hospital, but because it shows how effectively the company had pushed its particular way of thinking about the subject, to the point that even the hospital was conflicted about it. In other words, Disney had transformed desired commercial practices into legal realities to such an extent that it paved the way for legal expectations and aspirations and, hence, generated disputes about them. The fact that the hospital had recourse to law to argue the point is an indication that the commercial potential around intellectual property had begun to be normalised in such a way that it could be contested. The question of the elasticity of Disney's commercial practices foreshadowed the normative enquiry of the law. Or, to put it another way, how we think about intellectual property depends on its emergent qualities, and Disney's greatest legal achievement was the international propagation and actualisation of practices about the properties at stake.

By scrutinising the controversy between the hospital and Disney, we revisit some of the issues identified previously. For instance, the ways in which animation had developed a particular connection with children; the effects of industrial frameworks and corporate vehicles in linking and carving out opportunities for children's participation; and the doctrinal legal problems coalescing simultaneously around copyright, trademarks and designs. By shifting our focus to the specific dispute around the exploitation and circulation of *Peter Pan*, not just as a commodity but also as a gift, the chapter enables us to look further at changes in the way of thinking about intellectual property experienced in the twentieth century, changes that somehow erased concerns about its polity and propriety when addressed to children and exploiting the related rights.

Moreover, the chapter looks at the ongoing adaptability of intellectual property practices in capturing commercial opportunities, which in turn gave rise to a process whereby the boundaries between subject matter and advertising became more permeable. In so doing, we explore the bequest of the *Peter Pan* copyright to the hospital and the first administrative steps taken by the hospital to manage it. We have chosen to focus on the handling of intellectual property by the hospital as a contrast to Disney's commercial exploitation, since the path of litigation was characterised by a failure to understand what the other party was doing in relation to the property. We chronicle the dispute to reveal how the conflict between the parties merged with new forms of regulation in the administration of Barrie's gift, showing how business had seeped through the whole thing to such an extent that it gradually affected how the hospital handled the bequest of the *Peter Pan* copyright.

5.1 CHILDREN IN NEED

An introduction to the distinctive character of this legal dispute can be seen by highlighting an aspect frequently noted by journalists who reported the case in the 1960s – namely, the stark contrast between the two parties, described in terms akin to 'David and Goliath'.[1] While there was an evident disparity between the parties as legal entities, both in their geographical blueprint and the scale and remit of operations, it is also interesting to note the unusual position they occupied in this case. Disney, a successful commercial multinational enterprise in children's entertainment, notably appeared as the defendant, in contrast to its more usual role of experiencing the law from the other side of the courtroom, while trying to uphold

[1] 'Peter Pan hospital sues Disney' *The People*, 30 August 1964, 13; 'Action over Peter Pan by hospital' *The Guardian*, 10 March 1965, 4.

and enforce its intellectual properties.[2] The appearance of Great Ormond Street Hospital for Sick and Poor Children as the plaintiff was also odd since it was not the typical commercial litigation plaintiff.

The hospital was a medical establishment that had opened its doors in Bloomsbury in 1852.[3] While it was the first specialist hospital for children established in England, its foundation was also a product of a larger social concern around poverty and children's health. This concern coalesced into the perceived social need to provide a specific environment, to where children in need could be moved from their homes or the streets into hospital for care and treatment. In fact, the emergence of children's hospitals in the nineteenth century represented a new concept of childhood, with a special focus on the healthcare of poor and sick children, which coincided with the rise of paediatrics as an autonomous medical specialism.[4]

One of the defining characteristics of Great Ormond Street Hospital was its charitable foundation, as the state had not taken upon itself the role of establishing national or state-funded children's hospitals. This determined that the first decades of the hospital were characterised by a constant struggle for funds. It is well documented that literary celebrities such as Charles Dickens and Henry Morley supported this good cause in their writings and were instrumental in attracting donations to the hospital.[5] While most of the donations were monetary, charitable giving also began to comprise clothes and toys for children who might not otherwise receive a Christmas present. As discussed in Chapter 1, Charles Dodgson had also suggested the donation of rejected printings of *Alice in Wonderland* to sick children as a like-minded charitable act.[6]

2 See, for instance, *Walt Disney Productions v Souvaine Selective Pictures*, 98 F. Supp 774 (SDNY 1951) [USA]; *Walt Disney Productions v H. John Edwards Publishing Co. Pty Ltd* (1954) 71 WN (NSW) [Australia]; *Walt Disney Productions v Morey and Hannah Schwartz and Crockett Enterprises* (1955), [USA] docket 8231 (civil action), NARA, Philadelphia; *Walt Disney-Mickey Mouse Ltd and Willbank Publications Ltd v Lea Bridge Rubber Works* (1938) [UK]; see 'Snow White Copyright injunction sought' *Dundee Evening Telegraph*, 30 November 1938, 7; 'Disney copyright infringed' *Kinematograph Weekly*, 1 December 1938, 5.

3 Kevin Telfer, *The Remarkable Story of Great Ormond Street Hospital*, Simon & Schuster, 2008, 12, 25.

4 Katharina Boehm, *Charles Dickens and the Sciences of Childhood*, Palgrave Macmillan, 2013, 79.

5 Jules Kosky, *Mutual Friends: Charles Dickens and Great Ormond Street Children's Hospital*, Weidenfeld & Nicolson, 1989, 4, 84, 92; Leticia Fernández-Fontecha, 'Little patients: photography and the configuration of the sick child in Victorian Britain' in Jutta Ahlbeck, Päivi Lappalainen, Kati Launis and Kirsi Tuohela (eds.), *Childhood, Literature and Science: Fragile Subjects*, Routledge, 2017, 110–27; 112–3; Elizabeth M.R. Lomax, *Small and Special: The Development of Hospitals for Children in Victorian Britain*, Wellcome Institute for the History of Medicine, 1996, 33; Keir Waddington, *Charity and the London Hospitals, 1850–1898*, Boydell Press, 2000, 42.

6 See Chapter 1, 22, 24; see also the fundraising advertisement for the hospital with photograph of its 'Lewis Carroll Cot' (1905); GOS/14/241; GOSH Archives.

Although campaigns to raise public awareness and resources tended to be organised by the hospital, other donations came from external sources. In 1864, Queen Victoria sent hundreds of toys to children in the hospital and visited them on several occasions.[7] While these acts helped royalty to rehabilitate its public image after some scandals, they also benefited the hospital by raising its profile and attracting new donors. Toy manufacturers and retailers also joined the appeals, linking the sale of some of their products to benevolent ends. From a commercial point of view, the development of campaigns to raise charitable funds worked well as they served to connect their endeavours to the attention and sympathy already generated in the public. These associations were also commercially attractive since such public gestures augmented not only goodwill but also profitability, an aspect that was rapidly understood and recommended by advertising experts.[8] The paradoxical logic of selling commodities to make charitable gifts was perfectly exemplified by Kewpie, a cute cherub-faced character that became so intimately entwined with the support of hospital appeals that a so-called 'Kewpie philosophy' evolved, a term coined by the toy manufacturer to stimulate the desire for those dolls by appealing to the social responsibility underpinning their purchase.[9] The smiling face of the toy was fully protected by copyright and patents, and Kewpies were marketed as an antidote and solution to misfortune and illness because 'anything calculated to develop the milk of human kindness in a tiny heart deserves to succeed'.[10] The prospect of simultaneously meeting and courting a social obligation was also creatively appreciated in England by a toy company mentioned in previous chapters, Dean's Rag Book Co. This company went even further in drawing attention to charitable causes. It launched 'Tatters, the hospital pup', a doll which took the form of a dog in a begging position, with his paws bandaged, which was produced for the purpose of raising funds in aid of hospitals and other charities. The manufacturer committed to giving 12 per cent of receipts from its sales to charitable enterprises, claiming that 'every model of Tatters sold, helps a good cause'.[11] The following year a similar campaign was organised, now with another doll, 'Patient Pat, son of Tatters'.[12]

These schemes benefited from the public attention already mobilised and capitalised on a thirst to act for the betterment of society. While these campaigns

[7] Andrea Tanner, 'The sentimental hard-sell: establishing the idea of the children's hospital in Victorian London' (2004) 116(2) *Mélanges de l'École française de Rome: Italie et Méditerranée* 883–98, 891.

[8] 'Announcing the Kewpie Club' (1931) May *Playthings* 126.

[9] 'King Innovations, Inc.' (1931) August *Playthings* 21; 'What is Kewpie philosophy?' (1932) April *Playthings* 44; 'King Innovations, Inc.' (1932) July *Playthings* 77; 'King Innovations, Inc.' (1932) August *Playthings* 25.

[10] 'Rose O'Neill's soft Kewpies: the national symbol of fun and happiness' (1932) May *Playthings* 44.

[11] 'Tatters, the hospital pup' (1927) September *Games and Toys* 1; 'Tatters' in ibid. 36.

[12] 'Patient Pat' (1928) October *Games and Toys* 1; see also Dawn Cope and Peter Cope, *Dean's Rag Books & Rag Dolls*, New Cavendish Books, 2009, 215.

appealed directly to the public's heart, particularly because of the sentimental message embodied by these commodities, they were something of a double-edged sword, as campaigns of this sort were occasionally criticised as mercenary publicity stunts.[13] Such operations that seemed to take advantage of the unfortunate circumstances of children tended to blunt the public's kindness and generosity, despite the viability of charitable institutions possibly depending on such initiatives. Although we do not want to discuss here the specific caveats and problems associated with those gift-giving operations, and their religious roots connecting virtue and generosity, it is worth noting in passing that there were inherent contradictions.

The most interesting benevolent gesture ever received by a children's hospital came from a childless author, James Barrie. Unlike his predecessors, Barrie did not set up a charitable campaign nor did he depict the hospital sentimentally in his writings. Neither did he offer a percentage of his royalties or accept an invitation to join the hospital committee. Instead, in 1929, he found another way of helping. He assigned the copyright on his *Peter Pan* works to Great Ormond Street Hospital. This was confirmed in his will a few years later.[14] This imaginative gift to help the less fortunate immediately struck a popular chord. What could be a better act of generosity than transmitting such intellectual property to an institution that took care of sick and poor children. As the hospital itself put it, 'Peter Pan has brought already so much pleasure to countless children in health and happiness and in the future, it will be their benefactor also in pain and suffering'.[15] Although the gesture was widely publicised,[16] one of the interesting features of the bequest was the secrecy imposed by Barrie regarding the income generated by *Peter Pan*.[17] The hospital was not allowed to say how much it regularly received from the exploitation of the copyright and understood the bequest to be a form of donation directly connected to its goals and aims. This approach governed the conservative way the hospital handled the gift during the first decades. This view of the property as specially handed on to the charity was part and parcel of the *Peter Pan* gift and became inherent in the hospital's life and the identity of its wards. The gift 'inhabited' Great Ormond Street Hospital to such an extent that many even began to call it the Peter Pan hospital.[18] However, as discussed in greater detail below, it was not assumed that the hospital had any exclusive rights to the name 'Peter Pan'.

In the 1930s, the hospital also joined the trend of creating clubs for children. A Peter Pan League was founded to promote and collect voluntary contributions

[13] 'Announcing the Kewpie Club', above n 8.

[14] The gift was carried out by assignment on 14 August 1929 and was settled by one of the copyright experts of the time, Evan James McGillivray; see 'Instructions to Counsel to settle assignment and to advise'; 7 May 1929; GOS/6/4/2; GOSH Archives.

[15] James McKay, secretary GOSH, to James Barrie, 18 April 1929; GOS/6/4/2; GOSH Archives.

[16] 'Peter Pan: Sir J. Barrie's gift to hospital' *The Times*, 13 April 1929, 13.

[17] Jacqueline Rose, *The Case of Peter Pan or the Impossibility of Children's Fiction*, University of Pennsylvania Press, 1984, 87.

[18] 'Ageless Peter Pan gives gift to kids' *News Herald*, 18 February 1969, 4.

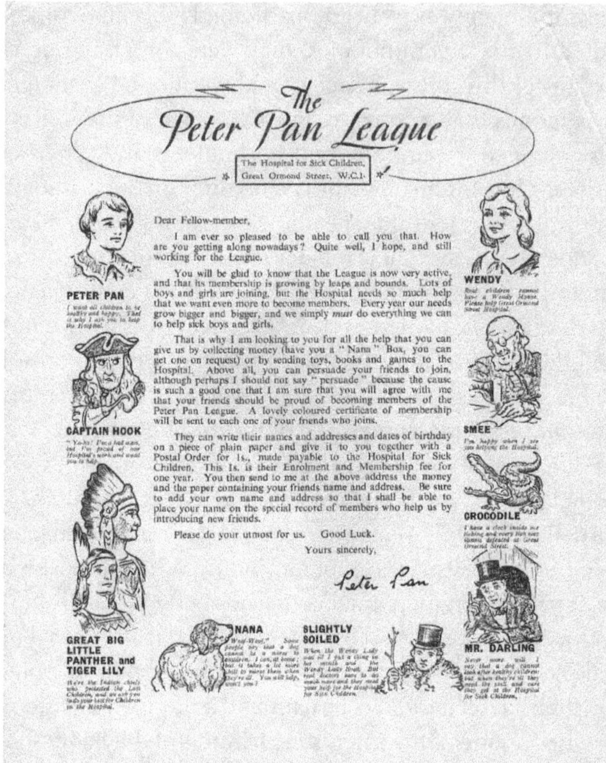

The Peter Pan League

The Hospital for Sick Children,
Great Ormond Street, W.C.1.

Dear Fellow-member,

I am ever so pleased to be able to call you that. How are you getting along nowadays? Quite well, I hope, and still working for the League.

You will be glad to know that the League is now very active, and that its membership is growing by leaps and bounds. Lots of boys and girls are joining, but the Hospital needs so much help that we want even more to become members. Every year our needs grow bigger and bigger, and we simply *must* do everything we can to help sick boys and girls.

That is why I am looking to you for all the help that you can give us by collecting money (have you a "Nana" Box, you can get one on request) or by sending toys, books and games to the Hospital. Above all, you can persuade your friends to join, although perhaps I should not say "persuade" because the cause is such a good one that I am sure that you will agree with me that your friends should be proud of becoming members of the Peter Pan League. A lovely coloured certificate of membership will be sent to each one of your friends who joins.

They can write their names and addresses and dates of birthday on a piece of plain paper and give it to you together with a Postal Order for 1s., made payable to the Hospital for Sick Children. This 1s. is their Enrolment and Membership fee for one year. You then send to me at the above address the money and the paper containing your friends name and address. Be sure to add your own name and address so that I shall be able to place your name on the special record of members who help us by introducing new friends.

Please do your utmost for us. Good Luck.

Yours sincerely,

Peter Pan

FIGURE 5.1 Peter Pan League, 1929
Courtesy of Archive Service, Great Ormond Street Hospital for Children, NHS Foundation Trust

and gifts which were then directly channelled to the fund for the reconstruction of its buildings (see Figure 5.1). Children collected charitable donations in money-collecting boxes with characters from *Peter Pan*, becoming involved in the adventure of helping to fund the hospital's wards and its little patients. The ubiquity of Peter Pan can also be observed in other activities which served to forge connections between patients at the hospital and children outside the hospital. Peter Pan himself was eventually portrayed in the League magazine as one of the patients of the hospital, and the League became a vehicle for fostering friendship among children. In many ways, the gift matched the motto of the hospital: 'the child first and always'.[19] And it helped to spread a note of happiness that inspired 'Peter Pan parties', 'Peter Pan days' and a variety of fundraising events that contributed to the hospital finances.[20] Although Peter Pan, and other characters such as Tinker Bell,

[19] Jules Kosky, *Mutual Friends: Charles Dickens and Great Ormond Street Children's Hospital*, Weidenfeld & Nicolson, 1989, 2; Telfer, above n 3, 31.

[20] Telfer, above n 3, 167.

proved to be valuable companions in the competition for attention and funds, the charitable character of the hospital as a not-for-profit organisation brought with it challenges in relation to the management of the copyright gift.

What did it mean to exploit a copyright gift? What could the hospital make of it? How to navigate the commercial world of licences, translations and adaptations? As Catherine Seville has noted, 'under the terms of the gift the hospital did not have the power to sell the copyright, but had all the powers of an absolute owner, and in particular to grant licences and make contracts for its exploitation'.[21] While all powers were granted, the hospital nevertheless found it problematic to decide on the proper way to exercise them, precisely because of the charitable character of the gift. The nature of the assignment and the bequest presented a puzzle in the shape of the dilemma between exploiting the copyright and at the same time honouring the gift: that is, exercising the rights in a way that it felt would please the donor. This meant that the *Peter Pan* copyright was primarily understood by the hospital in terms of a duty rather than a right. And the immediate consequence of this was that the hospital found it difficult to deal with requests for contracts and licences, particularly when Barrie was still alive. Interestingly, the hospital also felt uneasy when answering requests to sell commodities depicting *Peter Pan* characters. Just a few months after the copyright gift, it received applications for licences to manufacture Peter Pan garments and other products, such as figurines. Although it did not want to turn away efforts which could produce funds for the hospital, the hospital was not sure whether this type of exploitation of the gift was appropriate. It sought guidance from the theatrical agent acting for the hospital, who also found it problematic, but recommended contacting Barrie to see what he thought.[22] Barrie himself had said that the hospital could freely decide these 'trivial things', and the hospital did not want to continue bothering him with the outpouring of correspondence received.[23] From the very beginning, the hospital had been reluctant to go back to Barrie as it felt that pestering him over these matters might make him begin to regret the gift. Moreover, the sense of debt the hospital felt further reinforced its unwillingness to ask his advice, as it feared being seen as ungracious.[24] Yet, the slippery boundary between charitable events and copyright business became increasingly difficult to define. Would permission to use the *Peter Pan* characters or the play contribute to the hospital finances? Should the hospital discriminate among proposals and, if so, on what grounds? What would a suitable royalty rate be? Although the task of assessing requests was challenging, it occasionally required evaluating whether the proposed activities would harm

[21] Catherine Seville, 'Peter Pan rights: to die will be an awfully big adventure' (2003) 51(1) *Journal of the Copyright Society of USA* 1–78, 55.

[22] R. Golding Bright, Elisabeth Marbury Agency, to McKay, GOSH; 16 October 1929; GOS/6/4/6; GOSH Archives.

[23] Barrie to McKay, 20 October 20, 1929; GOS/6/4/6; GOSH Archives.

[24] H.P. Macmillan to Charles J.S. Harper (Waterhouse solicitors), 18 July 1929; GOS/6/4/2; GOSH Archives.

the value of the property and diminish the earning power of the play. It is no surprise that the assessment ended up being a commercial evaluation. But, more interestingly, the commercialisation of several activities stemmed not from the exploitation of copyright but from the equivocations caused by the announcement of the gift: that is, the desire to monetise use was not always a direct consequence of the way the hospital exploited the copyright gift but rather came from those who wanted to use *Peter Pan* and desired to contribute to the hospital's funds. In fact, some enquiries referred to private performances of *Peter Pan* with no charge being made for admissions, and hence presumably no copyright fee due. They nevertheless insisted on paying royalties to the hospital. And they tended to do so with an emotional plea: 'the children themselves are very anxious to pay them as they are for the hospital'.[25]

Ultimately, these endeavours demonstrated that turning copyright into a charitable gift embodied a curious paradox, an aspect that occasionally resurfaced in correspondence received by the hospital. In March 1936, an application for a Romanian translation of *Peter Pan* from a writer 'anxious to get Peter Pan into the hands of Romanian children' was framed as a charitable act, including a request for the relinquishment of any copyright fees.[26] The hospital hesitated but ended up rejecting the application precisely because of the awkward position the hospital was left in after this sort of request. As John Murray, vice chairman of the hospital, said: 'I am not at all sure that we have the right to give up royalties for the sake of charity considering that we are a charity ourselves'.[27] As it was, requests for the 'free rights of *Peter Pan*' or 'freedom from royalties' mushroomed, putting the hospital under pressure in different ways. It was not that some enquiries assumed that the charitable character of the gift meant copyright free but that some others incidentally asked for the proceeds of the activities to go to their own charitable institutions.[28] Although negotiations were often resolved with a modest and symbolic fee paid to the hospital, which always emphasised its obligation to children in need, they tended to show how the management of copyright was often caught up in an unusual scenario. The tension between charity and business prompted by the copyright gift often caused the hospital to take a conservative stance. On the one hand, the hospital considered that the gift was so distinctive to Great Ormond Street that it found requests from other charities to use the *Peter Pan* name in their titles or their appeals discomfiting.[29] As Herbert Rutherford, the house governor and secretary of the hospital stated in reply to one of these requests, the copyright of *Peter Pan* is 'something we guard

[25] Brockman to McKay, 21 July 1930; GOS/6/4/6; GOSH Archives.

[26] J.H. Adeney to Board of Governors, GOSH, 6 March 1936; GOS/6/4/105; GOSH Archives.

[27] John Murray to Rutherford, 13 March 1936; GOS/6/4/105; GOSH Archives.

[28] For instance, Editorial Juventud, the Spanish publisher asked the hospital whether the amount for the Spanish rights could go to a Spanish Children's Hospital; see Editorial Juventud to the Secretary, Great Ormond Street Hospital; 9 February 1932; CLC/B/119/MS16357/001; LMA.

[29] D.S. Crebo to Rutherford, 21 December 1954; GOS/6/4/2; GOSH Archives.

very jealously'.[30] On the other hand, the hospital was also initially reluctant to fully exploit its profitability since it did not seem appropriate. What we can see here is that the delineation of the copyright gift as property was in continuous operation and reassessment, not just from the reception of the gift from Barrie but also in the mundane practices that constituted its management by the hospital.

Given that the external associations potentially generated by the bequest were complicated, the hospital decided to set up a Peter Pan Committee. This administrative strategy gave a bureaucratic dimension to the copyright gift with a view to regularising its dealings and transactions. However, although this strategy incidentally served to provide a more consistent response to different enquiries, such as amateur performances of the play, it also contributed to slowing down those responses. Enquiries were routinely referred to the committee, and the management of the copyright gift became mainly reactive to enquiries rather than proactive in searching for opportunities for exploitation, a point to which we shall return later.

When the deed of the gift was prepared, Barrie recommended that his publisher and the hospital reach an agreement so that *Peter Pan* would continue under the literary imprint of Hodder & Stoughton.[31] One aspect that then came to the surface was that the firm had no agreement in writing with Barrie and had never had one. That is not to say that there was no agreement, only that the way Barrie dealt with this literary copyright had hitherto been informal.[32] In other words, Barrie had the habit of leaving the matter, including the royalty scales, in the hands of the publisher, reserving the right to decide himself on any matters of importance which arose. Indeed, the charitable gift provided the occasion for formalising the business, since it meant that for the first time a publishing agreement for *Peter Pan* was drafted and signed.[33] Here, it is worth noting that the gift triggered a regulatory effect on the expression of the various interests comprised in a copyright. Negotiation between the publisher and the hospital was necessary for the book to match the text with the illustrations, the copyright of which was owned by the publisher.[34] Although the literary copyright agreement was eventually reached as an exclusive licence to print and publish the *Peter Pan* books, the unusual character of the bequest to help sick and poor children also determined the sympathetic way the publisher approached

30 Rutherford to Crebo, 3 January 1955; GOS/6/4/2; GOSH Archives.

31 Percy Hodder Williams to McKay, GOSH, 6 June 1929; GOS/6/4/65; GOSH Archives.

32 Ralph Hodder Williams to Taylor & Humbert, 14 April 1953; J.M. Barrie Collection; Box 20, Folder 648; Beinecke Rare Book & Manuscript Library; Yale University.

33 Agreement for the publication of books known as 'The Peter Pan books' between the Hospital for Sick Children and Hodder & Stoughton Ltd, 22 October 1930 and supplementary agreements dated on 9 December 1930 and 26 April 1933; GOS/6/4/65; GOSH Archives.

34 This negotiation was necessary to continue the publication of *Peter Pan* in Kensington Gardens as the copyright in Arthur Rackham's illustrations had been assigned to the publisher, Hodder & Stoughton; see Andrew Birkin, *J.M. Barrie and the Lost Boys*, Constable, 1979, 147. For a history of the illustrations, see Maria Tatar, 'An introduction to Arthur Rackham's illustrations for Peter Pan in Kensington Gardens' in Maria Tatar (ed.), *The Annotated Peter Pan: The Centennial Edition*, W. W. Norton & Company, 2011, 237–48.

the negotiations. Reflecting on the publishing deal two decades later, the publisher wondered whether doing business with a charitable institution like the hospital had made the property less profitable than it would have been with a literary estate. Even more, the publisher let the hospital know it had given the '*Peter Pan* bequest' special treatment 'as something of a special charge upon us'.[35] The publisher appeared to recognise here that its contract with the hospital was characterised by the obligation arising from the gift – that is, as if the actual power of the charitable gift extended beyond the bequest and shaped the ways copyright was exploited. The gift had a similar effect in relation to other *Peter Pan* books, for instance *The Peter Pan Picture Book* published in 1907 with illustrations by Alice Woodward and a text adapted by Daniel O'Connor from the Barrie play *Peter Pan, or The Boy Who Wouldn't Grow Up*. The contract for the book was drafted and signed only after the bequest.[36]

Theatrical matters were most important for the hospital, as the performing rights attached to *Peter Pan* constituted a significant part of the bequest. The mode of governance that the hospital initially established for dramatic rights followed the same pattern as book rights: namely, granting an exclusive licence to the company that had already handled this side of the property before the copyright gift was assigned to the hospital. In the early 1930s, the hospital arranged an exclusive licence with Daniel Mayer Co. to produce the play on the stage. The relationship lasted for three decades, and, even though it appeared straightforward at first glance, it became muddled at times because of the intangible nature of the rights. That is to say, the distinction between play and book did not match the distinction between publishing and dramatic rights. Put another way, the sole and exclusive publisher appointed by the hospital, Hodder & Stoughton, had rights in all *Peter Pan* books, not only the story but also the play when it was printed. Nevertheless, the issues that occupied the Peter Pan Committee for decades were not only new arrangements or contracts but also identifying copyrights that the gift did not cover – for instance, the copyright or design rights in *Peter Pan* costumes or the copyright of the statue of *Peter Pan* in Kensington Gardens.[37] The reason the hospital wanted to throw light on these issues was not the desire to acquire those copyrights or engage in new contractual relations. Rather, these questions often concerned the hospital because some enquiries specifically referred to these matters. For instance, there was interest in producing dolls which were 'an exact replica of the various characters in the play, dressed as they are in the play'.[38] As we have seen, the administrative strategy taken by the hospital looked not only to reduce the complexity of handling the copyright gift but also to honour the wishes of the donor, James Barrie. However, the way those exclusive relations were initially structured and relayed to third parties was often

35 Ralph Hodder Williams to Rutherford, 26 January 1950; GOS/6/4/65; GOSH Archives.

36 A.W. Ready, George Bell & Sons to Ralph Hodder Williams, 15 August 1949; CLC/B/119/MS16352/001/002; LMA.

37 McKay to Butler, Charles Frohman Inc., 18 March 1931; GOS/6/4/2; GOSH Archives.

38 MacLeod to Rutherford, 8 July 1948; GOS/6/4/2; GOSH Archives.

FIGURE 5.2 Peter Pan window display at W. H. Smith & Son, Weston-super-Mare, 1953
Courtesy of Archive Service, Great Ormond Street Hospital for Children, NHS Foundation Trust

also caught up in the tension between charity and business. While the attempt to keep these balls simultaneously in the air was very successful, negotiations with third parties and new licensees raised some complexities.

The unique character of the copyright gift also troubled some prospective licensees and users who wondered about the role of the exclusive commercial enterprises that came into the picture to handle the copyright.[39] Furthermore, as the hospital routinely asked for the bequest to be publicised with the work, on its dust cover, title

[39] MacLeod to Rutherford, 2 March 1956; GOS/6/4/2; GOSH Archives.

verso, or any other embodiment of the play or the book, such an undertaking was held to be impracticable on certain media, particularly by those prospective licensees and users who kept charity and business in distinct compartments. For instance, an attempt to broadcast the play during the *Children's Hour* radio programme failed because of the limited airtime the British Broadcasting Corporation gave to charitable appeals and the policy of the corporation to offer a fair share of microphone time to each cause in their own prearranged programmes for charitable appeals.[40]

Although the management of the copyright gift for the play and the book was streamlined by the exclusive contracts, ancillary opportunities for exploitation gradually emerged. The hospital received an increasing number of requests not only for literary and theatrical projects but also for different media. Interestingly, the exclusive parties already enrolled, especially from the theatrical side, did not appear to be very supportive of 'allowing *Peter Pan* to be exploited in the mechanical field' (i.e. film, television and broadcasting).[41] These communication mediums could impact on the value of the theatrical goodwill and box office. Despite these reservations, the hospital began to entertain some of these possibilities, feeling justified in doing so for a number of reasons. First, these activities did not seem to contradict the logic of the gift as Barrie himself had already tried other modes of exploitation of *Peter Pan*: for instance, as a film, before his benefaction. Second, these forays clearly constituted new ways of bringing more regular funds to the hospital.[42] In the early 1930s the hospital had also appointed the same agents that had worked previously with Barrie. Leaving the direct exploitation of copyright in the hands of external trusted agents seemed then an appropriate way of handling the copyright gift. However, the hospital still viewed the copyright gift more as an obligation and a duty than a right.

Although the film agent was not very successful, almost a decade later, the hospital received an enquiry from Walt Disney Productions Ltd (US), for an exclusive licence covering the 'world animated sound cartoon rights in *Peter Pan*'.[43] The most significant obstacle to this agreement was the pre-existing contract Barrie had agreed for a silent film with Paramount, which could have stood in the way of the new contract. Although it was possible to ascertain the distinct nature of the rights transacted, cartoon and film, Disney wanted to avoid any potential risk before investing in *Peter Pan*. As a result, the hospital asked Paramount to facilitate the arrangement between

[40] Hamilton Marr, BBC, to the Secretary, GOSH, 7 December 1940; GOS/6/4/25; GOSH Archives.

[41] MacLeod to Rutherford, 26 September 1956; GOS/6/4/35; GOSH Archives.

[42] In 1924, a *Peter Pan* silent film was produced by Paramount after the producer acquired the rights granted by Barrie to a company called Famous Players Film Co.; see Agreement made between Barrie and Famous Players Film Co. Ltd, 19 August 1919; GOS/6/4/2; GOSH Archives.

[43] Rutherford to Walt Disney Productions, 2 February 1938; 'Board of Governors of the Hospital for Sick Children v Walt Disney; General Correspondence'; GOS/6/4/137; GOSH Archives.

Disney and the hospital and to 'bear the hospital's mind'. That is, 'not overlook the hospital's interest, which though commercial in one aspect, is one quite different in character in as much as we are a charity dealing with the welfare of the younger members of the community'.[44] This apparent complication was sorted out, but Disney lowered the amount of money offered. In any case, the hospital, as was its usual practice, insisted on inserting a preface in the cartoon to the effect that the copyright of *Peter Pan* was a gift to the Hospital for Sick Children and it reached an agreement with Walt Disney Enterprises for a modest sum.[45]

Another interesting aspect around the charitable nature of the *Peter Pan* copyright gift became apparent with the passage of the National Health Service Act in 1946. As the hospital was incorporated into the National Health Service (NHS), it was possible that the gift would become public or state property. This specific concern was exacerbated by an audit to which the hospital was subjected just a few years after the establishment of the NHS. In conversations with the auditor, the hospital became increasingly concerned that the gift could fall under the control of the Ministry of Health, entailing not only the loss of exclusive control of the property but also the loss of a considerable amount of money, which the hospital had been using for research and other purposes. This fear prompted the hospital to seek legal advice on how to persuade the ministry of the special nature of the gift.[46] It did so by shifting from the traditional view the hospital had adopted towards the copyright gift as an endowment to considering the copyright as a personal property held on trust for the specific charitable purposes of the hospital.[47] By changing the image of copyright, the hospital was able to defend the gift against the interpretation of the auditor. However, the impasse and reflexivity generated by the auditing exercise also had other consequences. For instance, it cemented the perception of the property as an asset, namely the notion that the copyright gift constituted a stream of revenue that required active engagement.[48] The review also made the hospital aware of the need to develop a closer and more systematic approach to the management of the copyright gift. A couple of years after the audit, the need to tidy up the administration of the copyright gift was recognised by Herbert Rutherford, the house

44 Rutherford to Paramount Pictures Ltd, 19 June 1938; 'General Correspondence' ibid.

45 Agreement between the hospital and Walt Disney Enterprises, 11 January 1939; GOS/6/4/137; GOSH Archives. One of the problems that would arise later in the litigation was whether the organisational changes in Disney meant that the contracts and obligations from Disney Enterprises were assumed by Walt Disney Productions. This was further complicated because, as we have highlighted in Chapter 4, Disney Enterprises was composed of different subsidiaries such as Walt Disney-Mickey Mouse Ltd, a company operating in London which was incorporated in 1931 and dissolved in 1966.

46 Rutherford to Winterbotham, 21 January 1950; GOS/6/4/104; GOSH Archives.

47 Winterbotham to Rutherford, 24 January 1950; GOS/6/4/104; GOSH Archives.

48 As Gordon Piller observed, 'the Ministry of Health became responsible for the running costs of the hospital, but the Board of Governors was permitted to retain and hold its own endowment funds'; Gordon J. Piller, 'The Story of the Hospital for Sick Children (1965)', 6; GOS/14/249; GOSH Archives.

governor and secretary of the hospital, because, as he said, 'things have, and partly I feel due to my own shortcomings, been *dealt with a little irregularly*'.[49] Here the regular norm of exploitation was arguably informed by a perception of commercial practice between private actors, ignoring, on the one hand, the special commercial identity of an NHS hospital and, on the other, the history of the bequest.

5.2 THE DISNEY TOUCH

For several reasons, it took Disney almost two decades to produce its own version of *Peter Pan*. Production was delayed mainly by the advent of World War II, but also by the prioritisation of other projects such as the making of *Pinocchio*. However, negotiations with the hospital in the late 1930s had already highlighted what the corporation wanted in return for its investment in *Peter Pan*. Disney's first concern when negotiating with the hospital was the potential for competition that could emerge with the exploitation of *Peter Pan*. Disney successfully introduced two provisions to shield its cartoon against competition in film and theatres. First, it introduced a ten-year restrictive covenant by which no other motion picture could be released in theatres in opposition to its version of *Peter Pan*. Second, it inserted a clause suspending the traditional annual performance of the *Peter Pan* play in the year of the Disney movie premiere. Here, we can see that Disney instituted a powerful strategic manoeuvre which had the combined effect of acquiring certain rights while blocking others. In other words, Disney enhanced its capacity to operate across media, even though it had not acquired rights in other media directly. These safeguards could be viewed as operations to capitalise on the amount of interest generated by the release of *Peter Pan*. But it is also possible to see them as intimately connected to the development of merchandising practices. In previous chapters, we have observed how Disney evolved the practice of exploiting characters through merchandise. These merchandising forays became more attractive to prospective licensees, such as toy manufacturers and retailers, when Disney blocked the possibility of competition from the rights owner: that is, when the Disney version of *Peter Pan* had already been secured as the one most likely to attract interest across media in the market.

Although initially the hospital did not pay much attention to these demands, the effect of these contractual strategies employed by Disney had already been highlighted in another negotiation that took place at around the same time that *Peter Pan* was being discussed with the hospital. In the early 1940s, Disney had also approached Helen Bannerman and her publisher to negotiate the rights of her racially problematic *The Story of Little Black Sambo*.[50] However, solicitors for

[49] Rutherford to Curtis Brown, 24 November 1952; CLC/B/119/MS16352/001/002; LMA (our emphasis).

[50] The commercialisation and merchandising efforts attached to Golliwogg-themed texts are briefly discussed in Chapter 2 at 47–8.

Bannerman and her publisher warned of the consequences that could be unleashed by clauses which would have given Disney 'far greater power than they need for the reasonable exploitation of their film'.[51] Interestingly, this contractual anomaly was deemed to be derived from the effect of the interplay between the clauses – a characteristic that, as the solicitor noted, 'seldom appear[s] in any film contract'.[52] The problem was not just the issue of giving so much promotional room for Disney to exploit, the real dilemma was the potential impact these operations could have on the original version. The legal advice was not to follow up with the negotiations with Disney because they 'put the original in serious danger'.[53] What was at stake here was the establishment of a privileged connection with children as audiences or consumers. To further illustrate this point, Bannerman's solicitor gave the example of the recent exploitation of *Snow White*, where a variety of small booklets published by Disney with its drawings were so successful that they superseded other versions. More significantly, the solicitor connected this strategy to the timely House of Lords decision of *King Features Syndicate, Inc. and Betts v O.&M. Kleeman Ltd*,[54] which, according to him, extended the right to continue selling merchandise as long as it did not infringe the copyright in the book.[55] That is, it allowed the Disney copyright to extend beyond the specific contracts for rights (i.e. publishing, cartoon or otherwise) that Disney had signed for the production and distribution of its cartoons.

Although the hospital did not realise the extent of this contractual anomaly when negotiating with Disney in the late 1930s, perhaps enthused by the Hollywood interest in *Peter Pan*, it is true that it did not sign the contract straight away. The delay was possibly because the agreement had yet to be ratified by the internal bureaucratic body through which the hospital managed and formalised the exploitation of the copyright gift, the Peter Pan Committee. This was then followed by a moment in which the negotiations were in danger of falling through because of Disney's insistence on securing merchandising rights.

In November 1938, the hospital withdrew its acceptance of the offer, preoccupied that it could not grant any merchandising rights. Interestingly, it was not that the hospital wanted to reserve them. Rather, the retraction was due to the belief that Disney was asking for something the hospital had never owned. In fact, the hospital had always considered that there was no copyright in the *Peter Pan* name, an aspect mentioned by Barrie himself when the assignment of the copyright gift was formalised. Moreover, the hospital assumed that being a charity forbade it from

51 Raymond (Chatto & Windus) to Medley (Field Roscoe solicitors), 15 July 1941; Correspondence, contracts and press cuttings relating to the works of Helen Bannerman; Add MS 88987/2/5; BL.

52 Ibid.

53 Medley (Field Roscoe solicitors) to Raymond (Chatto & Windus) 30 July 1941, 'Correspondence, contracts and press cuttings', above n 51.

54 [1941] AC 417, [1941] 2 All ER 403.

55 F.A.S. Gwatkin, McKenna & Co to Chatto & Windus, 29 October 1941, in 'Correspondence, contracts and press cuttings', above n 51.

manufacturing commodities or selling merchandising licences. This could also explain why the hospital had assumed that the name *Peter Pan* could be used commercially by traders. There were already several companies that used the name *Peter Pan* to sell their commodities even before the copyright gift. For instance, Cecil Coleman Ltd was a well-known London company which had been successfully making toys for children, labelled as 'Peter Pan', since the mid-1920s. Ironically, the most famous toy in that range was the Peter Pan store, a miniature shop with a cash register and exact miniatures of well-known brands of food and provisions such as Bovril, Oxo, Ovaltine, biscuit tins, OK sauce, Nestle's, Fry's Cocoa and other brands known to children.[56] Similarly, another company in Wolverhampton had been selling well-known juvenile bicycles and tricycles under the label 'Peter Pan' for decades before the negotiations between Disney and the hospital.[57] In sum, the mere existence of companies using the Peter Pan name to sell their commodities reinforced the hospital's assumption that it was not in a position to offer merchandising rights to Disney.

However, Disney refused to accept the hospital's attempt to withdraw from negotiations. Instead, the company argued that the hospital did not have the right, 'either legally or morally',[58] to abandon the deal since an understanding of agreement had already been reached by the parties. It is remarkable how quickly Disney acquiesced on several points primarily aimed at persuading the Peter Pan Committee to sign the agreement. The main obstacle was overcome by agreeing that the premiere of the *Peter Pan* cartoon would become a fundraising event for the hospital. This was not a problem for Disney, as charitable events could well elicit popular goodwill, especially when organised by Disney. Both Disney and the hospital would benefit from dedicating the premiere to the good cause of raising funds for the poor and sick children of the hospital. Regarding merchandising rights, the contract left them in a curious half-way position, assuming that the copyright held by the hospital and the merchandising operations proposed by Disney were not mutually incompatible. On the one hand, the hospital was to receive a percentage on the business carried out by Disney, and all merchandise would feature a statement to the effect that in purchasing the item the buyer would be helping the hospital. On the other hand, the specifics of Disney commercialisation practices were to be subsequently negotiated to distinguish them from other rights the hospital had already granted, mainly publishing rights. This meant that Disney ended up

[56] 'Peter Pan stores' (1926) September *Games and Toys* 70; 'Peter Pan stores' (1926) November *Games and Toys* 3; 'Peter Pan stores' (1927) February *Games and Toys* 5; 'Cecil Coleman Ltd' (1927) March *Games and Toys* 4.

[57] 'Peter Pan cycles' (1921) February *Toy and Fancy Goods Trader* 186; 'Peter Pan Cycles' (1921) June *Toy and Fancy Goods Trader* 94; 'Peter Pan toys' (1926) May *Games and Toys* 70; 'Peter Pan toys' (1927) August *Games and Toys* 66; 'Peter Pan products' (1928) August *Games and Toys* 62.

[58] McKenna & Co. to Winterbotham, 28 November 1938; 'General Correspondence', above n 43.

negotiating the publication of Disney books with Hodder & Stoughton. Again, this solution was no impediment at all for Disney. It was just the opposite, in fact, as it meant that its *Peter Pan* merchandising projects would be incorporated into specific contractual agreements. More specifically, the contract with Hodder & Stoughton helped to reduce the objections of the hospital to merchandising and, at the same time, allowed Disney to forge a crucial alliance and thus further develop the network of licences so fundamental to its operations.

As Chapter 4 showed, the enactment of a commercial infrastructure with licensees continued throughout the 1940s, albeit in a more refined manner. Just after World War II, the British subsidiary of Disney Enterprises, Walt Disney-Mickey Mouse Ltd, organised a luncheon mainly for Disney licensees, to announce two studio projects: *Alice in Wonderland* and *Peter Pan*.[59] This use of hospitality typically underpinned all Disney projects. The development of a system of licences depended upon a combination of public relations and a communication circuit that built up Disney's reputation among licensees and children as a reliable and trusted source. These qualities were promoted as hallmarks of the Disney brand fostered in Disney's main publications – the merchandising catalogue, *Mickey News*, *Mickey Mouse Annuals* and other bulletins that constantly nurtured this connection.[60] Other distinct communication relays, characteristic of the decade, were also employed, for instance, 'Disneygrams'.[61] Thus, Disney properties became valuable due to the commercial expectations the circuit generated. The children's parties and licensee luncheons, the parades and private gatherings, the previews and reviews, the advance information about forthcoming cartoons or the information about their success were all important mechanisms for establishing a network in which not only was everybody – traders, parents and children – informed about plans and features but also felt included. When we referred to 'animated properties' in Chapter 4, we were highlighting this feature that combined the central content with its promotional values and served to draw adults and children into helping to make these properties 'walk and talk'.[62] In other words, participation and reporting constituted a form of credit, a tactic rapidly understood by the corporation as it went about setting up a communication circuit among traders, parents and children. For there was no better way to augment goodwill than to build a business of hospitality and familiarity which enabled connected parties to participate and join in the success of its projects.

As Disney continued to announce its plans during the 1940s, the type of *Peter Pan* enquiries received by the hospital gradually evolved. In May 1944, a well-known

59 'My log' (1946) September *Games and Toys* 51–2.

60 See Chapter 4 at 141.

61 'Disneygrams' were a particular method for communicating commercial information to current and prospective licensees; see, for instance, Leggatt to Taylor, Disney, Mickey Mouse Ltd, 17 March 1953; CLC/B/119/MS16375/001; LMA.

62 Edward J. Davis, 'The Disney touch' (1948) August *Games and Toys* 104–5.

Scottish stationery company, Valentine & Sons, asked the hospital about the availability of 'greeting card rights' to *Peter Pan*. But, when the hospital replied in its usual fashion, inviting the company to send its proposal to the hospital for consideration by the Peter Pan Committee, the card manufacturer indicated that its interest was specifically regarding the characters from the *Peter Pan* film Disney had announced. Here, we can observe the normative effect of the communication circuit set up by Disney to motivate and instigate linkages. Although the cartoon had not yet been produced, and it would be almost a decade before its release, interest in the property had already been generated by announcements released by Disney.[63] The hospital replied that the copyright in the Disney characters would be owned by Disney, an answer that the card manufacturer had already anticipated since it had already come to an arrangement with Disney. However, the card manufacturer left an awkward comment when closing its correspondence with the hospital, explaining that the reason why the company had felt compelled to contact the hospital was that 'we were not quite sure how we were placed with you'.[64]

Presumably because the earlier negotiations between Disney and the hospital had been rushed to prevent the hospital withdrawing from the process, the contract had left several loose ends. This affected both merchandising rights and the nature of the rights actually transacted. The main concern was whether the rights acquired by Disney were for animated cartoons or films. As a result, the parties were left in an odd position, with different views about what they had agreed. This is not particularly surprising and should not have caused a major contractual obstacle. It is often the case that parties adjust their interpretation as their relationship evolves. But, at this precise moment, clarifying this issue was crucial for Disney because the studio had shifted its plans from the production of cartoons to feature films or to a combination of cartoons and live action pictures. Disney was already aware of how convoluted the interpretation of the contract with the hospital could be, so it tried to clear up any doubts about the agreement a few years after its signing. During the summer of 1945, Disney wrote to the hospital again to straighten out what it perceived as the problems of the original contract. Curiously, Disney proposed a bespoke new offer to the hospital: a small monetary contribution to the hospital from the company and, in exchange, a gesture from the hospital such as the naming of a room for Walt and decorating it with Disney characters. When the hospital received this new proposal, it replied in its conventional way. The proposal would be put up for consideration by the Peter Pan Committee, scheduled to meet in October of the same year. Anxious to settle the matter more quickly and disconcerted by this delay, Disney tried to force the matter, contacting the committee members prior to the

63 A similar enquiry came from publisher Abril in Buenos Aires, interested in acquiring the rights from the hospital to publish the books 'illustrated with the drawings taken from the picture which Walt Disney will produce in the near future'; see Pablo Terni to the Hospital for Sick Children, 2 July 1947; CLC/B/119/MS16357/001; LMA.

64 Valentine & Sons to Rutherford, 24 July 1944; GOS/6/4/12; GOSH Archives.

scheduled meeting. Unfortunately for Disney, nothing came of this attempt to 'clarify' the rights transacted. Not only was the proposal rejected, but the rejection letter caused additional trouble because the hospital's response was that it could not grant film rights to Disney, something that Disney argued it already owned.[65] This divergence in understanding between the charity and the commercial enterprise was reflected not only by the different way they viewed their agreement but also in their different tempos and manners of communication, interpretation and negotiation, which contributed substantially to their frequent misunderstandings and frustrations. In the following years, while work, treatment and 'audience research' tests were performed at the Hollywood studio,[66] Disney insisted on continuing with the attempt to persuade the hospital to reconsider this new offer. However, the hospital did not respond to the three or four letters sent by Disney. This was perhaps due to concern at the way Disney was interpreting the original agreement and pushing for a new version based solely on Disney's interpretation of its legal entitlements.

The disagreement between the hospital and Disney in determining the rights did not derive only from differing interpretations of the agreement, but it was also exacerbated by the way a distinction was drawn between rights and intangible property. Disney tended to separate the characters as a form of intangible property from the media in which they were to appear, such as cartoon or film. This 'emancipation', which was a requirement for merchandising to flourish, was an effect of the contractual arrangements and the distinct practices Disney had developed, for instance, promotional strategies which often advertised characters separately from the media.[67] The ongoing separability of characters from their original media can be seen in the examples mentioned in Chapter 4, which continued in the 1940s. We would like to pay closer attention to one of these technologies of consumption, the merchandising catalogue, as it acquired even greater relevance with the shift from animated shorts to full feature films that Disney initiated with *Snow White and the Seven Dwarfs*. The merchandise book provided an index or a kind of ledger for products bearing Disney characters, and hence a pool of ideas or 'angles' on things that had been done or could be done with them. While this facilitated the turning of characters into 'units' and 'properties' that could be transacted, it also profusely illustrated the range of commodities already licensed, which often run from nursery to teenage-oriented products.[68] Despite having several pages in colour and being a costly publishing endeavour, it is

[65] Rutherford to Levy, 19 November 1945, 'General Correspondence', above n 43.
[66] While the work had begun before the agreement with the hospital, a final treatment was achieved in March 1946; see Robin Allan, *Walt Disney in Europe*, John Libbey & Co., 1999, 219.
[67] This can be seen in the way Disney described *Mickey's News* as a 'bulletin for all who are interested in the application of Walt Disney characters to merchandise' (1953) *Mickey's News* 2; CLC/B/119/MS16375/002; LMA.
[68] 'Catalogue illustré' (1954) 1 *Le Journal de Mickey* 1; CLC/B/119/MS16375/002; LMA.

interesting that the catalogue was given away free to children, manufacturers and retailers. It was important that the catalogue circulate as widely as possible for it to function both as a kind of forecast for the cartoon or film and as a reference point for purchases, providing contact details for manufacturers to apply for further licences and wholesalers, retailers, or even children to enquire about products. While the special address to children and child-related entrepreneurs came together in the catalogue, the publication was another example of the logic of togetherness underpinning Disney as a business, characterised by an overall thrust to publicise achievements to attract newcomers to the Disney family. In a sense, it is not far-fetched to suggest that Disney, in so far as it created a 'system' to issue licences, became a sort of privately regulated intellectual property 'office', as licences were applied, examined, negotiated, granted and announced through these channels.

In the early months of 1953, the Peter Pan merchandising catalogue began to circulate among prospective licensees and interested parties. The publication was first given away at early showings of the animated feature that Disney had arranged in advance of its premiere scheduled for the spring. Interestingly, the catalogue included an acknowledgment of the Hospital for Sick Children together with images of merchandised products and hooks to 'attract family trade', illustrating what Disney described as 'the tremendous exploitation scope' of *Peter Pan*.[69] This publication, which was reissued several times throughout the year to incorporate new licences and products, was expected to produce several effects once it was disseminated. As one of the Disney employees told a licensee, 'we will be mailing these to a considerable number of store buyers, trade papers and others interested in this merchandise, and we hope they will help you materially in increasing your sales of lines based on both Peter Pan and other Disney characters'.[70] This incorporation in the catalogue did not arise solely from a Disney request but also because the licensees themselves were very interested in getting their products listed and photographed. They were able to achieve this advance release and coordinated circulation due to another key operation Disney developed over time, which constituted an important service to make licences even more attractive. Disney provided reference sheets to prospective users and invited them to come to their showroom in London to see replicas of the figurines used in Hollywood to produce the animated feature. The temporal logic of the enterprise was that the advance material Disney provided enabled manufacturers and retailers to prepare, copy and transfer the characters to their products. In other words, they were given the benefit of planning and aligning their commodities to the days on which the animated feature was going to be exhibited. It also allowed them to coordinate the release of publications 'at planned intervals' to coincide with film exhibitions, reissues or the Christmas season.[71] All

[69] Disney – Peter Pan Merchandising catalogue, 1953; 11; CLC/B/119/MS16375/001; LMA.
[70] Tuckwell to Hodder Williams, 31 August 1953; CLC/B/119/MS16357/001; LMA.
[71] 'Memorandum Hodder and Stoughton', 20 April 1953; CLC/B/119/MS16357/001; LMA.

these were examples of the productive use of information and exposure to capitalise and make the most of the property. And this attempt to synchronise commodities, film exhibitions and seasons was a frequent phenomenon, as Disney constantly advanced information about the playdates of *Peter Pan* for those firms in England who wanted to keep pace with the 'vastly accelerated tempo of the rest of the Disney Enterprises'.[72] Interestingly, one of the licensed manufacturers announced in the catalogue was Cecil Coleman Ltd, a company that had been selling Peter Pan toys for decades. The toy company was now enrolled by Disney to produce new lines featuring Disney's 'Peter Pan' and other Disney characters.[73] That this company, among others, became one of the Peter Pan licensees illustrates the large appeal and the practical convenience that the Disney programme offered toy manufacturers and retailers.

Disney's *Peter Pan* had its European premiere in London at the Leicester Square Theatre on 16 April 1953.[74] The studio had finally gone ahead with a Technicolor all-cartoon feature. In an article published in the *Radio Times*, Walt Disney justified the changes introduced in the play by reference to this method.[75] Although the personalised article casting Walt Disney as the author of the cartoon was a typical strategy used by the corporation to give a personal touch to a mass-produced feature, it also served to anticipate and respond to the predicted criticism the cartoon was sure to generate, an aspect the corporation was fully aware of in light of the *Peter Pan* audience research tests and criticism of its adaptation of *Alice in Wonderland* a few years earlier. However, despite such criticisms, Disney's method of producing a cartoon adaptation appeared to solve the divergent interpretation of the original contract between the hospital and Disney in 1939. As Disney had decided to make a cartoon, the hospital assumed that its interpretation of the contract had prevailed. That is, that Disney finally understood that it had only acquired rights for an animated cartoon.

Although the misunderstanding about the contract was thought to be solved, the sticking point of merchandising rights still lurked in the background. As some commentators have noted, the creative ways in which Disney had developed these rights took 'a quantum leap forward with Peter Pan'.[76] In relation to their potential scope, Ed J. Davis, managing director of Disney's London offices, exuberantly claimed 'the sky is the limit!'.[77] Less enthused, the hospital tried to impose a limit

72 Edward J. Davis, 'My American month' (1955) April *Games and Toys* 136.

73 'Cecil Coleman Ltd' (1953) *Mickey's News* 1; see also 'Peter Pan catalogue' (1953) May *Games and Toys* 122.

74 'Walt Disney's greatest! A new achievement in all cartoon entertainment! Walt Disney's Peter Pan. Leicester Square Theatre' *Mickey Mouse Weekly*, 18 April 1953, 12; '1953 is Disney Year: Peter Pan for Easter' (1953) *Mickey's News* 1, above n 67.

75 Walt Disney, 'Why and how I made Peter Pan' *Radio Times*, 12 April 1953, 5.

76 Susan Ohmer, 'Disney's Peter Pan: gender, fantasy, and industrial production' in Allison B. Kavey and Lester D. Friedman (eds.), *Second Star to the Right: Peter Pan in the Popular Imagination*, Rutgers University Press, 2009, 151–87, 180.

77 Davis, above n 72.

FIGURE 5.3 Leicester Square Theatre showing Walt Disney's *Peter Pan*, 1953
Courtesy of Westminster City Archives, A15A7891

on these rights just before the release of the Disney cartoon. In January 1953, an appendix to the original agreement between the hospital and Disney was signed to draw a distinction between merchandising and publishing. The hospital was troubled to see Disney had merchandised commodities such as *Peter Pan* colouring-in books, cut-out books and scrap books impinging upon the hospital's publishing rights and hence the copyright gift. By means of this new appendix, the hospital gave an 'additional right' to Disney so that the corporation could pursue its merchandising programme.[78] But this new right was subject to the important condition that these publications be negotiated with those exclusive licences the hospital had already reached, mainly the one with Hodder & Stoughton. Thus, the hospital sought to sidestep the problem in the hope that a solution would be negotiated between Disney and Hodder & Stoughton. In return, Disney agreed to give the hospital a royalty percentage of the proceeds arising from the publications based upon its cartoon, as agreed and cleared with Hodder & Stoughton. While the compromise between the hospital and Disney seemed clear, it is again worth noting the conservative stance adopted by the hospital when considering these

[78] H.F. Rutherford and Roy Disney, appendix to the agreement, accepted and signed, 7 January 1953; CLC/B/119/MS16375/002; LMA.

merchandising practices. As the hospital was primarily concerned with the ways in which these practices cut across pre-existing arrangements, it did not see them as opportunities. Rather it saw them as conflicting with contracts already reached with other parties. For that reason, the hospital also stated that it was not expecting any royalty from the remainder of merchandising operations carried out by Disney. Interestingly, the lack of enthusiasm showed by the hospital towards Disney's operations was in sharp contrast to the interest they elicited on the part of the main publisher of *Peter Pan*, Hodder & Stoughton.

Instead of seeing Disney proposals as encroachment on its rights, the publisher was delighted to connect these rights with the American corporation, as it saw them as great opportunities to stimulate its own business. For that reason, Hodder & Stoughton requested that the hospital extend its contractual relationship so it could exploit the subsidiary rights of the copyright gift.[79] A new rider to the contract was drafted for the licence to operate as a right so the publisher could engage in different methods of reproduction and adaptation of the book. In doing so, Hodder & Stoughton could also benefit from the attractive scheme set up by Disney, linking up its publications with the release of the animated version of *Peter Pan*. As a result, Disney arranged a licence with Hodder & Stoughton, who prepared and sent 'dummy' advance copies of Walt Disney *Peter Pan* books for approval and incorporation in the merchandising catalogue so that it could match its orders to the forthcoming playdates circulated by Disney.[80] A curious situation arose from this lucrative cooperation, as it prompted the main publisher of *Peter Pan*, Hodder & Stoughton, to become, at the same time, a licensee for the hospital and a Disney licensee. This was an awkward dual position that was increasingly difficult to sustain when the legal conflict between the hospital and the corporation escalated. However, it is true that for almost a decade this position alleviated tensions between the hospital and Disney. This can be seen in the way the publisher described its impression of the ways the Disney cartoon was affecting Peter Pan. According to the publisher, the Disney version had not harmed *Peter Pan* and was in fact advantageous to its publishing endeavours. Therefore, the hospital did not worry about possible encroachments on its rights.

The release of the Disney cartoon not only affected the publication of *Peter Pan* as a book but it also touched upon another important dimension: its performance as a play. As we have seen, Disney initially tried to freeze the traditional *Peter Pan* annual performance in the year of its cartoon premiere, a suggestion that was quickly discounted by the hospital when negotiating its agreement in 1939. Yet

79 In fact, Ralph Hodder Williams was one of the most active members of the Publishers Association, which formed a 'Subsidiary Rights Committee' to establish the interest of publishers to share in the proceeds from subsidiary rights such as film, broadcasting and television; see 'Subsidiary Rights'; Council Meeting Minutes, The Publishers Association, 19 October 1939; Publishers Association Archives.

80 'Disney film programme' (1953) August *Games and Toys* 62.

the release of Disney's cartoon sparked several requests which indirectly impinged upon the performance space traditionally occupied by *Peter Pan*. Perhaps the most interesting of these activities was the request for 'ice shows', a form of family entertainment that had emerged in the 1930s, becoming increasingly popular over the following decades.[81] While this popular spectacle echoed the parades mentioned in Chapter 4, the opportunity for these shows came directly from the frenzy generated by the Disney release. Again, it is possible to view these activities as part and parcel of Disney's customary strategy, which separated characters from their original context and exploited them across a variety of other media. But, more importantly, the request for 'ice show' rights precipitated a scenario similar to the one highlighted above – that is, a new set of coordinates for the consideration of the long-standing agreements and ties the hospital had with licensees. Here, the relationship affected was not with Hodder & Stoughton but with Daniel Mayer Co. Ltd, a theatrical producer that had been the holder of the exclusive licence to produce and represent the play in the United Kingdom since 1929.

The 'ice show' option presented by Disney was very attractive because the corporation offered an equal division between itself and the hospital. This would obviously amount to a substantial sum, which hospital managers felt they did 'not lightly wish to turn away'.[82] So tempting was the offer that the hospital sought advice about the propriety of granting licences to produce *Peter Pan on Ice*.[83] The resulting legal opinion on 'ice rights' was written in 1954 by Guy Aldous QC, a successful intellectual property barrister who would become the editor of a standard treatise on the law of patents.[84] Aldous gave his advice on the meaning to be given to a particular contractual term ('the regular speaking stage') included in the theatrical licence between the hospital and Daniel Mayer Co. Ltd and concluded that the hospital was free to license these shows, as ice rinks did not constitute a typical 'stage' for plays.[85] Predictably, Daniel Mayer Co. not only disagreed with the hospital about its way of handling the rights but was also disappointed that the hospital had entertained the possibility of 'ice shows' without bringing the theatre company into the conversation. In other words, the licensee felt neglected, and this disrupted and diminished the privileged connection it had thought it had with the play and with the hospital. Daniel Mayer Co. highlighted the special way in which it had exercised its obligations regarding the *Peter Pan* copyright gift. According to Daniel Mayer Co., its careful management had resulted in bringing *Peter Pan* to 'many children who would otherwise have no opportunity whatever of seeing it, thereby building up an audience of younger brothers and sisters who would clamour to be taken to the

81 'Ice show' *Life Magazine*, 20 May 1946, 50–4.

82 Rutherford to Lucas, 17 February 1954; GOS/6/4/93; GOSH Archives.

83 Instructions to Counsel to Advise, October 1954; GOS/6/4/34; GOSH Archives.

84 Guy Aldous, Douglas Falconer and William Aldous, *Terrell on the Law of Patents*, Sweet & Maxwell, 1965.

85 Opinion by Guy Aldous, 27 October 1954; GOS/1/39/1; GOSH Archives.

Daniel Mayer production in future years'.[86] However, the hospital now appeared rather excited about investigating the opportunities that lay at the boundary between rights, while the theatrical licensee insisted that the value of the play primarily emanated from the particular care it had taken to bring it onto the stage. Although in the end the hospital did not accept the offer for ice shows in the United Kingdom because it did not want to disrupt the long-established ties with Daniel Mayer Co., it did arrange for them to take place in the United States.[87]

The exposure to the commercial excitement that emerged with the release of the Disney cartoon ultimately impacted on the hospital's view of its relationship to the copyright gift; indeed, it animated a reconsideration of the property relations of the gift, over and above the specifics of legal rights. A vitalised commercial sense gradually shifted the conservative stance previously held by the hospital. More precisely, it began to transform its approach to the gift by connecting charitable purposes with business opportunities in ways the hospital no longer seemed to view as incompatible. Charitable fundraising was beginning to coincide with the managerial idea of exploiting the *Peter Pan* copyright gift efficiently and proactively. Thus, the idea took hold that the copyright gift should be treated as an asset; a financial consideration that, as we have indicated above, became more pressing once the hospital was incorporated into the NHS.

The hospital's reassessment of its approach came to the fore with the negotiation of broadcasting rights. Broadcasting rights brought to the hospital an opportunity that was apparently free from previous contractual constraints. Put simply, broadcasting rights were different from the double set of arrangements (publishing and performance) rooted in the initial setting of the *Peter Pan* copyright gift. The passage of the Copyright Act in 1956 also consolidated the perception that broadcasting rights were definitely separate from the right of performance in public.[88] Given that there was more room to negotiate and that the base for *Peter Pan* fundraising had broadened, the hospital was in a position to secure a profitable deal concerning television rights. This opportunity was realised with the live television version performed on the National Broadcasting Company (NBC) network in America in 1955, repeated live in 1956 and 1960. This new arrangement was interesting not only in terms of content, which was quite favourable for the network, but its most remarkable feature was the expedient way in which it was negotiated by the New York show business impresario, Peter Lawrence. Lawrence succeeded in getting Disney and NBC to agree on the television rights and for the hospital to receive a commission on the deal. This arrangement was highly unusual. Unlike previous copyright negotiations, this contract left the hospital out and brought Disney into the agreement. This was presumably thought to be the best way to proceed in the

86 MacLeod to Rutherford, 1 February 1955; GOS/1/39/1; GOSH Archives.

87 Rutherford to Curtis Brown, 5 June 1956; GOS/6/4/93; GOSH Archives

88 F.E. Skone James, 'The Copyright Act' (1956) 67(2) Winter *The Author* 38–40, 40.

light of the contractual protection Disney had originally arranged with the hospital to secure privileged exposure of its cartoon and launch a merchandising programme. And this could explain why it was later assumed that Disney temporarily held the television broadcast rights for *Peter Pan*,[89] a nebulous point that the hospital tried to clarify on different occasions, using different legal opinions. Nevertheless, the specific work that resulted from this agreement was a live TV version of the Broadway production of *Peter Pan*, starring Mary Martin, which made television history as one of the most-watched events ever.[90] While the impact of television on children's entertainment and the imponderables of intellectual property are something we explore in detail in the following chapters, this US production did have one important thing in common with Disney: the framing of the *Peter Pan* audience as both spectators and consumers.[91]

5.3 FALLING OUT

In the early months of 1960, the hospital appointed a new house governor, Gordon J. Piller, a well-known medical administrator, who would become the director of the Leukaemia Research Fund, a charity with close connections to Great Ormond Street Hospital.[92] Piller brought with him a set of remarkable strategies, linking public relations and charity fundraising initiatives.[93] This institutional entrepreneurship was distinctive not because of the campaigning and marketing techniques themselves but in their application to hospital management.[94] Under Piller's governorship, the administration of Great Ormond Street Hospital reconfigured the management of the *Peter Pan* copyright gift. The bureaucratic and conservative rigidity that had long characterised the hospital administration's management of the bequest shifted to a more flexible interpretation of the potential of the copyright gift.

Although this distinctive approach was connected to the need to raise funds and awareness for research into childhood cancer, it is worth outlining the changing

89 This point was mentioned in a legal dispute concerning the copyright in the videotaped productions; see *National Broadcasting Co. Inc. v. Sonneborn*, 630 F Supp 524, 532–3 (D Conn 1985).

90 The programme was seen by an estimated 55 to 60 million viewers; see Bruce K. Hanson, *Peter Pan on Stage and Screen, 1904–2010*, McFarland & Company, 2011, 246; John Krampner, *The Man in the Shadows: Fred Coe and the Golden Age of Television*, Rutgers University Press, 1997, 98.

91 Teresa Jones, 'Peter and me (or how I learned to fly): network television broadcasts of Peter Pan' in Kavey and Friedman, above n 76, 243–63, 249.

92 Board of Governors' Minute Books, 21 January 1960; GOS/1/3/9; GOSH Archives.

93 See, for instance, Gordon J. Piller 'Report on public relations in hospitals'; GOS/14/103; GOSH Archives.

94 Emm Barnes with Joanna Baines, *The Changing Faces of Childhood Cancer: Clinical and Cultural Visions since 1940*, Palgrave Macmillan, 2015, 89–116; see also Emm Barnes, 'Cancer coverage: the public face of childhood leukaemia in 1960s Britain' (2008) 32(1) March *Endeavour* 10–15, 14.

environment within which the hospital began to operate. The first important change was that the hospital began to keep a closer eye on negotiations made on its behalf. Just a few months after his appointment as hospital governor, Gordon Piller received a new offer to exploit *Peter Pan*. On this occasion it was for a film, and again it came from the Broadway impresario, Peter Lawrence. Lawrence mentioned that he was close to a movie deal with a firm called Berkeley Films. Although the negotiation resembled the one Lawrence had carried out for television rights, it prompted concerns which were communicated by Piller to the Peter Pan Committee at the hospital. A series of details made this offer unsatisfactory. First, the film company was not well known, and there was a need to discover more about who was behind it. Second, Piller noted that the draft for the sale of motion picture rights was unsatisfactory because it would re-engage the tensions surrounding the Disney contract. Furthermore, assignments of rights were not appropriate because the hospital was constrained from agreeing to this as an assignment was contrary to Barrie's wish and the terms of the bequest. Although this last point could be easily altered by making the assignment a licence, problems remained. On top of that, the offer did not seem particularly attractive from a financial point of view. Piller himself recognised the lack of a yardstick to judge whether 'the bargain Peter Lawrence had struck was reasonable'.[95] As part of the drive towards increased accountability at the hospital, proceeding with such a deal was not recommended. The Peter Pan Committee rejected the offer. This rejection was an example of the way hospital administrators were reconciling business and charity. They no longer saw the two activities as contradictory because 'as trustees, we are under a clear moral and legal duty to obtain the maximum financial benefit for the hospital'.[96]

One of the surprising features of the rejection of the deal was that it did not close the matter immediately. Peter Lawrence persisted in attempting to get the hospital to reconsider, framing his proposal in a variety of ways. He warned the hospital that litigation with Berkeley Films could ensue and that such a scenario would involve a legal case to which the hospital would be likely to be called to respond. Interestingly, Lawrence also tried to persuade the hospital that the deal he had secured was indeed financially attractive, particularly because Roy Disney had stated that he believed the copyright in *Peter Pan* would expire in 1963.[97] It is no coincidence that Disney approached the hospital again with an enquiry about the live action movie rights, an offer that was also rejected by the hospital in the forthcoming months. The reason why a *Peter Pan* live action film was becoming an attractive venture (particularly after the frustrated deal with Berkeley Films) circulated among Hollywood gossip circles. It was identified that the non-competitive covenant that protected Disney's

95 Piller to Agnew, 9 October 1961; GOS/6/4/141; GOSH Archives.

96 Anthony Sumption, chairman of the Peter Pan Committee, 'Peter Pan' *The Times Literary Supplement*, 11 January 1963, 3176.

97 Roy Disney to Peter Lawrence, 16 March 1954; 'General Correspondence', above n 43.

cartoon from competition from a feature film was about to end in 1963. Dissatisfied with the way the copyright gift was handled by external agents and now aware of inconsistencies that could put the hospital in a delicate position, the hospital's Board of Governors appointed Piller and a London solicitor, Peter Sneath, as joint agents for Peter Pan in May 1962. The rationale for this procedure was the need to place the management of the copyright gift under closer scrutiny. From then on, a systematic investigation of pre-existing contractual relations, the history of the gift and the term of copyright was carried out in order to be able to respond more quickly to further enquiries about the exploitation of Peter Pan. In addition to closer scrutiny of offers coming in, this set the scene for a slow transformation in understanding of the commercial property in the gift.

For the first time since the bequest, the hospital thought it could exploit *Peter Pan* directly. To ensure that its charitable status would not be affected, the hospital sought to establish a company to be called 'Peter Pan Merchandise Limited'.[98] The premise was for the hospital to license all merchandising rights in Peter Pan to this satellite company so it could arrange for subcontractors to manufacture commodities on its behalf. Disconcertingly, the hospital found that several Peter Pan trademarks had already been registered; a situation that made the registration of this company somewhat difficult. Most of these trademarks had been registered by the toy company mentioned above, Cecil Coleman Ltd, which had been operating for decades with the acquiescence of the hospital.[99] After several attempts to register 'Peter Pan Merchandise Limited', 'Peter Pan Trading Services Limited', 'Peter Pan Toys and other Merchandise Limited',[100] in March 1963 the hospital succeeded in registering a company called 'Peter Pan Productions Limited'.[101] The commercial nature of this enterprise was not deemed to conflict with the charitable endeavour of the hospital precisely because of the different approach that the hospital had started to take towards the opportunities presented by the copyright gift and its management.

The new management perspective was not just a controlling device, it was an attempt to renew the cycle of interest in Peter Pan. In doing so, it shaped the ways the hospital communicated with licensees. Despite initial reticence due to the inexperience of Gordon Piller and Peter Sneath, their agency generally revitalised relationships and transactions, incentivising not only the hospital but also licensees to alter their otherwise traditionally conservative view of the gift and to switch towards a more creative understanding of the copyright. To be more specific, the shift affected the way their contractual relationship was viewed because, as Hodder

98 Sneath to Boult, Wade & Tennant, 30 October 1962; GOS/6/4/98; GOSH Archives.

99 See, for instance, the trade mark Peter Pan No 692931 registered for cosaques (being crackers or bon-bons), games (other than ordinary playing cards) and playthings. 'Cecil Coleman Ltd' (1951) May *Games and Toys* 132.

100 Sneath to Piller, 31 December 1962; GOS/6/4/98; GOSH Archives.

101 Certificate of Incorporation, 7 March 1963; GOS/6/4/98; GOSH Archives.

& Stoughton reflected, 'we shall not continue in their good books unless we show liveliness in our stewardship of their copyright'.[102] By reinvigorating editorial projects around Peter Pan, that is, by finding new editorial lives for Peter Pan, the hospital's new administrative demands for productivity could be appeased. Of the opportunities specifically arising from this new framework, there were some noteworthy publications, such as the Penguin paperback version of *Peter Pan*. Although publishing was one of the obvious routes by which the relationship between licensees and the hospital was rejuvenated, merchandising was still an area which the hospital had not entered, for reasons mentioned above. Among the different factors contributing to the newfound interest in merchandising, and the formation of Peter Pan Productions Ltd as an associated company, was the importance Piller attached to public relations in hospital administration. It is no coincidence that, in 1963, one of this new company's first meetings was with an advertising firm. While this provided some access to child-oriented markets, Piller stressed that the type of exploitation of Peter Pan he had in mind was very specific and very much within the broader context of merchandising practices. Indeed, the bonanza of character merchandising in the early 1960s was a key reason why the plan he envisaged for the hospital was not considered inappropriate or extravagant. Merchandise bearing children's favourite characters were to be found across the high street. Piller himself bought a Noddy toy to show that 'this [was] the sort of thing I had in mind when suggesting Peter Pan Productions Ltd ought to license some firm to make similar models of all the characters in Peter Pan'.[103] In other words, the idea was to make the multiplication and proliferation of Peter Pan commodities an industry in its own right, as many others had done for different fictional characters by closer curating of licensing potential.

Peter Pan was no longer imagined as being limited to a specific play or text. Rather, it became a set of names or characters that could be advertised, licensed and manufactured. The hospital began to consider Peter Pan as an asset to be exploited across media, a trend comparable to the strategy Disney had been developing for decades. The hospital began to see these marketing operations as so alluring that it even contacted Disney to see if the company would be interested in getting on board, sharing expertise and contacts. This offer was quickly turned down by the corporation following the rejection by the hospital of its proposal for a new *Peter Pan* film. Soon after the formation of Peter Pan Productions Ltd, the hospital realised that the success of any merchandising programme by its subsidiary ultimately depended on the possibility of a new visual imagery, different from that of the Disney cartoon, which could attract a renewed interest in Barrie's Peter Pan bequest among children and adults alike. While trademarks for Peter Pan had been

[102] Memo from Paul Hodder Williams, Hodder & Stoughton, 9 January 1964; CLC/B/119/MS16375/001; LMA.

[103] Piller to Sneath, 5 November 1963; GOS/6/4/99; GOSH Archives.

registered by a number of manufacturers, a chance to work around those rights emerged from an enquiry about a new live action film of *Peter Pan*. A new release like this was important for Peter Pan Productions Ltd because it would facilitate the creation of new images and designs of Peter Pan that could be licensed.

This opportunity came in April 1964 when the American film director George Cukor met Gordon Piller at the Great Ormond Street Hospital for Sick and Poor Children. According to Cukor, the meeting was 'quite a story', not only because of the 'enormous, impressive and grim institution', as the hospital appeared to him, but also because of the difficulties he had had in arranging the meeting and attracting Piller's interest.[104] Indeed, he described Piller as the 'House Governor (whatever that means)'.[105] The comment highlights the apparent difference between Piller and the professional qualifications and demeanour of commercial agents, echoing Disney's frustrations and misunderstandings in negotiating with the hospital. Despite the hospital's efforts to embark on commercial ventures, there was still a considerable gap between the manners and expectations embodied in the Victorian hospital's policies and routines and Hollywood's more expedient approach. Cukor's difficulties in arranging the meeting and Piller's evasive responses were due to the hospital's initial wariness about accepting American proposals after its unfortunate experiences over previous negotiations with Berkeley Films and NBC.[106] However, the circumstances seemed a little different this time around. The call from Cukor was slightly more appealing to the hospital because of the way in which he presented himself and the proposal to the hospital. Cukor came in without an agent and contacted the hospital via the Society of Authors. Furthermore, he had just finished directing *My Fair Lady* and came already equipped with a professional 'setup'. But the definitive 'hook' that caught Piller's attention was the name attached to the project. Audrey Hepburn was the projected star of the new *Peter Pan* film. It was the idea of her as the star name that made Piller accept the meeting and caused the hospital to pay attention to the offer. The possibility of Laurence Olivier being cast as Captain Hook further beguiled the hospital.[107] It was possible to imagine how such a film could indeed create value in the property, giving a new life to Peter Pan beyond Disney's animated cartoon. There were other more interesting points discussed in this early negotiation. For instance, the hospital's associated company, Peter Pan Productions Ltd, was keeping merchandising rights in Great Britain and the

[104] George Cukor to Mel Ferrer, 28 April 1964; George Cukor Collection; 44; Folder 866; Margaret Herrick Library; AMPAS.

[105] Ibid.

[106] In fact, an examination of the terms and length of those contracts had made an important theatrical agency in New York lose interest in the right to handle and represent *Peter Pan*; see Report to the Peter Pan Committee on the visit to New York of Mr P. Sneath and G.J. Piller 19–23 November 1962; GOS/1/39/1; GOSH Archives.

[107] One of the clauses that the hospital became interested in negotiating was the 'consultation rights' on casting; see Goodman to Cukor, 1 June 1964 in George Cukor Collection, n 104 above.

Republic of Ireland. All interested parties decided to leave the final contractual details to their respective lawyers, but their preliminary impression of the possible deal was very optimistic. In fact, Mel Ferrer, Audrey Hepburn's husband and commercial partner in this enterprise with Cukor, was thrilled and began celebrating the accomplishment as a done deal. His main concern was not over any possible obstacle on the part of the hospital but rather at the distributor level. Indeed, he noted, 'we should not approach any other distributing companies until the property is safe in our hot little paws'.[108]

As a corporate vehicle to acquire the option and the licence for those rights, Mel Ferrer and George Cukor set about forming a joint venture. This scheme was aimed at keeping the risks to a minimum because (as discussed in Chapter 4) the main financial expenditure would come directly from distributors encouraged to invest in the film. Such an entrepreneurial operation would also generate an immediate capital gain for the venture. The film option agreement and licence, in which merchandising rights figured prominently, was drafted with the hospital. The negotiation was ratified by the Board of Governors of the hospital and news of the forthcoming deal appeared in the press. The deal was so close to being formalised that the parties began to make sure everything was ready to sign. Audrey Hepburn would sign the contract at the hospital premises, and she was going to be photographed with the statue of Peter Pan in Kensington Gardens, 'as this would be carried world-wide'.[109] The hospital was also very enthusiastic about the idea because it provided excellent publicity for its charitable work. However, the path to the film and the excitement about the project were dramatically interrupted by a letter sent by Disney's lawyers to Cukor and Ferrer a week after the news of the deal had begun to circulate. The missive was a sort of 'cease and desist' letter which questioned the legitimacy of the forthcoming deal, warning the film director and producer that Disney had acquired the rights upon which they produced a film titled *Peter Pan* from the hospital some time ago.[110] Moreover, Disney's lawyers explained that the title *Peter Pan* had been registered under the title registration rules of the Motion Picture Association of America and under comparable title registration rules in the United Kingdom. To conclude, the letter warned that if the Cukor film was produced and released, it would probably coincide with the reissue of the cartoon, so Disney would feel obliged to 'assert such remedies as may be available to us, including the rights we have established in the title as a permanently protected one and also our rights under the principles of unfair competition'.[111] While this letter obviously dimmed Cukor and Ferrer's enthusiasm, another communication ended up being even more troubling. Almost at the same time that

[108] Mel Ferrer to George Cukor, 25 April 1964, George Cukor Collection, n 104 above.

[109] Ferrer to Cukor, 21 May 1964, George Cukor Collection, n 104 above.

[110] Walt Disney Productions, to Mel Ferrer and George Cukor, 5 June 1964, George Cukor Collection, n 104 above.

[111] Wright, Wright, Coldwater and Mack to Piller, 5 May 1964; GOS/6/4/129; GOSH Archives.

Disney's lawyers sent the letter, the question of legitimacy surrounding this deal magically found its way to one of the most important Hollywood gossip forums, Hedda Hopper's column.[112] Although this is not the place to analyse the interplay between publicity and gossip as way of exerting power in the film industry,[113] the fact that this otherwise private correspondence suddenly appeared in public was a clear warning of the seriousness of the issue, as this sort of coverage was often responsible for 'making or breaking' films and careers. Even though the lawsuit between Disney and the hospital was converted into a dispute over the interpretation of their contractual relationship, it is reasonable to surmise that it was specifically the publication of this 'news' that scuppered the film project. No investor would participate in a project with such a cloud of uncertainty hanging over the property. To put it another way, the disclosure of the problems around the property short-circuited the profit strategy devised by the joint venture, in what is often described as the 'time of courtship'.[114] From this moment onwards, Cukor and Ferrer knew that it was going to be a struggle to turn the project into an attractive asset for investors, so they suggested delaying formalising the agreement until the situation was clarified. As one can imagine, this despondency and resentment also affected the hospital, which was convinced that Disney was frustrating a great opportunity for the management of the *Peter Pan* copyright gift and threatening the future revenue that it would bring to the hospital and its associated company, Peter Pan Productions Ltd. Here, we can see how invested the hospital was in trying to save the film project and how the hospital and Disney ended up bound together in the litigation.

On 1 July 1964, the hospital's solicitors wrote to Disney asking the company to withdraw the letter and issue an apology, emphasising how unfortunate it was that the party damaged by the letter was a children's hospital.[115] This request is interesting as it caused tensions between charity and business operations to resurface. Indeed, while the hospital believed that the situation was not going to escalate precisely because of the bad publicity this could bring to Disney, Disney remained firm in its response. Instead of apologising for or clarifying the letter, the corporation failed to see that any complaint could be made.[116] A few days later, the hospital decided to take legal action against Disney seeking three legal remedies. First, the hospital asked for a declaration that the hospital and its licensees could produce and release a

[112] Hedda Hopper, 'Hepburn and Cukor to film Peter Pan: but Disney owns title rights' *Los Angeles Times*, 14 June 1964, 78.

[113] On the connections between promotional campaigns and gossip in the film industry, see Kathleen A. Feeley, "Louella Parsons and Hedda Hopper's Hollywood: The Rise of Celebrity Gossip Industry in Twentieth-Century America, 1910–1950" (PhD thesis, City University of New York, 2004); see also Jennifer Frost, 'Hollywood gossip as public sphere: Hedda Hopper, reader-respondents, and the Red Scare, 1947–1965' (2011) 50(2) Winter *Cinema Journal* 84–103.

[114] Cukor to Ferrer, 10 June 1964, George Cukor Collection, n 104 above.

[115] Waterhouse & Co (GOSH Solicitors) to Walt Disney Productions, 1 July 1964; GOS/6/4/129; GOSH Archives.

[116] Warren, Murton & Co. to Waterhouse & Co., 7 July 1964; GOS/6/4/129; GOSH Archives.

film bearing the title *Peter Pan*, starring Audrey Hepburn. Second, the hospital sought an injunction to restrain Disney from objecting to this film and from threatening Cukor and Ferrer or any other person involved in the production. And, finally, the hospital sought an inquiry as to damages suffered by the hospital due to the breach of the 1939 agreement between the hospital and Disney.

5.4 MISSED OPPORTUNITIES

The hospital instituted proceedings so quickly because time was of the essence for the film project to have any chance of surviving. In hindsight, this turned out to be misguided. Litigation further threatened the prospect of resolving the issue quickly. The more adjournments and delays the proceedings had, the more likely it was that the film would never be made. However, expectations around the film and the conduct of the legal dispute highlight several important points. After the news of trouble over the rights got out, Warner Bros, one of the Hollywood studios first 'panting after the property' in the Cukor film, retreated.[117] Others, such as Paramount, followed suit. The domino effect of the news about controversy meant that one Hollywood studio after another suddenly lost interest, expressing their desire not to become involved in any contentious issue. According to the hospital's solicitor, this contagion was not only the effect of the news but had also been precipitated by another letter written by Disney to the film studios explaining its position, something he had been told but could not prove. At this point, almost everything Disney did was viewed suspiciously by the hospital. Interestingly, a few days before the hospital brought legal proceedings, George Cukor and Mel Ferrer thought of trying a different technique, a last resort to cool down the dispute: asking Disney to participate in their project as 'Disney financing and Disney distribution might resolve everything very neatly'.[118] This tactic was considered notwithstanding that they were appalled by Disney's attitude, particularly because the Great Ormond Street Hospital for Sick and Poor Children was ultimately the party most directly affected. For instance, Audrey Hepburn wrote to Cukor to say that she was 'quite terrified [by] Mr. Disney's gluttony. I can understand very well he wishes to protect his interests and investments but do not think he should rob "all those children" of the possibility of making a little extra for their hospital. We will find something else to do, I feel sure, but the Great Ormond outfit deserves more help'.[119] Although Cukor and Ferrer tried to figure out what Walt's position was in relation to the controversy and resolve it, the question was already in the hands of Disney's solicitors. They suggested that there was no personal attack here, only a routine procedure to assert what the company believed were its rights. However, the

[117] Ferrer to Cukor, 20 June 1964, George Cukor Collection, n 104 above.
[118] Ferrer to Cukor, 16 July 1964, George Cukor Collection, n 104 above.
[119] Hepburn to Cukor, 24 June 1964, George Cukor Collection, n 104 above.

possibility of an impromptu alliance with Disney vanished when the hospital's legal action against Disney began in the summer of 1964.

The hospital's decision to litigate was incentivised by a legal opinion by an experienced intellectual property barrister, A. D. Russell-Clarke.[120] He concluded that Disney Enterprises had committed a gross breach of its 1939 agreement with the hospital. According to the barrister, the infamous Disney's letter amounted to a slander of the hospital's title.[121] The only anticipated problem was a legal technicality with special significance for speeding up the proceedings. The multiplicity of companies and subsidiaries associated with Disney (mentioned in Chapter 4 and having gone through further changes in Britain throughout the subsequent decades) made it difficult to pin down the defendant. While it was suggested that it was important to ascertain which entity was the successor of Walt Disney Enterprises, the advice was to carefully ask for permission to serve the writ out of the jurisdiction – that is, to sue a company based in California, Walt Disney Productions Inc., in London. For the hospital it was important to sue in Britain as litigation was supposed to proceed more quickly there than in the United States. Although the proceedings were started and the writ was served, the choice of jurisdiction was a legal issue that emerged on appeal. Perhaps unsurprisingly, Disney was particularly slow in its replies, almost exhausting the time allocated for the procedure, an attitude that the hospital interpreted as 'using every device to delay matters'.[122] Even when the responses were given to the court, the possibility of amendment was pursued. For instance, Disney's defence first stated that Peter Pan was in the public domain in the United States and that Disney had acquired merchandising rights of Peter Pan: two points that the hospital argued were inaccurate but that demonstrated how central merchandising had become for both Disney and the hospital. Subsequently, Disney altered its defence halfway through the proceedings, which was interpreted by the hospital as 'an absolute trick'.[123] However, the judge ruled that the legal issue turned only on the interpretation of the original 1939 agreement between the hospital and Disney Enterprises with respect to whether or not the licence was limited to a sound animated cartoon film, which would not include live actors.

Alongside legal proceedings, alternatives to expedite a settlement were suggested by those eagerly waiting for a quick resolution of the conflict. Cognisant of the effect of the media portrayal of the dispute on the possibility of attracting investors, one of the suggestions made by Cukor and Ferrer was to use this publicity to their advantage, by planting what could be read as an 'independent' account of the

[120] A.D. Russell-Clarke was the author of *Copyright and Industrial Designs*, Sweet & Maxwell, 1951; see also A.D. Russell-Clarke, 'Design plagiarism and copyright reform' (1968) 116(5145) August *Journal of the Royal Society of Arts* 737–49.

[121] Opinion by Russell-Clarke, 24 June 1964, George Cukor Collection, n 104 above.

[122] Sneath to Cukor, 5 January 1965 in ibid.

[123] Cukor to Ferrer, 9 March 1965 in ibid.

litigation which fully exploited public sentiment towards the charitable status of the hospital and concern for vulnerable children. Although this proposal did not fully materialise, it was another example of how the parties were aware of the kind of effects that public attention could have in enabling control of the narrative surrounding what would otherwise be understood as a private controversy. The significance of headlines had been apparent from the outset, as the report about the conflict in Hollywood's gossip columns had arguably been one of the catalysts for the legal action. Suspicion about the strategic use of media among the parties resurfaced again with the reissue of Disney's *Peter Pan* cartoon at the end of 1965. The hospital was now concerned with the way Disney appeared to have eliminated any reference whatsoever in its promotional literature to the production being an 'animated cartoon'. Additionally, the reissue of Disney's *Peter Pan* was accompanied by an original marketing strategy that involved actors being lowered by helicopter in London. Amid fears over what they believed were calculated publicity manoeuvres connected to the legal controversy, the hospital sought an interlocutory injunction to restrain Disney from advertising any sound motion picture under the name 'Peter Pan' or 'Walt Disney's Peter Pan' without clearly indicating that it was an animated cartoon. The hospital's argument was that this promotional literature amounted to passing-off animated cartoons as if they were ordinary sound motion pictures with living actors. This publicity, the hospital argued, would deceive and mislead the public because no licence had been granted by the hospital for a film of this nature. This was a tricky claim to make out because it conflated the question as to whether the public could be deceived about the cultural content of the film due to its advertising, with a narrower question of whether the advertising constituted deception about the details of copyright licences.

The hospital's motion failed because the judge, Plowman J, determined that the absence of any reference in the promotional literature as to the nature of the film had had an effect contrary to that suggested by the hospital. In other words, the lack of reference in the advertising literature implied that the reissue was an animated cartoon and not a film with live actors. This interpretation ignored that the evidence of deception went beyond what was found in the literature. It included a stunt involving live actors. Plowman J's sympathetic view of Disney was on display in the judgment. He noted that his observation of the evidence was made 'as an ordinary member of the public who has grown up to know and love Walt Disney cartoons'.[124] Leaving aside these personal impressions, the judge concluded that he was still not satisfied that the publicity matter contained any of the representations that the hospital alleged, as in the mind of the public Disney was primarily associated with animated cartoons. The failure to obtain an injunction was obviously a setback for

[124] *Great Ormond Street Hospital v Walt Disney Productions Ltd*, 21 December 1965 (Plowman J); GOS/6/4/137; GOSH Archives; see also 'Peter Pan dispute' *The Times*, 10 March 1965, 5; 'Hospital fail in claim over Peter Pan' *The Times*, 22 December 1965, 5.

the hospital, particularly when coupled with the delays it was facing in getting the case heard. The hospital elected not to communicate this setback to George Cukor and Mel Ferrer as it was appraised as a minor legal incident that would have demoralised them.

Throughout this period, the ongoing correspondence between Piller and Cyril Hicks, the managing director of Peter Pan Productions Ltd, was constantly reflecting their discontent about Disney alongside trying to hold and maintain Cukor and Ferrer's interest in the *Peter Pan* film venture. They were aware that the producer and the director sometimes expressed the feeling of having been caught in the crossfire between Disney and the hospital. However, despite initial hesitations about whether to side with the hospital or not, Cukor and Ferrer became more irritated by Disney's tactics than the hospital itself. There is no better example of how emboldened they became than the way they reacted to *Mary Poppins*; the film released by Disney at Christmas 1964. *Mary Poppins* had been produced and announced together with a strategy that exploited the public sympathy for Julie Andrews, overlooked for Cukor's film of *My Fair Lady* made with Audrey Hepburn, despite Andrews having played the part of Eliza Doolittle on Broadway.[125] Cukor took a particularly dim view of the promotion of the new Disney film. He thought it was no coincidence that film critics tended to compare *Peter Pan* and *Mary Poppins*, emphasising that the latter was better. According to him, this was prompted by the Disney organisation, for 'I can't help but feel that there was some sort of briefing from Disney which caused the critics to compare the two. Walt's Grand Plan has become quite apparent'.[126]

The hearing finally took place in the spring of 1966, almost two years after the initial falling out between Disney and the hospital. The High Court judge, Buckley J, interpreted the original agreement between the hospital and Disney, signed in 1939, in the same way as the hospital – that is, that there was an obligation on Disney's part not to object to a film ten years after the premiere of the cartoon in 1953. In other words, the covenant Disney introduced to shield its cartoon from competition had already expired in 1963. However, the case became a little more complicated because Disney mounted its defence upon two further points, both of which had already been successful approaches used in film rights litigation (discussed in Chapter 4). First, Disney maintained that it had registered the title *Peter Pan* at the Motion Picture Association of America. Second, Disney contested the claim by arguing that it had acquired film rights from Paramount Films, the company that had produced the first *Peter Pan* silent film, having reached an agreement with Barrie in 1919. The two issues were closely interconnected with Disney's attempt to

[125] The interesting story here was that, despite her Broadway success interpreting *My Fair Lady* in the stage musical, Andrews was discarded from George Cukor's movie *My Fair Lady*, which starred Audrey Hepburn: see 'Disappointment' *Evening Post*, 19 December 1964; in MSS 5341/16/10; SLNSW.

[126] Cukor to Ferrer, 3 September 1964, George Cukor Collection, n 104 above.

strengthen the rights it claimed to own and, as we shall see below, in the way Disney and other Hollywood film production companies approached the film rights business. Disney changed a part of its defence to argue that it was the hospital's suggestion of an exclusive right to the title *Peter Pan* that it had really objected to in its warning letter to Cukor and Ferrer. While this position may appear complex at first glance, it can be summarised as a defence built upon the dispute over two distinct rights attached to the *Peter Pan* copyright gift: the right over the title (*Peter Pan*) and rights over the subject matter ('film' and not only 'animated cartoon' rights).

The first controversial point concerned the rights over the title (*Peter Pan*). Disney based its ownership claim on its title registration at the Hays Office, a US film industry bureau introduced in Hollywood in the mid-1920s designed to forestall government regulation of the industry (particularly around censorship), promote the mutual interests of members of the Motion Picture Producers and Distributors Association of America (MPPDA) and encourage an American vision and US terms of trade internationally. The Hays Office operated a register of film titles, listing the companies that owned 'rights' to them because, prior to films entering into production and release, it was difficult to ascertain who owned what. This also helped identity film rights agreements relevant to remakes, including sound and Technicolour versions of films. By helping avert the disaster of releases with the same or similar titles and stories, events that could severely impact on distribution prospects and box office returns, the registry facilitated the producer's capacity to raise capital from distributors and other investors.[127] In that sense, it was a bureaucratic vehicle to signal and reserve titles for attracting investments to the obvious benefit of the major studios who were the members of the organisation. This system also helped sidestep the many legal complexities that could arise with licensing film adaptation rights to books and plays, especially where copyright technicalities varied across jurisdictions and the United States was not a signatory to the Berne Convention. The registry documented claims mirroring the way Disney legal and merchandising practices operated. Titles were registered independently from any underlying material such as a book. A listing suggested a right to a form of intangible property far more expansive than a media-specific copyright or the words in a trademark registration. Inclusion in the list constituted an assertion of a right to produce the film of that title. But it also suggested that, downstream, there was a subsequent right to enter into an array of distribution and merchandising contracts with other parties based on 'the film'. The participation of all the major Hollywood studios in the registry bolstered their authority and control over film distribution and, where

[127] After the clarification of the book–play–film adaptation right in the Copyright Act 1911 (UK) on terms established out of liaison between Hollywood and the Society of Authors, there had been attempts to institute a similar bureaucratic system for registration of titles in Britain, but the Society of Authors concluded that it was too 'difficult a question to handle'; see Kathy Bowrey, *Copyright, Creativity, Big Media and Cultural Value*, Routledge, 2021, 111–40; Seville, above n 21, 56.

relevant, also associated merchandising. As only members of the MPPDA could participate in the register, the interests of external rights holders were invisible and effectively erased, unless the party litigated. As we will see below, Hollywood studios operated as if chain of title was proven through documentation based on the Hays Office register, and US courts treated it with respect.[128]

One way to understand why Disney ended up introducing this point in the lawsuit is to follow the approach it took when registering *Peter Pan*. In Disney's strategic plans to produce animated cartoons or films, the first step was to survey the title register at the Hays Office and use the search as a platform to acquire rights. In 1938, Disney requested information as to the registration status of the following titles: Mary Poppins, Winnie the Pooh, Doctor Dolittle, The Little Mermaid, Babar the Elephant, The Wizard of Oz, and Peter Pan. The enquiry anticipated Disney's interest in developing those projects in the future. The search for Peter Pan revealed a title registration made by Paramount Pictures. After agreeing with Paramount Pictures, Disney requested that the Hays Office transfer the listing of the title from Paramount Pictures' list to that of Walt Disney Productions. This context explained why Disney had registered the title in Hollywood, but the transaction and Hays Office registration was irrelevant to the owner of the copyright gift: the hospital. As a result, the judge dismissed the idea that this title registration scheme could have any effect on the claim. It was a self-regulated film industry policy which did not bind the hospital.[129] More specifically, Buckley J highlighted the difference between Hollywood and the Great Ormond Street Hospital: the hospital had 'nothing to do with the film industry and there has been no evidence [that has] led [me] . . . to the conclusion that the hospital knew anything about any system of registration of titles'.[130]

The second aspect Disney contended was that it had acquired a broader film right that supplemented the interest referred to in the 1939 agreement with the hospital. This justified the company's objection to the new licence issued by the hospital to George Cukor and Mel Ferrer for the film with Audrey Hepburn. As we have seen, the interpretation of the contract between Disney and the hospital was quite clear and referred to animated cartoon rights. Under the terms of the gift, the hospital did not have the power to sell the copyright, so it could only license Disney for an animated cartoon. However, the iteration Disney proposed as the relevant transfer was the film right agreement Barrie had entered into with Famous Film Players Co. in 1919 that led to a silent film version of *Peter Pan*. The interest Barrie had assigned was then transferred to Paramount Pictures and acquired by Disney. This convoluted chain traced an alternate history of the copyright in *Peter Pan*, but the scope of

[128] An interesting reference explaining the way this system worked can be read in *Johnston v 20th Century Fox Film Corp*. Court of Appeal of California, Second District, Division Three, 10 December 1947, 82 Cal App 2d 796 (Cal Ct App 1947).

[129] *Hospital for Sick Children (Board of Governors) v Walt Disney Productions, Inc.* [1966] 1 WLR 1055, 1063.

[130] Ibid. 1074; see also 'Peter Pan, Walt Disney and the sick children' *The Times*, 12 March 1966, 12.

the right suggested by Disney conflicted with the bequest by Barrie in which the copyright and all its reverted rights were given to the hospital. After a long discussion on contract law and the context in which the agreements took place, including the impact of the National Health Service Act 1946, the judge dismissed this point too, arguing that no consent was given by Barrie to transfer motion picture rights per se. The judge specified that these rights granted were limited to a right to make a silent film as that was the only technological and commercial possibility at that time.[131] The overall conclusion of the first instance court was that Disney had breached its contract with the hospital when it sent the warning letter to Cukor and Ferrer. An injunction to restrain Disney from objecting to the film and an inquiry as to what damages it had suffered was awarded to the hospital.[132]

5.5 CONSUMED

The outcome of the lawsuit was an undeniable legal success for the hospital, but the excitement was again short-lived. Despite the strength of the judgment, Disney announced an intention to appeal. The news that Disney was going to appeal was again widely publicised. This appeared to confirm early suspicions expressed by the hospital's solicitor that Walt Disney was spinning the case out as long as possible, 'as it would be in his best interests to do so'.[133] The news meant another delay that risked derailing the film project. For that very reason, the house governor of the hospital, Gordon Piller, decided to travel to Los Angeles in May 1966, just a few weeks after the judgment was handed down. The possibility of a meeting with George Cukor and Mel Ferrer was triggered by the Annual Meeting of the American Children's Hospitals Executive Council held in Boston, which Piller was attending. He suggested to Cukor that they could meet and 'take up where we left off two years ago'.[134] Here, we see again how the business of the copyright gift became part of the hospital's management agenda throughout the 1960s, and meetings and dispositions that could have been considered contradictory in previous decades now coalesced with the hospital governor's other activities, such as attending children's hospital conferences. Although the hospital tried to hold the parties' interest, news of the appeal made Mel Ferrer and Audrey Hepburn finally withdraw from the film project. Despite all the initial interest and efforts invested in the *Peter Pan* film, Ferrer wrote to Cukor that they had decided not to go forward after these new announcements, which were, in his view, another example of

[131] Ibid. 1068.

[132] 'Hospital wins in Peter Pan case' *Daily Mirror*, 12 March 1966, 19; 'Entitled to make a Peter Pan film, judge rules' *Birmingham Daily Post*, 12 March 1966, 9; 'Peter Pan, Walt Disney and the sick children', above n 130.

[133] Sneath to Goodman, 19 June 1964; GOS/6/4/129; GOSH Archives.

[134] Piller to Cukor, 17 March 1966, George Cukor Collection, above n 104.

'Disney's careful use of the press, particularly the trade press, which had the effect of scaring investors off while the legal battle was still pending'.[135]

Recognising the central place that the strategic use of the press played in diminishing the interest in the film project has important consequences for the way we think about the controversy. The significance of the case does not rest in the law report, in the parties' expectations of what the law could deliver, or even what authority the British law had. Rather, the most important feature of the case was the effect of its announcement and the fact that the judgment was going to be appealed. While the hospital and Cukor became increasingly irritated by news of the delay, Disney seemed to have a different attitude, which in turn reflected its organisational way of thinking. As Disney projects were segmented into different compartments and divisions, the corporation continued its routine operations around releases or reissues, such as *Mary Poppins* or even *Peter Pan*. This might explain why Disney's London office requested a licence to produce *Peter Pan* pop-up books in the middle of the proceedings, a request that was unsurprisingly rejected by the hospital. Similarly, another form of Disney promotional material, one that circulated while the litigation was going on, caught the hospital's attention. Disney had published a Peter Pan gramophone record including a small booklet. This publication was viewed with suspicion by the hospital as another breach of contract because under the 1953 agreement between Disney and Hodder & Stoughton a line had been drawn between publication and merchandising rights. As a result, the hospital suggested that its licensee, Hodder & Stoughton, consider whether this publication was a further encroachment on the book rights given to the company.[136] However, the publisher did not see the small booklet as an infringement of its rights.[137] The exchange about it reveals more of the extent of the fractured relationship between the hospital and Disney, the loss of trust and the hospital's growing irascibility, no longer considering that the dividing line between merchandising and publishing was clear at all. Perhaps the hospital's management also regretted the past practice of delegating responsibility for drawing the line to the two licensees. Hodder & Stoughton was, in effect, largely a beneficiary of any momentum and reinvention of the characters generated by Disney, or, if it had come to pass, by Cukor and Ferrer. The hospital was not in the same position. It had not stated clearly enough how far Disney could go with the rights it had been given. Notwithstanding the goodwill due to its status as a charity and the benevolent intention of the gift, this situation had left the hospital at a real disadvantage in managing its legal and commercial interests.

During the meeting in Los Angeles, the hospital was made aware that the Cukor, Ferrer and Hepburn triumvirate was breaking up, and that the option and licence

[135] Ferrer to Cukor, 4 April 1966, ibid.
[136] Sneath to Hodder Williams, 29 December 1966; CLC/B/119/MS16375/001; LMA.
[137] Hodder Williams to Sneath, 19 January 1967; CLC/B/119/MS16375/001; LMA.

which had been agreed was not going to be formalised. As such, the film was off the table. After two years, there was no obligation to continue the project in any form, so this did not come as a surprise. The hospital had started to consider the damages compensation enquiry ordered by the judge. However, identifying a reliable method for determining damages was problematic. For what was a film project that was cut off so soon worth? How successful could the *Peter Pan* film have been? How could the prospect of a valuable contract be translated into a concrete monetary value? The hospital interviewed accountants and other financial experts to find metrics for calculating the worth of such a film option and licence.

As might be apparent from our description of the lawsuit, George Cukor and Mel Ferrer never officially joined the case brought by the hospital against Disney. Although they eventually speculated on bringing another action against Disney based upon frustration of contract or alternatively joining the claim already made by the hospital, they never did so, keeping a low profile and not pressing the matter in court. The assessment of damages was based on finding a suitable model to plausibly estimate the projected financial performance of the frustrated Peter Pan venture. Because no model guaranteed an accurate prediction, the measure of past performance of films was investigated by the hospital. One of the benchmarks used was George Cukor's film *My Fair Lady*, as Audrey Hepburn had also appeared in its title role. Ironically, another motion picture used in the assessment was Disney's *Mary Poppins*. By looking at the profits of ten comparable films and the budget figures which Cukor had prepared before Disney came on the scene, the projected value of Peter Pan was estimated, and a representative figure of damages suffered by the hospital was proposed. However, the problem remained because 'it could go sky high as Mary Poppins did; but it could also go the other way'.[138] As Audrey Hepburn's agent, Kurt Frings, observed, 'never has a situation arisen where it is asked that an estimate be made of the profits of a picture that has not been done'.[139] Behind these uncertainties as to how to assess damages, the possibility of negotiating a settlement before lodging the appeal emerged. Disney offered a settlement framework in lieu of its decision to appeal on all issues.

Ultimately, the proposal for future relations between the hospital and Disney did not acknowledge any wrongdoing but was framed in a distinctively creative and outward-looking manner that pursued opportunities for all. Instead of looking at past deeds, it considered the future impact the new *Peter Pan* film could have on the animated cartoon and suggested the implementation of a collaborative working environment that could yield positive outcomes for all parties involved.[140] Although the proposal was commercially attractive, one could suggest that such

[138] Kurt Frings to Gordon Piller, 7 May 1968, George Cukor Collection, above n 104.

[139] Ibid.

[140] Warten Murton (Disney lawyers) to Waterhouse & Co (Hospital) 6 April 1966, George Cukor Collection, above n 104.

an expedient and business-oriented perspective was one of the factors that had propitiated the frictions and frustrations between the hospital and Disney in the first place. Moreover, the offer did not consider that the film project was unlikely to go ahead. As a result, the hospital did not accept the offer and Disney appealed on all issues. Once again, the appeal was amended at the very last moment, and Disney admitted its breach of the agreement, limiting the appeal to arguing that the court should not grant an injunction against an American corporation because it had no means of enforcing the judgment. In February 1967, the Court of Appeal unanimously upheld the hospital's claim and rejected the injunction point made by Disney.[141] The outcome was overwhelmingly in the hospital's favour, and Disney was denied permission to appeal further. Lord Justice Salmon came closest to expressing the outrage felt by the hospital. Salmon LJ referred to the 'cynical disregard' for its pledged word not to object to a new *Peter Pan* film exhibited by Disney's letter to Cukor and Ferrer, particularly because of the very serious financial loss caused to a hospital for sick children.[142] He added that he viewed the company's conduct as falling far below 'the generally accepted standards of commercial propriety. His Lordship could not believe that the man whose name the corporation bore approved of such conduct'.[143] As a result of the judgment, the hospital was then free to deal with the film rights and with other rights which had not yet been committed. However, it was too late for the film venture imagined by Cukor and Ferrer, as they had already moved on to other projects. The inquiry for damages continued for a couple of years, and a settlement with Disney for compensation was eventually reached.[144]

Although the controversy between the hospital and Disney centred around film rights, it had been triggered by the distinct commercial vision of the copyright gift nurtured by the hospital since the early 1960s. If the hospital had not changed its perspective on the copyright gift, the conflict would probably not have arisen. One of the characteristics of the managerial shift can be seen, as mentioned above, in the incorporation of Peter Pan Productions Ltd, an associated company specifically set up by the hospital with the aim of exploiting the merchandising rights. Such an incorporation crystallised the idea that business and charity were not incompatible, and that the hospital could immerse itself in the commercial world without betraying the bequest. The first attempt this company made to register trademarks laid bare that 'there remains very little that we can register in the name of Peter Pan

141 *Hospital for Sick Children (Board of Governors) v Walt Disney Productions, Inc.* [1968] CA 52.

142 'Disney men get Peter Pan rap' *Daily Mirror*, 15 February 1967, 6; 'Disney cannot stop Peter Pan movie' *Arizona Daily Star*, 15 February 1967, 10; 'Disney Productions fail in appeal over Peter Pan' *The Times*, 15 February 1967, 19; Frank Goldsworthy, 'Judges rap Disney company over Peter Pan promise' *Daily Express*, 15 February 1967, 7.

143 *Hospital for Sick Children*, above n 141, 75–6

144 The settlement was reached after the damages were mitigated by a new contract the hospital signed with Universal studios; see Piller to Dixon, 20 June 1970, GOS/6/4/135; GOSH Archives.

and it [was] obvious that the hospital have lost opportunity through being asleep in the past'.[145] While this perception of the past was not completely accurate, as previous hospital management had not even conceived of this possibility, the regret now felt after searching the trademark register and perceiving those instances as missed business opportunities was real.

However, the hospital started to explore other opportunities in different trades. Only a few things, such as fireworks, were a priori discarded as items that, 'from a paediatric point of view', were not considered appropriate.[146] But toys, soaps, greeting cards and cakes began to be considered as potential candidates for Peter Pan merchandising. While the pharmaceutical trade was relatively open to Peter Pan commodities, the confectionery and toy fields were constrained not only by Peter Pan trademarks already registered but also by merchandising operations developed by Disney. Although the hospital tried to register new designs, the US Patent Office first objected that some of them 'were similar to the Disney cartoon characters, which Disney registered some years ago'.[147] The hospital increasingly realised that the rise of commercial possibilities heavily depended on the development of a new image for Peter Pan and other characters such as Wendy, Tinker Bell and Captain Hook. One solution to this problem was to consider the services of external agencies with expertise in merchandising campaigns. For this, Peter Pan Productions Ltd considered a range of companies, from well-known advertising agencies to the firm in charge of the Beatles' publicity campaigns, attempting to assess which was the right one to help with the task of refreshing the Peter Pan brand. As it happened, the hospital finally selected Tuckwell & Associates, a company managed by a former Disney employee who had been involved in the Peter Pan merchandising programme in the 1950s.[148] While the following chapter assesses the significance of the rise of independent agencies for the development of merchandising rights in Britain, we would like to note here that Tuckwell became incidentally involved in sketching a new image for Peter Pan for the hospital. However, the final decision to launch new Peter Pan imagery was cancelled because

[145] Piller to Sneath, 12 March 1964; GOS/6/4/123; GOSH Archives. While the trademark Peter Pan had been registered and used for toys by Cecil Coleman Ltd, another firm that had registered and used the trademark for other classes around the world was R. and W.H. Symington & Co, Ltd, a corset manufacturer from Leicestershire making underwear, swimwear and children's clothes; see 'R & W.H. Symington & Co. Ltd – Peter Pan Trademarks – Provisional List' (c.1965)' DE 3730/129; Leicestershire, Leicester and Rutland Record Office. Further complicating the picture was the proliferation of other long-established Peter Pan brands in the marketplace. For instance, Peter Pan peanut butter was a well-known brand advertised and used in America since the 1920s; see Jon Krampner, *Creamy and Crunchy: An Informal History of Peanut Butter, the All-American Food*, Columbia University Press, 2013, 46–58.

[146] Piller to Sneath, 17 March 1964; GOS/6/4/123; GOSH Archives.

[147] Sneath to Piller, 21 January 1965; GOS/6/4/99; GOSH Archives.

[148] Sneath to Piller, 6 April 1965; GOS/6/4/99; GOSH Archives. The merchandising agency had been recommended to the hospital by Hodder & Stoughton; see Ewart Wharmby to Hodder Williams, 8 March 1966; CLC/B/119/MS16352/001/002; LMA.

FIGURE 5.4 Walter Tuckwell holding a Peter Pan drawing, c. 1963
Courtesy of Tasmin Overton

of the prospect of a new film.[149] The Cukor and Ferrer film project appeared as the key vehicle for a new version of Peter Pan beyond the one portrayed by the Disney animated cartoon. However, once the film project stalled, Peter Pan Productions Limited and its associated projects found it difficult to survive. In 1972, less than a decade after its formation, the company was dissolved.[150]

5.6 EXTENDED RIGHTS

During the dispute with Disney, the hospital chairman was Audrey Callaghan, wife of future Prime Minister Jim Callaghan. In 1987, Lord Callaghan introduced

[149] Similarly, the American publisher Scribner's had contacted E.H. Shepard, the children's illustrator of *Winnie the Pooh*, to do illustrations for a new *Peter Pan* in America, but Shepard rejected the proposal: see Shepard to Spencer Curtis Brown, 28 December 1960; EHS/C/2/2/50; Archives & Special Collections; University of Surrey.

[150] *The London Gazette*, 27 October 1972, 12691.

a bill in Parliament to ensure that the Great Ormond Street Hospital for Sick and Poor Children would continue to receive royalties despite the copyright expiration. It is our suggestion that the introduction of this bill was directly connected to political awareness of the controversy discussed in this chapter. The dispute between Disney and the hospital had meant that not only did the hospital miss a commercial opportunity to raise funds for sick and poor children but it also prompted a reflection on the representation of property, the significance of copyright, its length and the best way to manage it. The key term in judicial reflections on the relationship between the gift and copyright was perhaps 'propriety'. Instead of thinking about copyright as just a vehicle for profit, the chapter has argued that the understanding of copyright was entangled in ongoing practices that led to the copyright gift conveying different ways to perform its charitable character for children.

In the first decades of the management of the copyright gift, one of the interesting contractual relations that resulted was the arrangement with Disney in 1939. While the precise nature of the agreement raised several questions throughout the following decades, culminating in a protracted lawsuit between the hospital and the corporation, this chapter has argued that Disney's efficient managerial practices across media were in clear contrast to the hospital's traditional and conservative stance, which lasted until the 1960s. However, the shift in the hospital's attitude to the management of the *Peter Pan* copyright which followed led to an increased interest in merchandising as a source of revenue. Ironically, this change was one of the elements that facilitated the clash with Disney, which ultimately meant that no *Peter Pan* film was ever made. This fact was raised by a member of Parliament when the bill was discussed. As he observed: 'I know that those who advise the special trustees have met with a number of false starts when trying to get a film made'.[151] The parliamentary discussion revealed that the tension between charity and business that characterised the *Peter Pan* copyright gift to the hospital still polarised political opinion. Is there anybody against the idea of helping the Great Ormond Street Hospital? Of course not. But is copyright an appropriate means to do so? The answer was not so unanimous. Lord Willis perhaps represented those who felt uncomfortable about using copyright to 'subsidise the National Health Service' and asked whether there were not many other very good children's charities around beyond the Great Ormond Street Hospital equally deserving financial help.[152] Although these concerns were not considered and the amendment of the copyright statutes was

[151] HL Deb 10 March 1988, vol. 494, cc805–60 (Copyright, Designs and Patents Bill [HL] (Lord Jenkin)).

[152] HL Deb 10 March 1988, vol. 494, cc805–60 (Copyright, Designs and Patents Bill [HL] (Lord Willis)); see also Catherine Seville, 'Peter Pan rights: to protect or petrify?' (2004) 33(2) *Cambridge Quarterly* 119–54, 123.

accepted, they demonstrated a point that had already been made by some critics of the copyright expansion, such as Justice Laddie.[153]

Perhaps the most important question does not refer to the expansion of copyright or the distinction between charity and business but to what constitutes propriety in the exploitation of copyright, particularly in connection to a children's institution. Much of Disney's impact lay in its co-ordinated strategies to separate characters from their media in order to capitalise on their attachment to licensed commodities. Besides numerous innovations in advertising, consumption and public relations (only some of which we have mentioned in this chapter), one highly interesting outcome was the hospital's attempt to find a new image for Peter Pan which could compete with the Disney ideal. Although the strategy was frustrated by the cancellation of the film project, it shows the increasing cultural and commercial importance that merchandising agencies were acquiring in Britain. The next chapter will investigate how, in the mid-1950s, the professionalisation of merchandising agencies took place. It will also discuss their struggle to occupy a middle position between proprietors and children, and between manufacturers and commodities.

[153] These criticisms were made extrajudicially: see Hugh Laddie, 'Copyright: over-strength, over-regulated, over-rated' [1996] 18 *European Intellectual Property Review* 253–60.

6

The Rise of Merchandising Agencies

The rise of agencies specifically aimed at expanding the market for child-centred commodities based on intellectual properties is a mid-twentieth-century phenomenon. While previous chapters have explored the emergence of merchandising campaigns, their existence was tied to internal workings of specific corporations, institutions or settings such as Pat Sullivan Studios, Meccano Ltd or the Disney Corporation. These entities conceived merchandising activities not only as a source of revenue but increasingly as a way to enhance the circulation of what was initially considered to be their main product – the film, the toy or the animated cartoon feature. Their distinctive merchandising activities forged new relationships between child-focused markets and intellectual property negotiated by lawyers, agents and other professionals who were part of the corporate enterprise.

This chapter looks at the emergence of agencies in Britain which began to offer similar merchandise services as Disney, but outside the corporate structure in which these had initially been nurtured. The chapter shows how this development was tied to the opportunities engendered by the adjudication of television licences and the subsequent proliferation of television channels covering the whole British territory. The arrival of commercial television facilitated and stabilised contractual practices between agencies and sectors, such as the toy, publishing and food industries, eager to capitalise on the new medium. In the race for audience ratings, these agencies began offering merchandising campaigns to exploit programmes and their components (characters, titles and formats). A consequence of commercial television was the creation of specific departments or companies associated to television licence-holders linking the growth of television audiences to developing extended commercial opportunities. Their role gradually shifted from advertising and public relations to activities more closely related to intellectual property exploitation, such as merchandising. This involved looking at exclusive properties, not just from a protective point of view but also with a view to the potential revenue that contractual rights could generate. This focus changed the characteristics of goodwill which came to be understood not just as a feature exclusively embedded in the film, toy, or cartoon as such. It was constituted by coordinating the social life of the character-based media enterprise. As a result, a new profession began to evolve, aimed at developing programmes to engineer brand identities and 'properties', drawing owners, investors and children towards merchandising schemes and proposals.

The chapter follows these changes and the legal conflicts these activities generated: first, by giving a brief overview of the attempt to set up a company like Disney in Britain, G-B Animation Ltd; and, second, by tracing the rise and fall of the most influential independent British agency of the period, Walter Tuckwell & Associates. A former Disney employee, Walter Frank Tuckwell built a portfolio representing characters which linked commercial and legal opportunities elicited by television programmes and connected them to the emerging demand for child-related products. Through a look at the early days of this agency, it is possible to observe how the challenges and anxieties embedded in such a connection occasionally blurred the distinction between advertising and creation. This is not only a historical analysis of a specific period. Though the central focus is on the development and consolidation of the associated intellectual property issues, there is also a contemporary dimension, as shown by ongoing controversies relating to 'World Cup Willie', 'Betty Boop' and 'Hush Puppy', among others.

6.1 AFTER DISNEY

As mentioned in previous chapters, the transition from short films such as *Silly Symphonies* to feature films like *Snow White* shaped the studio-origination narratives that characterised Disney as a corporation. This move was facilitated by a training programme in the 1930s which aimed at streamlining the amount of work involved in making long feature films.[1] The transition also precipitated several organisational changes due to the economic pressures building up on Disney, which in turn resulted in a greater emphasis on corporate streams and merchandising activities to finance projects such as *Peter Pan*. While the dispute between Disney and the Great Ormond Street Hospital offered us a glimpse of the legal issues triggered by this shift and the corporation's method of creating business around properties (or properties around business), we would like now to follow the ways in which Disney's style and entrepreneurial practices were imitated in Britain a decade later. This specific focus is helpful in tracing the emergence of local merchandising agencies beyond Disney – that is, the appearance of a kind of expertise outside the American corporation in the same legal and commercial practices in which Disney had excelled.

1 The introduction of colour added another layer to industrial organisation in the studio: see Hannah Frank, *Frame by Frame: A Materialist Aesthetics of Animated Cartoons*, University of California Press, 2019, 117; Kirsten Moana Thompson, 'Quick – Like a bunny!' The Ink and Paint Machine, female labor and color production' (2014) 9 *Animation Studies*: http://journal.animationstudies.org/kirsten-thompson-quick-like-a-bunny.

The clearest attempt by the British film industry to make cartoons and animated features like Disney was the establishment of a subsidiary of the Rank Organisation: G-B Animation Ltd. What is remarkable about this experimental set-up was not only the effort to make similar cartoons but also the attempt to replicate the efficient industrial production and the legal and commercial strategies developed by Disney in order to compete with the American corporation.

In 1945, David Hand, a former Disney executive, was brought to England by J. Arthur Rank to develop its animation unit.[2] One of the veterans of the animation business, Hand had extensive experience in every branch of studio work, including drawing, action-timing and sound effects. However, he was specifically hired for his managerial skills and his pragmatic attitude.[3] As a supervising director at Disney, he became the second-in-command. As such, he was identified as the person most capable of heading what was initially imagined as Disney's British competitor. The launch of this venture required, as Disney had done in its transition to feature films, an ambitious recruitment and training programme for animators, technicians, secretaries and commercial agents. It also needed a location and specialist equipment to produce animated features on an industrial scale. After Hand's arrival, G-B Animation established its headquarters in Cookham, a small village in Berkshire, which had been the centre of operations of Odeon Films. Most of the recruits were ex-service men and women, but they also included former Disney employees. The special equipment the new venture acquired was also an attempt to rival, albeit on a minor scale, its American counterpart. It involved specially designed animator's tables, Bell & Howell cartoon film cameras, typewriters, duplicating machines and a 200-line telephone exchange.[4] The unit established a training scheme for would-be artists and animators, which involved learning the specialist techniques of animation.

One of the features central to this exercise was the making of the 'book of keys' from which character 'model sheets', mentioned in previous chapters, emerged. The book contained essential reference material, which served to coordinate work around both the production and distribution sides while the animated features took shape. On the one hand, these sheets specified and visualised characteristics for animators, juniors and in-betweeners to create the features.[5] On the other hand,

2 'Rank enters cartoon field and signs Disney Executive' *Kinematograph Weekly*, 22 March 1945, 46; 'British made cartoons' *Kinematograph Weekly*, 20 December 1945, 184; Geoffrey Macnab, *J. Arthur Rank and the British Industry*, Routledge, 1993, 131–6; Ken Clarke. 'GBA: a great British achievement' (1987) 19 April–June *Animator* 25–7.

3 This is what transpires from an interview he gave in 1973, see Michael Barrier, 'David Hand' in Didier Ghez (ed.), *Walt's People: vol. 1 Talking Disney with the Artists Who Knew Him*, Theme Park Press, 2014, 35–56.

4 'Dizzier Disney' *Birmingham Daily Gazette*, 6 September 1948, 2; 'Keen bidding expected for Rank Cartoon Equipment' *Kinematograph Weekly*, 20 April 1950, 47.

5 Model sheets were visual interpretations of the characters which circulated inside the studio together with exposure sheets, another type of document that included timing instructions and

commercial agents used duplicates of the sheets to encourage toy and confectionery manufacturers and retailers to take out licences. The sheets allowed licensees to produce a construction blueprint for their products, enabling them to adapt the character to their commodities while the cartoon was still being produced. In the meantime, in demonstrating the potential appeal of the characters to merchants, revenue in the form of intellectual property licences and advance payments to the animation unit could support production. Aware of the importance of these sheets to financing film production, animation companies specifically inscribed the copyright notice in the sheets. Indeed, this became a characteristic merchandising tool, followed by Disney and continued by other studios such as Warner Bros, as well as G-B Animation.[6]

Although G-B Animation was initially set up to create animated cartoon films for world release, it also engaged in the production of industrial short features for advertising purposes. The idea behind these assignments was twofold. Firstly, the Odeon and Gaumont exhibition circuit was controlled by the Rank Organisation, particularly the Saturday matinees.[7] Promoting advertising created inhouse to audiences made for a productive use of this circuit. Secondly, G-B Animation used these shorts to train newly hired artists in the skills of the animation business.

During the first years of its existence, the animation unit produced short commercials for different companies and brands such as Esso and Gillette. However, the most significant assignment was the series of short commercials commissioned by the chocolate manufacturer, Rowntree, and the advertising agency, J. Walter Thompson. This series of advertising films featured a cartoon character known as 'Coco' developed by the studio. The negotiation for the exploitation of this character reveals how Hand not only brought artistic and industrial techniques to G-B Animation but also the contractual manoeuvres Disney had developed to set up its business and profit from merchandising operations. Like Disney, G-B Animation separated the copyright in the character of Coco from the media in which it appeared, a contractual feature that puzzled both the advertising agency and the chocolate manufacturer. The issue appears to have been overlooked in the drafting process, as the advertising agency had assumed that when G-B Animation referred to the copyright in the character

other key information for the making of the animated feature. For a description of the in-between department, see Shamus Culhane, *Taking Animals and Other People*, St Martin's Press, 1986, 111–3.

6 Although devoted to a later period, there are some interesting references to the connection between model sheets and merchandising in Linda Simensky, 'Selling Bugs Bunny: Warner Brothers and character merchandising in the nineties' in Kevin S. Sandler (ed.), *Reading the Rabbit: Explorations in Warner Bros Animation*, Rutgers University Press, 1998, 172–92.

7 In fact, it is probable that there was an element of cross-financing whereby screening the shorts in Rank cinemas generated income for G-B Animation. However, as Macnab points out, 'even where the cartoons were being shown, in Rank's Odeon and Gaumonts, they were too far down the bill to generate much revenue'; see Macnab, above n 2, 135.

Coco, it meant the copyright 'in all *Coco* films'.[8] However, that was not the case. G-B Animation argued that if Rowntree wanted to use Coco in any context other than films (such as in print advertising campaigns) 'a licence would be necessary'.[9] The parties met a few times at Cookham to sort out the problems surrounding the rights to the property. Hand insisted that G-B Animation receive royalties not only for the film but also for press use of Coco. According to the confectionery company, the disturbing point was that G-B Animation saw these shorts as purely incidental to the production of entertainment films.[10] In other words, that the films made by G-B Animation and the character conceived therein were 'creations' on their own, and they consequently held their copyright.[11] More than this, the specificity of these contractual practices was such that it was not only the advertising agency and the chocolate manufacturer that found them baffling. As we have indicated in previous chapters, a range of solicitors, publishers and children's writers and illustrators had already found them problematic.[12]

While G-B Animation also produced educational films, the closest it got to reproducing a Disney style of entertainment was *Animaland*, a remarkable creative attempt to produce a cartoon series in Britain. The merchandising system developed by Disney, involving the creation of a specific department to issue and handle licences, was also mirrored. Copyright was announced to subsist in the characters of the series, a practice Disney had developed from its early stages. Moreover, licences were issued for a significant range of commodities, such as plasticine and balloons. Similar to Disney's approach, the programme involved the exhibition of the whole merchandise range in key locations, such as the Selfridge's Toy Shop at the Ideal Home Exhibition, one of the event's main attractions in the late 1940s. Furthermore, it tried to appeal to prospective licensees by letting them know that their commodities would be pre-sold since 'the characters were loved in advance by thousands of prospective cinema goers'.[13]

8 Meeting at York between Mr Rowntree, Mr Watson and Mr Tinsbury (J. Walter Thompson) at which a draft of the J. Walter Thompson letter to G-B Animation was left with Mr Watson for consideration, 6 September 1946; HAT50/1/158/2/1/1/11.

9 Meeting in London between Mr Palfery (G-B Animation) and Mr Sinclair and Mr Tinsbury (J. Walter Thompson), 26 August 1946; HAT50/1/158/2/1/1/11.

10 G.J. Harris to J.D. Watson, 10 March 1946 ('Coco Copyright'); HAT50/1/158/2/1/1/11.

11 Emma Robertson highlights these copyright problems of the character and also discusses 'the disturbing logics at work', mainly the racial stereotyping (in a context of decolonisation) in the figure of Coco; see Emma Robertson, *Chocolate, Women and Empire. A Social and Cultural History*, Manchester University Press, 2009, 41–5.

12 See Chapter 5 at 161. Another children's illustrator who was troubled by them was Winnie-the-Pooh's illustrator, E.H. Shepard, who wrote to his agent 'worried about the situation over Pooh with Disney Co. and wondered about how far they can go and how far is my copyright covered'; see Shepard to Curtis Brown, 12 July 1966; EHS/C/2/2/99; Archives & Special Collections; University of Surrey.

13 'They get into everything' *Daily Film Renter*, 21 February 1949, 1; 'Selfridge's Toy Shop at Olympia' (1949) April *Games and Toys* 98; see also 'Animaland's Merchandise' (1949) February *Games and Toys* 84.

The commercial programme did not turn out to be as successful as expected. Only nine cartoons eventuated. While it is tempting to compare the failure of the scheme to a box-office flop, it is worth investigating why the market and legal conditions necessary to coordinate films and merchandise did not function as smoothly as with Disney. There were significant risks inherent in relying upon an appeal to future goodwill to attract the interest of licensees to finance upcoming production, as newspaper rumours and gossip abounded about the prospects of the series. This included trade speculation that the main character was a 'corpse' because the Rank Organisation was going to close down the film studios and stop producing the animated cartoons.[14] The merchandising department of G-B Animation had to publicly state that the series was very much 'alive and kicking', and that there were at least 'nineteen films, some of which have not yet been shown and that there was still residual value of the films and reruns'.[15] However, despite a public attempt to counter the gloomy predictions about the longevity of the series, production soon ceased and the characters were quickly forgotten. Moreover, this failure demonstrated that, while it was relatively easy to persuade manufacturers to synchronise initial production of merchandise with the film's release date, it was more difficult to maintain the interest and keep the characters alive. The creation of goodwill required a communication strategy and associated infrastructure attached to film production and the other enterprises to support and promote the life of the characters. As we saw in Chapter 5, control of the news about upcoming releases was as important as securing the film rights because news and industry gossip had a clear impact on exploitation and circulation prospects for both film and merchandise. The potential to license the property in the character was undermined by doubts about the future of the cartoons. Although there was a grain of truth in some of the rumours, this was a problematic issue. The more doubts proliferated about the cartoon's viability, the greater the impact on its commercial prospects, leading to a withdrawal of support which in turn led to a reduction in investment in future cartoon production. In effect, industry gossip had damaged the potential to generate goodwill, and, as one commentator indicated, it was more than a coincidence that such rumours seemed to come from competitors.[16]

G-B Animation ceased its operations in 1950. While the attempt to compete with Disney was not successful, the influence of the British animation studio continued to be felt long after it closed, particularly because it had functioned as a training programme. In addition, G-B Animation was significant for having introduced a number of artistic, legal and commercial practices that continued in Britain under different guises and projects after the company closed down. While it is possible to

[14] 'My Log' (1950) April *Games and Toys* 84; 'The future of Ginger Nutt and company' (1950) April *Toy Trader and Exporter* 44.

[15] 'My Log', above n 14.

[16] 'More rumours are going around about the future of the David Hand coloured cartoons', *Daily Film Renter*, 23 November 1949, 5; 'Wardour Street gossip' *Daily Film Renter*, 20 February 1950, 4.

trace the career trajectories of former G-B Animation artists, many of whom moved into magazine comics after the studio closed, we would like to highlight the impact the studio had on merchandising practices, as those who had been trained to cut these deals ended up dominating the field in the following decades. John B. Myers, the head of the publicity department at G-B Animation, and Peter Barker, his assistant, both moved from the Rank Organisation to *Eagle*, one of the best-known comics of the 1950s. With them they brought artists to convert comic strips into toys, cards and games,[17] and both men continued their merchandising careers after they left *Eagle*.[18] Another agent who followed a similar career path, beginning at G-B Animation and moving on to different projects, was Walter Tuckwell. He was also an ex-serviceman, hired by Hand to commercialise animated features for the British animation studio. Ironically, he moved to Disney in the early 1950s to continue working as an agent commercialising characters before setting up the first independent merchandising agency in Britain.[19]

6.2 SNOWBALLING AS A TECHNIQUE

In March 1950, Myers sought financial support for a weekly publication for children and teenagers. He set out the vital ingredients for the project's success, predicting a profitable future if these recommendations were followed. With the financial backing of Hulton Press secured, the venture would eventually become very successful. Many post-war children in Britain, Australia and New Zealand still affectionately recall *Eagle* magazine, and its most popular feature, 'Dan Dare, Pilot of the Future'. The magazine was soon followed by the launch of its companion publications (*Girl*, *Robin* and *Swift*), with the prospective market being divided according to age and gender.

[17] 'New merchandising scheme' (1950) October *Games and Toys* 78; 'Our Artists in the Trade. No 3: Anthony Speer; staff artist to Hulton Enterprises' (1951) November *Toy Trader and Exporter* 78.

[18] 'It's all in the character £50,000,000' *Time and Tide*, 29 February–6 March 1968, 31; 'Peter Barker, Ltd' in 'Character Merchandise' (1963) June *British Toys* 14; 'Secure your Sooty licence: Peter Barker Ltd' (1963) September *Games and Toys* 79; 'Sooty: licence applications to Peter Barker Ltd' (1966) January *Games and Toys* 248; 'Ten years and onwards' (1966) September *Games and Toys* 4; 'Tuckwell Associates' (1966) September *Games and Toys* 12–13, 12; 'Merchandising for Q4' (1967) April *British Toys* 8; 'Merchandising for Cunard' (1968) March *Games and Toys* 64; 'The fantastically successful Sooty' (1970) July *Games and Toys* 48; 'Larry the Lamb is coming to television: enquiries should be made to Peter Barker Ltd' (1973) September *British Toys* 4; 'Woozy: all merchandising enquiries should be made to Peter Barker Ltd' (1975) September *British Toys* 10.

[19] 'Money in film merchandise: new British cartoon film industry' (1948) September *Games and Toys* 88–9; 'Tuck starts new company' (1956) September *Toy Trader and Exporter* 34; 'The independent character merchandiser arrives' *Advertiser's Weekly*, 9 November 1956, 9; 'Obituary: Walter Tuckwell' (1980) February/March *Games and Toys* 36 (describing him as 'the doyen of character merchandising').

Eagle magazine, a comics periodical, was launched with an aggressive marketing strategy – having its distribution on full sale or return – an initiative that caused the publisher to resign from the Newspaper Proprietors Association. Yet, the most interesting aspect of Myers' proposal was not the aggressive publicity campaign or the market segmentation but the use of a magazine as the basis for a comprehensive merchandising scheme. Although the idea of a children's comic was obviously nothing new, the novelty of the approach resided in the explicit focus on merchandising as a socio-legal programme to connect a variety of tasks, children and commodities. The key aim was to develop a sustainable and recursive commercial plan through which to capture children's interest in a multiplicity of activities related to the magazine – such as tie-ups, exhibitions and toys – a popularisation system that could generate several streams of revenue. Writers have tended to focus on the British credentials of *Eagle*, interpreting it as an initiative motivated by concerns over the Americanisation of childhood.[20] However, while Myers devoted some pages to the magazine content, the emphasis of his plan was on the material practices that could convert the idea into a commercial enterprise. As he stated, merchandising was a 'snowballing technique', an innovative commercial strategy that blended creative, legal and marketing features.[21]

Although the metaphor is now a cliché, it was not so at the time. It pointed out that as the ball rolled, more snow could be picked up with relative ease; the earning capacity of the enterprise depended not just on the initial consumer 'catch' but also on the development of a supportive context of consumption that maintained and even enhanced the magazine's popularity among children. In other words, the key was to create a practical environment for promotional events and initiatives to act as 'bait', attracting readers and converting them into consumers.[22] Such a setting was built on the opportunities created by the scheme that would, in turn, facilitate the magazine's circulation. A managerial effort would support the magazine to grow up alongside those who were going to become its avid readers. As would later be noted in a report on the magazine, 'one must catch one's readers at the moment they enter the relevant age group and never let them go'.[23] The proposal emphasised the need to develop commercial alliances in order to convert the venture into a sustainable and stimulating project. Among the different ways to give it a reliable trajectory was the periodical organisation of children's exhibitions and fairs. According to Myers, holding such annual events was an important strategy to generate goodwill. It was

[20] Graham Kibble-White, *The Ultimate Book of British Comics*, Allison & Busby, 2005, 112; James Chapman, *British Comics: A Cultural History*, Reaktion Books, 2011, 45–75.

[21] John B. Myers, 'A preliminary survey on merchandising and large-scale exploitation to be built-up on the regular publication of a juvenile paper, March 1950'; Box 13; Item 7; MM/CUA.

[22] As one trade journal observed, the very fact that Eagle-licensed commodities made an immediate appeal to children meant that parents could react against them, so retailers were specifically advised to follow a careful and tactful selling, that is, to stress the quality points of the merchandise; see 'Is this your business?' (1952) September *Fashions and Fabrics* 55.

[23] 'Hulton Press Publicity 1958/9: The Children's Papers'; Box 18; Item 14 (surveys); MM/CUA.

not only that the popularity prospects of *Eagle* and its featured characters would increase with the exposure heightened by the fairs, but that the events themselves would also provide trade connections with toy and clothing manufacturers and retailers.

The events in themselves were not conceived as profitable ventures in the short term. The arrangements would offer display and promotional opportunities that would lead to profit eventually through growing goodwill. Participation in such fairs would foster collaborative environments for licensees or prospective licensees to feel that they had the backing of the licensor, a corporation linked to the investor, Hulton Press. An ideal place for these events was suggested: the National Hall at Olympia. The proposal highlighted the need for 'something concrete to offer, the value of which [could] easily be explained'.[24] Property in the goodwill would emerge by association if the coordinating programme was professionally executed. In differentiation from earlier merchandising ventures that revolved around specific subject matter and fictional characters that animated the trade, merchandising was here better described as a practice geared towards an arrangement and co-ordination of commercial activities. These recommendations crystallised in different ways alongside the trajectory of the magazine.[25]

Myers also explained the legal technique upon which the merchandising scheme was to be based. Although we take licensing contracts for granted today, the time he spent explaining these practices demonstrates that merchandising was seen then as a special, and not-so-common, legal assemblage combining property, contract and marketing knowledge. As discussed in Chapter 5, licensing plans could go awry. In explaining the practice, Myers highlighted the characteristics of the licence, the contract – which played a pivotal role in scaling up the operations, as well as maintaining the status of the *Eagle* characters, such as 'Dan Dare', and enlarging their exploitation across different trade lines. Myers recognised that the Disney model licence would provide the best foundation for the enterprise: it was the one he had used in G-B Animation.

As with Disney, the merchandising department classified goods and services in the distribution and drafting of licences. It was thought important to be more and more specific and to divide them up as much as possible, breaking down these categories into different parts and specific opportunities. Instead of licensing goods and services, the approach was to imagine how many licences could be granted in each of the categories. In other words, the licensing opportunity was the primary commodity of the enterprise. In that sense, 'every category should be examined from

24 Myers, above n 21.

25 The most significant events co-ordinating these activities were the Hulton's Boys' and Girls' Exhibitions which began in 1956 at Olympia and broke all attendance records for the National Hall; MSS.179/1/32/45; MHC; see also 'Hulton's Boys and Girls Exhibition' (1956) September *Games and Toys* 73; 'Record breaking Hulton show' (1956) October *Toy Trader and Exporter* 41; 'Avenue of the FUTURE: Hulton Boys and Girls Exhibition' (1956) January *British Toys* 14.

the point of view of the number of licences available'.[26] The length of the arrangements and the possibility of withdrawal were also carefully highlighted since they constituted control mechanisms over manufacturers and retailers who remained in a contingent relationship of dependency. However, the most interesting ingredient of the licensing system was that, according to Myers, this facilitated the 'snowballing technique' mentioned above. Licensees were not merely individuals with a contractual relationship with the firm, they were participants in a community of licensees who were not in direct competition with each other. Once a licence was issued, future selling was less difficult and the business became 'ripe for intelligent opportunism', by finding new opportunities through building on the combined market intelligence of licensees.[27] An explanation of this commercial strategy given by Myers is instructive. Instead of issuing a licence to make all types of lampshades, he argued that it was preferable to make it susceptible to multiplication – in other words, to issue different licences for plastic, parchment and revolving lampshades. The active, expansive nature of licences involving trade lines was designed to make each licensed article complementary and not competitive, ideally with traders suggesting new lines. The whole point of establishing a licensing network was to construct a self-generating process, a system that possessed the capacity to reproduce licences by coordinating and matching opportunities. One consequence of seeing the property in this way was that it tended to conceptualise copyright not in terms of cultural subject matter but in terms of commercial activities centred on exclusive merchandising, licensing and franchising opportunities.

As Myers had predicted, a solid network of licensees connected to Hulton Press emerged in the early 1950s as the popularity of *Eagle* increased. The trade in goods connected to *Eagle* characters expanded significantly, ranging from guns to cowboy outfits, jigsaws, chocolate figurines and many other commodities geared towards children.[28] The appeal lay in the kind of engagement that licensees were offered. For instance, they were given special premiums, such as display and reference material based on the characters of the magazine for use in shops and exhibitions at specially discounted rates. Licensees were also attracted by the extensive readership and circulation. Self-generating commercial opportunities were enhanced by producing tensions that traders could reconcile by more active engagement in the enterprise. On the one hand, they were informed of facts and figures of interest and hence were left to wonder about a potential market out there. On the other hand, they were supplied with circulation figures and informed about the *Eagle* club,

[26] Myers, above n 21.

[27] Ibid.

[28] 'Hulton's games, toys and link with Eagle features has huge scope' *World's Press News*, 16 March 1951, 4; 'Eagle merchandise' (1951) September *Games and Toys* 128; 'Sales soar with Eagle' (1951) September *Games and Toys* 109; 'Eagle tie-up' (1952) May *Games and Toys* 126; 'Eagle licensees' (1953) December *Games and Toys* 68; 'More variety in toys' *The Times*, 21 December 1953, 4.

which had recruited more than a thousand members in the two years following the launch of the magazine. The club was indeed both a prospective market and a 'circulation-getter and holder'. Members were given special treatment, for instance, being offered subsidised activities, 'give-aways' and 'sponsored trips' because they were conceived as 'a voluntary body of publicists and helpers having considerable influence in their own sphere'.[29] That the club did not emerge as a spontaneous gathering but was designed as a public relations tool was confirmed by the editor of the magazine, Marcus Morris, when he said, 'We don't want children just wearing the *Eagle* badge. We want it to mean something to them and to the people who see them wearing them'.[30]

Rather than treating all of these events and marketing techniques as different activities, the scheme aimed to coordinate them and make them work together. Indeed, it is clear that membership numbers dramatically increased during the annual exhibitions at Olympia because it provided an opportunity for children to be invited to join the club should they want to enjoy special privileges such as access to a 'club only' gallery. Similarly, there was no better form of advertising than the press reports and photographs in different newspapers showing the children enjoying exhibitions.

Product diversification and trade expansion triggered by such marketing and promotional strategies meant that legal problems quickly emerged. In fact, one of the initial effects of merchandising activities was, as we have seen in previous chapters, to produce legal and contractual misunderstandings as activities were read in line with different categories of intellectual property rights. The first of these controversies came just a year after the magazine was launched, when the publisher successfully sued a holiday camp in Wales for its attempt to attract children and teenagers using the name 'White Eagle Holiday Camp for Boys'.[31] The action was brought in passing-off, with Hulton claiming that, due to the goodwill attached to *Eagle*, the camp's use of the term in its title would create a misapprehension that the two enterprises were connected. Hulton was granted an interim injunction to prevent the defendants from using the word 'Eagle' in any title for boys' holiday camps.[32] The dispute illustrated a complex issue that would remain controversial for

[29] Eagle Management, Budget Proposal. April 1951–March 1952; Box 16; Item 1 (club policy); MM/CUA; see also 'Eagle Club Rally' *National Newsagent Bookseller, Stationer*, 29 December 1951; 'Tractor tie-up with Eagle' *Advertising Weekly*, 13 September 1951; 'Mug of the week' *Peterborough Citizen and Advertiser*, 17 October 1952; Box 6; Item 1 (Eagle Cuttings); MM/CUA.

[30] Notes for Marcus Morris to speak at the Hulton Press Sales Conference, 26 April 1951; Box 16; Item 9 (Sales Promotion Branch: Early Days of Eagle Club); MM/CUA.

[31] *Hulton Press Ltd v White Eagle Youth Holiday Camp Ltd* (1951) 68 RPC 126.

[32] 'Claim to Eagle title' *Manchester Guardian*, 16 March 1951; 'Writ over a title' *Morning Advertiser*, 16 March 1951; 'Express involved in action on use of name Eagle' *World's Press News*, 21 March 1951; 'Hulton writ against Express and Holiday Camp' *World's Press News*, 22 March 1951; 'Hulton's claim to Eagle title: an important issue to the press, says KC' *Advertisers Weekly*, 18 April 1951; 'Hulton White Eagle action' *Newspaper World*, 10 May

years to come. While the law began to entertain the inherent possibility of consumer confusion between two different ventures (a magazine and a holiday camp), it is surprising that the evidence produced by the plaintiffs was framed to link the two ventures precisely by moving away from the publication, itself protected by copyright, towards other signifiers of goodwill such as figures and artefacts related to merchandising activities such as the *Eagle* club and badges.[33] In other words, the source of the reputation and associated goodwill shifted from manufacturing to the merchandising chain. In this way, merchandising practices began to contribute to a wider historical move away from legal delineations of rights with respect to specific goods and services, as recognised by the design and trademark register, to the brands themselves. This has been noted by some scholars as heralding 'a shift from product identification to the appreciation of the cultural meaning of that good'.[34]

A second controversy came from some educational and library sectors emphasising the harmful effect of comics on children. Although such criticism continued for decades, one of the features worth highlighting here is that *Eagle* and its companion magazines were praised precisely because they did not include violence and other 'American' influences. The fact that the founding editor of *Eagle* was an Anglican priest, who participated in debates trying to persuade public opinion of the educational value of the publication, helped to ease some of the criticism. Again, skilful marketing and advertising techniques targeting parents and educators were crucial in making the enterprise a successful one. That invitations to annual exhibitions were distributed among key people such as school headmasters helped to further enhance the magazine's image. Similarly, the exhibitions were conveniently timed at the end of summer to persuade parents to bring their children to the events. As Myers had anticipated, the 'quality, value and wholesomeness of the paper should encourage support from parents, schools, and even the church, and while this aspect, if detected by children, would have decidedly negative appeal, it may, nevertheless, carry considerable weight in future ancillary merchandising and exhibition projects which [were] outlined in his report'.[35]

Myers also highlighted the possibility of setting up lucrative merchandising plans outside and beyond Disney and different from earlier forms of merchandising such as that of Beatrix Potter characters, the more recent *Rudolph the Red-Nosed Reindeer* and the near contemporary 'Noddy'. As discussed in Chapter 4, while Disney had been the most prominent and sophisticated enterprise, its successful business model was mainly derived from a strategy built on film cartoon characters. A magazine like

1951; 'Interim injunction press in Eagle' *Newspaper World*, 19 April 1951; 'Holiday camp forbidden to use the name Eagle' *World's Press News*, April 20, 1951; Box 6; Item 1 (Eagle Cuttings); MM/CUA.

[33] *Hulton Press v White Eagle*, above n 31, 128–9.

[34] Mario Biagioli, Anupam Chander and Madhavi Sunder, 'Brand new world: distinguishing oneself in the global flow' (2013) 47(2) *UC Davis Law Review* 455–72, 466.

[35] Myers, above n 21.

Eagle was able to circumvent the film circuit dominated by the American corporation and produce a set-up to profit from the child-related commodities that emerged alongside the distribution of a print publication. A switch of media source could fend off the animated feature film merchandising virtual monopoly. Whereas films were exhibited in cinemas and animated film merchandise was distributed wherever licensed goods could be sold, the benefit of *Eagle*-licensed merchandise lay in the fact that newsagents had the opportunity of selling magazine and licensed products side by side. As well as the spatial distinction, it is interesting to note how Myers conceived retailers not only as distributors but also as consumers. He noted that 'as retailers stocked jigsaws, puzzles, children's books and even toys, the character or characters used on merchandise was already established in their minds, making them pre-sold customers for the merchandise'.[36]. In doing so, this was the first truly domestic merchandising programme in Britain. However, while the magazine proved successful as a merchandising programme, the next significant event that facilitated the emergence of a variety of agencies to follow suit came with the arrival of commercial television.

6.3 COMMERCIAL TELEVISION

Over the course of the 1950s, the number of merchandising projects increased dramatically. The main factor contributing to that growth was the arrival of commercial television in Britain. The impact this had on merchandising practices has seen some commentators associate the origins of character merchandising with the television era. Although this might not be completely accurate, as we have indicated previously, it is certainly true that the Television Act 1954 (UK) and its consequences were highly important factors in bringing professional maturity to merchandising agents in Britain. The creation and success of the first commercial television franchises helped to stabilise professional identities and contractual practices, making them increasingly common. Probably, as Brad Sherman and Leanne Wiseman have recently noted in relation to copyright, 'it is not technology *per se* that is of interest, so much as the changes that the technologies instigated and the challenges and opportunities that this created'.[37]

Commercial broadcasting provided an important impulse for new opportunities to consider the child as a consumer. Television differed from earlier media in that it developed a particularly intimate relationship between consumption and domesticity. Contrary to film and theatrical entertainment, in which consumption was frequently defined by the activity of going to the theatre or the cinema, television

[36] Ibid.

[37] Brad Sherman and Leanne Wiseman, 'Copyright: when old technologies were new' in Brad Sherman and Leanne Wiseman (eds.), *Copyright and the Challenge of the New*, Kluwer Law International, 2012, 1.

brought entertainment and information directly into the home. The advent of commercial television made the connection between the shop window and the television set and between the set and the shop-shelf all-pervasive. It was because of this that some advertising agents and trademark practitioners began to define television as 'advertising in motion'.[38] While this incursion into the private spheres attracted disapproval, mainly because children appeared to have become its most 'addicted' viewers and most vulnerable consumers, the medium was regulated in response to such condemnation. Even though commercial or competitive television was supported by revenue from advertising, criticism was defrayed by the separation of channels of trade – that is, advertisements from programme content. In other words, the advertiser's interest was temporally separated to suggest that it did not have any direct influence over the type of programmes broadcast. Another temporal incursion in response to criticism was the 'toddler's truce', a scheduling policy of no programmes between six and seven o'clock so that parents could get children to bed.[39] These kinds of restrictions faded over the years, but much of the historical development of broadcasting policy in this period was very much connected to both concerns over the rise of the child as a consumer and, at the same time, in making television more family friendly and safe for child audiences. Television turned out to be *the* medium of seductive popularity, emerging as the most important source to originate toys and children-related commodities in Britain. It was not that advertising could influence the programming, rather, it turned out that television programming had a significant influence on advertising. Television viewing figures provided crucial data for merchandising agents to demonstrate to merchants that child audiences were regularly attracted to a specific programme.[40]

The consortiums and start-ups that emerged around the bidding processes for commercial television franchises in the 1950s make a good starting point to trace the opportunities engendered by this new medium. Some applications, such as the one heralded by Hulton Press, emphasised their expertise in children's entertainment, particularly after the success of the *Eagle*. Others, such as an application submitted by theatrical impresarios put together by the publicity agent Suzanne Warner and Lew Grade, focused on talent management and show business connections as a main resource to service the needs of the new medium.

Although these applications were not initially successful, perhaps because of fears of monopoly and other political sensitivities, the chance to handle television-related issues and the possibility of intermediation arose. Several members of these failed applications shifted their position from being television-programming applicants to

38 Lyndon O. Brown, 'Advertising requirements of trademarks' (1954) 44 *Trademark Reporter* 794–802, 800.

39 David Buckingham, Hannah Davies, Ken Jones and Peter Kelley, *Children's' Television in Britain. History, Discourse and Policy*, British Film Institute, 1999, 83–4.

40 'Television Products Ltd and Character Licensing Ltd' (1958) January *Toy Trader and Exporter* 33.

offering subsidiary work in conjunction with programme controllers. Alongside the generation of creative content for children, they became agents to manage the licensed merchandising of television programmes, and, later, Hulton Enterprises took over the handling of ABC Television's merchandising.[41]

However, the theatrical impresarios' bid was far more ambitious and had a greater impact on the history of broadcasting. Although the initial bid was rejected, the group became a 'sub-contractor' of television services, emerging as one of the most important programme suppliers to the companies with broadcasting licences. Suzanne Warner herself set up two further legal entities in 1956, Television Products Ltd and Character Licensing Ltd, companies whose main strategic aims entailed the merchandising of products tied to television programmes.[42]

Suzanne Warner was a London-based Californian press agent who moved her interest from film to television after identifying the commercial opportunities and the potential value derived from the new medium. She foreshadowed the influential role of television in the development of the toy industry.[43] In an interview published just a month after the incorporation of the companies, she said, 'with the advent of commercial television, the toy trade stands on the verge of rocketing branded merchandise to the same heights that it has reached in the United States'.[44] Most interestingly, prospective licensees were directly addressed with advertising campaigns that focused on children, toys and their television connection as the main theme. For instance, the list of television programmes available for tie-ups was announced with the following caption: 'when he said he wanted a toy . . . he meant the toy he had seen on television!'[45] Similarly, a few months later, Warner inserted the following advert in toy trade magazines: 'children love to copy, especially their favourite television character'.[46]

Although the impact of advertising campaigns is hard to evaluate, what made these enterprises remarkable is that they clearly recognised the special place of the child as an active consumer connecting television and toys. The emphasis on specific consumer behaviour was evident in a new market where, according to Warner, the medium had 'created the demand'.[47] These new kinds of agencies could be characterised as intermediaries between television franchises and toy

41 'ABC Merchandising' (1959) April *Games and Toys* 62; 'Have a good character? We have good characters. We offer them to you' (1959) May *Games and Toys* 113.

42 'Suzanne Warner' *British Film and Television Yearbook*, 1956, 295; 'Television Products Ltd and Character Licensing Ltd', above n 40.

43 Olga Franklin, 'This year Santa is a blonde' *Daily Mail*, 15 December 1959, 6.

44 'The first travelling lady and the latest' (1956) September *Toy Trader and Exporter* 36–7, 36; see also (1956) October *Games and Toys* 70.

45 'Licensing enquiries to Suzanne Warner Television Products Ltd' (1956) October *Toy Trader and Exporter* 40; see also (1956) November *Games and Toys* 1.

46 'Suzanne Warner-Television Products Ltd' (1957) January *Games and Toys* 54; 'Suzanne Warner-Television Products Ltd' (1957) February *Games and Toys* 135.

47 'TV creates the demand' (1957) October *Games and Toys* 91; 'TV creates the demand' (1958) January *Games and Toys* 256; 'TV creates the demand' (1959) January *Games and Toys* 39.

manufacturers. Their activities triggered the exploitation and hence the arrival of children's television shows in Britain and also served to connect different trades aimed at children. Merchandising projects took up (if not creating themselves) the opportunities for common beneficial advantage, for instance, bringing together a toothpaste company, a toy manufacturer and a television series.[48]

Broadcasting histories have tended to focus on the discrete content of programmes, their broadcasters and regulators, and the technologies involved.[49] The central involvement of merchandising agents from the earliest days of television

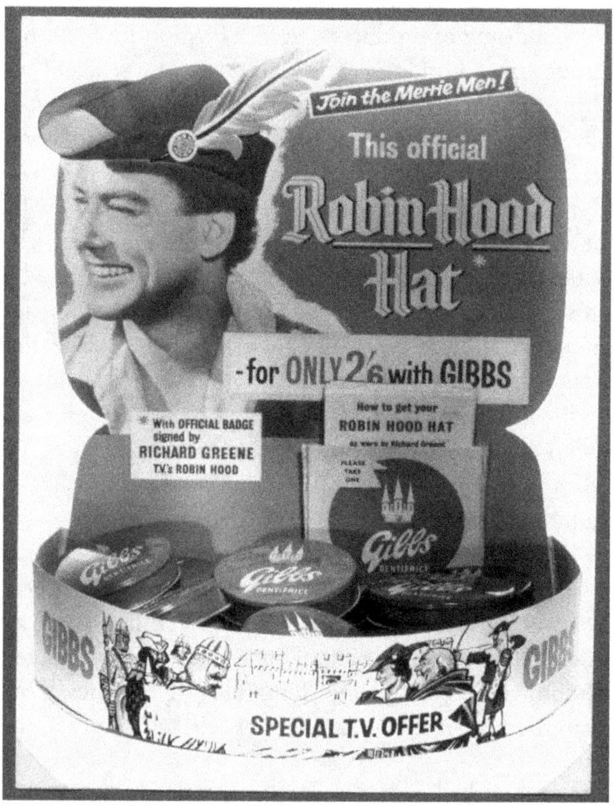

FIGURE 6.1 Robin Hood hat merchandise display on special offer with Gibbs Dentifrice, 1955
Courtesy of Unilever Art, Archives and Records Management, Port Sunlight

[48] This was the merchandising campaign around Robin Hood where Suzanne Warner was able to link up these different trade lines; see 'D & W Gibbs; merchandising operations – 1956' GB1752.EFL/DG/7/10/11; UARM; see also 'Further TV news' (1954) November *Toy Trader and Exporter* 55.

[49] For example, Michael Hilmes and Jason Jacobs (eds.), *The Television History Book*, BFI, 2003; Robert Dillon, *History on British Television: Constructing Nation, Nationality and Collective*

broadcasting and the scope of their activities in influencing what was broadcast has often been overlooked. However, it is difficult to imagine the success of many early transatlantic television series without the development of licensing regimes that made them commercially viable. Similarly, the stability of merchandising programmes became increasingly dependent on the television networks, which created opportunities for them to take off and evolve.

First, the serialisation of television shows enabled merchandising programmes to acquire and prepare their 'proprietary' effects. Although the capacity for development of merchandising schemes was contingent on the media conditions upon which to set up the snowballing process, the structure of television scheduling and programming provided appropriate templates and opportunities for some schemes to be accomplished. Second, television viewing figures turned out to be marketing tools for attracting further licensees into merchandising schemes. According to one commentator, 'commercial television has enormously widened the scope. And in Television Products Ltd, we are seeing the early signs of television branded merchandise promotion in Britain on a grand scale'.[50] This elucidates the way in which the television character was being increasingly promoted in order to attract investment and hence for its economic exploitation. As a result, it is no surprise that merchandising practices became ubiquitous. Curiously enough, the coming together of media and commercial techniques also produced interesting strategic partnerships and legal arrangements. Perhaps the most remarkable was the one formed between Suzanne Warner and a children's author, Roberta Leigh.[51]

Although it lasted for just a few years, their combined creative capabilities and negotiating skills paved the way for a number of projects aimed at children in the late 1950s. Their successful alliance was behind the television series *Twizzle*, Gerry Anderson's first puppet adventure. The contractual arrangements to produce this television series are particularly interesting because they offer a glimpse of legal practices around children's entertainment at that time. They illustrate how television and merchandising *rights* began to be split into distinct and separate agreements. In the summer of 1957, the television franchise for the London area acquired both the film and the merchandising rights of the forthcoming production on the very same day. However, the second set of rights were granted on the condition that the television contractor enter into an agreement with a third party, an agency to exploit the 'merchandising rights' over the television characters.[52] That the rights were granted on the condition of the appointment of an intermediary to exclusively

Memory, Manchester University Press, 2010; Mark Aldridge, *The Birth of British Television: A History*, Palgrave Macmillan, 2012.

50 'The first travelling lady' above n 44, 37.

51 'Television Products Ltd: scoop – Roberta Leigh joins as executive' (1954) November *Toy Trader and Exporter* 54.

52 'Twizzle: contract between Scribe Associates Ltd (MJ Clifford) and Associated-Rediffusion Ltd, 6 August 1957'; RL.

handle and implement a licensing regime shows how the contractual arrangements were designed to allow such a mediation. As soon as the distinction between film and merchandising rights was made, a legal space was opened for intermediaries to occupy and to 'manage' them.

6.4 COWBOYS AND CONTRACTS

While commercial television was still expanding its coverage and share of Britain's viewing public, the number of merchandising agencies also increased. Such a link evolved throughout the years, facilitating the institutionalisation of 'character merchandising' as a commercial practice and the emergence of merchandising agencies as a profession. The application of 'character' to merchandising, proper timing and efficacy-potential became 'a job for experts'.[53] By the end of the 1950s, it was noted that 'the tying-up or tying-in with popular characters of the telly had become an integral part of the toy industry both here and in America'.[54] Although this can be easily understood as a consumer quest driven by mutually advantageous interests, here we are more interested in connecting the emergence of a language of rights with the appearance of a legal space for competition. While a language of rights had been triggered by the media relationship between television and toy interests, judicial recognition took some time to coalesce. One of the curious features that reflects this development was the mushrooming of trademark applications in the toy field, not only from toy manufacturers but also from intermediaries.[55] For example,

[53] Notable evidence of this is the inclusion in a toy trade magazine of a regular section devoted to character merchandising 'whose intent [was] to keep the industry regularly informed of what [was] happening in this branch of trade activity' in (1956) September *Toy Trader and Exporter* 14.

[54] 'Toys, TV and tie-ups' (1959) September *Games and Toys* 95; 'Character merchandising today and tomorrow' (1963) September *Games and Toys* 78.

[55] 'No 770.974 ("Gunlaw") for all goods included in class 28 made by Character Licensing Ltd' in (1958) May *Games and Toys* 114; 'No 768.713 ("Hawkeye") for toys and games made by Television Products Ltd' in ibid; 'No 771.146 ("Popeye") for Jig-saw puzzles, games, etc made by Character Licensing Ltd' in 'Latest British Trade Marks' (1958) August *Games and Toys* 77; 'No B775.642 ("Dotto") for all goods included in class 28 (games, toys, etc) made by Television Products Ltd' in 'Latest British Trade Marks' (1958) October *Games and Toys*, 1958 120; 'No B781,920 ("Bat Masterson") for all goods included in class 28 (games, toys, etc but not including bats for games) made by Television Products Ltd' (1959) September *Games and Toys* 166; 'No 727,288 ("Shadow Squad") for toys and games (other than ordinary playing cards) made by Character Enterprises Ltd' ibid; 'No 788,290 ("The D.A.'s Man") for all goods included in class 28 (games, toys, playthings, etc) made by Character Licensing Ltd' (1959) November *Games and Toys* 96; 'No B789,087 ("Chi-Chi") for toys and games (other than ordinary playing cards) made by Character Enterprises Ltd' (1959) December *Games and Toys* 116; 'No 794,141 ("Four Just Men") in all goods included in class 28 made by Television Products Ltd' (1960) November *Games and Toys* 99.

Character Licensing Ltd, Character Enterprises Ltd and other merchandising agencies begin appearing as trademark applicants in the early 1960s.[56]

While these applications and registrations indicate a commercial rush evidenced by the shift in patterns of trademark registrations, as economic historians might argue,[57] they can be considered evidence of the legal re-conceptualisation of the boundaries of merchandising. When intermediaries began applying for trademarks in relation to television programmes, they did so in order to position themselves in the space of mediation and negotiation between toy manufacturers and television networks. More than the protective dimension of registrations, their attention to the register appears to have been precisely because of their need to offer 'something' suggestive of property ahead of the prospective deals that they were trying to forge. In so doing, the law also began to shift the perception of merchandising from a trade extension practice related to copyright to a matter increasingly connected to the law

[56] See also 'No 788,291 ("Dead or Alive") for all goods included in class 28 (games, toys, etc) made by Character Licensing Ltd' (1960) January Games and Toys 230; 'No 794,647 ("Biggles") for toys and games (other than ordinary playing cards) made by Character Enterprises Ltd' (1960) March *Games and Toys* 80; 'No 794,863 ("Four Feather Falls") for toys and games (other than ordinary playing cards) made by Character Enterprises Ltd' ibid; 'No 789,025 ("Airport") for games (other than ordinary playing cards) made by Character Enterprises Ltd' ibid; 'No B795,930 ("Knight Errant") for toys and games (other than ordinary playing cards) made by TV Network Merchandising Ltd' (1960) October *Games and Toys* 100; 'No 794,222 ("Tombstone Territory") for all goods included in class 28 made by Television Products, Ltd' (1960) November *Games and Toys* 100; 'No B794,226 ("Sergeant Preston of the Yukon") for all goods included in class 28 (games, toys, etc) made by Character Licensing, Ltd' (1960) December *Games and Toys* 84; 'No B794,960 ("Whirlybirds") for games (other than ordinary playing cards) and playthings but not including toy animals or toy aircraft made by Television Products, Ltd' (1961) March *Games and Toys* 108; 'No 788,289 ("Rifleman") for boxed games played with dice made by Character Licensing, Ltd' ibid; 'No B804,696 ("The Line-up") for toys and games (other than ordinary playing cards made by TV Network Merchandising, Ltd' ibid; 'No B707,857 ("Gil Favor") for toys and games (other than ordinary playing cards)' made by TV Network Merchandising Ltd' (1962) August *Games and Toys* 78; 'No 816,754 ("Mighty Mouse") for all goods in class 28 (games, toys, etc) but not including toy animals' made by TV Network Merchandising Ltd' (1962) September *Games and Toys* 128; 'No 826,157 ("Bootsie and Snudge") for all goods included in class 28 (games, toys, etc) made by TV Network Merchandising, Ltd' (1962) October *Games and Toys* 104; 'No 816,303 ("Deputy Dawg") for all goods included in class 28 (games, toys, etc) made by TV Network Merchandising, Ltd' (1963) February *Games and Toys* 158; 'No B838,653 ("Coronation Street") for all goods included in class 28 (games, toys, etc) made by TV Network Merchandising, Ltd' August (1963) *Games and Toys* 61; 'No B838,655 ("University Challenge") for boxed games and board games made by TV Network Merchandising, Ltd' (1963) September *Games and Toys* 126; 'No B839,329 ("Take-a-Letter") for board games made by TV Network Merchandising, Ltd' ibid; 'No 844,156 ("The Hillbillies") for boxed games, board games and jigsaw puzzles made by TV Network Merchandising, Ltd' (1963) December *Games and Toys* 72; 'No 858,140 ("Petticoat Junction") for all goods included in class 28 (games, toys, etc) made by TV Network Merchandising, Ltd' (1964) June *Games and Toys* 224.

[57] Paul Duguid, Teresa da Silva Lopes and John Mercer, 'Reading registrations: an overview of 100 years of trademark registrations in France, the United Kingdom, and the United States' in Teresa da Silva Lopes and Paul Duguid (eds.), *Trademarks, Brands and Competitiveness*, Routledge, 2010, 9–30.

of brands and trademarks. Perhaps the most obvious explanation of the shift in practice to the category of trademark comes from the fact that these intermediaries were not copyright owners themselves.

However, other factors gradually contributed to this juridical change. For instance, the passing of the new copyright legislation, which coincided with the Television Act 1955, brought with it some practical problems that directly affected the establishment of licensing regimes.[58] In particular, the new legislative distinction between design and copyright became an obstacle for the evolution of merchandising programmes if licensees had not registered their designs.[59] It is not a surprise then that companies such as Disney became particularly interested in the legislative impact of this distinction on their business strategies.[60] Instead of discussing the doctrinal distinctions further, below we consider the controversies surrounding an early television genre popular with children: television westerns. By doing so, it is possible to gain a deeper understanding of the working practices of merchandising agencies at the time. This focus not only throws new light on these practices, but also shows how the legal complexity around intellectual property was perceived locally and the strategies devised to overcome the problems encountered.

Above all, the western genre proved to be a particularly congenial merchandising medium, offering a commercial narrative to penetrate and assemble a child-focused market. What made westerns attractive to character-licensing firms was not just the 'character' itself and its media position from film to television but also its potential for accessories. The great play value of westerns offered merchandisers a commodity space carved out for children, who were given the option to choose from a rich repertoire of playsuits, toy holsters, play tents, hats, wigwams, rifles and revolvers, pistols and even fur caps, with participation in the market capable of attracting both genders. Moreover, merchandising schemes centred on television western stars also developed competitions and contests in order to attract and keep children as consumers.

Because of its enormous popularity and creation of differentiating features, the genre also became a fertile arena for disputes on the ways in which intellectual property could accommodate (or not) the property expectations generated after the arrival of commercial television. How these tensions played out specifically

[58] As noted by counsel's opinion to the British Association of Toy Manufacturers: 'the subject of copyright in relation to industrial design is very complex and, for example, the position differs in relation to designs created before 1st June 1957 and designs created after the date' see 'Opinion from Clifford-Turner and Co. Heinz H. Lorenz KC–Toy Works Limited', April 1963; BTHA Archives.

[59] 'Under the Copyright Act 1956, one cannot claim copyright where protection could have been obtained under the Registered Designs Act' in letter from J. Gwatkin to A.J. Hawkins (Roy Stewart & Co), 28 June 1957; Box 15; WB/AHC.

[60] Walt Disney Organization: overlapping of artistic copyright and copyright by way of registered design (1956), BT 209/577, TNA; see also Walt Disney Productions Ltd: memorandum relating to Committee on Industrial Designs Report (1963–1967) (Cmnd 1808), BT 209/429, TNA.

depended on local contingencies and legal strategies deployed in the disputes. However, it is worth highlighting that such controversies exposed an early troubled relationship between some toy manufacturers and merchandising agencies in Britain. The problem can easily be perceived by considering the elusive content of merchandising rights. What merchandising agencies were initially offering was 'manufacturing rights'.[61] Although there was advertising and promotional back-up obviously included in the package, merchandising contracts specified that the right given to licensees was the possibility to manufacture toys related to the television 'character'. In fact, the right was drawn up in a way that tried to maximise the exploitation of different trade lines, as we have noted above. Moreover, such a right became problematic for some toy manufacturers in Britain, who often considered that 'the paying of licensing fees for television or cinema characters [was] an imposition'.[62] After the outpouring of excitement that merchandising generated with the arrival of commercial television, we can observe this scepticism in a letter sent to the editor of the main toy trade magazine in Britain in which the unfairness of these licensing fees was criticised. Instead of looking at merchandising as a legitimate way to capture profits from creations, the correspondent argued that merchandising was a mere advertising technique that was mutually beneficial to the popularity of the programme and the toys. After asking whether manufacturers of toy cars paid royalties to motor-car manufacturers or manufacturers of toy dogs to the Kennel Club, and so on, he complained that 'the trouble in the world today is that too many people want it too many ways'.[63] Here, we can observe the difference in perspective: whereas merchandising agencies understood their right as a claim for royalties, several toy manufacturers were reluctant to accept that claim.

While some of those disputes were settled and an apology issued by the presumed infringer in different trade magazines, some toy manufacturers continued to press their case, making controversies more protracted and raising questions about the legality of merchandising practices. Interestingly, in their reluctance to comply, these manufacturers situated intellectual property rights at the level of practice and strategy, at the intersection between manufacturing and merchandising. Often at the centre of these controversies was Cheryl Playthings Ltd, a British toy manufacturer specialising in cowboy outfits. As a toy company making and selling a range of commodities from playsuits to holsters without paying licensing fees, it became the protagonist of several disputes concerning the merchandising practices of television westerns.

The first confrontation began in the mid-1950s, just before the serial *Davy Crockett* arrived in Britain. Produced by Disney, the programme was coming to

61 'Pinky and Perky' (1963) September *Games and Toys* 128; 'Selco holds merchandising rights to manufacture and sell on a world-wide basis' (1964) August *British Toys* 3.

62 'Letter to the editor: character merchandising' (1957) November *Games and Toys* 68

63 Ibid.

the London screen and television after enormous success in the United States. As often occurred with Disney, the release date was preceded by a merchandising campaign aimed at creating favourable conditions for the engagement of toy manufacturers. In the run-up to the launch, Disney organised a special event at the Harrogate toy fair, sponsored the publication of messages by Walt Disney himself wishing success to British manufacturers, and even incorporated an enquiry form for prospective licensees in toy trade magazines.[64] The American company was particularly organised and professional in preparing these campaigns, having established a specific department to handle merchandising operations in London. Although Disney launched a profitable programme around the western, the trouble in Britain arose in part because Cheryl Playthings Ltd was selling 'unofficial' merchandise, but also because it highlighted the fragility of merchandising operations as envisaged by Disney.[65] As noted above, Disney had historically grounded its licensing regimes using copyright as the basis to authorise and deal with toy manufacturers and retailers. Arguably, this was a more flexible intellectual property right than trademarks because it avoided stringent procedural conditions for rights to be acquired or maintained. The requirement of trademark 'use' or the prohibition of 'trafficking' in different national legislations was perceived as an obstacle for merchandising operations, as these were often based on the assumption of not directly using or assigning trademarks but licensing or purporting to license them.[66]

With the benefit of hindsight, Disney should probably have foreseen the problems with Cheryl Playthings Ltd, particularly after being involved in a series of disputes around the exploitation of *Davy Crockett* in America.[67] Rather than straightforward illegal counterfeits or unofficial merchandise, the avalanche of trademark registrations around the western showed the fragility of merchandising operations only grounded on copyright. Ironically, one of the most successful merchandising frenzies in the company's history exposed a Hollywood paradox: how can a private company claim copyright over a character in the public domain?

64 'Davy Crockett at Harrogate' (1956) January *British Toys* 7; 'Davy Crockett Merchandise' (1956) January *Toy Trader and Exporter* 82–3; '1956 is Davy Crockett Year!' (1956) January *British Toys* 17; 'Davy Crockett outfit: new lines at Harrogate' (1956) January *British Toys* 18; 'Davy Crockett, King of the Wild Frontier' (1956) January *British Toys* 21; 'Spotlight on Davy Crockett: aids to selling Crockett merchandise' (1956) April *Games and Toys* 90; 'A review of Davy Crockett merchandise' (1956) April *Games and Toys* 80–1.

65 Walter Partington, 'Davy Crockett goes to law' *Daily Express*, 23 May 1958, 7.

66 See *Re American Greeting Corporation's Application ('Holly Hobbie')* [1984] 1 All ER 426. The prohibition of trafficking was replaced by a more flexible understanding of trademark licensing and assignment; see ss24 and 28 Trade Marks Act 1994.

67 *Ex parte Crockett Seafood, Inc* 114 USPQ 508 (Comm'r Pat 1957); *Walt Disney Productions v Morey and Hannah Schwartz and Crockett Enterprises* (1955), docket 8231 (civil action); *Davy Crockett Enterprises v W.T. Grant Company* (1955), docket 8249 (civil action); *Davy Crockett Enterprises v Sears, Roebuck & Co* (1955), docket 8250 (civil action); NARA, Philadelphia. See also Paul F. Anderson, *The Davy Crockett Craze: A Look at the 1950s Phenomenon and Davy Crockett Collectibles*, R&G Productions, 1996, 53.

Against all odds, Cheryl Playthings Ltd fully resisted Disney's demand for copyright royalties by emphasising that the western was based on a well-known story in the public domain. There was never a lawsuit. This appears to suggest that Disney foresaw the risk of bringing the matter to trial and decided not to press the issue through the courts. However, the controversy continued over the next few months under a different guise before the Patent Office. When Disney filed an application for registration of a trademark in classes 28 ('toys') and 25 ('outfits'), Cheryl Playthings Ltd responded by opposing the registration.[68] Although the opposition was not successful and the application was eventually allowed to proceed, the dispute questioned not only the specific legal category but also the development of a particular system of value creation emerging around those categories.[69]

While the merchandising activities that used copyright as a legal vehicle to issue merchandising licences were being scrutinised, another American company engaged in similar business practices was monitoring the controversy closely. William Boyd Enterprises, a legal entity specifically incorporated to exploit another western, *Hopalong Cassidy*, had also expanded its licensing operations in Britain. During the summer of 1957, the American company found out that a British toy manufacturer was selling a line similar to its own outfits. Again, the cowboy trousers were produced by Cheryl Playthings Ltd, and a letter was sent to them to enquire about the similarity between the playsuits.[70] Although there were only slight variations, the British toy manufacturer responded that there was 'absolutely no question of any infringement'.[71] Internal correspondence from the American company shows a struggle to decide whether or not to sue the unruly toy manufacturer. There were several factors that contributed to such hesitation. First, the company's American management believed that it was not worth it financially to take legal action as the royalties of the British licensees were 'not considerable; probably no more than a couple of hundred pounds a year'.[72] Second, the lawyers had asked counsel's opinion as to whether there was any prospect of success should the case have gone to trial. Although there was some uncertainty as to the company's legal position after the change in copyright legislation in Britain a year earlier, it went ahead and instructed the leading copyright counsel in Britain, Edmund Purcell Skone James. His opinion was that if copyright in the photograph from which the British manufacturer had copied the trousers could be established, there might be a case. In contrast, some of the solicitors felt that 'embarking on any litigation' was not justified because it was 'a very dubious right'.[73] To complicate the matter even further, Cheryl Playthings Ltd seemed to have some connection with the film industry,

68 'Opposition to Davy Crockett Registration' (1956) June *British Toys* 5.

69 'Disney establishes right to Davy Crockett trade mark' (1958) December *British Toys* 4.

70 Roy Stewart & Co to Wolfin, Cheryl Playthings Ltd, 14 June 1957; Box 13; WB/AHC.

71 Wolfin to Roy Stewart & Co, 22 June 1957; Box 13; WB/AHC.

72 Hawkins to Cherry, 22 July 1957; Box 13; WB/AHC.

73 Brylawski to Deschamps (Langner, Parry, Card and Langner), 8 July 1957; Box 13; WB/AHC.

and the playsuit could have originated as part of a motion picture tie-up that had escaped the licensing organisation. The whole affair revealed, once again, the fragility of a licensing system, which was, as one of the merchandising agents put it, a 'dangerous state of affairs'.[74] It was internally suggested that a more careful managerial approach should have been followed in order to protect and register designs.

In any case, two months after the issue had come to the attention of the Americans, a 'cease and desist' letter was drafted by the lawyers based on a copyright photograph from which apparently Cheryl Playthings Ltd had made its design. Again, there was some hesitation, not only because the American company was afraid of circulating the letter around retailers but also in view of the 'defiant attitude of this concern'.[75] The letter finally reached its destination and Cheryl Playthings Ltd ceased using the design in question, stressing that it did so solely because it believed the matter 'only brought detrimental publicity to all concerned'.[76] Perhaps the most interesting issue underpinning the whole affair was the fear of a legal connection being perceived with the previous legal episode concerning *Davy Crockett*. In fact, the American company instructed its merchandising agent in Britain 'not to allow any letters regarding our situation to become involved in the *Davy Crockett* trade mark matter'.[77]

As the focus of the validity of licensing regimes shifted over trademark issues, Cheryl Playthings Ltd changed its strategy and started applying for registration of trademarks in relation to games and playsuits, many of which came from westerns.[78]

[74] Hawkins to Cherry, 22 July 1957; Box 13; WB/AHC.

[75] Brylawski to Cherry, 28 September 1957; Box 13; WB/AHC.

[76] Wolfin to Cherry, 21 October 1957; Box 13; WB/AHC.

[77] Cherry to Hawkins, 23 November 1957; Box 13; WB/AHC.

[78] 'No 789,707 ("Elfego Baca") for games (other than ordinary playing cards) and playthings'; 'No 790,980 ("Trace Hunter") for games and playthings (other than ordinary playing cards)'; 'No 788,346 ("Paladin") for games (other than ordinary playing cards) and toys, but not including toy vehicles'; 'No 788,944 ("Sugarfoot") for games and playthings (other than ordinary playing cards): all made by Cheryl Playthings Ltd' in (1959) December *Games and Toys* 116; 'No 789,439 ("Have Gun, Will Travel") for games (other than ordinary playing cards) and playthings made by Cheryl Playthings' in 'Latest British Trade Marks' (1960) January *Games and Toys* 230; 'No B789,789 ("Lucas McCain") for games (other than ordinary playing cards) and playthings made by Cheryl Playthings' (1960) February *Games and Toys* 211; 'No 794,680 ("Paladin") for games (not being chess and not being ordinary playing cards) and playthings but not including toy vehicles made by Cheryl Playthings' (1960) June *Games and Toys* 80; 'No 796,021 ("Johnny Ringo") for games (other than ordinary playing cards) and playthings made by Cheryl Playthings' ibid; 'No 797,199 ("Johnny Yuma") for games (but not including playing cards) and playthings, but not including dolls, toy animals made by Cheryl Playthings' (1960) October *Games and Toys* 100; 'No 804,678 ("The Rebel") for games (other than ordinary playing cards) and playthings by Cheryl Playthings' ibid; 'No 806,482 ("The Wrangler") for games (not including ordinary playing cards) and playthings made by Cheryl Playthings' (1960) December *Games and Toys* 84; 'No 811,188 ("Dondi") for games (not included in ordinary playing cards) and playthings made by Cheryl Playthings' (1961) April *Games and Toys* 108; 'No B791,529 ("Gil Favor") for games (other than ordinary playing cards) and playthings made by Cheryl Playthings' ibid.

This included well-known television series such as *Maverick*, *Bronco* and *Bonanza*.[79] This move paralleled the trend identified above, that is, the rise of trademark applications and registrations made by merchandising agencies.

The respective claims of toy manufacturers and merchandising agents were soon tested. Two trademark applications made by Cheryl Playthings Ltd were contested. The first one concerned an application by the toy manufacturer for the trademark 'Bonanza', the name of the famous American television series. The basis of the application was the intention of Cheryl Playthings Ltd to use the trademark when the programme was released and the denial of the existence of merchandising rights in Britain.[80] The second application referred to *Rawhide*, another well-known western series. It is worth noting here the source of the trademark opposition. The application was opposed by a merchandising agency, TV Network Merchandising Ltd, a recently incorporated legal entity in Britain which had been established with the aim of handling the merchandising of a television channel.[81] Both of Cheryl Playthings' applications were rejected, with the assistant registrar finding two ways to refuse the registration on discretionary grounds. First, it was determined that the intention to use the mark was contingent on the release of the film or the television programme.[82] Second, it was considered that the mark would be likely to deceive or cause confusion.[83] In reaching the decision, the assistant registrar also criticised the business practice followed by Cheryl Playthings Ltd of applying for trademarks in advance of foreign film and television programmes. The decision of the assistant registrar to refuse registration was appealed by Cheryl Playthings Ltd. Cross J, though only persuaded by the first argument – that Cheryl Playthings' applications

79 'Playsuits' (1959) September *Games and Toys* 140; 'Cheryl Playthings' (1965) February *Games and Toys* 142 (Maverick); 'No 791,194 ("Bronco Layne") for games (other than ordinary playing cards) and playthings, but not including toy pistols or any goods of the same description including toy pistols made by Cheryl Playthings Ltd' (1960) April *Games and Toys* 84; 'No 796,020 ("Bonanza") for games (other than ordinary playing cards) and playthings made by Cheryl Playthings' (1960) March *Games and Toys* 80.

80 *Bonanza TM* (unreported, 12 July 1961) (toys and games); see Christopher Morcom, *Character Merchandising*, CILIP, 1991), 17–18.

81 *Rawhide Trade Mark* [1962] 1 WLR 543; [1962] 2 All ER 86; [1962] RPC 133. The application was 'No 791,530 ("Rawhide") for board games, and boxed games, toys made of metal plastics or of wood, toy hats and toy playsuits, toy pistols and holsters therefore made of plastics made by Cheryl Playthings Ltd' (1961) February *Games and Toys* 182; see also 'Warning to the trade' (1960) October *Games and Toys* 39; 'Rawhide' (1960) November *Games and Toys* 90; 'Announcement to the trade by TV Network Merchandising' (1961) March *Games and Toys* 77; 'Rawhide' (1961) April *Games and Toys* 30.

82 Two years later, the trademark was applied for by the American television company, NBC; see 'No 825,645 ("Bonanza") for all goods included in class 28 (games, toys, etc) made by NBC International (Great Britain) Ltd' (1963) September *Games and Toys* 126.

83 Trade Marks Act (1938) s11 said: 'it shall not be lawful to register as a trade mark or part of a trade mark any matter the use of which would, by reason of its being likely to deceive or cause confusion or otherwise, be disentitled to protection in a court of justice, or would be contrary to law or morality, or any scandalous design'.

did not meet the legal standard of intention to use the mark – did proceed to confirm the decision to refuse the applications.[84]

One reading of this history is that these legal confrontations reveal Cheryl Playthings as a stubborn, almost vexatious litigant, a toy manufacturer trying to pursue every judicial tier to avoid paying any licensing fees. However, the disputes also indicate a much nuanced and more interesting tension between agents as professionals and legal actors. The late 1950s and the early 1960s was a crucial historical juncture for merchandising rights, a time when merchandising agencies sought to be acknowledged at the level of legal practice in Britain. Although the assistant registrar did not deal with the issues directly, this context is vital to understanding the role of intellectual property within a legal dispute about the relationship between manufacturing and merchandising. For the unruly and defiant toy manufacturer, the most important issue was not, in fact, simply the specific controversies mentioned, it was the attempt to persuade fellow manufacturers of what it perceived was an inherent trap of licensing regimes. In February 1960, Bernard Wolfin, director of Cheryl Playthings Ltd, sent a letter to the British Toy Manufacturing Association warning of the 'dangers and disservice being done to the trade by the uncontrolled menace of character licensing'.[85] He shared his experience with other members of the association, cautioning them that 'many licences are being sold for characters which are completely free from copyright, and could be used by all manufacturers without any payment, which shows the deliberate unconcern of these licensors'.[86] The association circulated a memorandum written by solicitors on the topic, but this failed to take an anti-licensing stance.[87] This was particularly disappointing for Cheryl Playthings Ltd since 'no collective stance was taken and it was left to the members' sole discretion to decide whether or not they embarked on the payment of royalties in connection with character licensing'.[88]

This argument was, by now, very much out of step with common industry practice. As discussed in Chapter 4, whether or not legally required, licensing had been part of the toy trade for decades, and the actions taken by merchandising agencies (and their utility to broadcasters) in the 1950s and 1960s had eroded any possibility of a collective position now being taken by the toy-manufacturing industry against licensing. Licensing agreements designed by merchandising agencies were so ubiquitous that the controversies in which Cheryl Playthings Ltd had been involved were not only triggered by proprietors or licensors attached to television

[84] Trade Marks Act (1938), s17(1).
[85] Wolfin (Cheryl Playthings Ltd.) to the members of the BTMA Council, 22 February 1960; BTHA Archives.
[86] Ibid.
[87] Memorandum by Clifford-Turner & Company on Character Licensing, 31 March 1960; BTHA Archives.
[88] Minutes of Council Meeting, 24 March 1960; BTHA Archives.

programmes but also by licensees: other toy manufacturers who perceived acquiring a licence as a preliminary step to developing their businesses.[89]

6.5 THE MAKING OF AN INDEPENDENT PORTFOLIO

Because the first merchandising agencies coincided with the arrival of commercial television, their services were committed to the channels with which they had become strategically connected. It is not insignificant that each of the legal entities set up by Suzanne Warner handled the licensing rights for different contractors (Associated Television on the one hand and Associated-Rediffusion on the other). Soon after the legal entities were established, new ancillary units were created in connection with the majority of commercial television outlets. For instance, Character Enterprises Ltd, later renamed TV Network Merchandising, was the institutional arrangement to exploit programmes broadcast by Granada Television.[90] As explained above, the agency occupied an important place in the legal history of character merchandising as it opposed the registration of trademarks related to television programmes by toy manufacturers. Ironically, the key characteristic of these agencies became their strength, as well as a potential weakness. Their dependence on television programmes acquired by such channels defined their dealings and limited their room for manoeuvre, producing a bottleneck effect.

There is, however, one agency that deserves special mention here: Walter Tuckwell & Associates. As happened with other agencies, the organisation was incorporated in the mid-1950s after the arrival of commercial television. Yet the agency was unique in that it was independent, created free of hierarchical constraints, and forged trade links with broadcasting and toy companies. The firm strove to develop a very varied portfolio of characters. In moving beyond an exclusive commercial environment, it paved the way for distinctive ways of thinking and developing licensing schemes. Rather than a subsidiary selling or licensing characters of its parent company for merchandising, Walter Tuckwell & Associates became an agency specialising in the commercialisation and licensing of third-party characters in merchandise.

An Australian educated in New Zealand, Tuckwell was a colourful entrepreneur highly competent in the exploitation of intellectual properties. His background meant that he recognised the rising value of merchandising in developing and creating markets for children. After his first job at G-B Animation, where he had

89 The specific toy manufacturer which had acquired a Disney licence and complained to Disney about Cheryl Playthings was Berwick's Toy Co Ltd; see 'Official Davy Crockett outfit by Cheryl Playthings' (1956) September *Games and Toys* 61 and 'Berwick's Toy – official "Walt Disney" Davy Crockett suits and hats' *Games and Toys*, September 1956, 82; 'Berwick's Toy Co. Ltd, Liverpool – the official "Walt Disney" Davy Crockett hat' (1956) October *Games and Toys* 111.

90 'Introducing Character Enterprises Ltd' (1959) April *British Toys* 11.

helped Myers and Barker with the merchandising campaign for cartoons, he went on to work for a well-known postcard publisher, and then to Disney, for whom he travelled to toy fairs, closed licensing deals and became involved in merchandising campaigns such as for *Alice in Wonderland* and *Peter Pan*.[91] Although there was obviously no specific professional path to becoming a merchandising agent, the career trajectory he followed prior to setting up his own agency made him a particularly suitable candidate. It paralleled the formative years of the professionalisation of the practice. It is not only that his varied expertise and broad skill-set drew from multiple media (film, publishing, television), but his name was already well-known to toy manufacturers, retailers and wholesalers.[92] While the institutional and personal relationships Tuckwell had forged in the toy industry were crucial and contributed to the decision to go it alone, the early stage of his small start-up was particularly risky because of the exclusive commercial environment generated by television franchises. Although the split between 'film' and 'merchandising' rights triggered by the advent of commercial television had carved out a lucrative environment beyond Disney, this was quickly occupied and fenced off by commercial television subsidiaries aiming to control revenues derived from the exploitation of the programmes broadcast by their companies.

Against that background, the best way to set up an independent company was to recognise an opportunity not yet identified by the newly emerging merchandising agencies. This meant shifting attention to popular children's characters that had yet to appear on television. Indeed, Tuckwell seized an opportunity to associate his new firm with a controversial but successful children's writer: Enid Blyton. Although Blyton had started commercialising her characters, notably Noddy, via a subsidiary company, and already had a literary agent, her various attempts to bring them to broadcast networks, particularly the British Broadcasting Corporation (BBC), had failed. While internal reviewers at the corporation had been constantly critical of her work, a polite rejection letter from the Children's Hour Department conveyed this more cordially: 'we have read a number of her stories and have always come to the conclusion that broadcasting is not quite the medium for them'.[93] However, after her engagement with Tuckwell, the characters began to proliferate in different media. Indeed, the merchandising programme was instrumental for Noddy, 'Big Ears' and other characters moving onto television channels. In 1958, less than two years after he was appointed as merchandising agent, Tuckwell had issued almost a

[91] See, for instance, Hodder & Stoughton, Ltd to Tuckwell, Walt Disney Mickey Mouse Ltd, 4 September 1953; CLC/B/119/MS16375/001; LMA and Walter Tuckwell, Walt Disney, Mickey Mouse Ltd, to LE Carroll, Macmillan & Co, 18 February1954; UoR MAC.

[92] 'Walter Tuckwell' (1956) October *Toy Trader and Exporter* 45–6; 'The independent character merchandiser arrives' *Advertiser's Weekly*, 9 November 1956, 9; 'Tuck – prince of character merchandising' (1960) September *Games and Toys* 83; 'Character merchandising today and tomorrow' (1963) September *Games and Toys* 78.

[93] Dearmer to Brimble, 23 September 1947; 'Blyton, Enid – Contributors'; BBC WAC.

hundred licences to more than forty manufacturing companies and got the character into the screen.[94] His work as mediator in making Blyton's characters a business proposition was successful, and her characters began to appear 'on almost every type of commodity – not only games and toys but clothing, toiletries, biscuits, calendars, postcards, cutlery, pottery, home furnishings and fancy goods'.[95] When the writer saw the impact of these merchandising practices, for instance, the publication of a glossy brochure in toy magazines, Blyton wrote to thank him for 'all you do for Noddy', adding, 'I've lost count of the manufacturers now'.[96]

While this alliance – a commercial arrangement between a merchandising agent and a children's writer – bears obvious similarities to other ventures mentioned elsewhere in this book, there were some notable differences. First, there was no legal entity formed here, through partnership or otherwise. Rather, the relationship was crystallised in a contract, giving form to an agency from which Tuckwell 'received twenty per cent of the royalties resulting from his introductions'.[97] Second, Blyton's personality and her promotion of her characters was described by a commentator as amounting to a 'one-woman industry', her entrepreneurial impetus to reach and establish child and juvenile markets was remarkable. Not only did she publish the *Enid Blyton Magazine*, set up children's clubs and write in toy trade magazines, she also became part and parcel of the licensing machinery. The new merchandising agency constituted by Tuckwell began with a client fully engaged with a fast-paced business and promotional aspects of character merchandising. Blyton, described by her literary agent as having 'a card index mind',[98] was directly involved in the bureaucratic and infrastructural side of the enterprise, giving her approval to prototypes, offering her thoughts on new licences and opportunities and leaving the agent enough room to act on her behalf. The enterprise continued successfully for a decade, and even beyond her death. Her correspondence sometimes reads like passages extracted from an intellectual property nutshell book, for instance, Blyton wrote: 'most of the goods are first class and I know you approve of that. A cheap or nasty product harms the original character'.[99] The more the characters were

94 While Noddy appeared first in commercial television in the mid-1950s, 'Noddy in Toyland' was a BBC production directed by McLean Rogers in 1958. Blyton asked Tuckwell not to select the well-known director Mary Field because 'as you know, she herself turned down the Fabolous Five books ten years ago as quite unsuitable for filming, and now, having been made to eat her words because of its great success, she is not really over-pleased'; Blyton to Tuckwell, 10 April 1958; TA.

95 'The fabulous Blyton: creator of Noddy – the modern Alice' (1958) May *Games and Toys* 68–70, 68; see also Sheila Ray, *The Blyton Phenomenon: The Controversy Surrounding the World's Most Successful Children's Writer*, André Deutsch, 1982, 49; Barbara Stoney, *Enid Blyton*, Hodder & Stoughton, 1974, 151, 160; see also 'Spear's Games: Noddy' (1956) February *British Toys* 13; 'Noddy's Musical Piano by Chad Valley' (1957) November *British Toys* 14.

96 Blyton to Tuckwell, 2 August 1961; TA.

97 See *Noddy Subsidiary Rights Co Ltd v IRC* [1967] WLR 1.

98 Stoney, above n 95, 140.

99 Blyton to Tuckwell, 30 September 1961; TA.

exploited, consumed and criticised, the more her name was becoming a character in its own right, making her famous signature a brand, which in turn fed back and contributed to the success of the enterprise.

Despite the advantages gained for the agency from this first signing, particularly in terms of capital being injected into the start-up, it also produced undesirable and unexpected side-effects. Perhaps the most significant problems that arose came from the attempt to replicate what was seen as an extremely successful formula. In February 1958, Tuckwell associated his firm to a well-known children's illustrator, Mabel Lucie Attwell. The expansion of the agency appeared appropriate since the new signing was also 'a shrewd businesswoman', as Blyton had been. Her creative output, mainly artwork featuring chubby-cheeked children, also seemed suitable for merchandising as it had already made some forays into stationery, toy-books, breakfast cereal and confectionery. Moreover, her business acumen was shown by her development of commercial undertakings to protect her interests. Although this bore some resemblance to the previous signing, Tuckwell decided to alter the arrangement to act not only as a merchandising agency but also as an artists' representative agency.[100] The relationship did not turn out to be as profitable as the one with Blyton. The art industry was a specialised environment difficult to navigate for a newly constituted agency without previous exposure to it. Also, Attwell proved unable to adapt to the fast-paced licensing scheme imposed by the agency (she was eighteen years older than Blyton). She had difficulty in overcoming a generational shift away from her artistic style, something made manifest in the attempt to move into a different media. For whatever reason, these chubby-cheeked characters did not make the transition into television, and hence it became difficult to persuade the toy trade to jump on the merchandising bandwagon.

The mode of entrepreneurship that characterised a merchandising agent became most visible at the industry's main event: the annual toy fairs. The fairs constituted a meeting ground for contacts (and contracts) to be made and nurtured. They did more than function as showcases of trade prospects; they were annual expressions of the market and future childhood crazes, constituting a hub to facilitate the social interaction between toy manufacturers, wholesalers and retailers. Neither toy producers nor distributors, merchandising agencies came to occupy the mediation space in these industry-oriented events, mainly by organising cocktail parties in which products and personalities came together.[101] Taking the form of receptions to introduce marketable characters to toymakers and distributors, or sometimes gatherings for people and personalities to meet one another, these parties were both social events and important occasions for building up portfolios of licensed

[100] 'Walter Tuckwell new agents for Mabel Lucie Attwell' (1958) February *Toy Trader and Exporter* 48; 'Mabel Lucie Attwell' (1960) September *Games and Toys* 137.

[101] 'Walter Tuckwell "Tom and Jerry"/ Charles Neufeld "Bendy Toys" cocktail party held at the fair' extract from *Toys International*, February 1974; Scrapbook 1; BTA; 'Standpix: Tuckwell-Neufeld cocktail party'; Scrapbook 1; BTA.

FIGURE 6.2 Group picture of a Tuckwell cocktail party at the Harrogate Toy Fair, c. 1964
Courtesy of Antony Neufeld

merchandise. The business idea probably came from Tuckwell's time at Disney, as the American company had already developed expertise in similar commercial rituals and congregations to energise merchandising programmes.[102] In any case, these marketing practices at the fairs constituted spaces for celebration, valuable opportunities to share information and entertain prospective and current licensees, as well as ways to keep them updated on all future developments concerning their programmes and opportunities to issue more licences on specific products or to review the products on which the licences were based.

While toy fairs were forums that facilitated exchanges for the incorporation and circulation of characters in the pipeline for merchandising, the reception environment created at the parties also allowed Tuckwell to showcase his own personality and charisma in order to make the transfers between toymakers and distributors happen. In fact, there were certain personal attributes, skills and talents that were

[102] 'At the Walt Disney Party' (1963) July *Games and Toys* 25. And it was also followed by other merchandising agencies; see 'TV network reception' (1961) March *Games and Toys* 50; 'My Log' (1962) March *Games and Toys* 39.

shared by these professionals: characteristics that were, in some way, fundamental to the job of a merchandising agent. First, merchandising professionals inherited and combined traits of advertising agents and other agents, literary or otherwise. Their expertise included promotional and sale ideas embedded in the contractual exploitation of characters. Furthermore, as their opportunities were sought after in toy circuits, travelling constituted part of their trade as contracts were obtained not only in local but also in international markets. Second, agents generally possessed some practical knowledge of intellectual property matters as the burgeoning application and registration of trademarks by these agents attest.[103] And third, becoming a merchandising agent involved regularly trying to persuade both sides of the trade that 'manufacturers, wholesalers, agents and retailers wanted good merchandise backed by great characters'.[104] Character merchandising shifted from being a legal complication in the trade to become 'a service for the toy trade',[105] coming together in the figure of the agent. Because of the split between ownership and exploitation, the virtue of the agent was that, in occupying a middle ground, the agent could smooth over tensions around ownership of the characters.

While Walter Tuckwell & Associates was particularly active in the toy trade, the lack of hierarchical position in the corporate infrastructure of television franchises did not pose an obstacle for the development of a portfolio of characters for licensing matters. Further, an interesting association Tuckwell pursued was with the BBC. As television viewing became equated with selling, and as the BBC had excellent coverage and accessibility, the lucrative possibilities inherent in BBC programmes were increasingly attractive to the toy trade. The BBC had historically been reluctant to establish a commercial undertaking for reasons explained in Chapter 7.

[103] See, for instance, some of the trademark applications filed by Walter Tuckwell & Associates: 'No 805,050 ("The Roaring Twenties") in all goods included in class 28' (1960) November *Games and Toys* 100; 'No 806,545 ("Sea Hawk") in all goods included in class 28' ibid; 'No 805,050 ('The Roaring Twenties' in all goods included in class 28 (games, toys, etc)' ibid; 'No B802,665 ("Bourbon Street Beat") in all goods included in class 28 (games, toys, etc)' ibid; 'No B798,172 ("Sea Hunt") in toys' (1960) December *Games and Toys* 84; 'No 811,484 ("Kookie") for combs, sponges and brushes' *Chemist and Druggist*, 25 February 1961, 202; No B802,324 ("Whispering Smith") in all goods included in class 28 (games, toys, etc)' March (1961) *Games and Toys* 108; No B802,399 ("Hawaiian Eye") in toys and games (other than ordinary playing cards)' ibid; No B805,051 ("Surfside 6") in all goods included in class 28 (games, toys, etc)' (1961) June *Games and Toys* 115; 'No 810,196 ("Bugs Bunny") in all goods included in class 28 (games, toys, etc)' (1961) July *Games and Toys* 58; 'No 809,391 ("Tenderfoot") in all goods included in class 28' (1961) August *Games and Toys* 72; 'No 818,114 ("Tumbleweed") in all goods included in class 28' ibid; 'No B811,936 ("Room for One More") for shooting games, card games (other than ordinary playing cards), dolls, puppets and toys' (1961) November *Games and Toys* 84; 'No 827,245 ("Calvin and the Colonel") in all goods included in class 28 (game, toys, etc)' (1962) May *Games and Toys* 89; 'No 832,444 ("Wagon Train") for games (other than ordinary playing cards) and playthings' (1962) December *Games and Toys* 74.

[104] Walter Tuckwell, 'Ten years and onwards' (1966) *Games and Toys* 5.

[105] 'Character merchandising' (1961) January *Games and Toys* 270; 'Big business in TV character merchandising' (1963) May *Toys International* 17–20.

Nevertheless, Tuckwell approached the public corporation offering his services in the late 1950s. It is possible that these initial contacts first made the corporation aware of commercial possibilities and expectations in this area, although the corporation did not have a clear understanding of what line of business the agency was in, rather imagining that they might be 'possibly advertising agents'.[106] Certainly, the epistolary correspondence from Tuckwell stirred some curiosity as the public corporation decided to arrange a meeting with him to find out what his merchandising agency involved.

The meeting took place at Broadcasting House, headquarters of the corporation, in June 1959. Tuckwell spoke of the possibilities around the exploitation of certain television programmes in the form of games and toys. Two interesting issues emerged. First, the corporation flagged that its policy was to deal only with principals (and not agents). Second, the agent not only offered his expertise in the toy trade, 'knowing the best manufacturers to use', but also stated that his proposal involved 'a constant and continuous attempt to get both the corporation and the games manufacturers in a succession of exploitation proposals'.[107] Despite the fact that the BBC did not entrust the Tuckwell agency with the rights, it did leave open the possibility of potential deals that could be agreed with toy manufacturers and retailers 'direct or by anyone acting on their behalf'.[108] From this point on, Walter Tuckwell & Associates became the main channel for stimulating and communicating a stream of proposals made from toy manufacturers to the corporation. This made the company virtually an external agency for the corporation. As a result of its mediation, toys and games based on a range of television programmes from the Canadian Mounties series *R.C.M.P.* to the sports programmes *Grandstand* and *Sportsview* were produced and distributed.

The mediation unfolded in a rather peculiar manner. Although this might confirm that intellectual property took place 'regardless of legal rights that may exist under the law',[109] here we would like to suggest that it indicates a prioritisation of contractual over proprietary relationships. During the summer of 1961, two years after the initial contact between the corporation and the agency, profitable arrangements continued to gather pace, boosted by the simplification of communications using 'forms [they] jointly devised'.[110] This permitted a succinct notification form for licence requests sought by manufacturers to facilitate the speeding-up of deals arranged and signed by the agency and countersigned by the BBC. The

106 G.M. Turnell, Assistant to the Head of Programme Contracts, 23 March 1959; (regarding the letter from Messrs Walter Tuckwell & Associates); R44/1,316/1; BBC WAC.

107 'Mr Walter Tuckwell: Record of the Interview' 4 June 1959; R44/1,316/1; BBC WAC.

108 Page to Tuckwell, 24 June 1959; R44/1,316/1; BBC WAC.

109 Kathy Bowrey, 'The new intellectual property: celebrity, fans and the properties of the entertainment franchise' (2011) 20(1) *Griffith Law Review* 188–220, 215.

110 Tuckwell to Grove, 25 August 1961; (regarding Gordon Murray's puppets); R44/1,316/1; BBC WAC.

infrastructure built into licensing regimes was dynamic and efficient. Streamlining and automation were especially important due to the bureaucratic ramifications of interacting with a huge public broadcast corporation. It prevented agency communications from getting lost. Yet the impact of the merchandising programme on the contractual practices of the corporation was even more profound, as the corporation had to assess whether these rights were even held by the corporation, a feature not introduced or even considered in previous contracts. It is noteworthy that the corporation's solicitor even suggested a definition of merchandising rights because there was rarely consensus on what these rights involved.[111]

The number of contracts facilitated by the merchandising agency for the corporation grew steadily during the early 1960s. A cursory glance at trade magazines shows a commercial relationship comfortably developing around programmes and characters such as 'Lenny the Lion', 'Andy Pandy and His Friends', 'Pinky' and 'Perky' and the 'Flower Pot Men'.

Merchandising rights for the most popular television characters on 'children's viewing time' developed in parallel with the agency's attempts to encourage toy manufacturers to apply for licences for series with the potential to 'win the hearts of more and more generations of children'.[112] Yet, the agency's main achievement did not come from the typical children's programmes broadcast during the week, but from a supposedly family sci-fi series aired for the first time on a weekend at the end of November 1963: *Dr Who*. Many factors, creative and otherwise, account for the merchandising success of *Dr Who*. A most interesting but often overlooked dimension was its scheduled transmission just before the main toy season. One of the techniques with which merchandising agencies attracted the toy trade was by predicting the forthcoming children's television shows that would achieve the best viewer ratings in periods that coincided with the seasonal demand for toys. As John Ellis has described, scheduling was 'television's key management tool, defining the nature of broadcast output'.[113] Television schedules became an important information tool for merchandising agents to garner interest from toy manufacturers, retailers, and wholesalers.

Nobody could have predicted in advance the viewing impact of *Dr Who*, and initially, due to low ratings and reviews, the BBC had little confidence in it.[114] However, particularly after the introduction of the space robots, the Daleks, it gained

[111] L.P.R. Roche to Grove, 27 April 1960 (proposed exploitation of merchandising rights); R44/1,316/1; BBC WAC.

[112] 'Andy Pandy' and 'Andy Pandy Licensees' (1960) September *Games and Toys* 146–7.

[113] John Ellis, 'Scheduling: the last creative act in television?' (2000) 22(1) *Media, Culture and Society* 25–38, 25.

[114] *Dr Who* screened the day after the assassination of President Kennedy, leading to low ratings and uncertainty around future production. See Kathy Bowrey and Michael Handler, 'Franchise dynamics, creativity and the law' in Kathy Bowrey and Michael Handler (eds.), *Law and Creativity in the Age of the Entertainment Franchise*, Cambridge University Press, 2014, 3–6.

in popularity, suggesting a particularly suitable vehicle for the initial investment of manufacturers and other firms in the toy and children's products trades. Many viewers, particularly children, were captured and fascinated by it. While the series became a very successful commodity in its own right, and was exported to different television markets, *Dr Who* toys and other children's accessories, driven above all by a Dalekmania, flooded the market.[115] The programme, along with its subsequent seasons and reruns, became a byword for the 'snowballing' process dreamt of by merchandising agents, as its ratings provided the pulling power for the development of the licensing regime.

The truly extraordinary success of the merchandising of the series had not been foreseen. The agency even ran out of the 'contract forms' to issue licences.[116] It was, however, almost too successful, at least for the agency. After realising the great revenue potential of merchandising, the BBC decided to reduce its commission and then to go ahead with its own merchandising department in 1966.

Walter Tuckwell & Associates could initially handle losing such an important account because the agency had already assembled a portfolio of characters sourced from other media companies. Because there was no clear affiliation to any single television franchise, the agency had become a sort of boutique, catering for the exploitation of characters derived from some American westerns, cartoons and other children's programmes. This meant that the agency was not dependent only on the source provided by the public corporation but was able to serve on merchandising programmes of television series broadcast by commercial television channels such as Associated-Rediffusion. One account handled by the agency at that time was Warner Bros. This enabled it to issue licences for Warner's television series and also opened the door for merchandising operations based on the *Bugs Bunny Show*. The association with Warner Bros immediately increased the agency's portfolio and enhanced the possibilities for characters to be licensed individually or as part of a series. In fact, the merchandising division of the American company had realised this potential and began to differentiate between (a) 'main', (b) 'lesser' and (c) 'incidental' characters with different rates.[117] Such flexibility offered licensees the possibility of participating in different merchandising operations adapted to their own needs and investment capacity. Walter Tuckwell & Associates conducted a particularly successful line of business for Warner Bros in Britain since local manufacturers who had licences to produce items based on the show reported

[115] David J. Howe, 'The Dalek invasion of toyshops' in George Mann, Justin Richards and Cavan Scott (eds.) *Dalek: The Astounding Untold History of the Greatest Enemies of the Universe*, Penguin Random House, 2017, 152–5.

[116] Peter Barker, Tuckwell & Associates, to Ann Fitch, BBC Enterprises, 23 December 1964; ('Dr Who- Licenses'); R120/20/1; BBC WAC.

[117] Harold Berkowitz, Warner Bros to Alfred Schneider, American Broadcasting Company, 9 January 1961; 'Bugs Bunny TV Merchandising – File 15554'; WBA/USC.

'excellent business'.[118] A telling indication of the success of the first few years of the relationship is that the agency expanded to incorporate the retailing side of the business, as Gamages and Selfridges, among other companies, came to recognise the value of character merchandise when stocking and selling consumer products for children.

During the 1960s, the agency added more foreign accounts, taking over the representation of King Features Syndicate and Metro-Goldwyn-Mayer in Britain.[119] These followed the pattern set out in previous accounts, which had already proved Tuckwell's reliability to American companies. Rather than being directly supervised by the television networks or studios to which they were agents,

FIGURE 6.3 Walter Tuckwell and Charles Neufeld reviewing a Bendy Toy (Tom & Jerry), *c.* 1965
Courtesy of Antony Neufeld

118 'Bugs Bunny now on TV: licence applications to Walter Tuckwell & Associates Ltd' (1962) September *Games and Toys* 85; 'Bugs Bunny' (1962) December *Games and Toys* 62; 'Great Bugs Bunny: Walter Tuckwell & Associates' (1963) January *Games and Toys* 225; 'Bugs Bunny lines from Berwick's' (1964) September *Games and Toys* 9; 'Walter Tuckwell on 1963 character lines and television on the continent' (1963) September *Games and Toys* 88.

119 'Popeye merchandise' (1964) March *Games and Toys* 34; 'MGM appoint Tuckwell' (1969) June *British Toys* 3; 'My Log' (1969) June *Games and Toys* 20; 'Walter Tuckwell & Associates' (1973) September *British Toys* 12.

FIGURE 6.4 Reference sheet, Warner Bros, by Walter Tuckwell & Associates, *c.* 1965
Courtesy of Tasmin Overton

Walter Tuckwell & Associates often reported to merchandising divisions of these companies. In other words, it functioned as an agency of agencies, a broker working with different agents and, hence, progressively acquiring knowledge, contacts and competencies in merchandising and marketing matters. Strategic relationships were used to compete against local merchandising agencies that emerged after the advent of commercial television; such strategies succeeded in broadening representation from different sources, making Walter Tuckwell & Associates the most important British character-merchandising agency in the early 1960s.

Although merchandising programmes have often been considered to be derivative or parasitic upon creative labour, they really entailed the co-ordination of aesthetic and managerial techniques. Such co-ordination contributed to the mutual transformation of brands into products and products into brands. Merchandising agencies not only strategically registered trademarks relating to the characters they were licensing – an important initial step that enabled them to forge and occupy a mediation space between manufacturers and media companies – they also worked in conjunction with artists to translate designs into toys and other goods aimed at children. Another effect of such creative mediation, particularly as undertaken by agencies such as Walter Tuckwell & Associates, was the cross-fertilisation between children's cartoons and television programmes by being referenced, drawn and translated into commodities. The global reach that shaped children's consumption experiences in the 1960s was achieved not from a top-down corporate strategy but from the media connections and material conditions through which these agencies on the ground arranged their merchandising operations.

It was in the midst of this prosperous trajectory that another profitable connection was made by the agency when Walter Tuckwell & Associates was appointed merchandising agents for the Football Association (FA). This assignment broadened the agency's horizons and brought new fields to explore commercially. The brief included the design of a character for the 1966 World Cup. Sporting events like this could be risky for merchandising agents and manufacturers as the character was really a mascot and the 'property' could be affected by external factors, such as the performance of the national team. However, the campaign (and the mascot) rode the wave of the team's progress, with the figure, a friendly looking lion named Willie, eventually lifting the trophy. Willie was creatively placed in different positions in newspapers.[120] The character featured in promotional events held in eleven centres in seven cities across Britain, with proceedings transmitted, followed and reported in different media. The campaign was not just remarkable for the proliferation of merchandise embodying the mascot (balls, balloons, dolls, mini-colour paints, puppets, stationery, T-shirts) or the extension of commercial activities of the agency to the retailing side. The aesthetic breadth in the approach to the brief was significant, showing the extent to which the agency had incorporated a creative side to its services. It was offering the creation of new images, as discussed in the Chapter 5 in relation to Peter Pan.

The mascot emerged from a series of sketches made by a freelance artist regularly used by Tuckwell & Associates. However, the final strategic selection was by the agency and the FA. While the copyright was advertised as owned by the FA, this should have been the effect of an assignment as the creative effort had been outsourced to Tuckwell, which in turn hired a freelancer.[121] A recent legal controversy regarding the exploitation of the mascot today reveals how the law finds it problematic to unravel these commercial entanglements.[122] One of the points tangentially discussed in litigation was the role of the organisations in the licensing operations. Although there was an attempt to depict the licensing regime as following a hierarchical model, it is probable that such a model never existed and that merchandising operations unfolded, as we have described, in a collaborative fashion. In fact, some of the legal conflicts generated decades later are rooted in these merchandising practices that make it difficult to trace the legal status of transactions concerning the material in question. While the tendency in intellectual property scholarship is to look at the subject matter defined with a high degree of

[120] 'World Cup Willie copyright would be available on request to all newspapers subject to the usual acknowledgment being made concerning the copyright' in 'FA Minutes; World Cup Organising Committee'; 31 January 1965; Football Association Archives; see also Ian Nannestad, 'World Cup Willie: how a lion with a Beatle haircut changed the commercial face of the game' (2008) 20 October *Soccer History* 8–11; 'World Cup character' (1965) September *British Toys* 12.

[121] The artist was Reg Hoye, described as 'one of the most experienced designers of boxes and show cards in the industry'; see 'World Cup Willie creator' (1968) March *Games and Toys* 20; 'World Cup Willie had been created by the Tuckwell Organisation' in 'Football Association Minutes': World Cup Organising Committee, 22 July 1965; Football Association Archives.

[122] *Jules Rimet v Football Association* [2007] EWHC 2376 (Ch).

abstraction, focused on bounding the intangible property with reference to copyright, design, or trademark specificities, merchandising campaigns operated in the opposite direction. They were preoccupied with increasing the general appeal of the character by broadening recruitment and establishing exploitation paths and campaigns to generate goodwill. It is at this point of practice, and out of collaborative participation, that a proprietary effect was elicited. The valuable property coalesced around the merchandising campaign that made up the enterprise, not just from plotting neat transactions concerning discrete exclusive rights.

6.6 THE DEMISE OF AN AGENCY

Tuckwell & Associates lost two clients almost simultaneously: the BBC in 1964 and Warner Bros in 1966.[123] After this, the portfolio of characters Tuckwell & Associates handled was reduced significantly. This circumstance and the profits achieved through the World Cup mascot inspired the agency to explore further the merchandising possibilities of mascots. The organisers of the Commonwealth Games, due to be held in Edinburgh in 1970, asked the agency to produce a mascot.[124] Similarly, a number of football clubs entrusted the agency with the task of designing and promoting lucky mascots for their own teams. However, this meant a shift in focus from children to sports fans, which not only constituted quite a different audience but also took the agency's business away from the media that had determined its formation: television. While football fans were recognised as 'the game's finest salesmen', there was no real snowballing opportunity. In other words, the building and extension of characters, their potential to evolve and to acquire a property form was more limited.

Despite the constraints of sports characters, the merchandising agency went ahead developing mascots for Burnley Football Club, Sheffield Wednesday and Birmingham City in the late 1960s. Their appearance can also be traced in the trademark registry, particularly in class 28 ('toys'), with mascots to be sold in new retail spaces in sports stadiums.[125] An interesting opportunity to reconnect with children occurred when Walter Tuckwell & Associates was approached to create a mascot for the 'Boy Scout' association in 1967.[126] The commercial horizon seemed

[123] 'Termination digest: Walter Tuckwell & Associates, December 1966' – File 155568 (Cartoon Character Toy Merchandising)'; WBA/USC.

[124] 'British Commonwealth Games (Scotland) Ltd: licence applications to Walter Tuckwell & Associates' (1969) August *Games and Toys* 43. Here Tuckwell & Associates was first asked to produce 'ideas' for a character similar to 'World Cup Willie'; 'Minutes of the Press and Public Relations Committee', British Commonwealth Games; 26 November 1968; ED27/380; NRS.

[125] 'Football mascots: apply to Walter Tuckwell & Associates' (1966) September *Games and Toys* 62 and less than two years later, see 'No 901,535 ("Ozzie Owl") for games, playthings and jigsaw puzzles made by Sheffield Wednesday Football Club Ltd' (1968) April *Games and Toys* 83.

[126] The name was changed to 'The Scout Association' in May 1967 (dropping 'Boy'), no doubt as part of the same updating process of the brand; see 'Stop Press: Walter Tuckwell & Associates Ltd and the Scout Association' (1967) December *Games and Toys* 117.

boundless. As the largest youth organisation in the world, the association seemed the epitome of a branded world. It was an institution defined by internal aesthetic distinctions in the form of badges, uniforms, tokens, emblems, flagpoles and related items specifically adopted for use within the movement.[127] With a network of shops for those items to be purchased, the Scout movement seemed the ideal space through which the merchandising agency could provide its services alongside the commercial chain. But the mascot, 'Skip', was a total flop.[128] While the character was devoid of charm and quickly jettisoned, its failure revealed a clash between the competing branding logics of the agency and the association. The merchandising campaigns that were most dynamic and successful were future-oriented processes geared towards the construction of a community, and hence concentrated on the advance exploitation of brands to produce goodwill. The Scout Association was more interested in the traditional 'scripting' of a community. In other words, the visions of childhood of the agency and the association were at odds with one another. The agency had an overtly commercial approach, seeing children as active consumers, reached through media promotion. The Scout movement constructed childhood as a separate, protected path along which it nurtured a specific set of values. It is no coincidence that the association had recently sought statutory protection for its new uniforms and badges.[129] It was looking for a distinct regime outside the law of trademarks in order to protect its insignia, emblems and badges to project a brand that had been primarily defined by civic and nationalist values, not recruitment into a covert commercial ethos.

Another flop was also a mascot designed to attract children. The client was not a sports club or youth association but one of the main attractions for children in the late 1960s: London Zoo. The character to be exploited was a cute, living polar bear cub called 'Pipaluk'.[130]

[127] 'My Log' (1968) February *Games and Toys* 26. Interestingly, the paraphernalia that surrounded the Scout Association had been the subject of litigation in a case that tried to distinguish between the laws of copyright and design; see *Pytram v Models (Leicester)* [1930] 1 Ch 639. The model commissioned by the Association was a wolfcub's head to be used a totem for poles which was held to be registrable as design so excluded from copyright; see Lionel Bently, 'The design/copyright conflict in the UK' in Estelle Derclaye (ed.), *The Copyright/Design Interface: Past, Present and Future*, Cambridge University Press, 2018, 171–225; 202; H.P.M. 'Totem poles' (1929) February *The Scouter* 44.

[128] The freelance artist hired by Tuckwell to design the mascot was again Reg Hoye; see 'World Cup Willie Creator' above n 121.

[129] The Chartered Associations (Scout Association) Protection Order No 1673 (1967); see also The Chartered Associations (Protection of Names and Uniforms) Act 1926 (16 & 17 Geo 5 c 26): An Act to protect the names, uniforms, and badges of associations incorporated by Royal Charter (4 August 1926).

[130] 'Pipaluk's arrived' (1968) April *Games and Toys* 49; 'My Log' (1968) April *Games and Toys* 26; 'Pipaluk' (1968) May Games and Toys 33; 'Don't miss the Pipaluk' (1968) June *Games and Toys* 1.

FIGURE 6.5 Walter Tuckwell and his daughter Tasmin with *Pipaluk*, 1968
Courtesy of Tasmin Overton

A craze centred on a polar bear cub had significantly increased visitor numbers to the zoo as well as boosting its revenue twenty years earlier.[131] However, problems with the new polar bear, Pipaluk, quickly emerged. First, the charter of the Zoological Society prohibited exploiting an animal, so in order to bypass the restriction the licensing scheme was arranged with a different company related to the society.[132] Second, as we have noted, there was a lack of connection to television, which had become the most important path to enhancing the value of the intangible property at stake. And third, as Pipaluk grew, he proved unexpectedly reluctant to entertain the public. As one journalist reported, the cute little bear rapidly 'grew, as nature intended, into the big rather severely introspective creature' and 'he did not, as the commercial promoters intended, develop much'.[133] While space for consumption such as the zoo gift shop expanded, the shortage of charisma

[131] 'Brumas' (1950) June *Games and Toys* 130. More than a decade earlier, 'Handy Pandy', a panda bear from the zoo had also become the model for toys commercialised by Dean's Rag Book; see 'Handy Pandy' (1939) February *Games and Toys* 185.

[132] This company was Zoo Restaurants Ltd; see 'Pipaluk' (1968) June *Games and Toys* 59.

[133] 'Baby Pipaluk was no match for Brumas' *The Guardian*, 18 January 1969, 3; 'Bear grows up' *Times Literary Supplement*, 20 September 1968; in Newspaper scrapbook ('Pipaluk'); GB 0814 HCA; ZSL.

demonstrated by the creature was insurmountable. As many agents came to recognise, it was preferable to pursue a campaign with inanimate material that came into being alongside merchandise than to focus on animals or even actors that were, by their nature, more unpredictable.[134]

The demise of Walter Tuckwell & Associates accelerated alongside the shifts in its portfolio of characters (or properties). Beyond the agency's creative design features, it increasingly became less efficient at capitalising on commercial opportunities, which in turn made it less interesting and less attractive. Failing to maintain a connection to the most important medium for capturing children's interest, television, meant that it encountered more and more difficulties selecting and creating durable properties. After the BBC decided to create its own department to handle merchandising and studios like Warner Bros developed their own international merchandising networks, the strength and variety that had once characterised Tuckwell's portfolio diminished. Alongside the loss of the most productive clients came the departure of its most talented agent, Richard Culley. With previous experience in advertising in New Zealand, Culley arrived at Tuckwell & Associates in 1963. Since then, he had worked closely in the development of the most valuable accounts the agency ever had, from World Cup Willie to *Dr Who*. After four years at the agency, he moved directly to a competitor; an agency called A. P. Films (Merchandising), later renamed as Century 21 Merchandising. This agency had also emerged from the relationship between a film production company and an independent commercial television station. It eventually acquired a toy company to control both licensing and manufacturing, but the growth of the merchandising business was such that it became an independent agency focused only on licensing.[135] The repertoire of characters handled by the agency came from Gerry Anderson's main film and television factory, Supermarionation. This included hits such as *Supercar*, *Thunderbirds*, *Captain Scarlet* and *Joe 90*. These series began to be exported to countries throughout the world, including the United States, Canada, Australia and Japan, offering Century 21 Merchandising global financial and licensing opportunities. As a merchandising manager, Richard Culley used his earlier experience at Tuckwell, deploying tie-ins, trade lists of licences to attract further licensees, promotional cocktail parties, contractual licence formulas, the circulation of advance reference sheets and scheduling information, and more.[136] In the mid-1960s, as new opportunities in juvenile and teenage

[134] Interview with Richard Culley, January 2015.

[135] Keith Shackleton, 'It's a supercar year' (1962) August *Games and Toys* 40; 'The Spacemakers' (1963) September *Games and Toys* 94; 'Thunderbirds merchandise is Go!' (1966) June *British Toys* 9.

[136] Century 21 Merchandising Ltd also applied for trademarks to be registered in Part A or B of the register; see, for example, 'No 852,738' ("Stingray") for all goods included in class 28 (games, toys, etc) made by A.P. Films (Merchandising) Ltd' (1964) May *Games and Toys* 90; 'No 863,519 ("Lady Penelope") for all goods included in class 28 (games, toys, etc) made by A.P. Films (Merchandising) Ltd' (1964) September *Games and Toys* 108; 'No 852,732 ("Fireball

audiences emerged, Century 21 Merchandising also began representing characters beyond television. It handled subjects as disparate as sport and musical celebrities, as well as characters such as the 'Pink Panther'.[137] Remarkably, these were joined at the agency by 'Rupert Bear', a strip which has featured in the *Daily Express* since making his initial appearance in 1920.[138] Despite its longevity, the strip had never been exploited by an agency before.[139] Within a year, *Rupert* was converted into a television series which ran for almost seven years on the independent television network. Although Disney, and to a lesser extent G-B Animation, had been doing similarly for decades, these modern agencies built on their predecessors' activities, bridging film and TV, animation and live action, while not being restricted to one production company.

6.7 COPYRIGHT PROMOTIONS LTD

In 1974, Culley left Century 21 Merchandising to set up his own agency. He was joined by David Cardwell, and they became joint managing directors of a company

X15") for all goods included in class 28 (games, toys, etc) made by A.P. Films (Merchandising) Ltd' (1964) November *Games and Toys* 78; 'No 869,042 ("Thunderbirds") for all goods included in class 28 (games, toys, etc) but not including toy birds or games or playthings utilising birds made by A.P. Films (Merchandising) Ltd' (1965) October *Games and Toys* 82; 'No B903,217 ("Captain Scarlet") for toys and games (other than ordinary playing cards) made by Century 21 Merchandising Ltd' (1968) April *Games and Toys* 83; 'No 905,912 ("Mysterons") for toys and games (other than ordinary playing cards) made by Century 21 Merchandising Ltd' ibid; 'No 903,214 ("Mysterphone") for toys and games made by Century Merchandising Ltd' (1968) July *Games and Toys* 47; No 905,707 ("Project Sword") for toys and games (other than ordinary playing cards) but not included toy hand weapons with cutting edge made by Century 21 Merchandising Ltd' (1968) August *Games and Toys* 50; 'No B906,380 ("Project Sword") for toys and games (other than ordinary playing cards) but not included toy hand weapons with a cutting edge made by Century 21 Merchandising Ltd' (1968) October *Games and Toys* 71; 'No B913,907 ("The Angels") for toys and games (other than ordinary playing cards) none being in the form incorporating or relating to angels made by Century 21 Merchandising Ltd' (1968) November *Games and Toys* 76; 'No 938,903 ("The Secret Service") for toys and games (other than ordinary playing cards) made by Century 21 Merchandising Ltd' (1970) June *Games and Toys* 50.

[137] 'The best for 1971: Pink Panther (Mrish-Jeffrey 1964), Scooby Doo (Hanna Barbera); Rupert the Bear (Beaverbrook Newspapers) UFO (Gerry Anderson) by Century 21 Merchandising Ltd' (1970) October *Games and Toys* 35; 'Century 21 sign Graham Hill' (1969) January *British Toys* 28.

[138] 'Century 21 to license Rupert' (1969) October *British Toys* 20; 'Rupert in character merchandising' (1969) September *Games and Toys* 28; 'Rupert Bear' (1969) November *Games and Toys* 42.

[139] Some toy manufacturers had been decades trying to secure a licence 'but Lord Beaverbrook would not permit it in his lifetime'; see 'Newfeld, Ltd (Bendy Toys)' (1970) July *Games and Toys* 36.

called Copyright Promotions Ltd.[140] The company's name is particularly telling because the business of merchandising agencies can be precisely defined as the promotion of copyright. Instead of acquiring properties, their task was to handle them and broker licensing deals to expand their profitability for venture partners. In doing so, intellectual property functioned as a lure to attract new commercial schemes for developing children's characters. In other words, through merchandising rights promoted by agencies, intellectual property and consumption came together as one.[141] The work of these intermediaries was situated at the border between rights. On the one hand, their business was predicated on the promotion and exploitation of copyright on behalf of rights-holders. On the other, the registration of trademarks, or even designs by third parties, impinged upon these operations. One way of circumventing this problem was by merchandising agencies themselves registering or opposing trademarks. Although this practice was subject to controversy in the early 1960s, in particular due to the statutory prohibition on stockpiling trademarks, the practice became normalised in the forthcoming decades. The aftermath of legal decisions and legislative changes will be explored further in Chapter 7.

Culley's career move replicated that of his mentor, Walter Tuckwell, two decades earlier. Not only did he leave a merchandising agency in order to set up his own company, but the first character taken on by his company, was Noddy, the very property with which Tuckwell had started his merchandising agency. Copyright Promotions Ltd was now appointed to handle negotiations with prospective licensees. The potential for merchandising was particularly attractive since around forty-six million Noddy books were being sold worldwide. It is not a coincidence that these figures, and the distribution of book sales by territories and languages, were the first pieces of information the agency requested before accepting the assignment.[142] The merchandising agency was instrumental in linking licensing operations to the making of a new *Noddy* television series.[143] Another innovative project took the character into an emerging form of mass communication media: audio cassettes. The most interesting aspect of this is how the project served to forge further contacts with publishers and phonogram

[140] 'Copyright' (1974) September *Toys International* 9; 'Takeover of Brit CPL by Culley and Cardwell' *Variety*, 29 May 1974, 41.

[141] Their presence is incidentally referred to in several intellectual property disputes, for instance, *Mirage Studios v Counter Feat Clothing Co Ltd* [1991] FSR 145 (Copyright Promotions Ltd); 'Hush Puppy' *Trade Mark Opposition Decision (o/099/98)* (Tuckwell & Associates); *Jules Rimet v Football Association*, above n 122, (Tuckwell & Associates).

[142] Cardwell to Hodder Williams, 6 May 1974; Ms 16352A/2; Enid Blyton (1958–1976); LMA.

[143] 'Focus on character merchandising and TV advertising: new Noddy series for television' (1974) September *Games and Toys* 38.

producers around the property. For example, when the agency contacted Blyton's publisher, Hodder & Stoughton, hoping to interest it in joining the audio-cassette project, it also asked to use the publisher's distribution network. Furthermore, the agency did not waste the chance for improving its connections with different trades, stating that 'these cassettes might be the opportunity to see whether there is some way in which we can use Hodder & Stoughton's catalogue for spoken word in the future'.[144] Thus, far from using the characters as ends in themselves, merchandising agencies were driven by working the opportunities that arose alongside the properties, seeking to carve out new projects.

While Copyright Promotions Ltd added more of Tuckwell's properties to its portfolio,[145] it also innovated with entirely unknown characters whose success exceeded even the highest expectations of manufacturers and retailers: the 'Mr Men'.[146] Because merchandising is a speculative exercise, it is difficult to pinpoint the reasons for the success of a character. However, there are several factors that contributed to the expansion of Mr Men which provide a window on how character merchandising operated. One of the reasons why Mr Men became so ubiquitous was that the artist behind them, Roger Hargreaves, had previous experience in advertising. Thus, instead of being a set of characters that were going to be advertised or merchandised after their creation, from the very beginning the character series had an advertising appeal. Mr Men was a collection of attractively simple drawings for children. Its format allowed the introduction of a host of new characters, and the way they were drawn and named meant that children found them very easy to copy and identify with.[147] Instead of being just a character that required programmes or instructions, the series was already a source that could clearly lend itself to merchandising invitations. Its flexibility increased the potential for collaboration at all levels of the trade. In that sense, it became a suitable resource for salespeople, advertisers and retailers alike to come together to plan projects and campaigns around their products. Even the Patent Office used it to advertise the value of intellectual property.[148] As such, the series evolved in a way that fulfilled what Myers had described as the best way to set up a large-scale exploitation programme.[149] Rather than looking at licences exclusively from the perspective of the manufacturer, or exclusively framing them as a contract for the

[144] Cardwell to McKenzie (Hodder & Stoughton) 10 October 1975; Ms 16352A/2; Enid Blyton (1958–1976); LMA.

[145] For instance, *Tom & Jerry*, see 'Cartoon exclusive' (1983) March *British Toys and Hobbies* 5.

[146] 'Notes and news' (1975) June *Games and Toys* 2; Ray Heath, 'How Mr Whiz is cashing in on the Mr Men' *Daily Express*, 29 January 1979, 25; 'Cardwell and Culley: the licensors' (1980) August *Toy Trader* 2.

[147] 'Books for Children' (1972) July *British Toys* 14.

[148] 'No wonder he's Mr Happy: he's worth more than a Mr Holbein' *The Guardian*, 19 March 1994, 8.

[149] Myers, above n 21.

FIGURE 6.6 Advertisement, Patent Office (*Mr Men*), 1994
Courtesy of University College London, Digital Media

copyright owner, the key was to inscribe the licensing potential in the products themselves. As Culley highlighted:

> another key component of our branding strategy was to present and promote the various characters as a group, or family, of related characters and brands. To this end, I suggested from the beginning that the back cover of each book have a grouping of the other characters depicted so that consumers who purchased one book would be made aware of, and encouraged to purchase, all of the other books. The point was to promote the books, and the merchandise, as an entire line featuring many different (but related) characters for consumers to collect.[150]

[150] 'Declaration of Richard Culley in support of plaintiff's motion for summary judgment' 3; *Thoip v Walt Disney*, 736 F Supp 2d 689 (SDNY 2010) 08 CV 6823; NARA, New York.

The exploitation strategy mimicked the seriality of television and film cartoons from the start, and in turn Mr Men appeared in animations. The series was the epitome of character merchandising because marketing and advertising techniques converged with product development.

The exploitation strategy affected both the contracts issued and the products developed. On the one hand, 'no licence was ever granted (in the United States) covering less than all of the *Mr Men* and *Little Miss* characters. One goal of the licensing programme, given the large numbers of characters in the family, was to distribute merchandise featuring many different characters so that consumers could collect them and select the characters they enjoyed the most'.[151] On the other, the link between the trademark and its embodiment was vital in the attempt to avoid boredom and obsolescence. Mr Men were marketed as irresistible to children because of their adaptability to a range of commodities. It was not that the characters were applied to the products; the products themselves blended with the characters. In other words, new shapes were introduced to a range of products such as chairs, toys, yogurts, soaps and balloons to adapt them to the individual characters.[152] In fact, a significant portion of toy inventiveness was absorbed by the association between merchandising agencies and product development, packaging, advertising and sales promotion. This idea of working 'under licence', which challenges the usual distinction between products and signs made in trademark jurisprudence, was what made Mr Men particularly successful.

The *Mr Men* series featured regularly on the BBC's 'Watch with Mother' slot, showing once again that television provided an enticing shop window and a fertile context of intermediation for investment and enterprise.[153] As one agent stated: 'without that television exposure there would not be a character to merchandise, or product to sell'.[154]

[151] Ibid. 4; see also 'Introducing … the Mr Men (Mr Happy, Mr Tickle, Mr Silly, Mr Bump)' in A31/62; Boots Archives.

[152] 'Agreement between the Boots Company Plc and Copyright Promotions Ltd', 29 November 1982; in 2726/3; Boots Archives; see also 'Character integrity' *Chemist and Druggist*, 6 October 1984, 614.

[153] The BBC Television (transmission) agreement for Mr Men was accompanied by a merchandising agreement between the BBC merchandising department (Television Enterprises) and Copyright Promotions Ltd; see 'Agreement between BBC Enterprises and Copyright Promotions Ltd', 21 September 1981; WW8/535/1; BBC WAC.

[154] 'Century 21 add their views to our remarks on character merchandising' (1969) January/February *Toys International* 11.

This chapter has shown the contribution made by merchandising agencies to children's markets, and indeed indirectly to the development of intellectual property practices. Chapter 7 further investigates the connections between intellectual property and consumption with respect to public broadcasting. It does so by sharpening the focus on the tensions felt within the BBC when commercialisation began to affect different aspects of its children's programming.

7

Troubles at the British Broadcasting Corporation

Broadcasting has played a pivotal role in the construction of the child as a mass-mediated subject. When children became a specific area of programming, wireless radio started to attract, engage and connect with them. It did so by addressing them individually in their homes, an aspect that increased considerably with the advent of new technologies such as television. The special programmes devoted to children did not only accompany them during the formative years, children of the interwar and post-war years were shaped by listening to and watching such broadcasts.

This chapter shows the distinctive ways in which the main broadcasting institution in Britain, the British Broadcasting Corporation (BBC), imagined, interacted with and addressed children, and how this, in turn, affected the ways its intellectual property practices evolved. Although we consider the distinct technological qualities of broadcasting, our focus will highlight a number of specific legal cases intertwined with the inception of merchandising at the BBC. In so doing, the chapter explores the conflict between Derek McCulloch, the director of the radio programme *Children's Hour*, and a breakfast cereal manufacturer over the use of the name 'Uncle Mac'. This commercial association was seen as affecting the public charter that defined the remit of the broadcasting institution.

The chapter then moves to look at the establishment of the merchandising unit at the public corporation. This brings into discussion a dispute generated by commercial appropriations of *The Wombles*, a well-known children's programme from the 1970s. It is difficult to understand these important cases in intellectual property law without situating them within the framework of the regulation of commercial broadcasting, the rise of merchandising agencies and the history of a special institution like the BBC. While some of these issues have already surfaced in previous chapters, here we will focus on how the connection with children intertwined with the contested ways in which broadcasting was understood as a public service. As John Elridge points out, 'since its inception the BBC has been a very special case. It represents a form of broadcasting informed by the concept of public service, a public corporation dependent on government funding but claiming a high degree of autonomy from the state'.[1] Looking at the constraints and media shifts of the institution itself gives us a glimpse into the legal changes and tensions experienced in different branches of intellectual property law. The broadcasting institution was a paradoxical entity, rife with contradictions emanating from a commitment to public service which also activated private consumption. Tensions were manifest in the negotiation of the lines between education, entertainment and the commodification of childhood, an impossible task at a time when, due to the penetration of mass media and popular culture, childhood itself automatically straddled all three dimensions at once. The BBC exemplifies how intellectual property became part and parcel of addressing and forming the child, first as audience and later as consumer.

This chapter traces the crucial position of the BBC in the scheduling and commissioning of children programmes as a point of departure for reflecting on the institution's concern with merchandising culture. Our view is that broadcast technologies had a decisive impact on the ways in which intellectual property shifted towards constituting children as both an object and subject of consumption. Firstly, the BBC played a significant role in developing a culture of participation for reaching and creating juvenile audiences. The measurement of audiences affected the way children began to be seen. Children were researched, quantified and attracted in diverse ways that led to a differentiation in expertise, with intellectual property exploitation practice increasingly isolated from research into childhood, and thus slipping beyond public scrutiny. Secondly, wireless furthered the expansion of a celebrity culture that had already been initiated by other media such as cinema. The chapter explores these two intertwined aspects and considers the specific historical circumstances of the issues faced by the BBC in attempting to deliver a public service that was not dictated by commercial motives.

7.1 CHILDREN'S PROGRAMMING

In December 1922, just a few days after the British Broadcasting Company Ltd (later Corporation) was registered, a special radio programme for children was broadcast for the first time. Broadcasting material geared towards children frequently included references to the importance of imagination, communication and play. John Reith, the director of the BBC, wrote a letter to *Meccano Magazine*, describing its young readers as (radio) 'licence holders of the future'.[2] The capacity of wireless communication to reach children and convert them into an audience enabled *Children's Hour* to become a defining feature of the BBC. The radio programme was unique,

[1] John Elridge, 'A very special case: the BBC from John Reith to John Birt' (1996) 2(2) *International Journal of Cultural Policy* 269–280, 269.

[2] John Reith, 'A message from the British Broadcasting Co' (1923) November *Meccano Magazine* 187.

with a curious history that resembles the history of the BBC itself. Indeed, it began almost at the same time as the corporation, and it ended its transmission when television took over as the most important medium. First produced locally on different radio stations, 'allowing certain national characteristics to emerge on the Scottish and Welsh sides of broadcasting',[3] the planning and programming of *Children's Hour* became increasingly standardised, particularly after World War II. One element that contributed to making the programme so popular across the country was its regularity: it was aired six days a week at the same time, between school and bedtime, preceding the six o'clock news bulletin. This converted the segment into 'a pause in the day's occupations'[4] and set children up around the wireless set.

At first glance, this could be considered a form of passive consumption of broadcasting material. The fact is that mechanisms and techniques were developed to stimulate the children's imagination and encourage their various interests. The programme soon began to attract their input and feedback. One of the earliest ways in which a special connection with children was established was through the creation of local clubs called 'Radio Circles',[5] the membership of which was fostered with badges, diplomas, membership cards and calendars. As we first explored with Meccano, these creative systems of reward increase a sense of belonging, autonomy and participation among children.[6] *Children's Hour* clubs initially appear to have been the result of bottom-up suggestions from listeners to ascertain 'how many children listened in'.[7] They served both as evidence of support and as an instrument to govern the relationship with young audiences. As a bridge between local stations and their audiences in the early years of radio, the clubs functioned as a means of establishing and imagining contact between the BBC and children from different parts of their local town.

While Radio Circles were crucial for the recruitment of young listeners, this type of engagement eventually raised concerns among commentators. Revealing a peculiarly British concern over public expression of emotion, listeners were identified as being overexcited at becoming members of these circles connected to *Children's Hour*. As wireless connection had opened distinct lines of communication, it also created opportunities for members' names to be heard and relayed on the radio. Club membership, birthday greetings and other club activities were also communicated on the airwaves. In the view of some commentators, this practice created an unfortunate and obsessive race for attention, a type of competitive bind which

3 Memorandum by Derek McCulloch, 6 February 1940; R/11/51/1; BBC WAC.

4 'Children's Hour: instructions: 1927'; R/11/57/1; BBC WAC.

5 In 1923, the corporation decided to form Radio Circles at all stations; see Minutes of the Annual Station Director's Meeting, 8 August 1923; CO 9; BBC WAC.

6 'Radio Circle party' *Western Morning News*, 29 December 1924, 3; 'The Children's Hour' *Manchester Guardian*, 4 January 1928; P129/1; BBC WAC.

7 'The Radio Circle' *Birmingham Daily Gazette*, 13 February 1928, 5.

fostered an egotistical spirit among juvenile audiences.[8] In other words, the personal triumph of hearing a birthday made public was judged likely to produce an unhealthy effect on children. While this could reflect moralistic or paternalistic views, the discussion over connecting with and engaging children became embedded in considerations over how to shape the notion of public service when programming for children. As some clubs collected money and fees, the corporation became worried about being associated with exploitative and profit-seeking activities. Although some stations strongly argued that, 'the money subscribed by circle members could be claimed to be their property and therefore independent of the funds of the corporation',[9] steps were taken to minimise these problems. For instance, fees were standardised throughout the country, programme money was not permitted to be used for club activities, and annual statements showing how the money was spent were made public.[10] Moreover, the corporation tried to shift clubs towards vetted social activities, such as those with charitable purposes because, in doing so, a different and more public and community spirit could be engendered. In that sense, some broadcasting stations saw the clubs as a 'means of social service',[11] with an interesting collateral effect: those activities supporting good causes were also observed as enhancing the corporation's 'own prestige'.[12]

For the most part, local stations found the Radio Circles valuable. Once described as a 'stroke of inspiration',[13] they engaged and mobilised juvenile audiences, linking a station with the population it served. The existence of these circles was considered a 'potential source of new licences'[14] and somehow 'responsible for the strong feeling of friendliness and goodwill which aided and distinguished the growth of the corporation'.[15] Even more, the correspondence generated by the circles 'elicited much information which was useful as an aid in programme-building'.[16] However, successful as they were, the BBC 'reluctantly' decided to end the circles in 1934, when *Children's Hour* shifted from local to national programming, and these radio clubs became unmanageable.

The different ways in which participation was structured across the clubs had produced, to the dismay of the corporation, a few recurring practical problems. The issues that cropped up were varied: from not having enough time to read out all the birthdays to a bewildering array of circles, corners, societies, or fairy leagues with active, dead, life, annual memberships, or even adults enrolled in some clubs.

8 Cecil Walton to John Kettelwell, 13 March 1933; R/11/57/2; BBC WAC.

9 Station Director, Sheffield, Relay Station to Head Office, 9 December 1927 (regarding Radio Circle party); R11/59; BBC WAC.

10 'Announcement, June 1927'; R11/58; BBC WAC.

11 Cecil Walton to John Kettelwell, n 8 above.

12 Station Director, Aberdeen Station to Director of Education, 13 June 1927; R11/58; BBC WAC.

13 'The Radio Circle' *Falkirk Herald*, 16 January 1926, 4.

14 John Kettelwell to Assistant Director of Programmes, 19 July 1932; R/11/57/1; BBC WAC.

15 Mr Appleton's Comments to Radio Circles; 16 August 1933; R/11/57/2; BBC WAC.

16 'Note: Children's Hour, December 1932'; R11/58; BBC WAC.

Despite complaints from local stations worried that they might become 'stereotyped dull',[17] the corporation tried to solve some of these issues by standardising the method of collecting subscriptions, issuing badges and distributing tokens. More importantly, it tried to divert this type of work and activities such as birthday greetings through non-microphonic channels. However, the search for ways to connect with children never ceased and different methods of developing channels of communication were thoroughly explored. In order to 'compensate for the loss of the bond' caused by the disappearance of the circles, different ways of getting in touch were encouraged.[18]

One of the regularly discussed schemes for maintaining personal contact with *Children's Hour*'s audiences was development of a children's magazine. Such an initiative was interesting and feasible because the corporation had already been involved in publishing ventures. The magazine or periodical could elicit different media iterations of the programme and was an ideal form to overcome some of the logistical troubles experienced with the clubs. Printing names of members on paper could solve the 'birthday problem' of the airwaves. However, the project did not come to fruition. This failure is nevertheless evocative of the struggle of the corporation in expanding the ways of reaching children across media. It is also an example of how the corporation could not (or did not want to) see the marketing potential of such a venture. The corporation did not think the periodical could work in tandem with broadcasting and considered that 'the better and more popular the periodical, the more it would undercut *Children's Hour* which surely should be heard and not read'.[19]

7.2 BROADCASTING UNCLES

Although Radio Circles were finally abolished, the priority afforded to fostering relationships between listeners and the corporation survived. Since the 1920s, the corporation had developed a set of practices in order 'to create in the child's mind a proper feeling of intimacy'.[20] Perhaps the most powerful strategy to attract children over the air was the technique of calling broadcasters 'uncles' and 'aunties'.[21] When

17 Station Director, Cardiff Station to Director of Education, 2 July 1927; R11/58; BBC WAC.

18 Kettelwell to Eckersley (cc Stobart), 18 January 1933; R/11/57/2; BBC WAC.

19 Kettelwell to Edgard, 13 March 1933; R/11/57/2; BBC WAC.

20 'Wireless in the nursery: influence of the new uncles' *Manchester Guardian*, 13 December 1923, 6; 'A leader for children' *Daily Mail*, 19 September 1925, 2.

21 Josephine Dolan, 'Aunties and uncles: the BBC's Children's Hour and liminal concerns in the 1920s' (2003) 23 *Historical Journal of Film, Radio and Television* 329–39; see also Stephen G. Parker, 'Teach them to pray Auntie: Children's Hour Prayers at the BBC 1940–1961' (2010) 39 (5) September *History of Education* 659–76; Katy Price, 'Gender and the domestication of wireless technology in 1920s pulp fiction' in Donald L. Opitz, Staffan Bergwik and Brigitte Van Tiggelen (eds.), *Domesticity in the Making of Modern Science*, Palgrave Macmillan, 2016, 129–50; Bridget Griffen-Foley, *Australian Radio Listeners and Television Viewers*, Palgrave Macmillan, 2020, 7–28.

broadcasters with 'cheery voices' called Uncle Caractacus, Uncle Rex or Auntie Sophie started addressing children, this was recognised as a way of drawing children towards the radio. Such a broadcasting feature created a paradox: individualising what was essentially a mass form of communication, allowing them 'to extricate themselves from the mass'.[22] The operation helped children to empathise and familiarise themselves with the otherwise anonymous wireless voices. Almost every radio station throughout the country had its own avuncular figures behind the microphones. The affective substrate was the hinge on which the relationship with child audiences, both present and future, was constructed. The attempt to court special audiences and to bond with children via a sort of amiable improvisation created by the medium also affected those broadcasters who came into being to play these roles and exercise those functions. For example, a former radio 'uncle' explained that the experience had made him feel responsible for the 'trust of a child in an unknown wandering voice'.[23] The use of titles suggesting an imaginary family connection to the child listener was facilitated by radio being a non-visual medium. The terms 'uncle' and 'aunt' served to mediate between (technological) filiation and (institutional) reproduction: that is, how to approach children without sounding too paternalistic became an important issue for the corporation. In fact, when some broadcasters reflected on their role, they saw themselves as 'relieving the parent or guardian from the task of entertaining the family for a time'.[24]

Although the kin-like relationship between family and broadcasters was useful in facilitating the construction of children as audiences, the corporation was careful not to undermine paternal or educational authorities. As wireless technology could be considered an invisible or vicarious adjunct to family life, it is not surprising that the corporation strategically positioned itself as 'uncles' and 'aunts', in other words, peripheral, yet close, relatives. This avoided the programme becoming too didactic, forging a personal link with children by giving the programme entertainment value. One of the ways in which paternal authority was not directly challenged was by the development of experiments in 'listener participation'.[25] This allowed children to emerge not as passive subjects but as respondents, figures invested with powers to vote and decide on, and contribute to, the design and content of programmes. As the corporation noted, children became the programme's 'court of appeal'.[26]

By the mid-1920s, the terms 'aunt' and 'uncle' were considered instrumental in furthering the popularity of the programme and 'in maintaining the happy and friendly relations between stations and local children'.[27] The familiar presenters

22 Stuart Ewens, *Captains of Consciousness: Advertising and the Social Roots of Consumer Culture*, Basic Books, 1986, 45.

23 C. A. Lewis, *Broadcasting from Within*, George Newnes, 1924, 100.

24 'Note by Derek McCulloch on Children's Hour war planning, 1942'; R/11/57/2; BBC WAC.

25 Gordon Stowell, 'The listener takes part', *BBC Handbook*, Jarrold & Sons, 1940, 80–83.

26 'The Children's Hour' *The BBC Yearbook*, 1931, 140–2, 142.

27 Minutes of the Annual Station Director's Meeting, 17 December 1926; CO 9; BBC WAC.

'really won children's affection'.[28] Despite being considered an 'asset',[29] such an informal approach was also sometimes considered 'too personal',[30] at odds with the professional attempt to cultivate a dignified demeanour in the corporation's relations with the outside world. As happened with Radio Circles, the overall policy of the corporation was to lower the enthusiasm and recommend that station directors 'detach themselves if possible, from the position of "uncle"[31] The corporation realised that excessive infantilising and sentimentality could be counterproductive. More so, when the term began to be used by outside artists, the corporation speculated that the 'excessive use of nicknames and pet names was detrimental, especially when applied to broadcasters who did not work in the programme'.[32] Several measures were proposed to alleviate such a friendly excess, for instance, avoiding diminutives like 'kiddie', 'auntie', and so forth,[33] eliminating the words 'uncle' and 'aunt' from print (but not the airwaves) or instructing broadcasters to introduce themselves not by their Christian names ('Peter', 'Geraldine'), but by their surnames.[34] Similarly, one of the earliest recommendations to local stations was to hire a woman because 'a lady was really the best for this hour, especially for the very small children'.[35]

Although these recommendations were not followed by all stations, the most interesting aspect of these attempts to alter nomenclature was that the identity of wireless 'uncles' and 'aunties' was often concealed. This reflected an ambivalent position on the part of the corporation towards publicising and producing broadcasting 'stars'.[36] When the corporation imagined children as audiences, it worked under the assumption that they were different from adults since 'children [were] not greatly impressed by great names. Prima donnas sometimes leave them cold, while they scream with delight at the familiar antics of a favourite uncle'.[37]

Despite, or because of, their ubiquity, the methods employed by 'uncles' and 'aunts' to connect with child audiences differed significantly. Their cheerful and intermittent personas became problematic when the corporation tried to justify its existence on the basis of efficiency and professionalism. As the corporation tried to combine informality with dignity, it found that the excessive 'chat' to fill time, the

28 'Suggestions for Children's Hour, 1924'; R11/21/1; BBC WAC.

29 Minutes of the Annual Station Director's Meeting, 17 December 1926; CO 9; BBC WAC.

30 'Children's Hour Programme Board', 26 November 1926; R11/52; BBC WAC.

31 Minutes of the Annual Station Director's Meeting, 16 December 1927; CO 9; BBC WAC; see also Minutes of Control Board Meeting, 5 January 1927; R3/3/3; BBC WAC.

32 Minutes of the Annual Station Director's Meeting, 27 May 1924; CO 9; BBC WAC.

33 'Report on *Children's Hour*; 27 July 1936'; R11/27/2; BBC WAC.

34 'Suggested Points for Memorandum to Station Directors' early 1927; R11/27/2; BBC WAC.

35 Minutes of the Annual Station Director's Meeting, 27 May 1924; CO 9; BBC WAC.

36 Station Director (Belfast) to Assistant Controller (Head Office), 22 December 1926; R11/27/1; BBC WAC.

37 'The Children's Hour' *BBC Handbook* 1929, 253–4, 254.

risk of cheapness, and the policy of avoiding publicity sometimes clashed with the style of some 'uncles' and 'aunts', particularly when they were in full flow.

Furthermore, the concept of public service upon which the corporation was built included the ban on advertising. While the corporation promised to guard 'against the intrusion into their programmes of any unauthorised advertising matter',[38] the line between broadcasting and advertising was often blurred. Even broadcasting concerts from retailers such as Harrods or Selfridges incidentally led to accusations of sponsorship or indirect advertising. It is worth remembering that the corporation was adamantly opposed to advertising during its programmes; it was, in fact, prevented from engaging in such activity by both its licence and charter.[39] The broad effect of these regulatory instruments was to forbid the corporation from advertising goods or firms on the radio. More specifically, the BBC was prohibited from receiving money or any valuable consideration in respect of any broadcast matter and from broadcasting any commercial advertisement. In practice, this meant that the corporation reduced 'credits' on the airwaves to a minimum. As no advertising was included in programmes, brands and proprietary names were inevitably affected. One of the areas of *Children's Hour* that came to be seen as sensitive was that of competitions; the policy of the programme became 'not to emphasise the question of giving a prize, a thing which the BBC did not approve'.[40]

Broadcasters and announcers who crossed the line and became 'too sympathetic' to brands or sponsors were reprimanded since neither the corporation nor its employees were permitted to profit from advertising.[41] The informal character of 'uncles' and 'aunts' contributed to this difficulty as it meant more careful monitoring of an elusive distinction between advertising and broadcasting. Impromptu or subtle references in presenters' scripts could not be easily vetted. The prohibition of advertising and the sense of obligation towards children had an important role to play in keeping the corporation separate from markets, including the toy, confectionery and other sectors primarily geared towards children. As a public institution, this gesture was seen not only as a way to enforce the BBC's licence and its charter but also as an instrument to generate goodwill. The way in which this reputation was generated, protected and channelled has been a constant theme in the history of the institution. It would also be relevant, as we will see, when the director of the *Children's Hour* tried to protect what he thought to be his intellectual property.

7.3 FIELDS OF ACTIVITY

Since the early 1920s, publishers, gramophone companies and other traders had become interested in linking their businesses with the *Children's Hour*. Most of the

38 Reith to the Newspaper Proprietors Association, 18 December 1924; R34/1; BBC WAC.

39 'Extract from memorandum relative to the BBC Charter and Licence, enclosed with letter from General Post Office, 19 February 1937'; Policy (Advertising); R34/1; BBC WAC.

40 Jenkin to DCA, 11 December 1935; R11/28; BBC WAC.

41 Reith to Phillips, the General Post Office, 25 May 1925; R34/1; BBC WAC.

subsidiary projects never materialised. This was not because the ideas and the possible turnover were not potentially successful or attractive but because of the distinct order of activities and commodities established by the BBC.[42] The corporation initially conceived children's programming as an end in itself, not a means to generate profit. In fact, the isolated publishing forays carried out by the corporation confirmed and reinforced the non-commercial route.

In 1924 the corporation began publishing a particular genre of children's books: Christmas annuals. Designed by different 'uncles' and 'aunts', the annuals were not designed for profit, but for tradition. They emerged from a desire to provide gifts for the wireless 'nephews' and 'nieces'.[43] Although this marked a shift in medium from microphone to print, the books and the programme remained directly connected. It was not just that the titles evoked the contact made by wireless in a creative way, but the compendia of written material – the 'goodies' – were mainly directed towards those already new, eager, mass-produced child-listeners. These publications ingeniously reproduced a familiar broadcasting style. The annuals were full of stories, short sentences echoing radio transmissions along with personalised, intimate writing resembling the ways in which 'uncles' and 'aunts' spoke on the radio. They included drawings, often depicting radio sets, wires and children. In fact, these children's annuals were geared towards orality, relying on and replicating wireless protocols by holding the individual child's attention through a mass-produced link. Despite the corporation's reticence in pursuing a commercial path, the paradox here is that, in a curious way, enticing and engaging with children across media became instrumental in converting the child into a special subject, specifically a consumer. When connecting with children, attracting their attention and eliciting feedback, the programme offered them possibilities and choices, stimulating their participation. Finding out what they were interested in listening to or might like to read foreshadowed the type of interconnectedness that would come with the advent of television.

Largely because these children's annuals foregrounded the dilemmas that the corporation would later face – a saleable object offered as a gift, a printed publication, or a public entity in private competition – the BBC tolerated them but explicitly tried to distance itself by first projecting them as 'unofficial' publications. A decade after the first annual based on the broadcast programme was published, the line drawn by the BBC to distance itself from these publications became increasingly blurred. In the mid-1930s, the physical appearance of the annuals changed considerably, signalling a shift in the way the corporation viewed its capacity to attract a child audience. A number of factors contributed to this change. First, *Children's Hour* was on the verge of becoming an independent division within the corporation, after the appointment of a new director, Derek McCulloch, popularly

42 Minutes of the Children's Hour Board Meeting, 13 May 1927; R11/17; BBC WAC.

43 Minutes of the Children's Hour Board Meeting, 16 March 1928; R11/52; BBC WAC.

FIGURE 7.1 *Children's Hour* annuals (1920–1950)
Courtesy of University College London, Digital Media

known as Uncle Mac, who had taken over the editorship of the annuals. Second, a literary agent had contacted the corporation expressing an interest in running the publication along 'more business-like' lines, changing its appearance to attract more readers. The agent had already acted for McCulloch during his literary career outside the corporation and had capitalised on commercial opportunities in the adventure and juvenile markets. The result of such mediation and bureaucratic intervention was reflected in the relevant annual's appearance. The new iteration came with photographs of *Uncle Mac* at the microphone and references to the corporation and the programme on the dust jacket. Likewise, the content was also slightly different as Compton Mackenzie, a well-known Scottish writer, contributed a foreword, and author's blurbs introduced each piece.[44] Another important difference was evident in the cover of the annual as the multiplicity of wireless 'uncles'

[44] 'Foreword to Children's Hour Annual'; Compton Mackenzie Papers; 25.7; Harry Ramson Center; University of Texas, Austin.

and 'aunts' curating the annual gave way to a volume edited solely by Uncle Mac.[45] In fact, the publisher and the literary agents had previously mooted the idea of Uncle Mac as the overall title for the annual but decided against this at the very last moment, opting for *Children's Hour* annual. These different marketing decisions produced an unexpected result, at least for the corporation, as it made the annual look 'completely official'.[46]

The most important change to the annual released in the mid-1930s was not only in the packaging or the presentation but also in the strategies used to engage children. The publisher and the literary agent went ahead with a marketing campaign that maintained the 'personal touch' promoted by wireless communication. In so doing, they drafted a postcard written and signed by Uncle Mac inviting children to buy the annual. While this might not be seen as a significant departure from previous broadcasting activities in fostering an economy of gifting and exchange, the campaign cleverly used the corporation's resources to refer to a different, less ephemeral, commodity. The postcards were sent primarily to children who had previously contacted the corporation, probably because *Children's Hour* had kept cards with the names and addresses of those who had written to or called the programme. Such information already gathered by the BBC served the publisher, editor and agent as the main marketing resource for the literary product. Although the corporation did not request 'the names and addresses of those children to go out of Broadcasting House' because it was the publisher carrying out the marketing operation, the use of the list was an opportunity to turn listeners into readers.[47] Strictly speaking, the exploitation of the list and its configuration as a trade asset was one of the earliest incursions of merchandising practices into the broadcasting corporation. The data generated by the broadcast programme became a source of advertising for other products. However, although the information provided by the corporation enabled the marketing operation, the BBC did not directly engage with the canvassing. Nonetheless, there were occasional complaints from parents who felt pressured by this practice. For instance, a father wrote to the corporation asking if it was right that an official of the BBC had used the information to boost the book of one publisher and whether that action was a form of direct and unfair advertising.[48]

While the corporation insisted that the annual was not a BBC 'publication',[49] several factors encouraged a perceived connection between programme and product. First, the radio programme began to generate data about its listeners via 'request weeks' and other participatory events that became increasingly attractive

45 'Children's Hour' *Radio Times*, 26 February 1937, 3.

46 Record of interview with Leonard Moore, 14 August 1936; R11/1; BBC WAC.

47 Leonard Moore to Jardine Brown, 12 October 1936; R11/1; BBC WAC.

48 Inman to McCulloch, 1 December 1936; R11/1; BBC WAC.

49 McCulloch to Inman, 2 December 1936; R11/1; BBC WAC.

to external companies eager to capitalise on that data. Second, the gradual reduction of the number of 'uncles' and 'aunts' signalled a shift in the corporation's culture towards a more professional 'touch'.[50] Although anonymity and collective authorship had previously paved the way for a legitimate position outside the marketplace, enabling the *Children's Hour* to play on the unknown identity of the 'uncles' and 'aunties',[51] the new corporate ethos became more flexible, making it a fertile ground for the rise of radio celebrities. One of those was Derek McCulloch (Uncle Mac), who had joined the BBC in 1926 and then the *Children's Hour* staff three years later. In 1933, he became the *Children's Hour* organiser and five years later, he was made the director of the programme. Strangely enough, he was initially viewed as lacking the skills to become 'an ideal broadcaster, basically because of a trace of an accent in his voice' and his propensity to 'mispronunciation'.[52] However, the corporation's internal assessment would become more positive a few years later in recognition of McCulloch's 'inventive mind' and his 'painstaking and industrious' efforts. His voice became 'known to and loved by countless children'.[53] Unlike previous 'uncles' and 'aunts', his interventions tended to be framed in the pursuit of recognition. While there might be different reasons for this, the result was the emergence of a media personality who fostered relationships outside the corporation. The name Uncle Mac mushroomed into different outputs – from annuals, books and newspaper articles to gramophone records – and marked his conversion into a broadcaster with a 'very large fan-mail'.[54] Such was the popularity of Uncle Mac that McCulloch was perceived as being 'jealous of other people shining on Children's Hour' and was viewed as a difficult colleague because he was 'liable to take offence and be on the defensive'.[55]

In the mid-1940s, McCulloch sued the manufacturers and distributors of a breakfast cereal called 'Uncle Mac's Puffed Wheat'.[56] That the defendant's business was this specific product is particularly interesting. Unlike other meals like lunch or dinner, breakfast has often been considered a meal requiring special marketing campaigns. Cereal companies had become keenly interested in advertising and

50 'The lost aunts' *Daily Mail*, 14 January 1927, 7; C.B. James, 'Children's Hour' *Daily Mail*, 18 January 1927, 8; 'Wireless uncles' *Western Mail*, 10 January 1927, 9; 'Changes in the Children's Hour – old informality lost' *Manchester Guardian*, 20 January 1937, 14.

51 'The Ideal Children's Hour from 2LO' *Evening News*, 15 June 1928; P129/1; BBC WAC.

52 B. E. Nicolls to Reith, 6 September 1926; L1/278/1; BBC WAC.

53 Collie Knox, 'Uncle Mac is made BBC Children's Hour Director' *Daily Mail*, 6 April 1938, 21; Rose McNamara-Wright, *Goodnight Children, Everywhere*, South Oxhey Publishing, 1998, 42.

54 'McCulloch, Derek' in Cyrus Andrews (ed.), *Radio Who's Who*, Pendulum Publications, 1947, 229; see also 'Uncle Mac's 1,800 letters' *The Observer*, 29 May 1938, 23.

55 'Record of an interview with Mr Derek McCulloch', 20 March 1941; L1/278/2; BBC WAC; see also Russell Twisk, 'Mac's your uncle' *The Observer*, 19 May 1991, 71.

56 The case is reported in *The Times*, 26 November, 6; 27 November, 8; 28 November, 8; and [1947] 65 RPC 58; [1947] 3 All ER 845.

branding strategies appealing to children. For instance, free gifts were regularly given away in packets of cereal breakfast foods. In the ensuing litigation, it was claimed that the defendant, Lewis A. May Ltd, had tried to attract children to the breakfast table by describing its product as 'beautifully crisp and crunchy', using slogans such as 'Uncle Mac loves children, and children love Uncle Mac'.[57] It is specifically the use of the name Uncle Mac that seems to have initially concerned McCulloch, since children would associate him with the breakfast cereal, assuming that he was endorsing it. The legal dispute between McCulloch and the cereal company has become a landmark case in passing-off, frequently featuring in intellectual property textbooks. However, the dispute emerged first as a case of copyright infringement, with McCulloch asserting copyright in his broadcast pseudonym. This was an ambitious claim since the literary work he claimed copyright in comprised of merely two common words the selection of which was rooted in a broadcasting tradition of effacing personalities and accents. McCulloch moved for an injunction to restrain the cereal company from continuing to sell or advertise in such a way as to associate his Uncle Mac character with the product. The case was dismissed, and the defendant escaped proceedings for infringement, but it did not alter McCulloch's belief that he had a proprietary title in his pen name.

In 1947, McCulloch brought another action against the same defendant based on passing-off. It is worth noting McCulloch's stubbornness in instituting legal proceedings not once but twice, bringing back the same complaint under a different guise. In lieu of copyright protection of the pseudonym, the new case claimed that the defendant had passed off McCulloch's professional name and that the public would be deceived and confused by the misrepresentation of an association with him.[58] One of the keys to understanding this persistence is McCulloch's sensitivity over a disability he suffered. His feeling was that some commercial phrases included by the defendant on the cereal boxes alluded to his physical condition. It was one of the 'various disgusting reasons … which convinced him of the necessity for bringing an action' and to sue again, now sure that the defendant was undoubtedly referring to him.[59]

However, the fresh attempt to secure injunctive relief also backfired with the court preoccupied with a lack of evidence supporting the construction of his claim of misrepresentation. Uncle Mac alleged the defendant had deliberately engaged in creative deception; hence the allegation of fraud became significant. Although fraud was not an element of passing-off law that needed to be proved, the failure to prove

[57] 'Uncle Mac's Puffed Wheat' *Essex Chronicle*, 29 September 1944, 2; 'Uncle Mac's Puffed Wheat' *Essex Chronicle*, 10 November 1944, 3; *Derek McCulloch v Lewis A. May (Produce Distributors) Ltd* [1948] 65 RPC 58, 62.

[58] When the defendant was sent a cease-and-desist letter threatening a lawsuit, the reply was a postcard sent while on holiday responding: 'I have ascertained that the name *Uncle Mac* has not been registered as a trade name in connection with any food product' in McCulloch to Nicolls, Director of Home Broadcasting, BBC, 5 April 1948; L1/278/3; BBC WAC; see also *McCulloch v May*, above n 57, 63.

[59] McCulloch to Nicolls, above n 58.

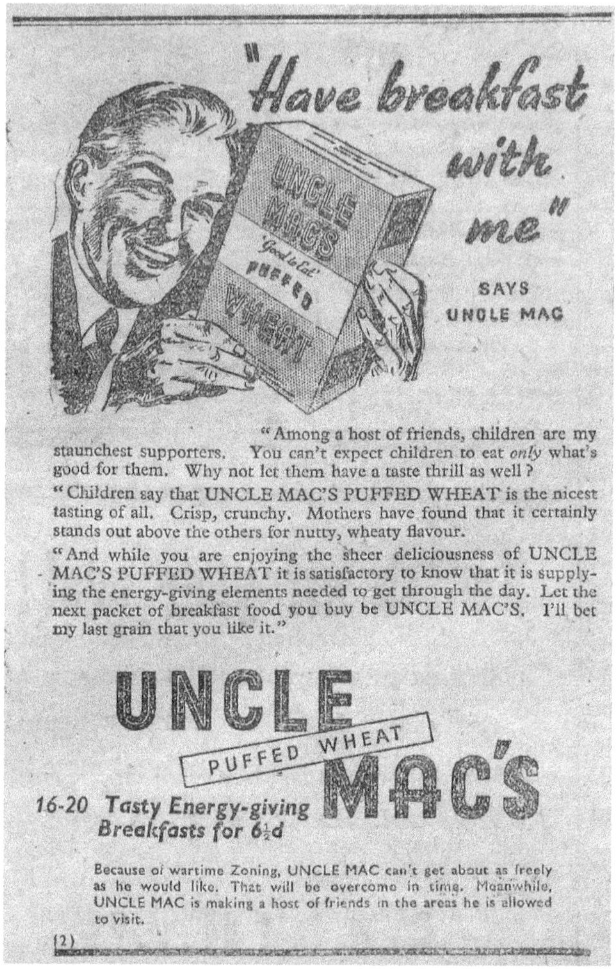

FIGURE 7.2 *Uncle Mac* cereal advert, 1944
The Essex Chronicle, 10 November 1944, 3. Courtesy of the Essex Chronicle © British Library Board

its existence significantly weakened and jeopardised McCulloch's case. It evidenced the lack of distinctiveness of the name Uncle Mac and the possibility that different traders and entertainers had in fact used the same or similar names in commerce. Taking into account that the technique of 'uncles' and 'aunts' to attract audiences of children was not a new practice, it became possible for the defendant to plausibly explain the reasons for his selection of the name as a trademark. Moreover, it was also easy to prove the existence of other 'uncles'.[60] Although McCulloch was able to

[60] For instance, the defendant was able to prove the existence of other entertainers using the same or similar pseudonym; see 'Uncle Mac and cereal label' *Manchester Guardian*, 28 November 1947, 8.

show the goodwill built up around his own use of the name, none of the main ingredients of passing-off, mainly misrepresentation and damage, were proved. As Justice Wynn Parry concluded, the prospect of damage to McCulloch's reputation was not real or tangible. As a result, McCulloch was unable to prevent the breakfast cereal from using the name Uncle Mac.[61] It is worth pointing out that scholarly references to the passing-off case frequently overlook the fact that it did not involve the merchandising of a 'real' person but rather of someone using a literary mask or pseudonym.[62]

The defendant, May, was represented by a leading figure from the parliamentary bar: Walter Monckton KC. Monckton was no expert in intellectual property but had expertise in cases involving the use of celebrity associations.[63] He had recently advised on the settlement of a controversy involving a film star, a case he described as exemplifying 'the commodity character of a celebrity'.[64] And, almost two decades earlier, Norman Birkett KC had presided over him in *Tolley v J.S. Fry and Sons Ltd*, an important decision on libel law – involving a well-known amateur golfer and a chocolate manufacturer – that went as far as the House of Lords.[65] The case centred on different legal principles to passing-off but shared some factual similarities with the 'Uncle Mac' case. For instance, in both cases the trade lines along which the defendant operated were typically child-oriented (chocolate and cereal). However, the main similarity resided in the two being legal cases focusing on advertisements, read and interpreted as if the plaintiffs, as a celebrity or a brand, were engaged in profitable enterprises. Cyril Tolley was an amateur golfer. His concern was that the suggestion of the advertising matter that he was endorsing products could tarnish his reputation and even threaten his amateur status. Similarly, the appearance of a BBC employee (McCulloch) on a cereal box could aggrieve him because he was contractually restrained from engaging in such activity.

61 'Uncle Mac loses action' *Manchester Guardian*, 29 November 1947, 3.

62 This point is often lost when a normative distinction between 'real' and 'fictional' characters is made; see Allison Coleman, 'The unauthorised commercial exploitation of the names and likeness of real persons' [1982] 7 *European Intellectual Property Review* 189–94; Allison Coleman, 'Character merchandising and fictitious characters' [1982] 10 *European Intellectual Property Review* 285–9; World Intellectual Property Organization, *Report on Character Merchandising*, Geneva, December 1994, 4–5; WP/NF/108.

63 A cursory glance at the law reports shows that, in the post-war years, a common litigating strategy for defendants in intellectual property controversies was to hire silks from the parliamentary and commercial bars. Those barristers were sometimes considered more prestigious and less esoteric than patent barristers, particularly in the landscape of courts and litigation. Moreover, their professional habitus was useful in framing property controversies as 'trade' disputes, raising suspicion around the possibility of rights engendering monopolies.

64 More specifically, he said, 'a film star is a very valuable commodity, to be treated rather as an exotic plant': see 'Vivien Leigh: defendant in lawsuit' *Birmingham Mail*, 23 February 1945, 1; 'Film star is exotic plant' *Daily Herald*, 24 February 1945, 3.

65 *Tolley v J.S. Fry & Sons Ltd* [1931] AC 333 (HL).

Despite the broadcasting restriction to becoming a subject of trade, McCulloch had become a *media* celebrity. His participation in and promotion of child-related activities, from Christmas cards to book competitions, had developed a celebrity-conscious persona, someone who used his pseudonym on headed paper, and even signed his private correspondence as Uncle Mac.[66] This is what really made the case curious: the wireless pseudonym had absorbed or consumed his real personal name; the public and the private boundaries had indeed blurred; and the legal case epitomised the underlying tension between the BBC and McCulloch. The hearing alluded to this at different points. For instance, a publisher of children's books gave evidence that he would have liked to refer to Uncle Mac, but the corporation did not allow it.[67] Similarly, a witness was asked what the BBC would do if McCulloch used his name in advertising without the consent of the corporation. Although the question was ruled out for having been formulated hypothetically, it implicitly referred to the existence of a dissonance between the corporation's policy and McCulloch's activities. In fact, as one BBC official observed, the corporation had never given permission to its employees 'for active participation in commercial activities'.[68] Such a remark indicated that the BBC was not interested in exploiting profitable ventures beyond broadcasting because it would have raised a number of accusations of contravening its charter and various internal rules. For that reason, McCulloch was told that the corporation 'would certainly never have brought the case itself'.[69]

The *Uncle Mac* case achieved a notable position in legal doctrine because it marked the establishment of a controversial legal test: the 'common field of activity'.[70] This was captured in the words of Justice Wynn Parry, who stated that, as a rule, in passing-off there should be a 'common field of activity in which, however remotely, both the plaintiff and the defendant were engaged'.[71] In other words, the rule elicited that no passing-off existed unless there was a common field of activity in which both parties operated. The law's relationship to that test and the value of the case as a legal precedent changed in subsequent decades, probably because of the

66 McCulloch to Farjeon, 21 November 1945, Add MS 88962/2/5; BL.

67 'Law Report' *The Times*, 26 November 1947, 6.

68 'Record of Interview, 16 December 1947; made by WJH'; L1/278/2; BBC WAC.

69 Ibid.

70 John Burke (ed.), *Current Law Year Book* 1947, Sweet & Maxwell, 1948, para. 3116; Frederick Honig, 'Lettre de Grande-Bretagne' (1948) August *La Propriété industrielle* 155–8, 158; R.G. Lloyd and the late F.E. Bray, KC, *Kerly's Law of Trade Marks and Trade Names*, Sweet & Maxwell, 1951, 518; John H. Andrew, 'The necessity for a common field of activity in the British law of passing off' (1963) 53 *Trademark Reporter* 1–16; Robert G. Howell, 'Character merchandising: the marketing potential attaching to a name, image, persona or copyright work' (1991) 6 *Intellectual Property Journal* 197–223, 206; David Howes, 'Inverted precedents: legal reasoning as mythologic' (1993) *Journal of Legal Pluralism* 213–29, 225.

71 [1947] 2 All ER 845; 65 RPC 58.

impact of television on merchandising practices, which enabled commercial 'fielding' to become an activity in itself. However, the perspective we offer here shows the specificity of institutional and historical constraints from which the 'common field of activity' test arose. While some legal scholars were critical of the judgment, arguing that McCulloch could have exploited the potential of his professional name in other fields, or referred to the decision as coming from an 'undistinguished High Court judge',[72] such critiques ignore important issues.

For instance, they do not consider the earlier proliferation of broadcasting 'uncles' and 'aunts', or the fact that the plaintiff, McCulloch, as a BBC employee, was prevented from pursuing commercial activities. Most importantly, they ignore consideration of the distinct way in which radio, as a mass communications technology, and the celebrity presence of a successful broadcaster challenged an imagined divide between the public space of communication and private consumption. McCulloch's entertainment forays constituted a variety of promotional and public appearances to enhance his popularity and that of *Children's Hour* across different media. While some legal scholars have considered the case as one of the earliest legal instances of merchandising,[73] such framing is problematic. It is not certain that McCulloch saw children's entertainment as a business venture. Described as 'the man with greatest pulling power among children', he was asked by local educational authorities to give talks to help the fight against juvenile crime.[74] Most of the activities could be described not only as charitable and educational ventures but also as instances of 'self-advertisement' or 'self-promotion'.[75]

The corporation did not seem to have an official policy on these 'ancillary' promotional activities, but it was certainly uneasy with those tendencies, since the profile of the celebrity presented a difficult problem for them. The corporation projected to the outside world the view that the BBC did not engage in the commercial sphere. That this message had been widely received can be seen from the example where one advertising manager of a cigarette company suggested framed sets of cigarette cards featuring 'radio celebrities' to be sent to Broadcasting House. It was presumed that the corporation would not accept them.[76] In terms of McCulloch's personal motives, it is also worth noting that the legal dispute against

[72] Leslie W. Melville, 'Towards a British law of unfair trading' (1971) 61 *Trademark Reporter* 375–96, 391.

[73] Jeremy Phillips and Allison Coleman, 'Passing off and the "common field of activity"' (1985) 101 *Law Quarterly Review* 242–68, 262.

[74] 'New job for Uncle Mac' *Daily Herald*, 21 January 1941, 3.

[75] The trouble of 'self-advertisement' was noted by some BBC officials when literature figures such as John Boynton Priestley began to work as broadcasters; see Ian Whittington, *Writing the Radio War: Literature, Politics, and the BBC, 1939–1945*, Edinburgh University Press, 2018, 41.

[76] Report of the Meeting of the W.D. & H.O. Wills Ltd (tobacco manufacturers) Branch Selling Committee, 14 August 1934; 38169/M/10/6; Bristol Record Office.

the breakfast cereal company was not focused on profit but on the negative moral association that advertising carried. For that reason, McCulloch only asked for nominal damages and an injunction.

The creation of this celebrity stemmed from a new dimension of connectivity – the closeness across space elicited by wireless technology. Even McCulloch hinted at this when he referred to his 'wireless' fame, acknowledging the role of technology in the constitution of a distinct mode of entertaining children.[77] The tension between the corporation and McCulloch specifically concerned ways of addressing and constructing children across media and whether that connection was limited to broadcasting channels. Their different perceptions of their roles and their boundaries became apparent again after the court hearing. Having lost the case, McCulloch was ordered to pay costs. In desperation, he approached the corporation for assistance as the financial burden of the case was 'a heavy one', and he had 'to mortgage [his] house'.[78] The response he received was that the BBC could not help since its revenues were public and it had a duty to administer the listeners' money properly. Two years later, McCulloch resigned from his full-time job at the BBC and joined a commercial newspaper, the *News Chronicle*.[79]

7.4 FROM PROMOTION TO SALES

One of the main difficulties McCulloch encountered was lack of support from the broadcasting corporation for his case, as his fame had shifted the boundaries between public service to private activities. In fact, the weakest legal point of his case resided in his failure to foresee that the corporation could not explicitly support such a legal claim. Limited by its charter and licence, the BBC could not 'officially' sanction or accept an employee profiting from or engaging in external activities, as this would contravene internal policies and lead to public scrutiny. That the commercial context involved children's broadcasting would have only heightened sensitivities. The BBC's lack of interest in the legal dispute needs to be qualified, however. Although it was not proper for the corporation to directly support merchandising operations undertaken by its employees, it was not totally against activities that helped to promote its programmes when carried out by external agencies. As we have seen in relation to children's annuals, the BBC allowed a publisher access to a cabinet with addresses of children who had contacted *Children's Hour*. The publisher used that valuable information by turning the addresses into commercial co-ordinates to target children connected with the programme, hoping to persuade them to buy the book.

77 McCulloch to Nicolls, above n 58.

78 Ibid.

79 'Uncle Mac quits Children's Hour' *Northampton Chronicle and Echo*, 13 July 1950, 1.

In the early 1950s, the corporation dropped the somewhat dated avuncular approach that governed the world of wireless and shifted towards different practices to constitute the child television audience. This child-centred move was internally marked by the appointment of Freda Lingstrom as head of the Children's Department in May 1951 and characterised by the production of *Watch with Mother*, a distinctive new children's television programme aimed at very young children. This explicit reference to motherhood through which pre-school children were addressed and entertained was accompanied by a particular aesthetics and schedule.[80] No longer constrained by the deliberate anonymity of the early days of broadcasting, from the beginning of the 1950s a distinct variant of merchandising operations emerged alongside these developments, pushed by the popularity and affection inspired by the first children's puppets and marionettes to make it to television: 'Muffin the Mule', 'Sooty', 'Andy Pandy' and 'Mr Turnip'.[81]

The shift from radio to television, with the spectacle of a genre of characters once confined to the stage now appearing in the home, also increased interest from companies hoping to profit from the success of these puppets. Television proved to be a particularly congenial medium for merchandising and advertising. It intensified the mode of attraction and relationship with children, as it constituted a visual register that contributed to the creation and development of 'brand-image' practices. Further, the advent of commercial television not only gave a fillip to toys allied to programmes, it also confronted the BBC with new ways of envisioning and fulfilling public service, imbuing the public corporation with a new competitive motivation to attract (or not to lose) children to overtly commercial outlets.

While the effect of competition on children's television had significant implications for the corporation's broadcasting remit and scheduling, it also affected internal policies and constraints concerning sponsorship and publicity. As an internal memorandum mused in 1950, 'the BBC, in its traditional children's role of favourite aunt, still presides over her vast table, but she is no longer alone. … Should she continue grimly to serve an emptying table or reconsider the menu?'[82]

The fact is that the corporation began to experiment with new ways of encouraging children to participate in their programmes to keep and grow its audience rates. As a result, television-based products and accessories specifically aimed at children mushroomed, principally in the form of toys, breakfast cereals and

80 See David Oswell, "Watching with Mother: A Genealogy of the Child Television Audience" (PhD Thesis, Open University, 1995).

81 'Introducing Muffin Junior' (1950) May *Games & Toys* 81; 'Mr Turnip-Balloons' (1952) July *Games and Toys* 90; 'Popular puppets' *Birmingham Gazette*, 18 December 1952, 6; 'Sooty toothbrush flute' (1956) January *Toy Trader and Exporter* 3; 'Sooty sweet shop' (1956) January *Toy Trader and Exporter* 7.

82 Memorandum by Richmond Postgate, 'BBC children's television', 6 July 1950; T16/45/1; BBC WAC.

novelties. These commodities paved the way for the next two decades in which the figure of the 'child and teenage consumer' took concrete shape.

One of the notable effects of television on the public broadcasting corporation was that it shifted its role in facilitating character-led merchandising. Although still reluctant to engage directly in these specific trade activities, it nevertheless passed information to manufacturers, confectioners and retailers that was crucial in enabling these commercial endeavours to take off. When receiving enquiries about the 'use' or 'registration' of trademarks concerning television characters or the 'rights of reproduction' of puppets and 'stars',[83] it relayed these requests to the performers, manipulators and artists behind the puppets who, the BBC reported, 'will no doubt write to you'.[84] In doing so, the BBC was immediately aware of the existence of commercial demands and the exploitation opportunities they presented. Similarly, the corporation facilitated connections between advertising agencies, manufacturers and retailers with the artists, puppeteers and performers behind those characters. For a business that depended so much on possibilities offered by connections and contacts, such mediation was critical. These exchanges enabled toy manufacturers, retailers and artists to create goodwill by getting closer to the child audiences assembled by the BBC. And they caused the corporation to reflect on these 'enterprising suggestions'.[85] After all, these contacts contributed to the promotion of television programmes, an increasingly important factor for the BBC, particularly after the advent of commercial television in the mid-fifties.

Another remarkable consequence was the rise of distinctive legal entities formed exclusively to deal with commercial sidelines. In 1949, the Muffin Syndicate Ltd was formed to issue licences for Muffin the Mule, the most famous puppet in the earliest days of television's *Children's Hour*.[86] Mimicking what had occurred decades earlier with film, the fictional character began to appear in different guises – from tin boxes to miniature puppets, from wallpapers to toilet soaps – featured on products authorised by the syndicate. A few years later, Sooty Concessions Ltd was incorporated with a similar concern to sanction products in relation to a different television character, a teddy-bear glove puppet.

[83] J. G. Wright (Kettering) Ltd (slippers) to BBC, 9 March 1950; Wallpaper Manufacturers Ltd (wallpaper) to BBC, 28 February 1951; R23/58; BBC WAC.

[84] G. M. Turnell, Assistant Head of Programme Contracts (AHPC), to Accrington Mills Ltd, 5 February 1952; R23/58; BBC WAC.

[85] Television Publicity Officer, BBC, to Head of Programmes, BBC, 13 March 1950; R23/58; BBC WAC.

[86] Adrienne Hasler, *Muffin the Mule*, Jeremy Mills Publishing, 2005, 19–20; Oswell, above n 80, 135; Jan Bussell, *The Puppets and I*, Faber & Faber Ltd, 1950, 39; 'Annette Mills, television's first star' *John Bull*, 9 September 1950, 12–3; 'Walt Disney of Great Britain', *News Review*, 6 April 1950 (thanks to Derek Johnston for this); see also 'Muffin Syndicate Ltd; company number 501789'; Companies House Archives; 'Muffin the Mule Syndicate' (1957) October *Games and Toys* 117.

FIGURE 7.3 Muffin the Mule wallpaper, 1949
The Muffin Syndicate, © 1949. Courtesy of Alexandra Palace and Will McNally

The Muffin the Mule syndicate was the business model and inspiration for converting this new puppet into a commercial enterprise.[87] This involved seizing merchandising opportunities, from becoming moulded and coloured as a toilet soap to 'going on the back of Kellogg's'.[88] Although these enterprises were first seen as 'ancillary' ventures, their importance increased as operations for furthering and maintaining merchandising practices became successful. While the Muffin syndicate handled the correspondence of a Muffin club to keep the BBC television-

[87] 'Sooty Concessions Ltd: company number 550858'; Companies House Archives; Geoff Tibballs, *The Secret Life of Sooty*, Ringpress Books, 1990, 28.

[88] 'Sooty's Magic Circle Game' (1955) October *British Toys* 19; 'Sooty books' (1956) September *Games and Toys* 110; 'Sooty stencil sets' (1956) May *British Toys* 12; 'New Sooty lines' (1957) January *Games and Toys* 160; Keith Happer, 'Sooty may now go commercial' *The Guardian*, 13 January 1968, 1.

favourite 'alive',[89] Sooty Concessions appointed different merchandising agents to sell opportunities around its sought-after glove puppet. Similarly, 'Prudence Kitten', another glove puppet, also developed a corporate personality in the early 1950s, when a distinct legal entity was set up to commercialise her.[90] As these business organisations exploited their corresponding characters via different media, from television to print, both the characters and the nature of the products and activities they licensed were affected. While passing-off doctrine maintained the importance of a common field of activity in order to grant relief, licensing projects considerably blurred the field of activities, contributing to a marketing revolution in which the identity of the brand became the product.

One of the most interesting corporate initiatives constituted *between* broadcasting and commercial design practices was Andy Pandy Ltd.[91] In the autumn of 1951, while the plan for the company to promote the Andy Pandy television puppet was taking shape, a trademark registration strategy was also considered. The formation of a legal entity to handle licensing enquiries not only acknowledged the 'sales appeal' that the puppet carried when applied to other products but also considered the registration of trademarks in different categories upon which the character was going to be applied.[92] For instance, 'soap' rights were discussed as licences were being negotiated with companies manufacturing different commodities.[93] A most remarkable feature of the company was its shareholding structure, a strategic combination of broadcasters and advertising and design entrepreneurs. The organisation accumulated members with different backgrounds and entrepreneurial skills. Lingstrom and her long-standing friend and co-creator, Maria Bird, became the controlling shareholders of the company. The other shares were allotted to Marcus Brumwell and Milner Gray, founders of the Design Research Unit and the Mass-Observation organisation.[94] When the corporation was formed, the broadcasters granted the company all rights in the use of and exploitation of Andy Pandy with the exception of BBC radio and television rights in return for its participation in the company.

89 'Muffin the Mule' *Johannesburg Star*, 4 February 1954; 'Puppet mule' *Brisbane Telegraph*, 28 February 1952; 'No business like puppet business' *New Zealand Woman's Weekly*, 28 April 1955, in Puppet Cuttings, 1932–1977; HA.

90 'Prudence Kitten Company Ltd: company number 00502743'; Companies House Archives; 'Prudence Kitten Co. Ltd' (1957) October *Games and Toys* 117; Gerald Morice, 'Round and about' (1952) 4(1) January *Puppet Master* 1–4, 2.

91 'Andy Pandy Ltd: company number 506797'; Companies House Archives.

92 Memo of meeting to discuss the promotion of Andy Pandy (Pre-formation Minutes), 30 October 1951; TGA 20046/1/3/3.

93 Board Meeting, 11 March 1952; TGA 20046/1/3/3.

94 'Facts about Andy Pandy', 27 November 1959; TGA 20046/1/3/1. For a general background of the Design Research Unit and the Mass-Observation organisation, see James Hinton, *The Mass Observers: A History, 1937–1949*, Oxford University Press, 2013, 217; Michelle Cotton, *Design Research Unit: 1942–72*, Walther Koenig Books Ltd, 2011, 12; Joe Brumwell, *Bright Ties Bold Ideas: Marcus Brumwell, Pioneer of Twentieth Century Advertising, Champion of the Artists*, Tie Press, 2010, 49–56.

Here, we can observe how the incorporation interacted with the transfer of ownership for the corporate form to become a means of conveying merchandising rights. The property assigned to the company by the BBC was not only the first trademark registration but also 'all non-broadcasting rights'.[95] The company relied on the combination of broadcasting information, design expertise and clerical assistance provided by the Design Research Unit.[96]

Among the different services rendered by the company was the artwork to apply or transfer the character to the goods to be produced. As head of the Children's Department at the BBC, Lingstrom had insider information about the extent to which the television programme was going to be exploited and shared the details with the rest of the shareholders. It is not simply that this information was important for the application for trademarks abroad. The establishment of contacts and the appointment of overseas agents to forward licence enquiries was influenced by knowledge of the BBC's plans. Likewise, design and advertising consultants in the company mobilised their networks and enabled goods bearing the characters to be manufactured, promoted and exhibited.[97] Although the company ended up appointing the renowned Walter Tuckwell as its merchandising agent, Lingstrom still played an active role in the governance of the company.[98] By negotiating licences and providing artwork to licensees, she tried to keep her two jobs separate. What is apparent is that, despite her prominent role at the public broadcasting corporation, she avoided public exposure of her participation in the private company. For instance, she declined the offer to become the chair of the board of directors as 'in view of her position with the BBC, she felt unable to serve'.[99] It is possible to argue that, unlike Derek McCulloch, who was eager for approval and public recognition, Lingstrom took a more discreet and careful stance, shielding her private and commercial ventures under a separate legal personality. In fact, the corporate legal form not only offered her a separation of spheres but also began to operate as a way of legitimising these contractual, copyright, and trademark arrangements within the broadcasting corporation.

Meanwhile, the *Uncle Mac* decision had encouraged some lawyers to believe that these practices were free and legal without the need for a licence from the

95 'Particulars of contract relating to shares allotted', 20 October 1952 in 'Andy Pandy Limited; Number 506797', Companies House Archives. The trademark was 'Andy Pandy No 690571 for games (other than ordinary playing cards) and playthings' (1952) February *Games and Toys* 112.

96 Minutes of Board Meeting, 15 January 1953; TGA 20046/1/3/3.

97 Milner Gray organised the exhibition of the Council of Industrial Design in Oslo, Norway (1952), and it is not a coincidence that the licensed toy exhibited there was Andy Pandy; see Milner Gray, 'Exhibitions in or out' (1952) 53(316) *Art and Industry* 119; Yunah Lee, "Selling Modern British Design: Overseas Design Exhibitions by the Council of Industrial Design 1949–1971" (PhD Thesis, University of Brighton, 2009), 378; and the correspondence in BW 2/421 Industrial Design Exhibition Norway (1952); TNA.

98 Minutes of the Board Meeting, 18 February 1958; TGA 20046/1/3/3.

99 Minutes of the Board Meeting, 15 January 1953; TGA 20046/1/3/3.

broadcaster, programme promoter, or celebrity in so far as new fields of activity were constituted.[100] This reading was, however, continually undermined by the establishment of distinct business organisations and agencies whose corporate aim was to promote puppet features beyond television and to carve out market fields for them. It is not just that these legal undertakings moved quickly to display copyright notices or register trademarks in Britain and elsewhere. At the same time, their activities weakened the *Uncle Mac* passing-off test of separate fields of activity through the provision of 'licence facilities' to exploit these characters in diverse ventures.[101]

As external companies, these operations marked out the profitable commercial ventures as separate from the BBC's engagement in public service. While some of the puppet creators, puppeteers and producers were or had been connected to the BBC in different ways, the creation of distinct legal entities attached to programme content veiled the possibility of commercial operations raising public criticism of direct involvement in conflict with the BBC's non-commercial charter. These companies served as headquarters, a reliable port of call for those manufacturers and retailers who saw licensing as a business prospect and an opportunity and did not want to get into legal trouble or waste time disputing rights. While merchandising agents instituted professional practices in terms of contractual norms, the significance of these distinct corporations handling and exploiting rights was due to other factors. In a fragile legal environment, at a juncture between copyright, design and trademark law, licences issued by these companies functioned as safeguards for manufacturers and retailers alike. In other words, they often fuelled each other by serving to provide a sort of contractual shield authorising them to manufacture or distribute television-related products. Although piratical copies obviously emerged in the somewhat grey legal zone beyond the licence, no legal cases were reported in these formative years, apart from the remarkable controversies cited in Chapter 6 concerning television westerns. This does not mean that there were no legal conflicts in Britain underpinning the exploitation of these television puppets in the 1950s. Rather, cases were either settled out of court, litigated abroad or just faded away.[102]

One of these rows broke out in Fleet Street between two rival newspapers. In 1956, the *Daily Mirror* launched its licensed *Sooty* comic strip and began to include characters that looked very similar to those from the long-standing *Rupert Bear*

[100] Sydney E. M'Caw, patent agent (Manchester) to the Independent Television Authority, 16 October 1957; 3995710 IBA/00577; ITA.

[101] Trade Mark registration No 571, 102 ('Muffin') in class 22 (games, toys and sporting goods), *Official Gazette of the United States Patent Office*, vol. 644, 27 March 1951, 969 (based on a previous British registration No 674,422, 12 November 1948); 'Trade Mark registration No 708812 ("Sooty") in class 28 (games, toys, etc.)' (1952) December *Games and Toys* 124; see also Minutes of Board Meeting (Andy Pandy Limited), 3 June 1954, TGA 20046/1/3/3.

[102] For instance, a dispute regarding the use of the name 'Andy Pandy' by the children's outfitters in Walthamstow was resolved out of court; see Minutes of Board Meeting, 9 December 1953; TGA 20046/1/3/3.

comic strip run by the *Daily Express*. The fact that the *Express* had lost the opportunity to secure *Sooty* despite having had the chance to do so contributed to a desire to take action. Max Aitken from the *Express* rapidly went to the paper's solicitors and requested advice from counsel. After receiving a very optimistic legal opinion from Skone James, the leading copyright barrister of the time, the *Express* decided to bring an injunction against the *Mirror*. However, before putting a writ, a letter was sent warning the *Mirror* that it was 'damaging property which is of considerable value' and that the paper must 'delete Rupert characters from the strip'.[103] Although Aitken had already speculated about the name of the judge who was going to hear the case (probably Diplock), no case was ever brought to court, as the *Mirror* 'immediately altered the strip'.[104]

The legal cases reported do not show the totality or even the whole range of conflicts that merchandising operations prompted. Among the effects triggered by these merchandising practices was that television programmes began to be seen not only as a unified whole but also in a fragmented manner, whereby its constituent parts, such as titles, stills, or characters, had potential asset value.[105] The corporation slowly began to consider some of these features as BBC 'material'.[106] While controversies often took place at the level of (trademark or copyright) use, they also resurfaced in registration systems constituted around intellectual property law. The link between legal incorporation and trademark or design registration became a characteristic feature of this business trend.

For instance, an attempt to register the design of 'Lenny the Lion', another television puppet popular in the 1950s, elicited a controversy which could be framed in juridical terms as the 'copyright/design' interface. Although the tension was fuelled by legal changes implemented in the Registered Design Act 1949 and the Copyright Act 1956 – reforms that sought to strengthen the distinction between the two regimes – broadcasting had already become embedded in both and was used as a vector to assess their interaction and scope. The Patent Office even contacted the BBC asking for the timing of the broadcasts to assess the registrability of the design.[107] While the point of the inquiry was to understand whether these broadcasts had prejudiced the registration of the industrial design on that puppet affecting the Registered Design Act 1949 s1B requirement that it be of a 'new and individual character', the informational value of broadcast programmes affected the constitution of intangible property.

[103] Aitken to Beaverbrook, 25 September 1956; BBK/4/182; Beaverbrook papers, PA.

[104] Aitken to Beaverbrook, 29 September 1956; BBK/4/182; Beaverbrook papers, PA.

[105] The agent of a television puppet already noted that merchandising operations would 'separate [Mr Turnip] from the television programme [Whirligig]'; Beresford to Turnell, 3 March 1952; R23/49/2; BBC WAC.

[106] Turnell to Platnauer Brothers Ltd, 30 April 1952; R23/49/2; BBC WAC.

[107] L. C. Stanes, Patent Office to the Director, BBC, 24 June 1957; 'Personal Files – Artists: Terry Hall'; BBC WAC

Yet, the most interesting correspondence between the Patent Office and the public broadcasting corporation took place in relation to the trademark application concerning Joey Laurie's puppet, Mr Turnip.[108] When the BBC applied as a joint owner of the trademark, the registrar of patents rejected the application because, he noted, 'it is common knowledge that the BBC is not a trading organisation'.[109] It is no surprise then that the BBC abstained from further attempts to register trademarks for its programmes. However, occasionally it did recommend that artists or their agents should register them themselves if they wanted to engage in merchandising.[110]

7.5 TELEVISION ENTERPRISES

Initially, the BBC did not have a direct interest in claiming rights for merchandising ventures. However, the steady flow of enquiries from toy and other manufacturers of child-related commodities received made it reconsider these trading arrangements.[111] Furthermore, as some of these puppets had been created by staff members, it could not avoid addressing the issue. Early attempts to deal with 'non-broadcasting' rights were characterised by sporadic, intermittent and unsystematic solutions.[112] For instance, in the early 1950s, the BBC started granting 'ex gratia' payments to employees who had created television puppets.[113] These occasional payments depended on the money the corporation received from the exploitation of the puppets in other fields.[114] This signified a minor change of attitude from the position taken in relation to the Uncle Mac activities a decade earlier. As noted already, while the BBC did not enter into any agreement to produce novelties or toys, it did not generally prevent external agents and companies from doing so. Yet, the main problem these agents and companies experienced in their interactions with the BBC was the lack of a central department to handle

[108] 'No 703564: Games (other than ordinary playing cards) and playthings. The BBC and J. Laurey' (1952) April *Games and Toys* 122.

[109] Stafford Clark & Co (solicitors) to Turnell (Assistant Head of Programme Contracts), 27 August 1953; R23/50; BBC WAC.

[110] R. G. Walford (Head of Copyright) to Assistant Head of Programme Contracts; 22 May 1962 (trademark registration for toys and games; Z Cars); R120/45/1; BBC WAC.

[111] See, for instance, the letter from the advertising company Mather & Crowther asking for the 'exploitation rights' of puppets used in various television programmes in the Children's Hour; Tupholme to Turnell, 23 January 1952; R23/49/2; BBC WAC.

[112] According to an internal memorandum, the uncertainty surrounding this issue was largely derived from 'a variety of uncoordinated behaviour in the past'; see 'Publicity and Advertising for BBC programmes and By-Products of Broadcasting', 30 October 1958; R44/892/1; BBC WAC.

[113] Administrative Instruction No 17; 30 May 1950 as amended on 11 August 1954; paras. 4–6; T16/472/2; BBC WAC.

[114] 'Consent and licence to use and apply the character design and name Mr Turnip to soap' 1 July 1952; R23/49/2; BBC WAC.

their enquiries. This meant that some of the attempts to exploit the material circulated between different departments within the corporation and no action was taken.

As explained in Chapter 6, Walter Tuckwell & Associates became the first merchandising agency that managed to navigate this bureaucratic maze, thus capitalising on the BBC's reluctance to handle merchandising rights directly. As a commission-based agency, Tuckwell succeeded in assembling a portfolio of television characters (or 'properties') and signed an exclusive agency agreement to handle merchandising rights for specific BBC programmes.[115] In this way, Tuckwell & Associates overcame the main difficulty experienced by 'one character' firms, which had 'to close down when the popularity of their protégé waned', often because of the discontinuation of the television programme.[116]

Several factors enabled the agency to achieve this ideal position. For instance, the experience Tuckwell had gained at Disney gave him expertise and knowledge, while the advent of commercial television opened the merchandising field to intermediaries and the proliferation of business organisations (mentioned above) to exploit the copyright and the characters facilitated the transactions. The existence of this corporate environment was an important factor in the emergence of merchandising agencies. In other words, merchandising agencies were well positioned when someone claimed to hold rights. This enabled them to act as intermediaries between the claimant and toy companies or other child-related manufacturers and retailers (as described in Chapter 6).

The competitive pressure brought about by the emergence of independent television had a decisive impact on the BBC's traditional monopoly, methods and policies. Although its constitutional position of 'no advertising' remained in place, the number of exceptions to this rule increased. As television was becoming a 'predominantly commercial world',[117] the relaxation of traditional policies was considered 'inevitable' by some.[118] Partly out of necessity and partly arising from strategic decisions to compete with commercial networks, the possibility of using the by-products of broadcasting to publicise programmes started to be considered. However, the most immediate concern was that earlier decisions had already highlighted the difficulty of drafting a general policy statement regarding merchandising activities arising from children's television programmes. For instance, the transfer of puppeteers to commercial stations gave rise to the fear that ad hoc arrangements regarding 'non-broadcasting' rights might be flagged in Parliament,

[115] Contract between BBC and Walter Tuckwell & Associates; 1 January 1960; R120/42/1; BBC WAC.

[116] 'Character merchandising' (1967) 116 October *Retail Business* 16–23, 16; see also 'Rent a character' *Sunday Times*, 10 September 1972, 65.

[117] 'Current and anticipated activities of BBC Television Enterprises department; Commonwealth Broadcasting Conference 1963'; T39/59/1; BBC WAC.

[118] The Solicitor to Miss Cawdell, 28 May 1954 ('Trade Names'); Policy ('Advertising in programmes') R34/963/1; BBC WAC.

or elsewhere, exposing the BBC to severe criticism for profiting outside broadcasting.[119]

This was one of the reasons why the BBC continued with its hesitant merchandising strategy, delegating the issue of 'non-broadcasting' rights to external agencies, such as Walter Tuckwell & Associates. This recourse to an external agency highlighted how merchandising rights had begun to acquire an important role in television scheduling and programming. In other words, 'non-broadcasting' rights had started to be perceived not just as a promotional operation but also as an additional source of income. The language used to describe the activity changed from 'disposing' the rights to 'exploiting' them.[120] This linguistic shift reveals a subtle change in perspective. While the BBC did not go out of its way to seek commercial outlets, it certainly did not disdain payment proposed by third parties for exploitation of programmes.

There were, however, two specific limitations apparently imposed on Walter Tuckwell & Associates. Firstly, the public corporation insisted that licences negotiated by the agency should not include any obligation to keep the programme on air. Secondly, Tuckwell's negotiations were limited to toys and games, confectionery and, incidentally, children's clothes based on television programmes, in an attempt to avoid licences over the field of apparent sponsorship of unrelated articles such as detergents.[121] It soon became evident that the distinction between promotion and income was not sustainable since boundaries between the two were often blurred during attempts to sell BBC television programmes overseas.

In March 1960, the BBC decided to set up Television Promotions, later renamed BBC Television Enterprises, a new department to handle the sale of television material.[122] What made this department significant was that it brought the purchasing and selling of programmes together as a single function. This signalled a new attitude towards the commercialisation of television rights abroad and highlighted the need to 'earn much needed dollars'.[123] Although a strong commercial impulse had traditionally been considered incompatible with the principles of public service broadcasting, the new focus on overseas sales reflected a relaxation of traditional principles. A changed attitude towards openly engaging in merchandising rights

119 Internal note by BBC solicitor on the agreement between the corporation and Miss Laurey ('Mr Turnip') 22 March 1955; R44/964; BBC WAC.

120 Minutes of meeting on 9 March 1961 to discuss the exploitation of rights in Television Programme Material. T16/472/1; BBC WAC.

121 Controller, Television Administration, to Head of Television Establishment Department, 13 March 1963; ('Z Cars'); R120/45/1; BBC WAC.

122 'BBC Promotions make sales in fifty countries' *The Stage*, 17 August 1961, 10; Asa Briggs, *The History of Broadcasting in the United Kingdom: vol. V. Competition 1955 and Beyond*, Oxford University Press, 1995, 712.

123 L. P. R. Rocha, BBC to Skone James, 2 November 1954; regarding the difficulty in selling the programme 'Guess my Story' to the Canadian Broadcasting Corporation because of a dispute concerning the underlying rights; R12/86; BBC WAC.

coincided with the making of coproduction deals such as *R.C.M.P.* (a series based on the Royal Canadian Mounted Police). These arrangements with foreign television stations demonstrated the importance of the Commonwealth as a distinctive broadcasting market with compatible production values and similar audience expectations. They also evidenced the importance of focusing on merchandising rights as part of a sales strategy, an approach that was soon increasingly adopted by the BBC.[124] The creation of Television Enterprises as a special department to foster commercial sales also removed the obstacle for the BBC to apply for trademarks in different fields at the Patent Office. Now a trader of rights in television programmes as well as a public broadcaster, the trademark applications for toy, confectionery, or children's clothes made by the BBC that followed the establishment of Television Enterprises went through smoothly.[125]

Television Enterprises operated on a self-supporting basis aiming at profitability. In that sense, it was quite different to the work carried out in any other department within the BBC. Crucially, distinct from the Children's Department and yet close enough to know about children's programmes, scheduling and rights, this internal organisational distance was important in mitigating the kind of public scrutiny remarked upon earlier. By separating questions of programming from questions of commercialisation, the distance created by the unit was instrumental in shifting the BBC's attitude away from observing merchandising practices passively to actively considering the rights upon which these operations were based. A few months before the department was set up, an internal memo had acknowledged that 'our attitude hitherto had been the fairly passive one of waiting for manufacturers to approach us'.[126] The possibility of changing this policy was the subject of inhouse consideration. The new department became a fertile ground for these conversations to take place since it was 'well placed and equipped to handle negotiations with manufacturers and publishers'.[127]

With this in mind, a few months after its creation, the department started to gather relevant commercial know-how. This included a productive talk with Frank Mincolla, MCA's merchandising director in New York. He shared different techniques to displace the risk from a broadcasting company to toy manufacturers and the type of royalty percentages common in the trade. Similarly, the new department examined the 'Benson formula', a shortcut referring to the ways in which Murray

124 Mark Farrell to Ronald Waldman, BBC TV Enterprises, 20 March 1963; R120/42/1; BBC WAC.

125 Trade Mark Applications No 896807 (class 30); 896490 (class 28); 896806 (class 25) made by the BBC regarding 'Adam Adamant'; R120/4/1; BBC WAC. In 1967, the application for class 25 was withdrawn, not only because the licensing negotiation became lengthier and the search in the Registry showed earlier conflicting marks but also because the television series had by then been dropped by the BBC.

126 C. D. Shaw (AHPC) to George Campey, Head of Publicity; 'Publicity through games and other toys', 20 January 1960; R44/892/1; BBC WAC.

127 Memo by Roy Williams, 'Exploitation of rights in television programme material', 29 November 1960; R44/892/1; BBC WAC.

Benson managed the merchandising and licensing department at CBS.[128] Coincidentally, at the time this was being considered, Benson was involved in the legal dispute that had surrounded the trademark registration of *Rawhide* (see Chapter 6). The BBC was interested in the legality of merchandising practices and paid attention to the outcome of the trademark case, asking Benson for further details because it was 'in the interests of all broadcasters that their programme titles should not be exploited by other interests'.[129]

Although the legal decision demonstrated that the Patent Office was sympathetic to merchandising agencies applying or opposing trademark applications, and the BBC had taken some steps to exploit rights via an external agency, the definitive push for the public corporation to fully embrace merchandising took a couple of years to materialise. While the extraordinary success of *Dr Who* made the BBC 'very conscious of the value of this form of exploitation',[130] it also exposed the need for policy reform to avoid criticism from those who worked with or supplied material to the BBC. In November 1965, the agents and the solicitors for Terry Nation, the creator of the *Dr Who* series, complained about the rejection of premium advertising offers and merchandising opportunities which, according to them, had severely prejudiced the income to both their client and the corporation.[131] Their complaints highlighted that the lack of commercial attention to these profitable opportunities was particularly problematic, considering that 'the public corporation ha[d] thought fit to create an independently operated body BBC Television Enterprises and the very name of this body distinguishe[d] it in operation from the normal operation of the corporation'.[132]

Ironically, the creation of the department meant that the corporation was now facing a new form of criticism, radically different from what the BBC was accustomed to. Instead of being accused of profiting from broadcast audiences, it was now criticised for the opposite: for not doing enough to maximise profit. After the establishment of Television Enterprises, the public corporation could be accused of failing to fulfil the public interests embodied in its remit by neglecting to satisfy the commercial expectations of the parties whom the corporation had contractual relations with. This tension facilitated a decision by BBC's management to engage a more elastic view of the way in which its public function was understood.[133]

[128] G. del Strother to John Grove, Television Promotions, 27 July 1960; R44/892/1; BBC WAC.

[129] S. G. Williams, Controller, Television Administration to Dennis Scuse, General Manager of BBC Enterprises, 24 November 1961; T16/472/1; BBC WAC.

[130] Lionel Clay, 'Stand by for the year of the Daleks' *Daily Mail*, 7 April 1965, 8; 'TV and BBC Enterprises' (1966) June *Toy Trader and Hobby and Model Stockist* 23–4.

[131] Beryl Vertue, ALS Management, to Dennis Scuse, 4 November 1965; T16/472/3; BBC WAC.

[132] Berger, Oliver & Co to Dennis Scuse, 17 November 1965; T16/472/3; BBC WAC.

[133] Board of Management Minutes, 21 December 1965, 'Commercial exploitation of the Daleks', and Board of Management Minutes, 14 January 1966, 'Premium advertising of products associated with BBC Programmes'; T16/472/3; BBC WAC.

The reassessment of the unit's operations that came after these discussions meant the end of the BBC's exclusive relationship with the external agency, Tuckwell & Associates.

Television Enterprises now began to issue licences in connection with series ideally suited for children on its own initiative, without the involvement of an agency.[134] This direct taking-up of merchandising by the department had a significant but subtle effect on the BBC's legal position when negotiating with third parties. Firstly, the interest in these 'subsidiary' rights began to figure prominently at the outset of negotiations to acquire or commission television programmes. Secondly, the standard contracts used by the corporation were updated to include a clause to try to secure merchandising rights ab initio and, where possible, a percentage cut of the exploitation of merchandising rights.[135] Television Enterprises not only functioned as an agency within the corporation handling merchandising rights of BBC programmes but also sought to act as a merchandising agency for third-party programmes commissioned by or licensed to the BBC. Here we can see how the department was useful in shifting the perception of merchandising from being a useful promotional tool to become a business in itself, created by the agency agreements signed by the public corporation.

One of the first instances in which Television Enterprises acted as a merchandising agent for a third party was in regard to *The Magic Roundabout*, a children's television series created by Serge Danot. The BBC proceeded to sign two contracts with DANOT, the company in which the copyright of the series was vested. In addition to a typical broadcasting contract that dealt with transmission rights, a collateral agreement was signed whereby Television Enterprises was appointed as the series' merchandising agency.[136] Similar kindred contracts underpinned the purchase or the commission of series like *The Adventures of Parsley* or *Bagpuss*.[137]

The person handling these commercial activities was a keen BBC employee, Roy Williams, who had been the liaison and contact with Tuckwell & Associates when the agency represented the corporation. By dint of his specific knowledge and expertise in these matters, Williams started working as an assistant to the business

[134] Roy Williams to the Assistant Head of Television Enterprises, 13 January 1966 (Harrogate Toy Fair); R120/36/1; BBC WAC.

[135] 'The Daleks are shooting into big business!' (1965) 10 October *Ariel* 1; (1966) October 'New BBC merchandising' *British Toys* 3.

[136] Agency agreement between the BBC ('Television Enterprises') and Société DANOT, 31 August 1966; R22/671/1; BBC WAC.

[137] Agency agreement between the BBC ('Television Enterprises') and FilmFair, 27 August 1968 ('The Adventures of Parsley'); T2/245/1; BBC WAC and the agency (merchandising) agreement between the BBC ('Television Enterprises') and Peter Firmin and Oliver Postgate ('Smallfilms'), 15 February 1973 ('Bagpuss'); WW3/16/1; BBC WAC.

FIGURE 7.4 Roy Williams surrounded by merchandise, 1968
Courtesy of Vanessa McElduff and Max Williams

manager at Television Enterprises. He then became exploitation and commercial manager, and head of merchandising a decade later.[138]

Although the commercial exploitation of *The Magic Roundabout* was thriving not only in Britain but also in Australia and other territories, and Television Enterprises was rapidly gaining a privileged position among the most important agencies in the late 1960s,[139] the unit's main challenge was to find its place within the BBC. Television Enterprises encountered no obstacles in the registration of trademarks for *The Magic Roundabout* or its characters: here acting on behalf of the copyright

[138] 'The BBC's selling arm' *The Stage*, 24 October 1968, 12; 'Character selling is big TV business' *Middlesex County Times and Gazette*, 2 June 1972, 15; Christopher Crouch, 'Roy Williams' (2013) February *Prospero Magazine* 10–11.

[139] 'Magic Roundabout' (1966) October *Games and Toys* 29; 'Merchandising venture with Magic Roundabout' (1967) August *Toys International* 3–4; 'Magic Roundabout' (1968) January/February *Toys International* 45; 'Magic Roundabout: BBC TV' (1969) January *British Toys* 32; 'BBC TV's Magic Roundabout at Selfridge's' in 'My Log' (1968) December *Games and Toys* 157; see also Pamela Redhead, 'TV transforms the UK toy industry' *Canberra Times*, 13 November 1968, 25.

owner, DANOT.[140] Similarly, the design of the puppets had already been registered by Serge Danot.[141] However, the dissolution of the DANOT company, after a dispute among its shareholders, put Television Enterprises in a rather difficult position when deciding the destiny of royalties arising from merchandising licences. Instead of getting bogged down in the controversy around who was entitled to the merchandising income, the department decided to alleviate tensions and focused instead on signing new licences on behalf of all the parties (potentially) concerned, holding the royalties in trust until the dispute was resolved. In doing so, Television Enterprises avoided litigation that could have put the department in the spotlight and ignited tensions within the BBC and beyond about the appropriateness of commercial activities being pursued by the department.[142]

The degree to which Television Enterprises struggled to assert its authority and fulfil its role inside the confines of the public corporation can be seen from the challenges that emerged in the exploitation of 'Joe', a character from the BBC series *Watch with Mother*. Television Enterprises acted for an external copyright owner, Alison Prince, but, in exploring the merchandising options for her, it found it easier and, more importantly, speedier to seek to deal with the publishing rights of *Joe* outside the public corporation. When Prince called the BBC publications department to enquire about the rights, no one there had even heard of the series. As a result, Television Enterprises sidelined the BBC publication department and pursued negotiations with publishers outside the corporation. It also complained internally about the inefficient handling of enquiries by its colleagues.[143] The relations with the publications department had been problematic since the early days of Television Enterprises. As noted in Chapter 5, the demarcation lines between merchandising rights on the one hand and publishing rights on the other were particularly difficult to draw. Merchandising often included magazines, comics, annuals and other children's publications. It is not surprising that this difficulty caused some internal frictions.[144] Yet, a minor but

[140] Alan Bylard to Frank B. Dehn & Co, patent and trademark agents, 23 August 1971; R22/671/1; BBC WAC.

[141] Registered Designs 922,517; ('Margotte'); 922,517 ('Zebulon'); 922,519 ('Pollux'); in the name of Serge Danot; 21 December 1965 (France) and extended to the UK until 8 June 1975; R22/672/1; BBC WAC.

[142] Curiously enough, Television Enterprises highlighted that 'I am sure that he (Danot) will appreciate the commercial sense in the Corporation's proposal'; see J. P. Colman to J. Coyne, 3 May 1972; R22/671/1; BBC WAC.

[143] Roy Williams to Alison Prince, 10 October 1966; R120/43/1; BBC WAC.

[144] For instance, the licences issued by Television Enterprises to Odhams Books Ltd based on *The Magic Roundabout* received criticism by the Publications Department; see Roy Williams to Head of Business, Television Enterprises, 7 October 1966; R120/36/1; BBC WAC. The reason was that BBC Publications also issued annuals based on television programmes for children; see 'New children's books' (1971) September *Games and Toys* 81; 'BBC publications' (1973) April *Games and Toys* 24.

persistent interdepartmental disagreement is most revealing of what was at stake in these internal controversies.

The disagreement concerned a rather innocuous attempt to include a display cabinet showing a selection of licensed items in the bookshop at the main headquarters of the BBC.[145] The publications department rejected this suggestion as inappropriate 'as it did not want their bookshops turned into toy shops'.[146] Although this might look at first glance as trivial, it highlights the controversial status of the new department within the institution. Television Enterprises was eager to emphasise the importance of internal publicity 'to show members of the staff the extent to which we are now engaged in merchandising'.[147] Such publicity and displays were deemed crucial to make everybody at the BBC aware that the point of contact for these products (and their deals) was Television Enterprises. In so doing, Television Enterprises tried to overcome the traditional ethos of scepticism that internally characterised the public corporation when commerce was even mentioned. It took more than two years for Television Enterprises to get a spot in the bookshop at Television Centre, supported by the Controller requesting 'that every branch of the Corporation works together for the purpose of the sale of BBC products of whatever kind'. Eventually, these communications had some effect.[148]

The relationship between Television Enterprises and the Children's Department was similarly conflicted. This can also be appreciated in the exploitation of *Joe*. When Television Enterprises was appointed as the merchandising agency for the series, the Children's Department raised its concern for the public image of the programme not to be undermined because of 'too easy sales of licences to people who will cheapen the product'.[149] Although the two branches of the corporation were kept separate to avoid conflicts of interest – that is, to prevent merchandising potential influencing programme decisions – some co-ordination was essential. For instance, the announcements made by the merchandising unit took special care not to pre-empt the press releases from the Children's Department about forthcoming new programmes. The information about BBC scheduling was key for Television Enterprises to connect programmes and products in closing deals with prospective licensees. However, since the advent of commercial television, the Children's Department at the BBC had struggled with the dilemma of competing with what it perceived was debasing standards in the education of children.[150]

145 Roy Williams to the Head of Business, Television Enterprises, 17 April 1964; R120/36/1; BBC WAC.

146 Dennis Scuse to General Manager, Publications, 28 January 1966; R120/36/1; BBC WAC.

147 Scuse to S. G. Williams, 10 November 1966; T16/472/3; BBC WAC.

148 S. G. Williams, Controller, Television Administration to General Manager, Television Enterprises, 25 January 1966; T16/472/3; BBC WAC.

149 Doreen Stephens to Roy Williams, 23 May 1966; R120/43/1; BBC WAC. In the mid-1960s, the department was temporarily called 'Family Programmes', the result of a merger between women's and children's programmes.

150 'Children's television; report of a meeting held on November 22, 1960'; T16/45/3; BBC WAC.

One distinctive way to broadcast programmes different from the 'Americanised' version of children's entertainment was to focus on puppets instead of cartoons or westerns. As we have seen, this concern encouraged the BBC to pioneer the scheduling of television puppets for children's entertainment. It also explains why it began acquiring the television rights of French animation series such as *The Magic Roundabout*, *Hector's House* and *Barnaby*.[151] The limited budget allocated to the Children's Department meant that the financial possibilities purveyed by merchandising prompted closer interdepartmental interactions. For example, the purchase of *Barnaby* was facilitated by the incorporation in the contracts of an advance commission against merchandising income.[152] This financial operation significantly reduced the price for the corporation, and it demonstrated how Television Enterprises could play an important role in Children's Department acquisitions. Despite or because the public corporation failed to acquire the merchandising rights in other series it purchased, such as *The Man from U.N.C.L.E.*, which typically saw merchandising rights remain with the originating producer or an external agency, Television Enterprises began to focus on the commissioning stage of BBC children's television series.[153] By intervening at that initial stage when the proposals selected by the Children's Department were considered, a mutually beneficial interdepartmental connection was achieved, based on income being guaranteed against merchandising revenue. On the one hand, the special commitment of the Children's Department to fulfil the public service remit for children was not sacrificed. On the other, Television Enterprises hereby found a way to normalise its activities within the parameters of the public corporation.[154]

It is therefore possible to see how such upfront capital arrangements reframed merchandising rights and shaped the negotiations of many children's programmes throughout the late 1960s and the 1970s. Television Enterprises facilitated the investment of the public corporation in projects such as *The Herbs*, *The Adventures of Parsley*, *The Wombles* and *Paddington*.[155] All these series were

151 'Magic Roundabout' (1968) May *Games and Toys* 41; 'Another French puppet series for BBC TV' (1968) September *British Toys* 18; 'BBC's TV star: Hector's House' (1968) November *Games and Toys* 51; 'Hector's House' (1969) March *British Toys* 19; 'BBC Enterprises presents: Barnaby' (1974) July *Games and Toys* 15; 'The Magic Roundabout: merchandising enquiries' (1974) December *Games and Toys* 3.

152 Purchased Programme Agreement (Television) No 1148 ('Barnaby'), 26 September 1972 to which another agreement on the representation of merchandising rights was attached: contract between Etablissement Prolic and the BBC ('Television Enterprises'), 9 October 1972; WW3/3/1; BBC WAC.

153 Gordon Smith to Assistant Head of Business, Television Enterprises, 23 March 1966; R120/36/1; BBC WAC. 'Television sets the trend' (1967) October *Games and Toys* 3.

154 These operations became increasingly important to help the BBC cut financial losses; see 'Successful year for BBC Enterprises' (1974) May *Games and Toys* 34; 'BBC Enterprises help BBC to cut losses' (1975) May *Games and Toys* 16.

155 'The Herbs' (1968) July *Games and Toys* 27; 'Notes from Harrogate' (1972) December *British Toys* 14; 'News from BBC Enterprises' (1973) October *Games and Toys* 6; 'A great bunch of characters' (1979) October *Games and Toys* 15.

produced by a British animation studio called FilmFair, which offered the public corporation a financial stake in the property. One of the notable features of these projects was the centrality of merchandising and character licensing for all parties involved. The income guarantee functioned as a mechanism to recoup investment while the percentage cut taken by the unit was seen as a tool to generate profit for the public corporation.

7.6 LICENSING AS A YARDSTICK

The Wombles was one of the instances in which the BBC decided to invest in the development of a children's television series. It came after the public corporation revealed that the time devoted to children's television programmes was going to be increased by forty per cent; a decision influenced by the boom period of colour television. The project appealed both to Television Enterprises and the Children's Department for several reasons: firstly, the expertise and experience of the animation studio (FilmFair); secondly, the transmission life projected for the series; and, lastly, the fact that Elisabeth Beresford, the literary creator of *The Wombles*, was the wife of a well-known BBC sports commentator, Max Robertson. Among the features that attracted all parties concerned was the environmentally minded message embedded in the series.[156] The 'social conscience' that characterised *The Wombles* was perceived simultaneously as a valuable educational ingredient and an ideal space for licensing, resonating with the recipe for branding success that many marketing experts would suggest decades later.[157] The contractual situation underpinning the commercial venture was, however, complicated from the outset. Unlike previous projects, this was conceived as a triangular venture. FilmFair and Television Enterprises dealt with Wombles Ltd, a company in which not only Robertson and Beresford, but also two marketing and advertising agents, had shares.[158] While this was not considered to be an insurmountable obstacle at the beginning, as time passed the issue started to complicate co-ordination of the licensing regime.

In May 1972, an agreement between the three parties was reached, demonstrating how the BBC was able to engineer a creative solution, blending the educational needs of children's broadcasting with the economic resources arising from merchandising. According to the commercial manager of Television Enterprises, Roy Williams, the approach was appropriate not only financially but also because, as the licensing agency for the enterprise, 'it ensured that we can exercise control over

[156] 'Wombles: a background'; ABC Publicity Material C612T1 ('The Wombles'); NAA.

[157] See, for instance, Peter Dauvergne and Jane Lister, *Eco-Business: A Big-brand Takeover of Sustainability*, MIT Press, 2013.

[158] In fact, the principal activities of the company were originally centred around marketing and advertising activities such as 'to act as trade consultants and advisers in production, management and exports of products of all kinds'; see 'Wombles Ltd'; company number 995585; Companies House Archives.

the type of products that are produced and identified with the BBC programmes'.[159] This managerial appeal worked well within the boundaries of the BBC, still haunted by the circumspect attitude to protecting its reputation that had shaped its operations for decades.[160] As such, the mediation of Television Enterprises was crucial in enabling the other two companies, Wombles Ltd and FilmFair, to come together.

However, one of the issues that made the arrangement particularly intricate was the different way in which copyright was envisaged by the parties. Although there was a recognition that Beresford had created the characters, the visual treatment of the series and its puppets were going to be designed by FilmFair. Hence, the animation studio saw itself as a developer of the property. As Television Enterprises was licensing agent for both Wombles Ltd and FilmFair, the question of copyright ownership of merchandising rights was left open and subject to negotiation. The parties also went ahead with several practical ways and techniques to accommodate their different views of the property. Firstly, a protocol to distinguish between merchandising and publishing was established, so Beresford could continue dealing with publication rights of *The Wombles*. Secondly, and most importantly, FilmFair and Wombles Ltd decided to share merchandising royalties on an almost equal footing after deducting the commission fee taken by the agency, Television Enterprises.[161] This strategic view prioritised management of copyright over ownership, showing how the most important element for the parties to agree on at this moment was not the copyright title or ownership but their respective share in the profits arising from its exploitation. It also demonstrated that the parties recognised television as a decisive driving force and launching pad for making the property profitable.

Although this is an indication that the dynamic between media, contract and property underpins many intellectual property projects and their assumptions, we would like to continue exploring the concrete entanglement behind this children's television series, implicated in a well-known passing-off case that took place a couple of years later. The financial perspective through which the project took off satisfied all interests involved in the venture: FilmFair, Wombles Ltd and the BBC (in the form of Television Enterprises).

The programme was first aired in Britain in February 1973. Despite or perhaps because of the constraints on commercial advertising affecting the BBC, the advertising skills of the investors and entrepreneurs were channelled into the project itself

[159] Television Enterprises invested £4,500 in the form of advance royalty on the understanding that a sum of £5,000 would be recovered as a first charge against merchandising income after the deduction of a commission of 25 per cent of gross receipts; see Roy Williams to Senior Assistant (Sequences) Purchased Programmes, 25 May 1972; WW8/496/1; BBC WAC.

[160] Catherine Johnson, 'Trading Auntie: exploitation and protection of intellectual property rights during the BBC's monopoly years' (2009) 7(4) *New Review of Film and Television Studies* 441–58.

[161] The split was 49 per cent (FilmFair) and 51 per cent (Wombles Ltd); Record of telephone conversation, 3 July 1972, between Roy Williams (BBC TV Enterprises), Clutterbuck (FilmFair), John Hanson and Terry Flounders (Wombles Ltd); WW8/496/1; BBC WAC.

and the promotional activities surrounding it. As mentioned above, Wombles Ltd had its own marketing and advertising experts.[162] Similarly, FilmFair was composed of a mixture of creative and advertising people.[163] This meant that the three parties all played different parts in promoting *The Wombles*. Their activities, in turn, determined a particularly elastic exploitation of the television series, covering not only the programmes and the characters but also the development of a scheme called 'Rent a Womble', the recording of a very successful hit pop song, and even the possibility of producing special television episodes for specific markets. These marketing operations made the venture an example of media cross-fertilisation.[164]

While Television Enterprises was incidentally concerned with the 'over-exposure' of the series, the merchandising campaign was nevertheless particularly profitable and connected the programme and its characters, such as 'Great Uncle Bulgaria', to many children's products.[165]

Much of the foregoing discussion bears directly upon the idea that the licensing of *The Wombles* was not a straightforward process. In fact, Television Enterprises became increasingly worried about the lack of liaison between the parties as they pursued what they understood as being within the scope of their legitimate interest and the chaos this brought to the customary way of establishing a licensing regime. The unorthodox setting in which the project was structured and the conflicting ways in which it was taken forward meant that the activities impinged upon the orderly scheme traditionally followed by merchandising agencies, such as Television Enterprises, whereby licences were carefully issued not to conflict with other licences already granted. This overlap of activities caused some tensions between the parties, which constantly tried to redefine their respective roles in the project, and hence their corresponding stakes in the property. On the one hand, Wombles Ltd reacted to complaints by Television Enterprises by emphasising that the credit line for merchandising on commodities ought to 'read licensed *through* BBC Television Enterprises and not *by* BBC Television Enterprises'.[166] Essentially, this highlighted that Television Enterprises did not hold any merchandising rights for *The Wombles* but was only given the right to act as the licensing agent. On the other

[162] 'Marketing a name' (1975) January *Toys International* 54.

[163] 'Cross-fertilization' *Television Mail*, 9 February 1973, 2.

[164] As Terry Flounders, the marketing consultant for Wombles Ltd, explained when selling the programme in Australia, 'the combined efforts of television, films and music (giving us exposure); books (giving us authority); media co-operation (giving us popularity); and merchandising (giving us money) must all be present to achieve the cult proportions we have enjoyed in at least two markets, the UK and, to date, New Zealand'; see Report from Terry Flounders to Elisabeth Beresford, 1976 (Australia); Box 4 (Memos); Wombles Archive; NCCB.

[165] Bill Hagerty, Clifford Davis and Kenneth Hughes, 'Womblemania' *Daily Mirror*, 16 December 1974, 14–5; 'Wombles colouring sets' (1973) October *Games and Toys* 24; 'The Wombles on note boards and badges' (1974) July *Games and Toys* 14; 'Success of Letraset Wombles' (1975) August *Games and Toys* 19.

[166] Original emphasis. John Hanson, Wombles Ltd, to Roy Williams, 18 February 1976; WW8/495/1; BBC WAC.

hand, FilmFair reopened an issue that had previously seemed to have been settled for good: the distinction between merchandising and publishing. As we have observed in Chapter 5, this distinction is inherently unstable because many children's commodities are situated at the boundary between merchandising and publishing rights. FilmFair tried to return to the distinction between 'very clearly text-predominating' and 'picture-predominating' books to suggest that it should be receiving more royalties for boundary-crossing products such as gift books. FilmFair also asked Television Enterprises to act as an arbiter in these cases; a suggestion that the BBC bluntly rejected.[167]

The running tension surrounding the project not only affected its exploitation but also its legal protection. Wombles Ltd included warning notices against pirates in trade journals with the acquiescence of Television Enterprises but made no mention whatsoever of FilmFair.[168] Similarly, it planted a newspaper piece about 'illegitimate Wombles' aimed at alerting traders that Wombles Ltd had appointed a solicitor to deal with unlawful practices.[169] The reason for this publicity was the perception that piracy was damaging the value of licences.[170] But again, the reference to the animation studio was missing. Asking for a newspaper rectification, FilmFair noted that 'the fact that your article did not mention my company's name but placed the ownership of *The Wombles* entirely in the hands of Wombles Ltd could have negative repercussions amongst associates and potential clients who might consider that we have been exaggerating our proprietary interest in *The Wombles* in order to boost the importance of our company'.[171] Putting the record straight, the newspaper published another piece explaining that 'the big money in children TV programmes is in character merchandising. Every sale of a Womble product made legally under licence is money in the till for BBC Enterprises, Wombles Ltd. (Miss Beresford's company) and FilmFair'.[172]

One of the effects of the television programme was that Wombles Ltd hired a patent and trademark firm to manage the portfolio of marks tied to the series and its characters. This involved watching and securing design and trademark registrations and recording registered users in different classes and across the jurisdictions in which the television programme was sold.[173] More interestingly, Wombles Ltd also wrote to magazines and newspapers requesting that they should not use terms such as 'wombling' or 'wombleisation', in an attempt to avoid the fall into genericism of

[167] Roy Williams to Graham Clutterbuck, 30 August 1983; WW8/496/1; BBC WAC.

[168] 'Warning: it is illegal to use the Womble mark without a licence to do so' (1974) November *Games and Toys* 5; 'Infringement of copyright' (1974) November *Games and Toys* 18.

[169] Lorana Sullivan, 'Will the real Womble please stand up' *Sunday Times*, 22 June 1975, 49.

[170] 'Womble Pirates (Newspaper Clipping)', June 1975; WW8/495/1; BBC WAC.

[171] Clutterbuck (FilmFair) to Richard Wilsher (*Sunday Times*), 23 June 1975; WW8/495/1; BBC WAC.

[172] Lorena Sullivan, 'The six-inch tall superstars' *Sunday Times*, 17 August 1975, 37.

[173] Abel & Imray, Patent Agents to A.P. Williams, Denton Hall & Burgin, 4 March 1975; Box 5 (Merchandising); Wombles Archive; NCCB.

FIGURE 7.5 Wombles warning advert, 1974
Games & Toys, November 1974, 4. © British Library Board. Courtesy of the British Toy and Hobby Association

the trademark.[174] It also appointed a solicitor to monitor and take action against what it perceived as unlawful activities. After succeeding in stopping a magazine publishing articles about a pop group called *The Woffles*,[175] a company selling unauthorised posters, and a well-known pirate selling T-shirts printed with the characters images,[176] it failed in its attempt to secure an injunction against a company using the name Wombles Skips Ltd, which in turn became an important case in the law of passing-off.[177]

[174] Wombles Ltd, Minutes, 11 June 1975; Box 6 (Minutes of Meetings); Wombles Archive; NCCB.
[175] Wombles Ltd, Minutes, 29 January 1975; Box 6 (Minutes of Meetings); Wombles Archive; NCCB.
[176] Wombles Ltd, Minutes, 20 May 1974; Box 6 (Minutes of Meetings); Wombles Archive; NCCB.
[177] *Wombles Ltd v Wombles Skips Ltd* [1975] FSR 488.

In hindsight, it is possible to see why it failed. However, taking into account the expansive nature of the promotional and licensing scheme that surrounded *The Wombles*, it was not so clear at the time how the defendant, a skip company, could so easily avoid liability. Wombles Ltd tried to get an injunction against the defendant because of the poignant irony triggered by its company name. While the television series was about characters that collected rubbish left on the green, the defendant was a company selling skip bins used for the collection of builders' rubbish. Furthermore, the anti-litter connotations and the environmental concern of the series were specifically used by Wombles Ltd and Television Enterprises as vectors to enhance the merchandising and educational potential of the series, serving as key selling points to attract prospective licensees.[178] For instance, Schweppes Ltd was approached by the merchandising assistant of BBC Television Enterprises because 'they are now printing a message on the back of their non-returnable bottle labels'.[179] Likewise, Wombles Ltd was negotiating a licence with Spearhead, a company manufacturing tin trays and waste paper bins.[180] Although Wombles Ltd had not registered *The Wombles* trademark for skips, the licensing operations were getting close to this kind of activity. Arguably, the aspect that seemed to confirm that its case was going to succeed on the passing-off action was that the Registrar of Companies wrote back to Wombles Skips Ltd apologising for registering the company, arguing that he had never heard of *The Wombles* and offering to refund the skip firm's registration fee and to register it again under a new name.[181]

In July 1975, the hearing on the application for an interlocutory injunction took place. Walton J refused to grant it, ordering instead for a speedy trial. He did so by referring to the 'common field of activity' doctrine mentioned earlier. In other words, that to establish passing-off it was necessary for there to be a common field of activity, and here there was no such common field between the parties. Interestingly, he summarised the activities of Wombles Ltd as follows: 'The plaintiff company exploits the rights for money. It does not develop the rights: it takes the rights and exploits them for money'.[182] While it is arguable that the exploitation of rights was more creative than the description given by the judge, it is true that, if the plaintiff had a case, this could be demonstrated at the speedy trial. But having failed to secure the injunction, the licensing system established by Wombles Ltd, Television Enterprises and FilmFair was provisionally impacted. Fun Products

[178] 'The Wombles: character merchandising with a social conscience' (1973) November *Games and Toys* 33.

[179] A. D. J. Hanson, BBC Television Enterprises, to Terry Flounders, Wombles Ltd, 26 July 1972; WW8/496/1; BBC WAC.

[180] Wombles Ltd, Minutes, 11 June 1975; Box 6; Wombles Archive; NCCB.

[181] Ibid.

[182] *Wombles v Wombles Skips*, above n 177; see also 'The Wombles lose battle over rubbish' *Daily Mail*, 19 July 1975, 10; 'Wombles sorted out' *Birmingham Daily Post*, 19 July 1975, 13.

Ltd, which was selling unauthorised stickers of the characters, even called Wombles Ltd's solicitor enquiring whether the judgment meant that the company was 'now able to produce their stickers without licence'.[183] The response was clearly negative, requesting Fun Products to sign an undertaking that it would not infringe again and would get a licence. Perhaps because of the uncertainty and frustration generated by the court failure, Wombles Ltd continued suing other pirates but was now strategically joined by other licensees.[184]

During preparations for the trial against Wombles Skips Ltd, a similar legal case was heard by the same judge.[185] This case was important because it revealed in more detail how Walton J conceived the business of character merchandising. It concerned another character from a television series, *Kojak*, which had first been broadcast by the BBC during the summer of 1974. The coincidence of the cases indicates the extent to which licensing activities were becoming a ubiquitous aspect of legal practice.[186] Although the law of trademarks had already facilitated these activities, thus allowing merchandising agencies to oppose trademark registrations, the use of names from titles and characters was still legally possible for those who seized the opportunity.[187] Merchandising activities were discussed in the *Kojak* case because the defendant was the licensee. Although the defendant explained what character merchandising was and how it was shaping the legitimacy of its business, Walton J was unimpressed, and the defendant lost the case. However, what united *The Wombles* and *Kojak* cases was the emphasis the judge put on evidence.[188] This focus is particularly interesting because the final decision over the conflicts depended on the demonstration of public awareness of licensing activities, as turned out to be the case in many legal disputes to come.[189] As *The Wombles* and *Kojak* cases were interlocutory proceedings, our view is that they should not be interpreted

[183] Wombles Ltd, Minutes, 4 August 1975; Box 6 (Minutes of Meetings); Wombles Archive; NCCB.

[184] *Wombles Ltd and Manchester Leathercraft Co Ltd v Boris Supplies and Co*, 1 March 1976 (statement of claim), in Hugh Laddie, *Opinions* 1975–1976; QMIPA; see also the reference to 'Pirates' in 'Historical notes for guidance on the development of the Wombles in New Zealand, July 25, 1975'; ABC Publicity Material 'The Wombles', NAA: C612T1.

[185] *Taverner Rutledge Ltd v Trexapalm Ltd* [1975] FSR 479.

[186] As the commercial practice became pervasive, legal advice about it grew exponentially; see Hugh Laddie, 'Whitbread London Limited: Opinion, 29 August 1974'; 'Cartoon Bags Limited: Opinion, 18 August 1975'; 'Cinderella Trade Mark: Opinion, 16 November 1975'; 'Universal City Studios et al, v Barry Merchant Ltd: Indorsement on Writ, 12 March 1976' in Hugh Laddie, above n 184; and '"Schweppes" Drink: Copyright Opinion, 28 April 1978'; 'Topps Chewing Gum Inc: Footballer' 8 September 1975'; 'Kojak Trade Mark, 6 July 1976'; Robin Jacob, *Opinions*, 1976–1978; QMIPA.

[187] See also *Re Holly Hobbie Trade Mark* [1984] 19 RPC 329.

[188] *Taverner Rutledge v Trexapalm*, above n 185. Trexapalm was a UK company with a licence from Universal City to make and sell 'Kojak lollies'. The claimant was another UK company, Tavener Rutledge, that had been selling 'Kojakpops' without any licence.

[189] See, for instance, *Children's Television Workshop Inc v Woolworths (NSW)* [1981] RPC 187, 193; *Mirage Studios v Counter Feat Clothing* [1991] FSR 145.

as denying the legality of merchandising practices, or even as firmly reinforcing the doctrine of the common field of activity as a matter of principle, but rather the opposite. Since the question was left open to evidence, the emphasis shifted to a matter of legal strategy, extending into the question of the proof around the other two ingredients of the action for passing-off, namely misrepresentation and damage to goodwill. Not surprisingly, the main type of advice given by barristers in the period before the trial was to remain especially careful with trap orders and hence to be watchful about use of the phone, or any other media contact with the public. Moreover, they often requested the disclosure of Wombles Ltd licensing contracts, as the requirement of goodwill across fields was to be evidenced through those documents.[190] Although these may appear to be legal technicalities, and so they are, it is important to highlight their social implications. Firstly, the reference to the public awareness of the connection between the fields paved the way for consideration of the behaviour of the average type of consumer to which these commodities were addressed, children, to emerge as an object of inquiry and debate. Secondly, the disclosure of Wombles Ltd licensing contracts suggested that licensing practices could serve as a yardstick to measure the plaintiff's proprietary interest. To put it another way, the dynamic between contractual practices and merchandising activities could in fact help to constitute, develop and potentially limit the intangible property and/or goodwill.

The absence of other parties profiting from *The Wombles*' licensing system in the case is rather remarkable. FilmFair did not join the proceedings because no images of the characters were used by the defendant. Neither did BBC Television Enterprises participate, albeit the counsel for Wombles Skips Ltd thought they would do so.[191] The reason for this lack of support could be the difficulties around the management of merchandising rights mentioned above. However, the most probable reason is the BBC's wary attitude towards litigating these matters.[192] As the case was settled, we will never know. Nevertheless, the fact that BBC Television Enterprises was now embracing commercial activities aimed at children distinguishes the case from the Uncle Mac decision. This point is often overlooked by legal scholars and commentators alike. We consider it significant. What marks the difference between the two disputes is the historical relationship between intellectual property and children's consumption that had flourished around merchandising. By the late 1960s, and after investing in several children's television series, the BBC not only considered it possible but also saw it as desirable to include commercial aspects. Denis Scuse, the director of Television Enterprises, observed that 'it is

[190] '*Wombles Ltd v Wombles Skips Ltd*: request for further and better particulars of the statement of claim, 8 September 1975' in Jacob, above n 186.

[191] '*Wombles Ltd v Wombles Skips Ltd*: note, 8 September 1975' in Jacob, above n 186.

[192] However, two decades later it was possible to observe how BBC Enterprises had shifted its circumspect attitude to litigate over merchandising rights; see *BBC Worldwide Ltd v Pally Screen Printing Ltd* [1998] FSR 665 (1998).

impracticable to separate the commercial and public service aspects of broadcasting'. He added that 'any public service of whatever kind must be run in a business-like and therefore commercial way'.[193]

Previous concerns surrounding the exploitation of intellectual property in relation to children's consumption had begun to dissipate. In June 1979, two years after *The Wombles* decision, a conference entitled 'Character Merchandising and the Law' was organised in London to discuss the legal implications of these commercial practices.[194] The event brought together barristers, solicitors, merchandising agents and marketing executives and was sponsored by the publisher of a magazine that would become the leading intellectual property journal in the late twentieth century: the *European Intellectual Property Review*. Interestingly, the publication began with several influential articles about the topic and case notes about merchandising disputes, which often turned on to how to categorise the intellectual property right at stake, ways to prove it and the need for law reform.[195] No mention can be found there of tensions between public service and profit, or the marketisation of children's culture through intellectual property. Perhaps this was because not even the BBC saw them as contradictory any longer.

[193] Denis Scuse, 'The commercial aspects of public service broadcasting' (1969) July *EBU Review* 21–4.

[194] 'Character Merchandising and the Law' Cumberland Hotel, London, 19 June 1979, European Study Conferences Ltd.

[195] Christopher Morcom, 'Character merchandising – a right, or mere opportunity' (1978) October *European Intellectual Property Review* 7–10; Louis Stevenson, 'Protection of character merchandise rights under UK Copyright Act 1956' (1979) March *European Intellectual Property Review* 66–70; Karen J. Schulman, 'Case comment: Starsky and Hutch: copyright in film frames?' (1979) May *European Intellectual Property Review* 143–6; Geoffrey Hobbs, 'Passing off and the licensing of merchandising rights: part 1' (1980) February *European Intellectual Property Review* 47–52; Geoffrey Hobbs, 'Passing off and the licensing of merchandising rights: part 2' (1980) March *European Intellectual Property Review* 79–82.

Conclusion: Unsuitable for Children

The Oxford-educated medical doctor, Jonathan Miller, was a well-known author and producer associated with the oddball satire *Beyond the Fringe*, and it was this theatre revue that helped establish the careers of Alan Bennett, Peter Cook and Dudley Moore. Thus, not only was Miller a member of a community of artists, actors, writers and comedians, but he was also a key figure within an arts intelligentsia.

In 1965, Miller took over as editor and presenter of BBC flagship arts magazine programme, *Monitor*, supported by Huw Wheldon. Wheldon, through an association with the head of the Children's Department, Freda Lingstrom, had moved from being a BBC publicity officer in 1952 to fronting the BBC children's skill and talent demonstration programme *All Your Own* (1952–1961). Wheldon was also a producer in the 'Talks' department. Through this managerial role Wheldon became responsible for *Monitor* when it was launched in 1958. Wheldon's managerial oversight further increased with his appointment as Controller of Programmes, Television, in 1965, giving him ultimate responsibility over BBC productions and programming.[1]

However, Miller's association with *Monitor* was to be short-lived. Within a year the programme was cancelled. Nevertheless, there were sufficient funds left to support an original production. Wheldon accepted a proposal by Miller that he direct and produce a film adaptation of Lewis Carroll's *Alice in Wonderland* for the centenary year of the book's first publication. It could be screened as the BBC Christmas Special for 1966. Miller recruited his friends, including internationally celebrated performers such as Peter Cook, Alan Bennett, Peter Sellers, Leo McKern, Michael Redgrave and John Gielgud (filling in after Frankie Howerd dropped out) to play key roles. 'Alice' was to be played by someone without stage

[1] British Film Institute, Screen Online, 'Wheldon, Sir Huw' (1916–1986) www.screenonline.org.uk/people/id/473425.

experience, 'not pretty but curiously plain, sallow and priggish, more Rosetti than Tenniel like'.[2] He cast an unknown thirteen-year-old girl, Ann-Marie Mallik.

There had, of course, been many versions of *Alice* over the years. This included Disney's *Alice Comedies* (1926)[3] and, three years after copyright expired, a 1951 feature-film-length Disney musical colour film animation. This film had also been broadcast in black and white on the *Disneyland* television programme. The broadcast included host Uncle Walt's introduction to the story: an avuncular, suited Disney stands decorating a Christmas tree, acknowledging the importance of the 'holiday season'. He then explains to viewers the English tradition of a children's Christmas pantomime featuring a children's classic, going on to briefly introduce Dodgson. Disney holds up the cover of a Disney cartoon picture book edition of *Alice in Wonderland*, then we glimpse a scene, and it fades into the animation.

Miller sought to offer a more British, historically inspired Victorian reading of childhood in honour of Dodgson's achievement. His aim was to be entertaining. The film was to be visually rich and sumptuous, dreamy but not sexualised. With a nod to the Beatles, Indian sitar master Ravi Shankar provided much of the soundtrack. Miller told an interviewer that Dodgson was a man interested in logic who used a fairy story to play around with language games for his own entertainment. But subconsciously

> he [Dodgson] was describing what it was like for himself perhaps to grow up – the anxieties he felt about growing up and particularly his anxieties which all Victorians felt -er- in respect of the innocence of childhood um- not just simply to mention ... to the social structure, but some feelings which the Victorians seemed to have ... – about the feeling that the [sic] childhood was some special place ... Er – where curious values of perception and insight were preserved, which then decayed as one grew up.[4]

Miller's ambition for *Alice* reconnects with Chapter 1 where we have outlined other dealings beyond text, through which Dodgson expressed and managed anxieties surrounding the child's place in the world. Dodgson created merchandise and experiences for children mindful of the priority of preserving the child's innocence and imagination. He used his copyright to express a patriarchal concern for the child, only authorising the development of productions, including books, plays and high-quality wares, that he considered suitable. Dodgson also maintained a personal attachment to and investment in *Alice* productions. Accordingly, parents and friends of the individual child could trust that this content was suitable for children. Miller did not engage in any similar process of negotiating the line between innocence and exploitation. The story of *Alice in Wonderland* was now, as Disney identified, a

2 'Miller in Wonderland', press clipping, Alice in Wonderland (Talks); T51/9/1; BBC WAC.

3 See Chapter 4 at 119.

4 Transcript of interview: Jonathan Miller, 11 November 1966, General Division Sound, Alice in Wonderland, File 3: T51/9/3; BBC WAC.

children's classic, and Miller's fidelity to Dodgson's story was apparent. As the book was in the public domain, no negotiation over adaptation rights was required. However, the public broadcaster still had an obligation to ensure any particular content broadcast was appropriate for the BBC audience. Though it contained no overt violence or sexual scenes, Wheldon shifted the broadcast to three days after Christmas and delayed the time slot beyond family friendly hours to nine pm. The broadcast, or at least the implications of the BBC changing the timeslot, fed a moral panic. Miller's *Alice* was critically acclaimed, but the film was judged a public relations disaster for the BBC.

Unpacking why this happened, why it was thought by many within the BBC, and by members of the press, public and politicians, that the film was unsuitable for children provides a useful vehicle for examining the thematic connections between the first and later chapters. A historically informed, languid vision of childhood exploring ideas of childish logic, trust, vulnerability and anxieties about what is lost in adulthood did not need to be defended by the BBC as creatively justified. But, by 1967, the BBC's judgement of creative choices was overlaid with expectations about the nature of the children's market. The kinds of commercial productions that had been promoted by intellectual property licensing agreements since the 1930s had become so ubiquitous that these relations now completely dominated comprehension of the children's market – even for a public broadcaster. Miller's disinterest in mainstream commercial fare and, perhaps, the impossibility of bridging a Victorian simulacrum with contemporary expectations of appropriate content for children rendered the film incomprehensible to many. The BBC was hounded for spending public money on a film that could frighten, baffle or bore innocent viewers and their parents. In analysing what happened to Miller's *Alice*, in this final chapter we highlight, once more, how expectations of intellectual property had changed across the twentieth century so that a multinational corporate approach to cultural commodification became the norm. The gulf between Dodgson's original *Alice* and expectations flowing from Disneyfied versions was so insurmountable that Miller's production was now considered avant-garde.

NEGOTIATING *ALICE* AT THE BBC

Reflecting divisions of labour within the organisation, there are two kinds of files related to the staging of the *Alice* production at the BBC. Combined, these reveal the nature and extent of negotiations. The BBC Television Enterprises file contains mundane communications about merchandising opportunities anticipated. Early correspondence was very enthusiastic, identifying three commercial opportunities: sound recordings, international film sales and *Alice* products.[5] Two LPs packaged in time for Christmas were envisaged. This led to negotiations with recording

[5] Alice in Wonderland (Merchandising) 1966–67; R120/8/1; BBC WAC.

companies, who were only interested in a sound recording of Ravi Shankar and company's musical arrangements. A contract was presented by RCA Victor, but it fell apart due to uncertainties about who could clear copyright in the original compositions by Shankar and other musicians. Furthermore, the BBC could not license rights where it involved performances by musicians who had participated in the original recordings, possibly also including BBC staff, because the contracts had only covered the right to a UK broadcast.[6] With respect to international film sales, pre-sale interest was withdrawn once it became known that the film was in black and white. The only solution identified here was to get Miller to agree to later reshoot the film using the same cast, with Lord Snowdon serving as colour consultant. A proposed new Hanna-Barbera *Alice* cartoon was not thought a relevant factor impacting commercial prospects. With regard to character merchandising, 'the scope here is endless .... By our own publicity drive (and bearing in mind that is yet to come) we have already done half the work. It only needs someone to maximise the situation'.[7] However, no one stepped forward, as rumours of production issues circulated within the BBC.

As *Alice* was a commissioned programme, the 'Talks' file contains internal correspondence about production logistics including matters dealt with by executive producer, Stephen Hearst; Huw Wheldon's comments in his capacity as controller of television; post-screening complaints requiring a formal response; records of switchboard feedback; audience surveys; and press clippings.[8] It is clear that original expectations were of an international hit due to the star power participating in the film. Although performers' fees on offer were modest because of BBC budget limitations, this was manageable thanks to Miller's ability to entice friends to participate and because the artistic credentials and names attached served as a drawcard for others. Miller also shared an agent with some of the stars, such as Alan Bennett, and he had had prior dealings with other agents from *Beyond the Fringe* days. The decision to film in black and white was supported because of the BBC budget and Miller's vision. An assurance was made that, while live hedgehogs had been called for, these would not be harmed in the croquet scenes and 'neither humanity nor the animal kingdom will have anything to complain of'.[9]

Some audience complaints were anticipated from the start. On viewing the first rough cut, Wheldon remarked:

> My first and overwhelming conclusion is that I am pleased that we put such enormous capital expenditure into this programme, pleased that we took what

6 See, for example, Catherine Dyson to J. M. L. Stone Esq., 14 November 1966; R120/8/1; BBC WAC.

7 'Alice in Wonderland', Undated Correspondence, File 3: T51/9/3; BBC WAC.

8 Alice in Wonderland (Talks); T51/9/1; T51/9/2; T51/9/3; BBC WAC.

9 Stephen Hearst, 'Hedgehogs in "Alice in Wonderland"', 24 June 1966; T51/9/3; BBC WAC.

> was from all sorts of points of view, a considerable risk. I am pleased because it is a deeply interesting reading of the story . . . .
>
> Equally I am as anxious as I am pleased. Anxious, because while the gold is there it is also largely obscured at the moment. The simplest way of putting it is not that the film is too long and needs trimming; but that it is miles too long and need re-editing.[10]

Following two pages of suggestions, he concludes:

> I am full of admiration. I do seriously and deeply congratulate you on what is a real piece of work. Did I not think this I would not be so bold or so brutish as to suggest, as I do very strongly suggest, that your most difficult and at the same time your most decisive work is still to come.[11]

Wheldon suggested it was crucial that the 110-minute film be cut to 80 or 75 minutes. Miller actually cut the film to 73 minutes, but Wheldon still decided to change the screening hour. This decision was endorsed by the Board of Management, which viewed the film as 'a near masterpiece' but one that many viewers might regard as 'confusing'.[12]

AN 'X-RATED' ALICE IN WONDERLAND

Wheldon's decision to shift the time slot led to front page headlines in the tabloids appearing at the end of November, well before the film was to be screened: 'The BBC slaps an X on Alice in Wonderland' (*Daily Mail*); 'Curious and curiouser: TV's Alice is not for the young' (*Daily Express*); 'For adults only: the BBC's view of Alice in Wonderland' (*The Sun*); 'TV Alice in Wonderland too horrific for children' (*Daily Mirror*).[13] The film was characterised as a psychological drama out of Miller's own imagination that introduced sexual undertones, with unusual directorial decisions such as presenting the natural appearance of actors whose faces he thought represented the relevant animals, rather than using costume masks. He also permitted actors to improvise. It was further criticised for its claimed £25,000 cost to tax payers.

Wheldon wrote to the editor of the *Daily Mail* rebuking the claim that it was X-rated or horrific. He thought it would have gone 'over the heads of the little ones' so decided to move it past children's hour (five or six pm) or whole-family viewing time (seven or eight pm).[14] He told the *Daily Express*: 'I was worried that parents might

[10] From Controller of Programmes, Television, to Jonathan Miller, 15 September 1966; T51/9/3; BBC WAC.

[11] Ibid.

[12] General Manager, Television Enterprises, File Note, Controller Meeting, March 1967; T51/9/3; BBC WAC.

[13] Undated clippings; T51/9/1; BBC WAC.

[14] Huw Wheldon, Controller of Television, 'Personal Letter to the Editor', *Daily Mail*, 1 December 1966.

think it is a children's production just because it is *Alice*'.[15] A press release was also issued to this effect, which also claimed that, '9 o'clock was our first and only decision about the timing of the programming'.[16] Wheldon's actions, and subsequent explanation that 'Alice did not go wrong',[17] contributed to the view that the film was designed for an adult audience, further feeding into the mainstream commercial construct of children's fare. Miller's defence did not disrupt this perspective:

> I regard *Alice* as a Victorian fantasy about the pains and perils of growing old. There is an enduring melancholy which outlasts the fun .... The animal heads, the fur, the whiskers conceal real Victorian types. The more one goes into the story, the more one sees it as an account of what a young girl thinks of the adult world.[18]

A press preview screening was organised on 15 December 1966. The reviews overwhelmingly commented that, while not appropriate for very small children (who would be bored), there was nothing in it that made it unsuitable for other children. *The Times* noted: 'I could see no reason why the children should not be kept up late to see it. It is still a children's story, faithful almost entirely to the Carroll text'.[19] When the film finally screened on Wednesday 28 December, it was viewed by 12.5 million – 26 per cent of the viewing audience.[20] The switchboard logged 129 complaints, many of which mirrored the tabloid press coverage, with 54 calls in appreciation.[21] The film was decried in the British Parliament by Lord Willis as 'self-indulgent'. He identified the cause of the problem as the adaptation having been made without the involvement of those responsible for BBC children's programmes.[22]

Miller was disappointed by his treatment by BBC Publicity and feared his film would only be seen once. However, it was felt that the controversy could draw in a new audience, and the second screening, described as a 'film *re-creation* by Jonathan Miller', was scheduled. Advance publicity provided by Humphrey Burton, head of Music and Arts, noted:

15 Philips Phillips, 'For adults only: The BBC's view of Alice in Wonderland' *The Sun*; T51/9/1; BBC WAC.

16 'The placing of Alice in Wonderland', a note from Huw Wheldon, Controller of Programmes. BBC-TV; T51/9/1; BBC WAC.

17 Peter Knight, 'Alice did not go wrong, says BBC', *Daily Telegraph*; T51/9/1; BBC WAC.

18 Phillips, above n 15.

19 Newspaper Summary, 16 December 1966; BBC WAC.

20 'Alice in Wonderland', 16 February 1967; T51/9/1; BBC WAC. Rohan McWilliam, 'Jonathan Miller's "Alice in Wonderland"' (2011) 31(2) *Historical Journal of Film, Radio and Television* 229, 241.

21 BBC Office Log, 28 December 1966; T51/9/2; BBC WAC.

22 'Children's television programming', HL Deb 3 February 1967, vol. 279, cols. 1127–40, per Lord Willis.

> The BBC film of *Alice* attracted more coverage in the national Press before it was even completed than any other feature of its kind. When it was transmitted last December, it became the main television talking topic of the week. Whatever the controversies, praise was high:
> 'brilliant, in a class by itself'
> OBSERVER
> 'What it isn't: It isn't sweetly pretty or Disney or charming. It's fascinating and fearful, beautiful and mad'.
> THE SUN[23]

It was rescreened on Sunday, 2 April 1967, at 4.35–5.50 pm. A later time slot was no longer felt necessary. It attracted 5 million viewers – 9 per cent of the viewing population.[24] An audience analysis noted that publicity and word-of-mouth had affected views of it, with first-time viewers reacting more unfavourably than repeat viewers. Many first-time viewers were assumed to have watched it because of the adverse publicity. Some repeat viewers reported that, having recovered from the shock, they could better appreciate the originality of Miller's film. Surveys of those who watched with children reported that, while it did not frighten them, they showed no enjoyment.[25] The *Daily Mail* and *Yorkshire Evening Post* organised child reviewers. These responses were positive, though one expressed disappointment it was not frightening, 'nowt compared with Batman'.[26]

So how did we get to here?

NEGOTIATING INTELLECTUAL PROPERTY

Intellectual property constructs – like authorship, the copyright work, design right, patent or trademark – operate within a self-referential world of rights-owners and abstract intangible properties. These legal constructs are ciphers for much more complicated social and commercial relationships. The legal focus on the origins of rights masks the layers of cultural and business negotiations that effect investments surrounding the creation, production and distribution of cultural commodities. The assignment of rights and the issuing of licences to various corporations are held together and remain connected by marketing that continues to attribute an association with a particular originator. But the creator's perspective of these transactions is rarely studied, and the cultural and business dynamics of the trade are poorly theorised in intellectual property scholarship.

This book has argued that the twentieth century not only produced an international infrastructure for exploitation of intellectual property rights but that a

[23] Executive Producer, Music and Arts, to Mrs Cox, 'Alice in Wonderland repeat'; T51/9/3; BBC WAC.

[24] 'An Audience Research Report, "Alice in Wonderland"', 2 April 1967; T51/9/1; BBC WAC.

[25] Ibid.

[26] McWilliam, above n 20, 241.

number of exploitation practices changed the significance and perceived content of these rights, leading to a narrowing of the range of questions thought relevant to ask about the law's role in education in cultural consumption. The very idea of intellectual property expertise that emerged in the twentieth century was tied to servicing commercial exchanges between multinational corporations and subsidiary enterprises, built upon original creative acts and with little consideration of the concerns of audiences and consumers who engage with these productions about commercial intrusions into childhood.

In Chapters 1 and 2 we saw how Dodgson and Beatrix Potter respectively approached their responsibilities as authors and creators of commercial interest in children. Though Potter was far more actively interested in understanding her financial opportunities than Dodgson, she considered that her status as author was connected to larger cultural questions about the role of aesthetics and manufacturing in British society. The family of wares bearing her imprimatur did not necessarily all flow from her personal negotiations in trade, but her lack of control over mass production and distribution of wares connected to her creativity frustrated and angered her. She understood that the way intellectual property and trade law intersected limited her capacity to express herself as a commercially successful artist and writer, but that it was trade policy, not intellectual property rights, that mostly dictated her market opportunities.

The development of Meccano, explored in Chapter 3, also linked intellectual property rights to an understanding of international market dynamics. However, here there was a modern social project embedded in the toy: the making of the 'Meccano Boy'. Patents, copyrights and trademarks were all deployed by Meccano Ltd, but these were not the only drivers of commercial activity. Children themselves helped the company to construct a market for the toy by internationalising business opportunities around the forms of play embodied by Meccano. Appreciating and constituting the market in this manner was a remarkable strategy that anticipated other corporate attempts to link intellectual property and consumption in the twentieth century. Moreover, the educational and professional connotations of the enterprise helped defray concern over the commercial dimensions attached to participation in Meccano's experience of play, display and fraternal enjoyment. Understanding the social and commercial underpinnings of the making of the Meccano Boy helps explain both the rise and demise of this company, as Meccano Ltd struggled to compete with the tighter organisation of children's markets constituted by film and television.

In considering the unique features of film and television markets, Chapter 2 contrasts the unbridled enthusiasm for *Felix the Cat* and its chaotic commercial exploitation to the steady, well-co-ordinated activities that developed to promote *Mickey Mouse* and friends. In both cases, it was the broader exploitation possibilities that supported the original film productions, and the possibility of licensing, that led to new corporate connections, distinctive company structures and assertions of exclusive international intellectual property rights. The benefits accrued to Disney Enterprises were due to its more tightly calibrated approach to intellectual property licensing, with merchandising practices centred upon agency arrangements, managed separately to rights in the film.

Chapter 5 adds further nuance to the account of Disney's legal and business practices and their ongoing ramifications, showing how the Disney approach to managing intellectual property impacted on the ostensibly non-commercial activities traditionally identified with charitable gifts. Based on the bequest of J. M. Barrie, the Great Ormond Street Hospital's initial exploitation of *Peter Pan*'s copyright aimed to provide financial resources for needy children within paternalistic notions of charity and love. This impulse was gradually eclipsed by recognition of the commercial opportunities that Peter Pan presented, and which were proposed to the hospital by others keen to benefit from a profitable association with Peter Pan. Tensions regarding the administration of the bequest were heightened with Disney's licensing of the characters and its ongoing overshadowing of the traditional exploitation of *Peter Pan* as a play or a book. The need for legal clarification of licences repeatedly led to contractual misunderstandings in the relationship between the corporation and the hospital and even a reassessment of the best way to deal with the copyright gift. That is, a transactional regard for commercial self-interest gradually displaced considerations of propriety, trust and care for children. The Barrie gift came to be overlain with a concern for efficiency, exemplified in the view that the trustee's responsibility was to maximise wealth creation through improved licensing practices. A return to the more traditional reactive administration of intellectual property became untenable, it now seeming financially irresponsible and careless not to actively exploit the copyright gift. However, without appropriate corporate resources or dedicated management expertise, the hospital's efforts to compete with the Disneyfied adaptations of *Peter Pan*, and to create new interest in 'the boy who wouldn't grow up', struggled to come to life.

How the idea of distinctive intellectual property management expertise further developed and advanced after the arrival of television, with and without the support of legal institutions, is taken up in Chapter 6. Corporate management of the social life attached to cultural commodities was first introduced in earlier chapter discussions of Meccano, Felix and Mickey Mouse. We note a significant shift in these dynamics, occurring from the 1950s onwards, where specialist agency services were deployed, unrelated to the commercial ambitions attached to particular media originators or production houses. A new class of independent licensing agencies, exemplified by Walter Tuckwell & Associates, began to create intangible property through licensing activities, focusing especially upon the exposure generated by children's television programming. They promoted merchandising suggestions for toys, accessories and other products linked to anything capable of evoking a connection to these television programmes. Such suggestions included mascots, cartoon characters, stars and costumes suggestive of archetypes like 'Robin Hood' and cowboys. Conversely, previously under-exploited characters like 'Noddy', and new ones featured in programmes such as *Dr Who* and *Mr Men*, were also promoted as opportunities for the character trade. In tracing the rise of agency activities, this chapter reminds readers once more of the law's ambivalence toward entrepreneurialism and the importance of mediators to enable and facilitate legal changes. Legal institutions remained mildly unsupportive of the broad mobilisation of copyrights and trademark concepts and were sceptical of the view that these rights conveyed meaning beyond specific media expressions, trade contexts and registration processes. Yet, licensing agencies operating as intermediaries, brokering the interests of media owners and other traders, became a formula for market success. This service also helped dissipate the potential for organisational tensions that arose surrounding decisions about the content of children's programming and the pursuit of commercial activities targeting the child.

The penultimate chapter tracks how the BBC developed its distinctive reputation and presence in children's markets. Initially, this included careful consideration of the terms for engaging children's radio audiences, ensuring that the participation of BBC personnel would not breach the broadcasting charter by constituting direct engagement in commercial activity. However, with the advent of commercial television, this fine legal distinction between broadcast rights and character-merchandising rights proved difficult to maintain. In theory, distinctive departmental divisions separated the commissioning of programmes from their promotion and created a defensible separation of scope and responsibility by differentiating the public broadcasting service from private commercial activity. However, the two spheres and competences began to blur in practice, as Lingstrom, head of the Children's Television Department in the 1950s, developed children's entertainment, such as *Andy Pandy*, alongside her involvement in a private company called Andy Pandy Ltd. While she had a foot in both camps, this was not recognised internally as a conflict. The creation of a separate department in the 1960s, BBC Television Enterprises, to internally handle exploitation was not a complete capitulation to market forces. However, prospects for merchandising unavoidably impacted upon decisions about the kind of content that it was felt desirable to commission. Furthermore, with some programmes such as *The Wombles*, the idea that the BBC was merely disposing of merchandising rights and licensing *through* BBC Television Enterprises, rather than BBC Television Enterprises actively exploiting the rights, was already unsustainable. As became apparent in litigation, licences with third parties were needed as a legal reference point to identify the precise scope of the BBC's commercial interests, or, in other words, to identify what intellectual property and goodwill the BBC created when it commissioned this entertaining eco-education children's programme in the 1970s.

The significance of the BBC's active engagement in marketing to children had clearly not been recognised at the time of the Parliamentary denouncement of Miller's *Alice* film in 1966–1967. The accompanying explanation that the scandal would have been avoided if the Children's Department had been responsible for commissioning the film was made in the context of criticising the 'low level of programmes' on commercial television. Lord Willis said:

> I am in the same position as most adults, if not all of them. All we can do is guess and grope in the dark about what really attracts children and how they will react to programmes .... We should all agree that television is a powerful medium, and that children (I am speaking largely of that section of the population aged 12 and under) are the most vulnerable and most important section of our community; and that therefore this is a question we cannot afford to ignore or overlook ....
>
> My main criticism today is directed against the Independent Television Authority and the commercial companies associated with it. With rare exceptions, they are just not doing their job in this particular area of television.[27]

It is not our contention that commercial activity prevented concerns about the commodification of childhood being raised or heard. Rather, the significance of this intellectual property history is in pointing out how licensing by corporations or intermediaries directly shaped the production, circulation and consumption of cultural content, and how this proceeded with little scrutiny. Across the twentieth century, the stewardship of the creator linking intellectual property licensing to questions of aesthetics, concern for the well-being and education of the child and the production of quality goods has been gradually lost. In place of those questions, we have seen the emergence of a different kind of intellectual property expertise. This represented a new kind of managerial entrepreneurship, where commercial actors treated the world as their family and treated copyrights, patents, design rights and trademarks as children to be cajoled into compliance with projects for success, where business partnerships were cemented around licensing agreements.

[27] Lord Willis, above n 22.

Index

CAMBRIDGE INTELLECTUAL PROPERTY AND INFORMATION LAW

Titles in the Series (formerly known as Cambridge Studies in Intellectual Property Rights)

Graeme W. Austin, Andrew F. Christie, Andrew T. Kenyon and Megan Richardson *Across Intellectual Property: Essays in Honour of Sam Ricketson*
Brad Sherman and Lionel Bently *The Making of Modern Intellectual Property Law*
Irini A. Stamatoudi *Copyright and Multimedia Products: A Comparative Analysis*
Pascal Kamina *Film Copyright in the European Union*
Huw Beverley-Smith *The Commercial Appropriation of Personality*
Mark J. Davison *The Legal Protection of Databases*
Robert Burrell and Allison Coleman *Copyright Exceptions: The Digital Impact*
Huw Beverley-Smith, Ansgar Ohly and Agnès Lucas-Schloetter *Privacy, Property and Personality: Civil Law Perspectives on Commercial Appropriation*
Catherine Seville *The Internationalisation of Copyright Law: Books, Buccaneers and the Black Flag in the Nineteenth Century*
Philip Leith *Software and Patents in Europe*
Geertrui van Overwalle *Gene Patents and Clearing Models: Patent Pools, Clearinghouses, Open Source Models and Liability Regimes*
Lionel Bently, Jennifer Davis and Jane C. Ginsburg *Trade Marks and Brands: An Interdisciplinary Critique*
Jonathan Curci *The Protection of Biodiversity and Traditional Knowledge in International Law of Intellectual Property*
Lionel Bently, Jennifer Davis and Jane C. Ginsburg *Copyright and Piracy: An Interdisciplinary Critique*
Megan Richardson and Julian Thomas *Fashioning Intellectual Property: Exhibition, Advertising and the Press, 1789–1918*
Dev Gangjee *Relocating the Law of Geographical Indications*
Andrew Kenyon, Megan Richardson and Ng-Loy Wee-Loon *The Law of Reputation and Brands in the Asia Pacific*
Edson Beas Rodrigues, Jr *The General Exception Clauses of the TRIPS Agreement: Promoting Sustainable Development*
Annabelle Lever *New Frontiers in the Philosophy of Intellectual Property*
Sigrid Sterckx and Julian Cockbain *Exclusions from Patentability: How Far Has the European Patent Office Eroded Boundaries?*
Sebastian Haunss *Conflicts in the Knowledge Society: The Contentious Politics of Intellectual Property*
Helena R. Howe and Jonathan Griffiths *Concepts of Property in Intellectual Property Law*
Rochelle Cooper Dreyfuss and Jane C. Ginsburg *Intellectual Property at the Edge: The Contested Contours of IP*
Normann Witzleb, David Lindsay, Moira Paterson and Sharon Rodrick *Emerging Challenges in Privacy Law: Comparative Perspectives*
Paul Bernal *Internet Privacy Rights: Rights to Protect Autonomy*
Peter Drahos *Intellectual Property, Indigenous People and their Knowledge*
Susy Frankel and Daniel Gervais *The Evolution and Equilibrium of Copyright in the Digital Age*
Edited by Kathy Bowrey and Michael Handler *Law and Creativity in the Age of the Entertainment Franchise*

Sean Bottomley *The British Patent System during the Industrial Revolution 1700–1852: From Privilege to Property*
Susy Frankel *Test Tubes for Global Intellectual Property Issues: Small Market Economies*
Jan Oster *Media Freedom As a Fundamental Right*
Sara Bannerman *International Copyright and Access to Knowledge*
Edited by Andrew T. Kenyon *Comparative Defamation and Privacy Law*
Pascal Kamina *Film Copyright in the European Union* (second edition)
Tim W. Dornis *Trademark and Unfair Competition Conflicts: Historical-Comparative, Doctrinal, and Economic Perspectives*
Ge Chen *Copyright and International Negotiations: An Engine of Free Expression in China?*
David Tan *The Commercial Appropriation of Fame: A Cultural Analysis of the Right of Publicity and Passing Off*
Jay Sanderson *Plants, People and Practices: The Nature and History of the UPOV Convention*
Daniel Benoliel *Patent Intensity and Economic Growth*
Jeffrey A. Maine and Xuan-Thao Nguyen *The Intellectual Property Holding Company: Tax Use and Abuse from Victoria's Secret to Apple*
Megan Richardson *The Right to Privacy: Origins and Influence of a Nineteenth-Century Idea*
Martin Husovec *Injunctions against Intermediaries in the European Union: Accountable but Not Liable?*
Estelle Derclaye *The Copyright/Design Interface: Past, Present and Future*
Magdalena Kolasa *Trade Secrets and Employee Mobility: In Search of an Equilibrium*
Péter Mezei *Copyright Exhaustion: Law and Policy in the United States and the European Union*
Graham Greenleaf and David Lindsay *Public Rights: Copyright's Public Domains*
Ole-Andreas Rognstad *Property Aspects of Intellectual Property*
Elena Cooper *Art and Modern Copyright: The Contested Image*
Paul Bernal *The Internet, Warts and All: Free Speech, Privacy and Truth*
Sebastian Felix Schwemer *Licensing and Access to Content in the European Union: Regulation between Copyright and Competition Law*
Daniela Simone *Copyright and Collective Authorship: Locating the Authors of Collaborative Work*
Emily Hudson *Drafting Copyright Exceptions: From the Law in Books to the Law in Action*
Graeme Gooday and Steven Wilf *Patent Cultures: Diversity and Harmonization in Historical Perspective*
Mark Burdon *Digital Data Collection and Information Privacy Law*
Tanya Aplin and Lionel Bently *Global Mandatory Fair Use: The Nature and Scope of the Right to Quote Copyright Works*
Edited by Niklas Bruun, Graeme B. Dinwoodie, Marianne Levin and Ansgar Ohly *Transition and Coherence in Intellectual Property Law: Essays in Honour of Annette Kur*
Alexander Peukert *A Critique of the Ontology of Intellectual Property Law*
Brent Salter *Negotiating Copyright in the American Theatre: 1856-1951*
Patrick R. Goold *IP Accidents: Negligence Liability in Intellectual Property*
Péter Mezei *Copyright Exhaustion: Law and Policy in the United States and the European Union* (second edition)
Jose Bellido and Kathy Bowrey *Adventures in Childhood*
Henning Grosse Ruse-Khan and Axel Metzger *Intellectual Property Ordering Beyond Borders*

For EU product safety concerns, contact us at Calle de José Abascal, 56–1°,
28003 Madrid, Spain or eugpsr@cambridge.org.

www.ingramcontent.com/pod-product-compliance
Lightning Source LLC
LaVergne TN
LVHW010341220926
848484LV00004BB/1077
9781108485913